Gender and Crime: A Reader

Gender and Crime: A Reader

Karen Evans and Janet Jamieson

 Open University Press

Open University Press
McGraw-Hill Education
McGraw-Hill House
Shoppenhangers Road
Maidenhead
Berkshire
England
SL6 2QL

email: enquiries@openup.co.uk
world wide web: www.openup.co.uk

and Two Penn Plaza, New York, NY 10121-2289, USA

First published 2008

A catalogue record of this book is available from the British Library

ISBN-13: 978-0-335-22523-1 (pb) 978-0-335-22522-4 (hb)
ISBN-10: 0-335-22523-3 (pb) 0-335-22522-4 (hb)

Library of Congress Cataloguing-in-Publication Data
CIP data applied for

Typeset by RefineCatch Limited, Bungay, Suffolk
Printed in Great Britain by Bell and Bain Ltd., in Glasgow

Fictitious names of companies, products, people, characters and/or
data that may be used herein (in case studies or in examples) are not
intended to represent any real individual, company, product or event.

The *McGraw·Hill* Companies

Contents

Series editor's foreword

This is the second collection of readings to be published as part of a new series in the McGraw-Hill/Open University Press series, Readings in Criminology and Criminal Justice. The purpose of this series is to offer a student-friendly approach to the kinds of issues and debates that are central to the contemporary discipline of criminology. Despite the proliferation of textbooks claiming to offer a wide coverage of the issues within criminology and the criminal justice system, it is inevitable that such books frequently do not do justice to the needs of the undergraduate curriculum beyond year one. The intention of this series is to fill this gap. Indeed the changing nature of the criminology undergraduate market makes its own claims for more readily available material beyond the standard textbook. In particular, the modular system of curriculum delivery means that in order to deliver courses of an appropriate standard, tutors require readily available and easily accessible material to support their courses. Collections of readings that address the core features of the criminology curriculum provide an essential starting point for students and tutors alike, especially in the light of the increasing number of journals and other outlets which may not be that easily accessible or subscribed to by all libraries, electronic developments notwithstanding. Lack of availability of a wider range of material has a detrimental effect on the discipline and the student experience. The intention of this series is not only to fill this gap, and as a result do better justice to the debates in the discipline, it also provides the opportunity for the nominated editors, and the series itself, to make a mark on the discipline, by both stretching and contributing to the boundaries of the discipline. This collection by Karen Evans and Janet Jamieson achieves just this.

It is now over 30 years since the publication of Carol Smart's ground-breaking book *Women, Crime and Criminology* (1977). In it she, among others at that time, posed some key questions for the discipline of criminology around the extent to which mainstream assumptions were embedded in both its theory and its practice. Her work exposed the ways in which these assumptions resulted in particular understandings and images of the female offender and the female victim of crime. In the intervening years, criminology has become much more sensitive to the need to challenge these assumptions, yet at the same time has developed theories and practices that recognise that crime is disproportionately committed by males (Braithwaite, 1989). Evans and Jamieson's readings chart a path through the historical legacy of the debate initially established by the work of Smart and others, and explore its contemporary legacy. Divided into five parts, this reader maps the theoretical, empirical and practical developments that have endeavoured to identify the ways in which gender, as opposed to sex, differently informs criminology the discipline as well as criminology the practice. Parts 1 and 2 are focused around 'engendering the agenda' in respect of women as offenders in the case of Part 1, and women as victims of crime in the case of Part 2. In each of these selections the reader is encouraged to think critically about both how gender has informed the criminological response and understanding of female offending and female criminal victimisation, what the different theoretical responses to these understandings might look like, and how those different theoretical approaches render some features of the gender question visible and others not. In essence, both of these sets of readings ask us to think about questions such as: when is gender the salient variable, for whom, and what impact does it have on, for example, black female offenders on the one hand or male victims of domestic violence on the other? The next two selections of readings, Parts 3 and 4, take us further down the road in our critical appreciation of criminology's appreciation of these questions. These selections encourage the reader to think about the different ways in which womanhood and manhood are constructed within criminal justice practice. Part 3 addresses questions relating to the ways in which the gendered processes of social control, that particularly focus on women's sexuality and thereby their femininity, ensure that they 'grow up good' (Cain, 1989) and contribute to contemporary concerns about female criminality. Part 4 explores the ways in which understandings of masculinity contribute to understanding why it is that men seem to be particularly predisposed to criminality (qua Braithwaite, 1989, referenced above). Again both of these selections of readings reiterate the importance of thinking about the question of how and under what circumstance these understandings take their toll on individuals.

The final selection of readings explores the extent to which it is important for criminology to appreciate the international dimensions of the gender and crime question. The importance of understanding the impact of different cultures on criminological theory and practice is placed alongside the persistent evidence of cross-cultural female criminal victimisation and male criminality that reiterates the significance of the gender and crime question for the criminological agenda. In a powerful conclusion, Evans and Jamieson set out the achievements and the challenges that the gender and crime question has posed for criminology. They argue that unless the question of gender remains at the forefront of criminological endeavours, the question of backlash notwithstanding, criminology will fail to offer an agenda that is suitably informed by an understanding of social justice that strives to be attentive to humane constructions of both victims and offenders, whether or not they be male or female.

The journey that Evans and Jamieson take us on through this selection of readings and their analysis of it is significant for the future intellectual and practical life of criminology and criminal justice practitioners. Suitably armed with a critical understanding of the nature and impact that gender has on the social construction of both victims and offenders facilitates simultaneously a more complex and more subtle appreciation of the impact that crime differentially has on individuals' everyday lives. Evans and Jamieson clearly link the importance of this kind of understanding with the questions of social inequality and social justice. The agenda they set in the light of this link is a powerful one that criminology needs to be constantly alerted to. This reader makes sure that this is achieved.

Professor Sandra Walklate
Eleanor Rathbone Chair of Sociology
University of Liverpool
January 2008

References

Braithwaite, J. (1989), *Crime, Shame and Reintegration*. Cambridge: Cambridge University Press.
Cain, M. (ed.) (1989), *Growing Up Good*. London: Sage.
Smart, C. (1977), *Women, Crime and Criminology*. London: Routledge.

Publisher's acknowledgements

The editors and publisher wish to thank the following for permission to use copyright material:

Smart, C. (1977) 'Criminological theory: its ideology and implications concerning women', *Sociology*, 28(1). Reproduced with permission of Blackwell Publishing Ltd.

Rice, M. (1990) 'Challenging orthodoxies in feminist theory; a black feminist critique', in Gelsthorpe, L. and Morris, A. (eds) *Feminist Perspective in Criminology*. Milton Keynes: Open University Press.

Chesney-Lind, M. and Pasko, L. (2004) 'Girls' troubles and 'female delinquency', in Chesney-Lind, M. and Pasko, L. *The Female Offender: Girls, Women and Crime*, 2nd edition. Thousand Oaks/London/New Delhi: Sage Publications. pp. 9–30. Reprinted by permission of Sage Publications, Inc.

Worrall, A. (2004) 'Twisted sisters, ladettes, and the new penology: the social construction of 'violent girls'. Reprinted by permission from *Girls' Violence: Myths and Realities*, edited by Christine Alder and Anne Worrall, the State University of New York Press © 2004, State University of New York. All rights reserved.

Brownmiller, S. (1975) 'Women fight back', from *Against our Will: Men, Women and Rape*, by Susan Brownmiller, published by Secker and Warburg. Reprinted by permission of the Random House Group Ltd.

Stanko, E. (1987) 'Typical violence, normal precaution', in Hanmer, J. and Maynard, M. (eds) *Women. Violence and Social Control*. Basingstoke: Macmillan.

Gilchrist, E, Bannister, J., Ditton, J. and Farrall, S. (1998) 'Women and the "fear of crime" challenging the accepted stereotype', *British Journal of Criminology*, 38(2).

Dobash, R.P. and Dobash, R.E. (2004) 'Women's violence to men in intimate relationships: working on the puzzle', *British Journal of Criminology*, 44.

Hudson, A. (1989) ' "Troublesome girls": towards alternative definitions and policies', in Cain, M. (ed.) *Growing Up Good. Policing the Behaviour of Girls in Europe*. London: Sage.

Gelsthorpe, L. and Loucks, N. (1997) 'Justice in the making: key influences on decision-making', in Hedderman, C. and Gelsthorpe, L. (eds) *Understanding the Sentencing of Woman*. London: Home Office Research Study 170. Reproduced under licence.

Gelsthorpe, L. and Morris, A. (2002) 'Women's imprisonment in England and Wales: a penal paradox', *Criminal Justice*, 2(3). Reproduced by kind permission of Sage Publications Ltd.

Chigwada-Bailey, R. (2004) 'Black women and the criminal justice system', in McIvor, G (ed.) *Women who Offend*. London/New York: Jessica Kingsley Publishers. Reproduced by permission of Jessica Kingsley Publishers.

Messerschmidt, J.W. (1993) 'Structured action and gendered crime', in *Masculinities and Crime*, Maryland: Rowman and Littlefield.

Collier, R. (2004) 'Masculinities and crime: rethinking the "man question" ', in Sumner, C. (ed.) *The Blackwell Companion to Criminology*. Oxford: Blackwell.

Carlen, P. (1994) 'Gender, class, racism and criminal justice: against global and gender-centric theories, for post-structuralist perspectives', from *Inequalities, Crime and Social Control* by George Bridges. Reprinted by permission of Westview Press, a member of Perseus Books Group.

Snider, L. (2003) 'Constituting the punishable woman. atavistic man incarcerates postmodern woman', *British Journal of Criminology*, 43. Reproduced by permission of Oxford University Press.

Radford, L. and Tsutsumi, K. (2004) 'Globalization and violence against women-inequalities in risks, responsibilities and blame in the UK and Japan', *Women's Studies International Forum*, 27(1). Reproduced with permission from Elsevier.

Jamieson, R. (1999) 'Genocide and the social production of immorality', *Theoretical Criminology*, 3(2). Reproduced by kind permission of Sage Publications Ltd.

The publisher directs the reader to the original publications for the full list of references.

Every effort has been made to trace the copyright holders but if any have been inadvertently overlooked the publisher will be pleased to make the necessary arrangement at the first opportunity.

Introduction: gender and crime – the story

Women are typically non-criminal: they have lower rates of crime in *all nations, all communities* within nations, for *all age groups, for all periods of recorded history*, and for practically *all crimes*.

(Leonard, 1982: 1, emphasis in original)

Gender is a key and enduring determinant of likely involvement in offending behaviour yet the relative importance of gender has not always, nor indeed accurately, been reflected in the development of criminological thought. Indeed, the development of criminological knowledge has always proceeded on the assumption that 'crime was men's work not women's' (Walklate, 2001: 26). So the study of 'criminal man' has dominated the development of criminological thought, and 'criminal women' have been largely excluded. This selection of readings provides an important corrective to this criminological proclivity to neglect gender. Focusing explicitly on questions of gender and crime, it guides the reader through a range of classic and ground-breaking studies, highlights key contributions and debates, and provides an indication of the new directions an engendered criminology may take us in the coming years

This first introductory chapter charts the shifting contours of criminological interest in the question of gender in order to provide the reader with the necessary contextual background to explore and appreciate the nuances and contributions of the selected readings which comprise this reader. It demonstrates the ways in which a critical engagement with questions of gender have interacted with, challenged and contributed to the development of criminological thought. It highlights the deficiencies of the 'malestream' tendencies of much criminological endeavour and outlines how a 'gendered perspective' (Walklate, 2004: 16) has not only served 'to render the issue of women and crime more visible' (Walklate, 2004: 47), but also to 'dismantle or fracture the limitations of existing knowledges, boundaries and traditional methodologies' (Gelsthorpe, 2003: 8) employed within criminology.

'Malestream' criminology

Early criminological theories looked for an explanation of offending behaviour in an individual's genetic characteristics and psychology. Since, at all times and across all regions of the world, rates of recorded crime show much higher rates of offending for males than for females, the positivistic 'Lombrosian project' (Garland, 2002: 8) concluded that there was something in the biological, genetic or psychological make-up of the criminal which set him apart from the 'normal' citizen. Since not all men committed crime – there was after all a 'law-abiding majority' – it was considered that there must be something deeply flawed in the individual (male) criminal's body or mind. Where such positivist studies of crime and criminality stumbled upon the female offender, she is portrayed as an aberration from the norm. For example, Lombroso and Ferrero (1895) asserted that the criminal woman was genetically disadvantaged and driven by primitive – 'atavistic' – physiological characteristics; Thomas (1907) viewed her as more masculine than feminine; Freud (1933) asserted that she was unable to come to terms with her essential femininity and suggested a delinquency driven by 'penis envy', or the desire to be a man (Klein, 1973: 89); while Davis (1981) argued she was driven by 'unnatural' sexual desires. Departing from this perspective somewhat, Pollak (1950) asserted that women's ability to conceal sexual arousal and menstruation is indicative of her deceitful and manipulative character which not only enables her to commit crimes by stealth but also to propel men into criminality on her behalf, safe in the knowledge that she can rely on the chivalry of men to do her bidding and to protect her from harm and prosecution.

Following one of the 'great creative explosions in modern sociology' (Heidensohn, 1996: 128) emanating from the University of Chicago in the 1920s, later studies moved to sociological conceptualisations of crime causation and looked alternatively at the specificities of the social and cultural experiences contributing to criminality. However, the ongoing conviction that 'the delinquent is a rogue male' (Cohen, 1955: 140) meant that a 'cavalier androcentrism' has remained a defining feature of criminological endeavour (Chesney-Lind and Pasko, 2004b: 15). Indeed, seminal studies addressing juvenile gangs (Thrasher, 1927); social disorganisation theory (Shaw and McKay, 1942); strain theory (Merton, 1938); subcultural theory (Cloward and Ohlin, 1960; Cohen, 1955); control theory (Hirschi, 1969) and differential association theory (Sutherland and Cressey, 1978) unapologetically focused on the delinquent male. Even labelling theory (Matza, 1964), which focused on societies' attitudes and reactions to particular forms of behaviour perceived and labelled as deviant, failed to explore systematically how society reacted to women's transgressions – whether of a sexual or criminal nature.

Each of these theories displays a strong sense of sympathy with the lot of the male delinquent who is portrayed as actively seeking solutions to what are viewed as exclusively male problems (Naffine, 1987). Their implicit exclusion and dismissal of girls perpetuates negative conceptualisations of femininity, which is characterised as passive and conformist and is accompanied by the assumption that a woman's status and experiences are contingent upon form-ing and sustaining a successful partnership with a man (Naffine, 1987). Con-sequently, females who do offend are denied the energy, intelligence, creativity and agency of their male counterparts, and their delinquent activities are associated with stereotypical cultural sex-role expectations that are character-ised as leading to sexual rather than criminal transgressions (Walklate, 2001).

These 'malestream' theories are hugely contradictory and flawed. They are also blatantly sexist in their assumptions and, it has been argued, inherently misogynistic (Klein, 1973). However, certain of their assumptions – crime as biologically determined, the inherent passivity of the female, the chivalry of men towards female offenders, the criminality of men and the conformity of women, and the problematic nature of female sexual expressiveness, continue to resonate in more contemporary accounts of female offending.

Challenging the 'malestream'

The impetus to challenge these 'malestream' criminological assumptions and explanations emerged with the 1960s Civil Rights, anti-war, New Left and stu-dent movements in North America, Europe and Australia (Bryson, 1992). New ideological frameworks served to question the social mores, values and institu-tions of the post-war era and alongside more general calls for an end to oppression and discrimination in all its forms, what has been termed a 'second wave of feminism' blossomed. This second-wave feminism essentially began as a 'liberal protest' within an American society that was seen as failing to deliver to women 'the promises of independence, self-expression and fulfil-ment' central to the American Dream (Bryson, 1992: 159). It rapidly developed in all kinds of directions with activists attempting to fashion social change with respect to a myriad of issues, including equality in the work place, the recogni-tion of the value of women's work within the home and women's rights to control their own bodies (Morash, 2006: 107). Second-wave feminist theory and activism not only raised profound challenges to the discrimination against, exclusion of and (mis)representation of women, but also provided an important fillip to 'gendered' interrogation and enquiry within the social sciences, in gen-eral, and with respect to crime and the criminal justice system in particular.

Indeed, the social and political upheavals emerging in the 1960s elicited challenges to existing modes of thought within many academic disciplines, including literature, history, philosophy and sociology (Heidensohn, 1996; Naffine, 1987). With regard to criminology, the angry young men within British criminology of the 1960s and 1970s sought to transform the discipline away from the study of the individual towards the study of 'the structural inequalities and power relations of capitalist society' (Newburn, 2007: 246). In particular, Taylor et al.'s *The New Criminology*, published in 1973, comprised an influential text. Critiquing earlier theories as 'predicting too little bourgeois, and too much proletarian criminality' (Taylor et al. 1973: 107), Taylor et al. championed the use of Marxism, symbolic interactionism, and labelling and subculture theories to provide, as the subtitle of their book attests, a 'fully social theory of deviance'. Yet notwithstanding the 'symbiosis between the intellectual and political projects' of the then ascendant critical criminology and feminist scholarship, this 'new criminology' was silent with regard to the 'singular experiences of and concerns of women' (Stevens, 2006: 18).

Given the strong 'masculinist' tendency (Heidensohn, 1996: 154) within criminology, even criminology of a radical persuasion, it is perhaps no surprise that it is within the scholarship of female social scientists themselves, often, though not necessarily, inspired by feminist discourses, that a gendered lens was applied to women's relationship to offending and criminality. Carol Smart's *Women, Crime and Criminology* provided the influential text which arguably transformed and structured succeeding criminological debates regarding the gendered understanding of crime, criminal justice and victimisation. Smart concluded that criminology must 'become more than the study of men' (1976: 185), recommending that such study should be situated with regard to the economic, political, moral and sexual realities of women's position in society.

In the wake of Smart's scholarship, a plethora of divergent writings by other female academics have endeavoured to counter the marginalisation of women within criminology by ensuring that their experiences should be made known and that their perspectives on the question of crime be taken into account. Even if not espousing a defined feminist philosophical framework, their wish was that the actions and experiences of women be put centre stage. So the first notable engagements with the question of gender emerged from early feminist critiques of the omission, marginalisation and stereotypical treatment of female offenders within criminological writings. The works of Bertrand (1967; 1969); Heidensohn (1968); Klein (1973) and Smart (1976; 1977) comprised the initial forays into the 'lonely and uncharted seas of human behaviour' (Heidensohn, 1968: 171) characteristic of the study of female criminality. These pioneering writers provided justifiably outraged, robust and, at times, scathingly humorous accounts of the sexist and misogynistic representations of female offenders perpetuated by extant criminological theories. Furthermore, the imperative to place women inside the criminological focus, which ensued in the wake of these critiques, brought many issues to the fore which simply had not been previously considered by the male-dominated discipline.

Our first selection of readings on 'Engendering the agenda' reveals how poorly the discipline of criminology dealt with the problem of women as offenders and the extent to which this neglect obscured the view of so many criminologists for so many decades. It also illustrates how early feminist critiques were rapidly transformed and developed into women-centred empirical enquiry which, by emphasising questions of women's relative agency and autonomy, illustrated the complexity of female criminality and established a more 'realistic, humanising conception of women's offending' (Stevens, 2006: 26).

Woman-centred epistemology

Studies around gender and crime often employed explicitly feminist research techniques. Previous frameworks of knowledge, it was argued, had proved blind to issues of gender because they had been based on outdated and masculinist discourses and methodologies which looked for scientific and universalist explanations for criminal behaviour. Feminist scholarship, by utilising more qualitative research techniques designed to empower the (female) research subject and to tap in to the reality of women's experiences (Harding 1987; 1986; Stanley and Wise 1983), revealed the female offender as an individual struggling to make her mark within a world which constrained her opportunities for meaningful activities and her ability to make different choices.

As feminist research methods began to be employed increasingly within criminology, researchers began to uncover some very interesting relationships which had hitherto remained stubbornly hidden from view. Far from their transgressions being unidimensional in nature and concentrated around the violation of sexual norms, women were discovered as participating in a wide range of offending behaviours, such as theft, fraud, burglary, violence, arson and the supplying of drugs (Carlen 1988: 57). In addition, feminism's stated intention to study and challenge the oppression of all women allowed researchers to uncover previously unexplored dimensions of power and the patriarchal social relationships which shaped and severely limited the choices women could make. Rather than presenting simple causal connections to explain the offending behaviour of girls and women, these research techniques exposed the inability of existing theories to understand the nature of female offending and at the same time cast doubt on their fitness for purpose in explaining male offending. In particular, they exposed the folly of considering offenders as a unitary group and their offending as driven by simple explanatory variables. The vulnerability of many female offenders gave the lie to those theories of criminality which dominated establishment ideas of the criminal and which emphasised the rational choice exercised by offenders or which saw them as driven by individual pathology. Once this was revealed for female offenders, academics were furnished with a powerful critique of existing criminology which applied as much to theories of male offending as it did to the theories of female offending. Once gender had been demonstrated to be such a key consideration for criminology, feminist scholarship also called for the variables of class and race to be inserted into understandings of criminality. This paved the way for a whole host of writings which revealed the oppressive practices employed in the control and surveillance of other subordinated and excluded groups, once again turning the focus of criminology to new directions.

Discovering 'the victim'

The study of victims was to prove one such new direction, and the reporting of women's victimisation has been one of the most successful interventions in the field of criminology. A consideration of the impacts of crime upon the victim which was emerging from the implementation of victim surveys in the USA, from 1967, and the UK, from 1977, not only served to 'permanently alter the criminological agenda' (Zedner, 2002: 420), but also provided a further platform from which to render visible the experiences of girls and women as *victims* of crime. This focus on women's and girls' experiences of victimisation questioned the traditional criminological focus on 'the randomised and somewhat romanticised, crimes of the public sphere' (Stevens, 2006: 45) and the tendency of some more radical areas of the discipline to fetishise or revere the offending person as society's rebel. The uncovering of the 'dark figure' of crime – those crimes which go unreported or unrecorded – provided a fundamental challenge to criminology to expose the invisible – often female – victim. Feminist scholars responded to this challenge and their work served to reveal the 'hidden and privatised nature of much violence against women' (Carrington, 2002: 116) – at the hands of men – and the high rates of distress it caused (Hanmer and Saunders, 1984; 1987). Indeed, Young (1988: 171) asserts that the 'moral entrepreneurship' integral to this feminist endeavour served to highlight not only domestic and sexual violence, but also child physical and sexual abuse, areas of crime which had previously been widely ignored within criminological enquiry.

Early scholars working in the field of victimisation were often driven by their activism as feminists. They set out to change the world not only to document it, and brought with their work a determination that the violence women suffered could not be 'glossed over, excused, tolerated or ignored' (Carrington, 2002: 128). Indeed, feminist activism on these issues has not only provided economic and practical resources for women seeking refuge from abuse (Pizzey, 1974), but also has elicited more sensitive legal, policy and practice responses to vulnerable victims (Zedner, 2002). Furthermore, the deconstruction of male violence and sexual violence with regard to issues of rape, child abuse and domestic violence has not only served to illustrate the gendered nature of these crimes, but also the lack of power available to women within a culture and legal system imbued with normative assumptions regarding male power and female subjugation (Brownmiller, 1975b). Of course, this emphasis on women's relative powerlessness was in stark contrast to the characterisation of crime as rebellion and resistance integral to more radical/critical criminological thinking in the same period (Corrigan, 1979; Hall and Jefferson, 1976; Taylor, 1971; Young 1971). For example, early work on female prostitutes focused on the reality that women's bodies could be treated as saleable commodities in illegal marketplaces and that women were all too often forced into crime through poverty or the violence of men (Barry, 1979).

The discovery and exposition of the invisible, yet highly distressing, nature of women's victimisation served to 'undermine the notion that fear of crime is largely irrational and without basis' (Young, 1988: 171). Indeed, the recognition of the need to take crime seriously from the perspective of the injured – often female – victim proved an influential consideration in the emergence of 'left realist' criminology in the 1980s. Left Realism's concern to find solutions to crime within a more radical framework than had hitherto been possible, spawned a mini-industry of research into the fear of crime which placed gender and the fears experienced by girls and women firmly on the agenda (Crawford et al., 1990, Jones et al., 1986). However, it took another feminist working within the field of criminology, Elizabeth Stanko, to point out that it was not enough to see gender as merely another variable in a typology of fear. The fear of crime for women, she argued, was, in reality, a fear of men. Stanko (1987) knitted the problem of male power into the criminological garment and revisited the ways in which fear of men controls and limits women's behaviour in a variety of ways. Some of the early second-wave feminists had contended that all men were potential rapists, and while this slogan soon had its day within the women's movement, Stanko's work, and those with whom she collaborated, demonstrated that male power did serve to keep women in a state of fear. Although it was by now acknowledged that all men did not exercise their power in the same ways, this work revealed that the potential threat of victimisation by men was ever present for women and that young girls were socialised into particular, defensive, behaviours at an early age.

The second part of this reader entitled 'Engendering the victim' is illustrative of feminist and gendered incursions in relation to the study of victims. The selected readings not only serve to challenge and transform criminological assumptions regarding the gendered nature of female victimisation, but also to highlight the diversity and subjectivity of gendered experiences of criminal victimisation.

The significance of social control

The socialisation of and limitations placed upon the female half of the population are explored in the readings on 'Gender and social control'. Arising from the feminist movement of the 1960s, this area of scholarship declared an interest in the ways in which regulation, social control and the criminal justice system subjected masculine and feminine behaviours to different norms and social rules (Lees, 1986). The imperative for girls to 'grow up good' (Cain, 1989) in order to fulfil the pervasive domestic expectations of them being a wife, a mother and a carer, it was argued, embedded expectations regarding 'appropriate' female behaviours and served to subject girls and women to greater constraints and controls than their male counterparts (Carlen, 1983: Heidensohn, 2002, Oakley, 1981), with women themselves often policing and disciplining their own bodies and behaviours (Heidensohn, 2002; Smith, 2005). While the pervasiveness of dominant discourses of femininity usually act as a 'highly effective system of controls and bonds which make criminality a damaging and difficult course for women to take' (Heidensohn, 1996: 195), some girls and women are unable or unwilling to conform successfully. Hence a gendered scrutiny of the constructions, treatment and experiences of these women in their interactions with state institutions and agencies provided further valuable insights into and critiques of extant criminological knowledge.

A striking and resonant insight has been that concerns relating to the sexuality and sexual reputation of girls have proven particularly significant in their likely involvement with state welfare and criminal justice agencies (Lees, 1986; 1989). As Klein has explained, 'the theme of sexuality is a unifying thread in the various, often contradictory theories' which have made up much of criminology's canon of work (1973: 101). Indeed as Cain reiterates 'feminist criminologists had begun to point out the continuity between the ways in which women and girls are pressured and schooled into conformity by the criminal justice system and the ways in which they are controlled by a myriad of other institutions and structures in society at large' (1989: 1). Thus, while there is a traditional implicit acceptance and encouragement for young men to 'sow their wild oats', sexually active young women are deemed to be 'out of control' and 'in moral danger'. As Muncie observes, 'the disobedient or runaway young women and the "unfit" teenage mother are far more likely to be candidates for intervention than the disobedient, runaway or sexually active heterosexual young man' (2004: 210).

The plethora of informal means exerted to control the activities and behaviours of girls and women are, of course, replicated in their treatment within the criminal justice system (Carrington, 2002). Concerns regarding the treatment of these women by criminal justice systems began to emerge in 1980s initially centred on the competing discourses that women were either likely to be treated with chivalry – and consequently protected from the worst excesses of law and punishment – or condemned as doubly deviant (Lloyd, 1995) – and consequently treated harshly with regard to prosecution and pun-ishment. The consensus emerging from a range of empirical studies in relation to these contradictory hypotheses is that women can sometimes be treated with leniency by the criminal justice system, especially if they are considered as conforming in most aspects of their gender role, but they are more likely to be dealt with more punitively if they step outside of accepted stereotypical female behaviour in other areas of their life (Worrall, 1990).

Concern regarding women's treatment within the criminal justice system has spurred on an important debate regarding whether women should be treated equally before the law or whether gender-sensitive treatment and inter-ventions should be encouraged. MacKinnon (1987) has argued that there is a danger in any approach focusing on issues of equality without acknowledging the male structures of power which create the legal and penal system within which we operate. In a system which presumes the male experience to be the norm, the equality approach poses a real threat for women in the prospect of 'equality with a vengeance', whereby the principle of equal treatment will result in women being treated the same as men (Smart, 1990: 79). In this way the specificities of women's experiences may be lost in the clamour to treat every-one 'equally' and result in the gross spectacle of women prisoners manacled to hospital beds while giving birth because not to do so might attract the charge of favourable treatment for women. In addition, a system based on 'equal treatment' would most probably mean incorporating into female punishment all that is wrong with the current male-centred system, so accepting its racism, its discriminatory practices and its ethos of control and punishment. By con-trast, Carlen (2002a) has argued that a criminal justice system which is responsive to consideration of women's particular needs would be more pro-gressive and closer to a system based on social justice. Such a system would acknowledge that offenders should be treated differently depending on their particular situation, their familial responsibilities; any special needs they might have; the circumstances of their offending; their vulnerability and their history of prior victimisation. To incorporate sensitivity to difference within sentencing and treatment policies could also help to improve conditions for men, who can be similarly vulnerable and should be similarly individually assessed.

Notwithstanding such differences of opinion an empathy for the female offender and their fate within the criminal justice system and the conviction that it is better to do something than to do nothing (Carlen, 2002a, Hannah-Moffat, 2002) has inspired the pursuit of gendered reform of imprisonment and crim-inal justice interventions from the 1990s to the present. However, this pursuit of gender-sensitive responses and interventions has been overshadowed by a manifest increase in punitiveness towards all offenders since the early 1990s, which is arguably most starkly illustrated by the inexorable rise in female incarceration across western jurisdictions (Gelsthorpe and McIvor, 2007; Heidensohn and Gelsthorpe, 2007). Hence gendered approaches to the issue of crime control have most recently sought to explain and understand this increasing propensity to incarcerate women, and to scrutinise 'the logics and strategies of governing' (Hannah-Moffat, 2001: 5) that perpetuate and intensify resort to incarceration. The selected readings addressing 'Gender and social control' serve to illustrate how normative gendered expectations of female conduct are inextricably connected to girls' and women's interaction with, and treatment by, state and criminal justice agencies.

Interrogating masculinity

A consideration of the ways in which women are controlled and manipulated both within and outwith the criminal justice system has been a key factor in understanding the offending behaviour of women and the limits placed on their choices to behave differently. The control of women's sexuality, the limits that have been placed on their economic and social opportunities, the poverty in which many live and must raise families, all affect their life chances, constrict their choices and strip them of the power to act. As the feminist intervention into criminology has reminded us, much of the control of women is played out in their private lives. However, radical criminology had constructed a markedly different view of the working-class male as closely controlled, monitored and constrained in the streets and in the public sphere more generally. Economically marginalised young men, and young black men in particular, were perceived as 'criminalised' by mainstream institutions and thereby victims of state power, their criminality constructed by moral panics concerning troublesome male behaviours, police targeting of working-class youth and discriminatory law and order practices (Hall, 1978; Lea and Young, 1984). A feminist critique of this perspective questioned where it left the female victims of male power and aggression and led Scully to enquire 'whether abusive men are the agents rather than the objects of social control' (1990: 33). Many male crimes, she argued, were largely ignored by the legal system, especially when they were interpersonal, and she went on to state that, rather than challenging existing relations of domination and control, 'both sexual and racial violence are attempts to maintain, rather than challenge, existing power relations; both demonstrate that social control is not the monopoly of the state' (Scully, 1990: 33).

The readings on 'Engendering masculinity' pick up on these emergent themes. Any analysis of gender and crime quite quickly concludes that males appear much more inclined to criminality than females – and that females are very often their victims. This is as true of the crimes of the powerful – those which occur in the corporate board rooms, in cabinet governments, in times of war and in the name of capitalist efficiency and profit – as of the powerless. Our story of gender and crime continues by focusing on the 'masculine turn' evident in criminology from the 1990s. Within the context of public debates regarding crime, criminal justice and the politics of 'law and order' scholars such as Connell (1987; 1993; 1995), Messerschmidt (1993b; 1997; 1998; 2000), Hearn (1987; 1998) and Jefferson (1992; 1994b) sought to address 'what it is about men . . . not as working class men, not as migrants, not as under-privileged individuals but as men that induces them to commit crime' (Grosz, 1987, cited in Gelsthorpe and McIvor, 2007: 340). This concern with the 'maleness' of crime was played out against the backdrop of the postmodern challenge to criminology's modernist-inspired project to find a universal response to a universal problem. Indeed, the 'universalising positivistic meta-narratives' upon which criminology was founded were deemed no longer applicable to the inherently pluralistic, subjective, contingent and insecure experiences which characterise contemporary social life and 'deconstuctive replacement discourses' were pursued (Stevens, 2006: 57).

Arguably, at this point any future for feminist/gendered study within the auspices of criminology appeared quite bleak as one of its most vociferous and influential champions, Carol Smart, chose to abandon criminology altogether, provocatively stating that 'it is very hard to see what criminology has to offer feminism' (1990: 84). Yet, notwithstanding the marked resistance to post-modern ideas within criminology and victimology, Walklate argues that rather than diminish the prospect of gendered criminological enquiry postmodern-ism's concern to 'give voice to diversity' has not only led to a re-examination of the category of 'woman', and the way this has been used to delineate all women, but also 'a blossoming literature on masculinity and masculinities' (2001: 50). This literature deploys a largely feminist methodological approach and theoretical perspective utilising the insights of a decade or so of work on gender and crime led by female scholars to apply similar questions and analysis to the problem of males and crime (Collier, 1998: 5–6). Connell's sophisticated conceptual model of 'hegemonic masculinity' as the dominant discourse of an idealised masculinity has proved pivotal to this genre of studies. The hegemonic ideal valorises the masculine characteristics of aggression, pride, risk-taking, competitiveness and the 'macho' (Collier, 1995: 18–19), and places the white, heterosexual breadwinner and provider in a position of dominance. Connell (1995) recognised that at any given time there were likely to be multiple masculinities hierarchically ordered by age, social class, racial difference and sexuality to produce social relationships based on degrees of domination and subordination (Jefferson, 1994b: 12). Thus while many men strive for the hegemonic ideal not all will succeed, and those who are not white, heterosexual or monied are most likely to be in a position of subordinated masculinity.

Although Connell made few observations about the criminality of males, his insights have been used to attempt to understand the offending behaviour of boys and men. Messerschmidt (1993b; 1997; 1998; 2000), in particular, has explored the dangers inherent in both hegemonic and subordinated masculinities, highlighting the violence and aggression which social stereotypes of masculinity confer on the lives of men and that which they learn to mete out to others, especially those considered as lacking in power and force. Thus the male 'over-involvement' in crime can be understood not as an essential characteristic of men and boys but as a practice, an engagement in a 'wide range of activities which all need to be understood within the context of gender relations' (Newburn and Stanko, 1994: 4). Masculinity is 'accomplished' in many differentiated ways, but under dominant patriarchal ideologies which are inherently violent and misogynistic these traits tend to rise to the surface and become normalised.

Women, of course, can never achieve the status conferred by 'hegemonic masculinity'. From the time of Lombroso onwards, however, it has been posited that female offenders take on, or already possess, elements of masculinity which subsume their femininity. One thesis which emerged in the 1970s and attached itself to the feminist project – but was certainly not of its making – was the 'liberation hypothesis' typified by the work of Freda Adler (1975). Adler argued that women, in their struggle for equality, were taking on male values

and attitudes and that their involvement in crime was a function of their struggle for liberation and their attempts to be just like men. It was not until the
1980s that the accumulated weight of both qualitative and quantitative evidence resoundly demonstrated the inherent flaws of the liberation thesis (Box,
1983; Box and Hale, 1983; Burman et al., 2000; Joe and Chesney-Lind, 1998;
Maher and Curtis, 1995; Maher and Daly, 1996; Steffensmeier, 1978), which
not only failed to account for the lived experiences of many women and girls
which were far from any notion of a liberated ideal, but also the complex ways
in which men and women respond to gendered norms and expectations, and
how such norms and expectation are reflected and reproduced in their offending behaviours. Yet the charge that females are becoming more like men and
that this is fuelling an increase in their offending persists to this day.

Our selected readings on 'Engendering masculinity' reflect the diversity of
the scholarship which has emerged to address the 'man problem' in respect of
criminality and to explore the relative importance of the concept 'hegemonic
masculinity' in explaining the gendered nature of male crime. The readings are
particularly significant as they serve to consolidate the transformation of the
gendered lens to one which critically engages not only with female but also
male experiences in relation to criminality.

Widening the critical gaze

Our final part of the reader attempts to provide some insight into the history of
the present. Arguably the character of criminology in the twenty-first century
reflects the conditions of late modernity, the 'culture of control' and 'new' forms
of governance (Foucault, 1991; Garland, 2001; Loader and Sparks, 2007;
Rose, 1999; 2000) which are often global in nature. Arguably, within such a
context an exclusive focus on domestic, or indeed as some might say paro-
chial, concerns are no longer an option (Gelsthorpe, 2002: 127). Hence our
last selection of readings, 'International perspectives' reveals how the study of
gender within criminology has more recently culminated in an acknowledgement that the discipline needs to divert its focus towards other cultures,
incorporating much more diverse perspectives into its field of vision. Perhaps
an unsurprising but nevertheless deeply depressing theme within these readings is the truth that women are more often victimised and that men remain
most often the perpetrators of crime across very different cultural boundaries.
Nevertheless, this recent focus on diversity builds on the necessity of looking
at difference rather than sameness, which the focus on gender within criminology has demonstrated as both revealing and enlightening.

A gendered criminological future?

Despite the insights which we have outlined in the preceding paragraphs, and
the ongoing attempts of feminist and other scholars since the late 1960s to

highlight the significance of gender to the discipline of criminology, the view that the male delinquent is the legitimate object of study remains so firmly entrenched it can be considered as continuing to be guilty of 'gender myopia' (Stevens, 2006: 18). Stevens reminds us that the ascendent critical criminology of the 1970s failed to engage with the experiences and concerns of women despite the 'symbiosis' of its intellectual and political projects to those of feminist scholarship (2006: 18). Likewise, Walklate (2001) argues that in the 1980s the criminological endeavours of administrative criminology and radical left realism did little to rectify the omission of female criminality. Furthermore, the evident fascination since the 1990s with 'actuarial' techniques and 'what works' approaches valorises an evidence base almost exclusively derived from studies of the male offender (Hedderman, 2004). Even Garland's key contribution to debates regarding the nature of contemporary crime control – as explicated in his 'Culture of Control' thesis – is perceived as problematic in its neglect of the 'gendered dimensions' of crime and of criminal justice (Heidensohn and Gelsthorpe, 2007: 407).

Acknowledging such challenges, our final chapter 'Gender and crime: the legacy?' demonstrates how the application of a gendered lens has continued to shape contemporary criminological knowledge, and concludes that concerns for individual and social justice demand that the 'criminological gaze' continues 'to see and to speak' gender (Cain, 1990: 11), not only to protect the insights gained to date but also to critically document the 'diversity and specificities' (Walklate, 2004: 210) of the ongoing relationship of gender to crime, victimisation and criminal justice.

Part 1
Engendering the agenda[1]
Introduction

The first reading in this volume is representative of early feminist incursions within the criminological enterprise. Carol Smart's 1976 text, *Women, Crime and Criminology*, is widely recognised as particularly significant in instigating and legitimating the study of 'women and crime' (Carrington, 2002; Gelsthorpe, 2002; Heidensohn, 2006; Newburn, 2007; Stevens, 2006). Providing a flavour of the analysis presented within this text, the opening reading is inspired by the 'overwhelming lack of interest' (Smart, 1977: 89) in female criminality within criminology and the 'sexist ideology' (p. 6) integral to those theories which do address female criminality. Smart details how criminological theories serve to deny female offenders any agency, complexity or diversity by perpetrating 'common-sense' explanations emphasising the significance of hormonal and biological imbalances and hence the 'abnormality' and 'unnaturalness' of women who commit crimes. Smart alerts us to the potential harms that can arise from the association of female criminality with individual pathology – being 'sick' – particularly with regard to the propensity to 'treat' as opposed to punish these women. Taking issue with the questionable benefits of 'chivalry' and 'paternalism', Smart warns of the unjust and severe responses which are likely to be forthcoming for women who offend – responses which are justified on the basis of seemingly humanitarian concern to return them to their 'natural' place and role within society as passive and feminine and dependent upon and subordinate to men.

Smart's (1976: 185) clarion call that 'criminology must become more than the study of men and crime' inspired a plethora of studies and writings on the subject of 'women and crime' which served to render 'women visible' and ensure that they were no longer represented as a 'mere gargoyle-like stereotype' (Heidensohn, 1996: 17). However, it became increasingly apparent that

---

[1] Title taken from Heidensohn (2006: 3).

attempts to construct women as a 'unitary subject' (Carrington, 1998: 80) served to erase the 'intra-sex specificities among women' (Carrington, 2002: 119). Indeed, the endeavours of 'black feminist criminology' (Arnold, 1995; Rice, 1990; Russell, 1992) provide a percipient reminder of the need to widen the parameters of criminological concern to not only incorporate gender but also the diversity of experiences that 'gender' can encapsulate. As Gelsthorpe and McIvor (2007: 323) eloquently observe 'we are rarely just men or women, Black or Asian or White, but rather situate ourselves on a number of social and cultural planes'.

The second reading in this part, by Marcia Rice, challenges criminology to address such diversity. Rice outlines the peripheral treatment accorded to black women's experiences by both black and feminist criminologies arguing that the black woman's experiences of gender, race, class, crime and the criminal justice system – compounded by the historical context of slavery and colonialism – are likely to be qualitatively different to those of black men and white women. Rice then persuasively asserts the need for a sophisticated and nuanced approach to the study of crime which is theoretically and method-ologically capable of addressing the specificities of the black woman's experi-ence. Ultimately for Rice the 'black feminist perspective' is characterised by a commitment to 'eradicating oppression in all its forms as it affects the lives of men and women' (p. 25).

The increasing awareness of the need to locate female offending with regard to age, class, race, status, power, and so on, alerts us to the complexity and multiplicity of experiences that precipitate criminality. Indeed, a series of seminal studies have not only served to 'engender' criminology (Heidensohn, 2006: 3), but also to emphasise that the 'essential criminal women does not exist' (Carlen, 1985: 10). For example, Carlen (1985) and Worrall (1990) high-light the importance of economic marginalisation in making sense of why it is some women offend; Hudson (1989) notes how the sexualisation of female juvenile delinquency means that girls are often criminalised by the welfare and justice agencies with whom they come into contact; Leibrich (1993) observes the complex interplay of risk and protective factors in inducing desistance from and persistence in offending behaviours; and Phoenix (2001) and Saunders (2004) stress the multiplicity of contradictory factors which precipitate and sustain women's involvement in sex work. In mapping and seeking to under-stand women's broad pathways into crime these studies demonstrate that a gendered understanding of offending must engage with women's (and men's) experiences of economic and social disadvantage and their histories of abuse and victimisation (Gelsthorpe, 2003).

The third reading in this section highlights the unique and particular nature of the factors that may contribute to female criminality. Focusing on how status offences, such as running away from home and 'ungovernability', constitute the prime referral route to official social control agencies for girls, Chesney-Lind and Pasko demonstrate how recourse to delinquency may be a consequence of the strategies girls enact to escape and survive physical and/or sexual abuse. In effect, they argue that all too often girls' responses to experiences of victimisation are being criminalised. Given the 'invisibility' of girls within a juvenile justice system preoccupied with the maleness of the juvenile delinquent, Chesney-Lind and Pasko stress the need for a greater understanding of how gender, race and class shape the evident differences in not only an individual's offending experiences but also their life chances.

Continuing this focus on the prospect of 'criminalising' girls' problematic behaviour the final reading in this part outlines the potential social, political and personal repercussions of (mis)representing female offenders. Notwithstanding the evidence of Burman et al's (2000) study regarding the rarity of female violence and their finding that girls' resort to violence is in no way irrational, hysterical and pathological, the vexed question of female violence is eliciting much criminological, political and popular interest. Indeed, respectable fears regarding the 'unstable', 'out of control' and 'emotional' violent female offender abound (Burman, 2004: 38). Accordingly, the final reading in this part provides a powerful example of how the detail and nuances of gendered accounts of offending are susceptible to the vagaries of public anxieties and political will.

In the final reading, Worrall observes that since the early 1990s the UK has witnessed a series of 'moral panics' in relation to youth crime, for example 'rat boy' (the case of an elusive persistent young offender), the 'child killer' (in response to the murder of Jamie Bulger) and, most recently, the 'violent female offender'. Notwithstanding a paucity of empirical evidence, the latter has resulted in the (re)construction of violent girls as 'twisted sisters' (p. 35) which has interacted with a paradigm shift from welfare to justice responses to youth crime to shape girls' experiences of the youth justice system. Consequently, more of the problematic behaviours of 'bad' girls are being redefined as criminal, and there is an increased likelihood of this problematic behaviour being dealt with under the auspices of criminal as opposed to welfare systems. Worrall concludes that the net result is the greater criminalisation and incarceration of girls.

Suggestions for further reading:

Carlen, P. (ed.) (1985), *Criminal Women: Autobiographical Accounts, Diana Christina, Jenny Hicks, Josie O'Dwyer, Chris Tchiakousky and Pat Carlen*. Cambridge: Polity Press.

Taking a back-seat role as editor, Carlen presents a collection of autobiographical accounts of female offending which provides a compelling insight into the complexity, rationality and purpose of offending within the lives of women.

Batchelor, S., Burman, M. and Brown, J. (2001), 'Discussing violence: let's hear it from the girls', *Probation Journal*, 48(2): 125–34.

Presenting findings from a study undertaken in Scotland relating to the place of violence within girls lives, this article challenges some of the traditional thinking about violence which has primarily been derived from research on boys and young men.

Phoenix, J. (2001), *Making Sense of Prostitution*, 2nd edn. London: Palgrave.

A fascinating theoretical and empirical account of both the attractions and the pitfalls of being a street prostitute in contemporary Britain.

Stevens, A. (2006), *Confronting the 'Malestream': The Contribution of Feminist Criminologies*, Issues in Community and Criminal Justice Monograph no. 7. London: NAPO.

This is an engaging and accessible text which provides an overview and assessment of feminist incursions within the discipline of criminology.

1.1

Criminological theory: its ideology and implications concerning women
by Carol Smart

Criminological theories have rarely been concerned with the analysis of female criminality. Typically criminologists have either been content to sub-sume discussion of women offenders under 'general' theories, that is to say they have implicitly assumed the female is dealt with in discussing the male, or they have dealt with them exceptionally briefly in the way that other 'marginal' or 'special' categories are treated. The reason offered for this over-whelming lack of interest is that within the population of known offenders, female offenders constitute a statistically much smaller proportion than male offenders. With the exception of offences like shoplifting and soliciting, the number of female offenders nowhere exceed the numbers of male offenders known to the police. But this statistical 'insignificance' alone cannot fully explain why so little work has been attempted in this area. Rather the relative absence of work on crimes by women may be considered as symbolic of the nature of the discipline of criminology. Traditional criminology in both the UK and the USA has always had close links with social and penal policy-making bodies with the result that research has tended to be directed towards areas officially designated as social problems. Female criminality has not generally been treated as a particularly important or pressing social problem, not only because of its comparative rarity, but also because of the nature of the offences committed by women. Official statistics, which are themselves a problematic source of information in criminology (Hindess, 1973; Wiles, 1970), indicate that women engage mostly in petty offences and, with the exception of prostitutes, most appearances by women in court are for first offences. Women do not seem to pose a serious recidivist problem therefore; nor a threat to society, and so fail to constitute a real problem to the agencies of social control. Failing to become a pressing social problem has meant that studies of female criminality have not received much official support or finance with the result that traditional 'control oriented' criminology has also shown a lack of interest in this area.

The lack of attention devoted to the question of crimes committed by women and their treatment has given rise to the present unsatisfactory understanding of female offenders and the offences they commit. There has been virtually no development of our knowledge in this area with the result that ostensibly scientific works predicated upon unexplicated ideologies have been allowed to stand uncriticized. Recognition of the under-development of criminology and sociology in this area is explicit in Ward's statement to the U.S. National Commission on Crimes of Violence that:

> Our knowledge of the character and causes of female criminality is at the same stage of development that characterised our knowledge of male criminality some thirty or more years ago.
>
> (Ward, 1968)

As a consequence of this lack of development the ideology and method-ological limitation inherent in some of the classical works on female criminal-ity still inform contemporary studies and, furthermore, are reflected in the treatment of female offenders.

This paper is therefore concerned to reveal the ideological foundations of the major theories of female criminality, in particular the culturally rela-tive, commonsense conceptions of women on which they are based. I shall concentrate on the works of Lombroso (1895) and Pollak (1950), whose theories are still influential, as well as the work of Cowie, Cowie and Slater (1968) whose analysis of female delinquents reveals the influence of the early theorists. The second part of this paper will focus on the possible implications of the ideologies inherent in these studies of female criminality.

The ideology of theories of female criminality

The most significant ideology which informs both classical and contemporary accounts of female criminality is a sexist ideology. It is sexist not because it differentiates between the sexes but because it attributes to one sex socially undesirable characteristics which are assumed to be intrinsic or 'natural' char-acteristics of that sex. Such an ideology arises because the socially structured and culturally given nature of the assumptions informing these theories are not treated as subjects for analysis; rather common-sense understandings are taken for granted as a suitable platform from which to commence theorizing. Working within the natural attitude, adopting culturally given understand-ings of the nature of sexual differences and in particular the characteristics attributed to women, the theorists concerned provide merely a scientific gloss for common-sense understandings. Myths about the 'inherent' evil in women or their lack of intelligence and ability and their 'natural' passivity therefore abound in these studies and they are used uncritically to supply 'evidence' for either the greater or lesser involvement of women in crime.

An equally persuasive theme implicit in most accounts of female criminality, which also stems from the uncritical attitudes of the pioneers in this field,
is that of biological determinism. Biological determinist accounts may take
two forms, although they are rarely mutually exclusive. Firstly women who
have committed offences are perceived to have been motivated by fundamental biological bodily processes. For example, menstruation or the menopause,
by affecting the hormonal balance in the body, are taken to be precipitating
factors leading some women to commit criminal acts. In such cases action is
seen to be directly related to, or even directly produced by, hormonal or
biological imbalance. Secondly, and more significantly, the female biology is
perceived to determine the temperament, intelligence, ability and aggression
of women. In this case it is usually argued that women are 'naturally' averse to
crime and hence any involvement in criminal activities is treated as symp-
tomatic of a fundamental physical (or more recently mental) pathology. As a
consequence of biological factors assuming such a key status in studies of
female criminality it has followed that female offenders have been treated as a
homogeneous group. Such factors as class, status, power, age, culture and so
on are not considered as pertinent to an understanding of female criminality
even though these variables are now accepted as relevant to the study of male
criminality. As a result, therefore, of both the creation of a narrow stereotypical perception of women which relies upon culturally constituted understandings of the nature of female sexuality and the belief in biological
determination, those women who do commit offences are judged to be either
criminal by nature (Pollak, 1950) or pathological because they deviate from
the 'true' biologically determined nature of woman which is to be law abiding
(Cowie et al., 1968; Lombroso, 1895). The latter perspective which treats
female offenders as pathological is prevalent in both classical and contemporary criminological theories, one consequence of this being the continuing
implementation of policy decisions predicated upon an understanding that
criminal activity by women is a product of pathology located within the individual rather than an exemplification of meaningful action. Indeed it has
become a 'popular' belief that women who commit criminal offences are
'sick' and in need of psychiatric treatment; it is to a much lesser extent that this
'sick' analogy has been adopted in the treatment of men as men are generally
assumed to be rationally responsible for their actions while women are not.

   This theme of the biological basis of female criminality which has
become so entrenched in official and academic explanations was first fully
formulated by Lombroso in his work entitled *The Female Offender* published
in 1895. It is of course true that Lombroso employed biological factors to
account for male criminality but with few exceptions this school of thought
has been repudiated. As Shoham maintains,

   Today . . . . ., the Lombrosian myth in criminology, and the few contemporary adherents to the biophysiological approach to the genesis of

crime, are considered a sad episode which retarded the development of the field by almost half a century.

(Shoham, 1974: 167)

This is undoubtedly the case with most of Lombroso's theories and yet the ideological content of his work on female criminality persists in contemporary explanations. In particular his assertion that most women, with the exception of the rare 'born' criminal, are 'congenitally . . . less inclined to crime' and his belief that women's 'natural' passivity and conservatism robs them of the initiative to break the law have become a predominent part of the ideology in contemporary criminological and sociological theories.

The work of Cowie, Cowie and Slater (1968) is perhaps the best exemplar of a modified form of the ideology inherent in Lombroso's work. In analysing the differences between male and female delinquency they state,

Differences between the sexes in hereditary predisposition (to crime) could be explained by sex-linked genes. Furthermore the female mode of personality, more timid, more lacking in enterprise, may guard her against delinquency.

(Cowie et al., 1968: 167)

Clearly, Cowie, Cowie and Slater and other theorists who adopt similar positions, have taken no cognizance of cross-cultural studies nor of historical data which reveal that, rather than there being only one 'female mode of personality' there are a multitude of culturally and historically based sets of attitudes and expectations that influence the consciousness or personalities of women, thus producing gender-related behaviour. To suggest, for example, that women are 'more lacking in enterprise', or in the case of Lombroso, lead more sedentary lives because of their genetic structure, is to ignore the social situation facing many women which gives no opportunity or outlet for active or creative behaviour.

Interestingly, Lombroso maintains that one sure sign of criminality in women is the *lack* of a maternal instinct. This deficiency was perceived to mean that 'psychologically and anthropologically' the delinquent woman belongs more to the male than the female sex. But this belief, which is echoed in Cowie's work, is based on not only biological determinism but also on a confusion between sex and gender. As Ann Oakley (1972) has pointed out sex is a biological term and gender a social, cultural and psychological term such that for a woman to act in a socially defined 'masculine' way does not mean that she is sexually or biologically abnormal. However, where gender appropriate behaviour is seen as biologically determined women who adopt 'masculine' forms of behaviour become labelled 'masculine' themselves and this has connotations of 'maleness' which are seen to be linked to hormonal or genetic abnormalities. Cowie et al. in fact failed to distinguish between sex and gender at all, they state,

> Is there any evidence that *masculinity or femininity of bodily constitution* plays any part in predisposing to delinquency and in determining the form it takes? (Emphasis added.)

In response to this question they maintain,

> Delinquents of both sexes tend to be larger than controls, and overgrown by population standards . . . Markedly masculine traits in girl delinquents have been commented on by psychoanalytic observers. . . . *we can be sure that they have had some physical basis.* (Emphasis added.)
> (Cowie et al., 1968: 171–2)

The point is that female delinquents are not perceived to be merely adopting behaviour more usually associated with males, they are portrayed as being chromosomally or genetically abnormal. This means that the 'treatment' of such offenders becomes justifiable, the aims, intentionality and rationality of the deviant act are overlooked and the social and cultural conditions under which the act took place can be relegated to the vague status of 'environmental' factors whose only role is to occasionally 'trigger' the inherent pathology of the deviant. Crime and delinquency can thereby be treated as an individual, not social, phenomenon.

Inherent in this 'individual pathology' model is a control oriented ideology which serves to locate the causes of 'problems' in specific individuals and which supplies the relevant knowledge and understanding to develop the appropriate technologies and social policies for controlling deviant members. Criminological theorizing thereby becomes a means of providing new technologies for control or, failing that, a means of legitimating current policies which become justified as forms of treatment rather than punishment. Moreover, while such theorizing is not concerned to provide the subjects of its study with the means to change their social situation and status it does provide a damaging anti-intellectual diet for its consumers which in fact serves to mystify the social phenomenon under research. For example, the way in which Cowie, Cowie and Slater present their evidence is worth noting for they attempt to appeal to the reader's 'senses' rather than intellect or critical faculties. They have a tendency to invoke 'commonsense' and concepts of the 'natural' to support their claims rather than relying on credible, scientific evidence. Rather than reducing the influence of their work however, their anti-theoretical and anti-intellectual approach may be conducive to acceptance by policy-makers who perceive themselves to be concerned with 'practical' issues and not theoretical ones. For example, Cowie et al. state,

Common-sense suggests that the main factors are somatic ones, especially hormonal ones . . . . . (Emphasis added.)

and again later,

It is more natural to suppose that the male-female difference, both in delinquency rates and in the forms that delinquency takes, would be closely connected with the masculine or feminine pattern of development of personality. (Emphasis added.)

(Cowie et al., 1968: 170–1)

This debunking of a theoretical and intellectual approach to the topic may be seen as the witting embrace of ideology.

I have implied that the work of Pollak (1950) is also of considerable significance to the present state of our knowledge of female criminality. His work is broadly within the same ideological tradition of Lombroso and Cowie but the conclusions he draws show some interesting variations. For example, he does not assume that fewer women than men commit crimes; in fact, he argues that women are the most able criminals as biologically and socially they are well equipped for lying, deceiving and trickery. Consequently, he argues that they commit heinous crimes but are never apprehended and he thereby gives considerable support to the theological and common-sensical view that women are inherently more evil than men. He maintains in fact that women instigate crimes and manipulate the gullible male sex into enacting them, in other words women are the cause of the downfall of others. The ability to be manipulative is, according to Pollak, due to the physiologically based fact that women can conceal their 'positive emotion' during sexual intercourse while men cannot as they must achieve an erection. He argues,

It cannot be denied that this basic physiological difference may well have a great influence on the degree of confidence which the two sexes have in the possible success of concealment and thus on their character pattern in this respect.

(Pollak, 1950: 10)

Thus, rather than considering the implications of the sexual politics which produce a situation in which many women face sexual intercourse when they are neither aroused nor willing, Pollak takes this example as a basis for further assumptions about women's ambiguous attitude towards 'veracity' and deceit.

There are numerous other examples in Pollak's work where his uncritical, anti-feminist presuppositions lead him to make authoritative but unsubstantiated statements about the origins of female criminality. In this respect his work cannot be differentiated from other ideologically informed works like Lombroso's and Cowie's. Where he does offer an important variation however, which is uniquely significant in terms of its implication, is in relation to the treatment of female offenders by the Courts and police. He maintains that the chivalrous attitude of men towards women, which is based on a misconception of women as gentle and passive creatures, leads them to treat female offenders more leniently than their male counterparts. He states

> One of the outstanding concomitants of the existing inequality between the sexes is chivalry and the general protective attitude of man towards woman . . . . . Men hate to accuse women and thus indirectly to send them to their punishment, police officers dislike to arrest them, district attorneys to prosecute them, judges and juries to find them guilty and so on.
>
> (Pollak, 1950: 151)

Such beliefs are still extremely prevalent both in common-sense and criminological accounts, in spite of evidence which reveals that in sentencing, magistrates are more likely to be influenced by a previous record or the seriousness of the offence than the sex of offender (Walker, 1973. 300) and that in some cases, particularly in so-called moral offences, female offenders are actually treated more severely (Chesney-Lind, 1973) than male offenders. The implications of this ideology of chivalry and male benevolence are discussed in the next section.

The implications of the ideological content of theories of female criminality

The implications of theorizing have frequently been overlooked by those sociologists or criminologists who perceive themselves merely to be observers or recorders of everyday life. Yet social theories do have indirect social implications either by confirming common-sense and culturally located beliefs or by altering the consciousness of people in their everyday lives through a criticism and demystification of accepted values and beliefs. Allen recognizes this when he argues that,

> Theories enter into the ideological process and emerge in an abbreviated, often vulgarized, sloganized form embedded in language and thought processes alike. They form the basis of common-sense attitudes. They are transmitted through the family, enter into folklore, get expression through the mass media. In a variety of subtle ways conventional theoretical explanations enter the conscious of individuals and provide them with instant explanations.
>
> (Allen, 1974: 10)

Although this process by which theories are translated into common conceptual currency will influence the actors own perception of self, our concern here is more with the way in which particular 'scientific' theories of female criminality, operating with conceptions of social science which indicate an interest in technical control rather than emancipation or liberation and emphasizing the biological and pathological nature of criminal offences, may have influenced and/or legitimated the conceptualizations of policy makers such that female criminality is, or continues to be, interpreted as a biologically-rooted sickness.

Indeed there is a clear trend within the English penal system towards adopting a concept of 'treatment' for offenders rather than, or in association with, punishment. This development may be simply indicative of an 'official' recognition of more 'efficient' means of controlling criminals than have been available in the past but it may also indicate a change in the conception of the motivational basis of criminality away from the classical concept of responsibility to a more positivistic orientation which emphasizes individual pathology.

The development is most marked in penal policies relating to female offenders. For example one consequence of the adoption of the 'sick' analogy for understanding what is defined as criminal motivation, is the transformation of Holloway from a prison to a secure psychiatric hospital in which women will receive psychiatric treatment related to their perceived individual psychological 'needs' rather than to their offence (Faulkner, 1971). The assumption underlying this policy is that to deviate in a criminal way is 'proof' of some kind of mental imbalance in women. This position is quite consistent with other assumptions about the mental instability of women in general employed to explain or account for the mental health statistics which indicate that women suffer from mental illness more frequently than men. In fact mental illness has been perceived as an alternative to crime for women (Bertrand, 1973) – both crime and mental illness being treated as phenomena emerging from common 'causes' rather than as possible rational and logical action (Laing, 1968). Nigel Walker lends some credence to this practice when he states that,

> Certainly in practice women offenders have a higher chance of being dealt with as mentally abnormal ... We cannot however exclude the possibility that psychiatrists' diagnoses ... are being influenced by the ... proposition ... that there is probably something abnormal about a woman delinquent.
>
> (Walker, 1973: 300)

The implications of the adoption of the 'sick' analogy in the treatment of female offenders does not merely rest with the introduction of therapeutic methods and the removal and denial of responsibility for action. It in fact creates a situation in which realistic and potentially self-determining educational and vocational courses are intentionally excluded or reduced in importance. The women in the new Holloway will not be able to work, except for therapeutic or general domestic work. They will not be given the opportunity to learn skills which will fundamentally improve their life-chances, not only because the average stay in Holloway is so short, but also because it is not the principal aim of penal policy for women. In fact their typically dependent status will be confirmed and their ability to control or possibly change their lifestyles further damaged. Penal policy for female offenders is geared to preserving the typical female role, its intention is to make women and girls adapt to their pre-given passive social role which by definition is thought to preclude deviant behaviour. The criminological theories discussed in the preceding section (with the exception of Pollak's work) all provide a justification for this policy because they support commonsense understandings of the 'natural' role and behaviour of women. Even if it is impossible to show that these theories of female criminality have precipitated some of the changes in the treatment of female criminals it can still be argued that the ideological basis of such works offers a 'scientistic' legitimation of social policy oriented towards an adoption of the 'sick' analogy, the development of more effective techniques of control and the perpetuation of the subordinate position of women.

Lastly, in considering the implication of these ideologically informed theories of female criminality, we must return to the idea of chivalry and male benevolence propounded by Pollak. While it is possible that sexual discrimination plays an important part in differential arrest and sentencing policy, it is misleading to assume that this discrimination is always in favour of the female sex. In fact it is difficult to reconcile the view that the police and legal system are staffed by 'chivalrous' men with reports on the treatment of female political prisoners (Davis, 1971), prostitutes (Davis, 1966; Millett, 1975) and raped women (Griffin, 1971; Weiss and Borges, 1973) It would seem that if sexual discrimination is an influential factor in the treatment of women it is not a simple variable that always leads to greater leniency. However the belief in chivalry and leniency has become a part of our (mis)-understanding of the operation of the legal system and it has served to conceal the existence of unfavourable attitudes towards female offenders and the real injustice often meted out in the name of benevolence and paternalism (Chesney-Lind, 1973; Terry, 1970). The very existence of chivalry is synonymous with an inequality of power between the sexes in which a woman must depend on a man for her protection. Women must deserve their protection however, and women and girls of a 'bad moral' character who lose their rights in this respect, leave themselves open to the full force of outraged morality. It should also be remembered that the morality co-existent with chivalry imposes double-standards on men and women, frequently condoning the same behaviour in one sex while punishing it in the other. As Chesney-Lind maintains,

> These labels (immoral, incorrigible) allow for the same abuses that characterize the labels of 'sick' or 'insane' – that is, the 'saving' or 'helping' of a girl often justifies more radical and severe 'treatment' than does the punishment of a male law violator.
>
> (1973: 57)

The practice of sending adolescent girls to Approved Schools (now community homes) for being found 'in need of care and protection' or for being in 'moral danger' is an example of the double-edged nature of chivalry and paternalism. The Home Office statistics for 1960 reveal that while 95 per cent of boys are sent to Approved Schools for committing offences, only 36 per cent of girls are similarly committed. Consequently 64 per cent of these girls are committed to penal institutions without having committed any criminal offence (Richardson, 1969). The justification for this discrimination is often couched in humanitarian terms, for example as a form of protection or as an opportunity for moral guidance, but in practice it would seem that juvenile girls are punished severely for behaviour which is usually overlooked in boys. A similar case can be made for prostitutes who are socially stigmatized and punished for their behaviour while their clients remain respected members of society. Such inequitable treatment finds its justification in the ideology which underpins most of the theories of female criminality. Once it is accepted that deviant females are sick individuals or that they are naturally inclined to wrongdoing and this is combined with a belief in the 'benefits' of chivalry and paternalism it is not surprising that Cowie can make the statement that,

> These girls had to be removed from society into the security of a residential school much more for their own sakes than to protect society. *And yet, if one looks at their deliquent acts, they are of a very petty and trivial kind.* (Emphasis added.)
>
> (Cowie et al., 1968: 166)

The frequent injustice and the severity of the 'treatment' of female offenders or adolescents involved in so-called sexual or moral deviations is therefore veiled in humanitarianism. Moreover because the courts and other agents of social control reflect the double-standards of morality implicit in our sociosexual mores and because their attitudes towards women are informed by a common-sense understanding of what a 'natural' female should be, negative discrimination towards women in 'sexual' offences, including rape cases, is overlooked. Theories of female criminality have tended to preserve this mystification and to justify the differential treatment of male and female offenders in terms of unexplicated assumptions about the 'true nature' of men and women. They have in no way served to clarify our understanding of a complex issue. It is to be hoped that new trends in the sociology of deviance and criminology will not merely replicate the major limitations of existing studies of female criminality by treating this phenomenon as marginal to a general understanding of the nature of crime in contemporary society.

1.2
Challenging orthodoxies in feminist theory: a black feminist critique
by Marcia Rice

Over the past decade feminist criminologists have been challenging stereo-typical representations of female offenders. Despite these advances, black women and women from developing countries have been noticeably absent from this discourse. However, in part as a result of a surge of writings by black women (for example, Amos and Parmar, 1984; Carby, 1982; Mama, 1984; Bhavani and Coulson, 1986), there are now attempts to incorporate black women's experiences into feminist writings (Carlen and Worrall, 1987), though few attempt to develop perspectives which take into account race, gender and class simultaneously.

[. . .]

The contribution of feminist criminology

Given the history and theoretical objectives of feminist criminology, one might have assumed that the monolithic, uni-dimensional perspectives employed by traditional theorists would have been abandoned for a more dynamic approach. But, almost without exception, feminist criminological research – from the late 1960s to date – has focused on white female offenders. Pioneering writings by Heidensohn (1968) and Smart (1976) and more recent writings by Carlen and Worrall (1987) and Morris (1987) have all adopted an essentialist position with regards to the construct of 'women' and have paid little attention to the relevance of race. Sexist images of women have been challenged, but racist stereotypes have largely been ignored.

(White) women and crime

Since the 1970s, feminist criminologists have launched a critical attack on male-dominated theoretical premises in criminology. The basic point which they make is that these expositions are not theories of women's crime but stereotypes which perpetuate sexist ideologies of women. Feminists insist that many of the assumptions made about female criminals are incorrect – they are based on middle-class notions of morality and behaviour – and that the focus on biological and social pathologies to explain both crime and conformity is inadequate.

Central to these arguments is the belief that notions such as 'femininity' and 'sexuality' are constructs, not objective givens. But, this said, feminist writers have made little reference to the different cultural experiences and socialization patterns of black women. There is a failure to situate, for example, discussions of sex roles within a structural explanation of the social origins of these roles which are influenced by black women's racial and sexual experiences and their general position in society (Malson, 1983). Gender differences are assumed to be universal, irrespective of race (or class).

This is clearly not so. Despite significant changes in family structures in Britain, the popular representation of the family is the husband/father as the economic supporter of his wife and children and the wife/mother as the full-time domestic worker and child carer. This idealization does not touch on the experiences of black (or working-class) women. It not only excludes them, but distorts the particular gender roles adopted by them (Lewis, 1977; Carby, 1982; Malson, 1983). I provide two examples of this.

First, as a result of economic pressures and cultural distinctions, black women in Britain are more likely than white women to be single and full-time employees on low wages and are less likely to be primarily dependent on a man. Thus, in 1986, 40 per cent of West Indian women worked full-time compared with 20 per cent of white women and 25 per cent of Asian women. Moreover, *Social Trends* (Central Statistical Office, 1988) indicates that most women from ethnic minorities work soon after the birth of their children out of the necessity to provide for their families. Female-headed households are common amongst West Indians; yet the matriarchal family structure (coupled with low rates of marriage and high rates of illegitimacy) is viewed as 'pathological'.

Second, black girls develop early on a particular set of subcultural values which stress strength, independence, resilience and perseverance and which are necessary in the face of a racist and sex-segregated labour market (Riley, 1981; Bryan et al., 1985). However, these qualities, when judged by ethnocentric standards, are viewed as 'unfeminine'. Feminist writers have challenged neither of these stereotypical representations.

(White) women and the criminal justice system

Also since the 1970s a number of feminist researchers have investigated a series of issues pertaining to the discriminatory practices and sexist ideologies present in the criminal justice system. They have covered a range of areas – women as defendants (Edwards, 1984), probationers (Worrall, 1989) and prisoners (Carlen, 1983). While there has been some acknowledgement that black women are not dealt with in the same way as white women (Eaton, 1986; Morris, 1987), no research has been carried out in Britain which compares the sentences of black and white women. This is an important point as a failure to consider the potentially different experiences of black women may invalidate the research findings. Race may be as important as gender, if not more so.

Research into women's imprisonment has covered a range of topics – experiences in prison (Carlen, 1983; O'Dwyer et al., 1987), prison discipline and medical services (Mandaraka-Sheppard, 1986) and post-prison experiences (Wilkinson, 1988). Most of the studies point out that the majority of women are there not because of the seriousness of their offence or their criminal record, but rather as a result of their different and 'unacceptable' lifestyles. Particular emphasis has also been laid on the patriarchal ideologies which attempt to reinforce traditional modes of feminine behaviour on women in prison.

Almost without exception the bulk of the research carried out on women in custody has referred to 'women' (cf GLC, 1985) as a homogeneous category and has ignored the interaction of gender, race and class. For example, there is hardly any recognition of the special problems which black female prisoners encounter during their sentence on remand or after release. There is an assumption that all women are equally disadvantaged. For example, O'Dwyer, Wilson and Carlen write:

Women in prison suffer all the same deprivation, indignities and degradations as male prisoners. Additionally they suffer other problems that are specific to them as imprisoned women.

(1987: 178)

This statement is inadequate as it stands: it does not acknowledge the added problems of the isolation of and discrimination against black women. Bryan et al. (1985), for example, point to the fact that a higher percentage of black than white women in prison are on prescribed psychotropic drugs. This requires explanation. Furthermore, many black women serving long sentences are not indigenous but are from West Africa and are serving sentences for drugs offences. This group of female prisoners, often awaiting deportation, have special needs; for example, contact is usually severed with their families and there are problems of communication.

Feminist criminologists have paid more attention to race in research on women's victimization. Hall (1985), for example, found that black women were much more likely to be assaulted than white women because black women's economic situation tends to exacerbate their vulnerability, particularly as they work unsocial hours and rely on public transport. But while feminists have readily acknowledged that sexism is an important explanatory factor in the physical and sexual assault of any woman, they have been slow to see that racism is a further precipitating factor in attacks on black women. One black woman in Hall's survey sums up the significance of this:

> There's a particular fear of white men that Black girls grow up with. We know they think we're hot, sexual animals, that we're always available. It goes back to slavery. What they think about us sexually is part of the racism.
>
> (1985: 48)

There is another point to be made here. Some feminist criminologists, in arguing for longer sentences for offences against women, have ignored the discriminatory impact this is likely to have on black (and working-class) men.

Feminist research methods

Feminist theories have prided themselves on developing a method of inquiry which reconsiders the relationship between the researcher and the subject (McRobbie, 1982). Therefore, most of the research done by feminists has used methods which allow some participation by subjects in the research process. However, despite claims by feminists to be representing the subjective experiences of *all* women, much of the research has yet to prove its relevance to black women. In hooks's words:

> White women who dominate feminist discourse today rarely question whether or not their perspective on women's reality is true to the lived experience of women as a collective group.
>
> (1984: 3)

Feminist theorists have assumed that, as women, they were qualified to make assertions and generalizations on the grounds that all women's experiences are reducible to gender. However, as McRobbie pointed out in a different (class) context:

> No matter how much our past personal experience figures and feeds into the research programme, we can't possibly assume that it necessarily corresponds in any way to that of the research subjects.
>
> (1982: 52)

This must apply even more so when the researchers are white, middle-class feminists. Ramazanoglu makes clear the reasons for this:

> [They] can live in communities where marriage is unnecessary . . . can choose to avoid families, have the power to counter some of the effects of

patriarchy, [can] exercise considerable control over reproduction and their own bodies, [and] are far removed from the experiences of the majority of women. They are unusual in the extent of the choices they can exercise, and in the lack of contradictions in their personal lives – in short, they are highly privileged.

(1986: 85–6)

In sum, feminist criminologists have developed a theoretical approach which emphasizes the significance of patriarchal oppression and sexist ideological practices. The main problem with this is that, in assuming a universal dimension of men's power, this approach has ignored the fact that race significantly affects black women's experiences in the home, in the labour market, of crime and in the criminal justice system.

Ethnocentrism and feminist theory

Black women, like most other women, experience some degree of sexual oppression. However, this fails to acknowledge the complexity of gender considerations and the significance of other social taboos such as ethnicity and economic marginality. Kate Millett defined patriarchy as 'a set of social relations which has a material base in which there are hierarchical relations between men and solidarity among them which enables them in turn to dominate women' (1970–25). This unqualified focus on men's domination does not allow for the historical specificity of patriarchy which has meant that oppression is not experienced in the same way by all women or expressed by all men (Davis, 1981; Anthias and Davis-Yuval, 1983; Mama, 1984; hooks, 1989).

To take the first point. While accepting that relationships between black men and black women are likely to be as sexually oppressive as those experienced by white women, the historical experiences of black women compound their situation and produce a more complex mesh of struggles both within and outside the family. The experiences of black women as chattels under slavery and colonialism has meant that social relations were often mediated and bound up with economic as much as sexual reproduction. Thus, to understand the unique oppression of black women, we need to consider their experiences as black *people*.

We need to note also that black women do not comprise a homogeneous group, although the majority share a similar class position. Black women are further subdivided in terms of ethnicity. For example, there are differences in histories and experiences between Afro-American, Afro-Caribbean and Asian women (Anthias and Davis-Yuval, 1983). Finally, the relationship between black women and black men is not necessarily analogous to relationships between white women and white men; black women experience sexual and patriarchal oppression by black men but at the same time struggle alongside them against racial oppression (Davis, 1981; hooks, 1982).

With respect to the second point, the hierarchical relationship on which patriarchal oppression is premised assumes that black men naturally occupy a similar economically privileged position to white men. However, in Western industrialized countries black men have been socially and politically disadvantaged to an extent which has limited their power both in the family and in society in general.

One of the consequences of the employment structure in capitalist countries has been reliance on the labour of black women which has reduced their dependency on black men. This has contributed to the complex social and patriarchal relations in which black women are involved and stands in contradiction to the conception of the family which predominantly white feminist academics have endorsed. The traditional model of the family is based on ethnocentric ideals of the dependent married women with a male patriarchal head of the household. Black women's relationship to the family is then presented as deviant or pathological. This is reiterated in discussions of the black family in feminist theory where the dominance of black women in the family is portrayed as both a cause for consternation and an explanation for structural weakness.

An example is the work of Shulamith Firestone (1981) whose theories are based on the ethnocentric assumption that black women's experiences of racism can be understood simply as an extension of sexism (see Simons (1979) for a critique). She denies the significance and impact which the added dimension of racial oppression has for black women. However, the testimony of black women bears witness to the complex interaction of sexist and racist forms of oppression occurring simultaneously. To quote Bryan et al.:

Our relationship with men – both black and white – has meant that in addition to racism, black women have had to confront a form of sexism and sexual abuse which is unique to us. But it is impossible to separate our understanding of sexism in our community from its context in a racist society because popular acceptance of racist stereotypes of black women, black men and black juveniles not only compound our sexual oppression but have also become internalised.

(1985: 212)

Nor does Firestone's thesis acknowledge the status hierarchy which exists between black and white women. Hooks explains that white women may be victimized by sexism, but racism enables them to act as exploiters and oppressors of black women (and men):

Black women are in an unusual position for not only are we collectively at the bottom of the occupational ladder, but the overall social status is lower than that of any other group. Occupying such a position we bear the brunt of sexist, racist and classist oppression. Racist stereotypes of the strong, superhuman black woman are operative myths in the minds of many white women, allowing them to ignore the extent to which black women are likely to be victimised in this society and the role white women play in the maintenance and perpetuation of that victimisation.

(1984: 14)

Thus it is not just or simply that black women are subject to 'more' disadvantage than white women. Their oppression is of a qualitatively different kind. Women's experiences of oppression in social or patriarchal relations cannot be reduced to those of white middle-class women. Ethnocentric feminist analyses are not adequate. In areas as diverse as women's employment (Barrett, 1980; Beechey and Whitelegg, 1986), the family (Barrett and McIntosh, 1982) and crime (Smart, 1976; Carlen, 1983; Heidensohn, 1985[a]; Morris, 1987), the history of racism and its implications have been ignored. The significance of this intellectual exclusion or marginalization is far reaching. Joseph (1981: 95) has pointed out that to speak of women, all women categorically, is to perpetuate white supremacy because it is white women to whom the comments are addressed and for whom they are most appropriate. Barrett and McIntosh recognize this: 'Our work has spoken from an unacknowledged but ethnically specific position: its apparently universal applicability has been specious' (1985: 25). They appreciated the need for such work to be overhauled and re-examined in order to remove ethnocentricism.

Towards a broader framework

Since neither feminist criminologies nor black criminology adequately account for the crimes of black women – the former focuses exclusively on gender and the latter on race – one has to look beyond these perspectives for a more comprehensive understanding. This is not an easy task; it demands a more sensitive and complex set of analytical tools for understanding race and gender relations than currently exists (Brittan and Maynard, 1984).

There are various possible reformulations. First, if the problem is defined in terms of ethnocentricity, then the remedy could be a reconceptualization of the basic notions employed by feminist criminologists. For example, the category of 'women' and characterizations of 'femininity' and 'masculinity' could be constructed in ways which acknowledge black women's experiences (and black men's). The ideology of 'femininity' as it is usually portrayed lends support to the view that women have low crime rates and that women's crimes are trivial and insignificant (Carlen, 1985; Carlen and Worrall, 1987). Neither of these statements is necessarily true of black women.

Second, feminists could simply insert references to black women without altering their underlying theoretical premises. But ethnocentrism is not a 'problem' which can be eradicated simply by grafting black women onto the conceptal framework. Nor do black women want to be grafted on to feminism in a tokenistic manner (Carby, 1982: 232). Black feminists have argued that, by focusing primarily on patriarchal oppression and by not fully considering the significance of race and racism, feminist theory has oversimplified the position of black women who experience the triple oppression of racism, patriarchy and class discrimination. They have argued also that the racism in economic, social and political institutions must be confronted and theories based on cultural pluralism must be developed.

Third – and this is the approach I advocate – the remedy could be to develop a perspective which is both situational and interactive (Bourne, 1984). By this is meant an approach which recognizes that race, class and gender are ideological constructs which overlap and take on particular significances at particular periods in history and which require three levels of analysis: the macro (which involves examination of historical, economic and political influences), the middle-range (which involves consideration of cultural ideologies) and the micro (which includes identification of geographical location, age and other demographic factors).

One of the central elements in developing a black feminist perspective is the development of black consciousness and 'recognising that black women and white women have different histories and different relationships to present (and past) struggles in Britain and internationally' (Bhavani and Coulson, 1986: 82). Black feminists are therefore interested in describing the ways in which racism not only divides but draws together gender identities and how gender is experienced through racism. This particular discourse locates racism as central to feminist theory and practice. Thus a viable black feminist perspective would give full consideration to *all* women. In the words of Smith, a black American feminist:

Feminism is the political theory and practice that struggles to free *all* women: women of colour, working class women, poor women, disabled women, lesbians, old women – as well as white economically privileged heterosexual women. Anything less than this vision of total freedom is not feminism, but merely female self aggrandizement.

(1982: 49) (my emphasis)

Taking this wider approach, research would not simply address two race/gender groups (that is, black men and white women) but would include black women and white men (Smith and Stewart, 1983). Thus research into the effects of racism would explore whether or not this is experienced differently by black men and black women and research into the effects of sexism would explore whether or not this is experienced differently by white and black women. It would not assume that the experiences of each group were the same.

A black feminist perspective

By focusing primarily on gender and patriarchy, feminists have been constrained by their own limiting definitions. This stance, as I have shown, omits consideration of the complex process of oppression experienced by women (Brittan and Maynard, 1984). The histories of racism and sexism have meant that, as each social group cuts across racial, ethnic, sex and class lines, experiences vary as to degrees of discrimination and oppression. The forms and intensity of oppression are shaped by relationships between the oppressor and the oppressed and these are constantly renegotiated, reconstructed and re-established in their relative positions. My point is that oppression cannot be conceptualized in abstract and global ethnocentric terms such as patriarchy, but has to be seen as a set of dynamic relations based on concrete and specific situations.

Historically, the struggles of black men and white women have not always signified the liberation of the entire social group which they were representing, that is, black *people* and *all* women. As bell hooks succinctly states:

> White women and black men have it both ways. Black men may be victimised by racism but sexism allows them to act as exploiters and oppressors. White women may be victimised by sexism but racism enables them to act as exploiters and oppressors of black people. Both groups have led liberation movements that favour their interests and support the continued oppression of other groups. Black male sexism has undermined struggles to eradicate racism just as white female racism undermines feminist struggle.
>
> (1984: 14–15)

Black feminist politics was constructed out of a disillusionment with the peripheral treatment of black women by black liberation and feminist movements. In Britain, for example, black women committed to improving the quality of life of black women in particular and of black people in general have organized activities around such issues as immigration, employment, housing and education policy (Zhana, 1989). One of the distinguishing features of their work is their definition of feminism. A traditional definition is centred on advocacy of the political, economic and social equality of the sexes. Many black feminists believe this to be inadequate and propose an alternative framework.

Black feminists have been engaged in a process of extending the parameters of conventional definitions of feminism which are alien to many of them into a movement which is more relevant to their experiences (Davis, 1981; hooks, 1984; 1989). For the majority of black women, feminism is not just about equal rights for women but involves a much broader commitment to eradicating oppression in all its forms as it affects the lives of men and women. This approach recognizes the similar economic pressures from the state on black people in developed countries and on those suffering from imperialist oppression.

Drawing on this experience, black feminists in Britain and elsewhere have attempted to develop a theoretical perspective which recognizes the constraints of a racially structured, patriarchal capitalism (Bhavani and Coulson, 1986: 89). The emphasis is on the pervasiveness of racism in economic, social and political institutions through which black women's and black men's oppression is manifested (Bryan et al., 1985). The inclusion of men in a black feminist perspective is based on the realization that the liberation of women through challenges to patriarchal structures cannot be successful unless *all* repressive ideologies and practices are eradicated. Black women have added to the potential power of feminism as they have explored wider collective struggles against imperialism and racism (Hull et al., 1982; hooks, 1984; 1989). What these women have demonstrated is the possibility of a liberating feminist theory capable of being translated into practice.

Conclusion

If feminist criminologists wish to take account of black women's criminality then they must think carefully about the framework which they are using to analyse women's involvement in crime. Feminists must not include black women solely to add an extra edge to the victimization or offending patterns of women. Black women do not represent a homogeneous group and, as such, should not be grouped together and referred to as a common 'other'. Finally, the issues relevant for black women are applicable to the social, economic and political development of all. In essence, then, I would suggest:

1   Theories of black women's criminality should not be based on ethnocentric models or racist stereotypes which construct an inaccurate picture and which ignore important differences between female offenders.

2   Criminology should avoid the use of universal, unspecified categories of 'women' and 'blacks' in theoretical discussions and in research. Homogeneity cannot be assumed.

3   The significance of race and racism must be seen as integral to any analysis of (women's) criminality. There is insufficient research which analyses how gender roles and differential opportunity structures are affected by racism as well as sexism and which considers the implications of this for female offenders.

4   Comparative studies, on the basis of race, sex and class, should be carried out to determine how black and white women (and men) are dealt with in the criminal justice system.

5   Following the sentiments of Smart (1976: 85), studies of (women's) offending should be situated in the wider political, economic and social sphere.

6   The experiences of (black) women should not be investigated in a manner which separates the researcher from the subject. There should be a dynamic exchange which involves participation and consultation at all stages in the research process.

   [. . .]

1.3

Girls' troubles and 'female delinquency'
by Meda Chesney-Lind and Lisa Pasko

Every year, girls account for over a quarter of all arrests of young people in America (FBI, 2002, p. 239). Despite this, the young women who find themselves in the juvenile justice system either by formal arrest or referral are almost completely invisible. Our stereotype of the juvenile delinquent is so indisputably male that the general public, those experts whose careers in criminology have been built studying 'delinquency,' and those practitioners working with delinquent youth, rarely consider girls and their problems.

[. . .] [T]his invisibility has worked against young women in several distinct ways. First, [. . .] despite the fact that a considerable number of girls are arrested, explanations for the 'causes' of delinquency explicitly or implicitly avoid addressing them. Second, major efforts to reform the way the juvenile justice system handles youth were crafted with no concern for girls and their problems within the system. Finally, although girls are no longer completely forgotten at the academic and policy levels, there still exists a paucity of information on girls' development, survival strategies, and pathways to criminality. This dearth of knowledge means that those who work with girls have little guidance in shaping programs or developing resources that can respond to the problems many girls experience.

[. . .]

Boys' theories and girls' lives

Feminist criminologists have faulted all theoretical schools of delinquency for assuming that male delinquency, even in its most violent forms, was somehow a 'normal' response to their situations. Girls who shared the same social and cultural milieu as delinquent boys but who were not delinquents were considered by these theories somehow abnormal or 'over-controlled' (Cain, 1989). Essentially, law-abiding behavior on the part of at least some boys and men is taken by these theories as a sign of character, but when women avoid crime and violence, it is an expression of weakness (Naffine, 1987).

None of these traditional theories address the life situations of girls on the economic and political margins because they were not looking at or talking to these girls. So what might be another way to approach the issue of gender and delinquency? First, it is necessary to recognize that girls grow up in a different world than boys (Block, 1984; Orenstein, 1994). Girls are aware very early in life that, although both girls and boys have similar problems, girls 'have it heaps worse' (Alder, 1986).

Likewise, girls of color grow up and do gender in contexts very different from those of their white counterparts. Because racism and poverty are often fellow travelers, these girls are forced by their color and their poverty to deal early and often with problems of violence, drugs, and abuse. Their strategies for coping with these problems, often clever, strong, and daring, also tend to place them outside the conventional expectations of white girls (Campbell, 1984; Orenstein, 1994; Robinson, 1990).

The remainder of this chapter [. . .] deal[s] with two aspects of these gender differences. First, the situation of girls who come into the juvenile justice system charged with status offenses and other trivial offenses is considered. Next, the unique issue of girls' violence and girls' gang membership is explored. These two discussions explicate the unique ways gender, color, and class shape the choices made by girls – choices our society has often criminalized.

Criminalizing girls' survival: abuse, victimization, and girls' official delinquency

Girls and their problems have been ignored for a long time. When gender was considered in criminological theory, it was often a 'variable' in the testing of theories devised to explain boys' behavior and delinquency. As a result, few have considered that some, if not many, of the girls who are arrested and referred to court have unique and different problems than boys. Hints of these differences, though, abound.

For example, it has long been known that a major reason for the presence of many girls in the juvenile justice system was because their parents insisted on their arrest. After all, who else would report a youth as having 'run away' from home? In the early years, parents were the most significant referral source; in Honolulu, 44% of the girls who appeared in court in 1929–1930 were referred by parents (Chesney-Lind, 1971).

Recent national data, although slightly less explicit, also show that girls are more likely to be referred to court by sources other than law enforcement agencies (such as parents). In 1997, only 15% of youth referred for delinquency offenses, but 53% of youth referred for status offenses, were referred to court by sources other than law enforcement entities. The pattern among youth referred for status offenses, in which girls are overrepresented, is also clear. Over half of the youth referred for running away from home (60% of whom were girls) and 89% of the youth charged with ungovernability (half of whom were girls) were referred by entities outside of law enforcement, compared to only 6% of youth charged with liquor offenses (68% of whom were boys; Poe-Yamagata & Butts, 1996; Pope & Feyerherm, 1982; Puzzanchera et al., 2000). Additionally, girls are more frequently committed for status offenses than are boys: 9% of girls in training schools were committed for status offenses, compared to 1.5% of boys (Poe-Yamagata & Butts, 1996, p. 24).

The fact that parents are often committed to two standards of adolescent behavior is one explanation for these disparities – one that should not be discounted as a major source of tension even in modern families. Despite expectations to the contrary, gender-specific socialization patterns have not changed very much, and this is especially true for parents' relationships with their daughters (Ianni, 1989; Kamler, 1999; Katz, 1979; Orenstein, 1994; Thorne, 1993). Even parents who oppose sexism in general feel 'uncomfortable tampering with existing traditions' and 'do not want to risk their children becoming misfits' (Katz, 1979, p. 24).

Thorne (1993), in her ethnography of gender in grade school, found that girls were still using 'cosmetics, discussions of boyfriends, dressing sexually, and other forms of exaggerated "teen" femininity to challenge adult, and class and race-based authority in schools' (p. 156). She also found that 'the double standard persists, and girls who are overtly sexual run the risk of being labeled sluts' (p. 156).

Contemporary ethnographies of school life echo the validity of these parental perceptions. Orenstein's (1994) observations also point to the durability of the sexual double standard; at the schools she observed, 'sex "ruins" girls; it enhanced boys' (p. 57). Parents, too, according to Thorne (1993), have new reasons to enforce the time-honored sexual double standard. Perhaps correctly concerned about sexual harassment and rape, to say nothing of HIV/AIDS, 'parents in gestures that mix protection with punishment, often tighten control of girls when they become adolescents, and sexuality becomes a terrain of struggle between the generations' (Thorne, 1993: p. 156). Finally, Thorne notes that as girls use sexuality as a proxy for independence, they sadly and ironically reinforce their status as sexual objects seeking male approval – ultimately ratifying their status as the subordinate sex.

Whatever the reason, parental attempts to adhere to and enforce the sexual double standard will continue to be a source of conflict between them and their daughters. Another important explanation for girls' problems with their parents that has received attention only in more recent years is that of physical and sexual abuse. Looking specifically at the problem of childhood sexual abuse, it is increasingly clear that this form of abuse is a particular problem for girls.

Girls are, for example, much more likely to be the victims of child sexual abuse than are boys. In nearly eight out of ten sexual abuse cases, the victim is female (Flowers, 2001, p. 146). From a review of community studies, Finkelhor and Baron (1986) estimate that roughly 70% of the victims of sexual abuse are female (p. 45). Sexual abuse of girls tends to start earlier than that of boys (Finkelhor & Baron, 1986, p. 48), girls are more likely than boys to be assaulted by a family member (often a stepfather; DeJong, Hervada, & Emmett, 1983; Russell, 1986), and as a consequence, their abuse tends to last longer than boys' (DeJong et al., 1983). All of these factors cause more severe trauma and dramatic short- and long-term effects in victims (Adams-Tucker, 1982). The effects noted by researchers in this area move from the well-known 'fear, anxiety, depression, anger and hostility, and inappropriate sexual behavior' (Browne & Finkelhor, 1986, p. 69) to behaviors that include running away from home, difficulty in school, truancy, drug abuse, pregnancy, and early marriage (Browne & Finkelhor, 1986; Widom & Kuhns, 1996). In addition, girls who have experienced sexual abuse in their families are at greater risk for subsequent sexual abuse later in life (Flowers, 2001).

Herman's (1981) study of incest survivors in therapy found that they were more likely to have run away from home than a matched sample of women whose fathers were 'seductive' (33% vs. 5%). Another study of women patients found that 50% of the victims of child sexual abuse, but only 20% of the nonvictim group, left home before the age of 18 (Meiselman, 1978).

National research on the characteristics of girls in the juvenile justice system shows the role played in girls' delinquency by physical and sexual abuse. According to a study of girls in juvenile correctional settings conducted by the American Correctional Association (ACA; 1990), a very large proportion of these girls – about half of whom were of minority background – had experienced physical abuse (61.2%), and nearly half said that they had experienced this abuse 11 or more times. Many had reported the abuse, but a large number said that either nothing changed (29.9%) or that reporting it just made things worse (25.3%). More than half of these girls (54.3%) had experienced sexual abuse, and for most this was not an isolated incident; a third reported that it happened 3 to 10 times, and 27.4% reported that it happened 11 times or more. Most were 9 years old or younger when the abuse began. Again, although many reported the abuse (68.1%), reporting the abuse tended to cause no change or made things worse (ACA, 1990, pp. 56–58).

Given this history, it should be no surprise that the vast majority ran away from home (80.7%) and that of those who ran, 39% had run away 10 or more times. Over half (53.8%) said they had attempted suicide, and when asked the reason why, said it was because they 'felt no one cared' (ACA, 1990, p. 55). Finally, what might be called a survival or coping strategy has been criminalized; girls in correctional establishments reported that their first arrests were typically for running away from home (20.5%) or for larceny theft (25.0%; ACA, 1990, pp. 46–71).

Detailed studies of youth entering the juvenile justice system in Florida have compared the 'constellations of problems' of girls and boys (Dembo, Sue, Borden, & Manning, 1995; Dembo, Williams, & Schmeidler, 1993). These researchers found that girls were more likely than boys to have abuse histories and contact with the juvenile justice system for status offenses, whereas boys had higher rates of involvement with various delinquent offenses. Further research on a larger cohort of youth ($N = 2,104$) admitted to an assessment center in Tampa concluded that 'girls' problem behavior commonly relates to an abusive and traumatizing home life, whereas boys' law violating behavior reflects their involvement in a delinquent life style' (Dembo et al., 1995, p. 21).

This suggests that many young women are running away from profound sexual victimization at home and, once on the streets, are forced into crime to survive. Girls who are sexually abused are more likely than abused boys to run away from home as a direct result of their sexual victimization. As long-term runaway youth, these girls are more likely to engage in a prostitution lifestyle, which is highly correlated with other future problems and victimizations, such as AIDS, depression, and rape (Flowers, 1987, 2001; Widom & Kuhns, 1996). The average age of entry into prostitution for girls in the United States is 14; this makes sense when considering that the rate of child sexual abuse is highest for girls when they are age 12 to 17 (Flowers, 2001, p. 146; O'Toole & Schiffman, 1997).

Interviews with girls who have run away from home show, very clearly, that they do not have much attachment to their delinquent activities. They are angry about being labeled as delinquent yet engage in illegal acts (Chesney-Lind & Shelden, 1998). A Wisconsin study found that 54% of the girls who ran away found it necessary to steal money, food, and clothing to survive. A few exchanged sexual contact for money, food, or shelter (Phelps, McIntosh, Jesudason, Warner, & Pohlkamp, 1982, p. 67). In their study of runaway youth, McCormack and his colleagues found that sexually abused female runaways were significantly more likely than their nonabused counterparts to engage in delinquent or criminal activities, such as substance abuse, petty theft, and prostitution (McCormack, Janus, & Burgess, 1986, pp. 392–393).

The backgrounds of adult women in prison underscore the important links between women's childhood victimization and their later criminal careers (Snell & Morton, 1994). Women offenders frequently report abuse in their life histories. About half of the women in jail (48%) and 57% of women in state prisons report experiences of sexual and/or physical abuse in their lives (Bureau of Justice Statistics, 1999).

Confirmation of the consequences of childhood sexual and physical abuse on adult female criminal behavior has come from a large quantitative study of 908 individuals with substantiated and validated histories of victimization. Widom (1988) found that abused or neglected girls were twice as likely as a matched group of controls to have an adult crime record (16% vs. 7.5%). The difference was also found among men but was not as dramatic (42% vs. 33%). Men who had been abused were more likely to contribute to the 'cycle of violence,' having more arrests for violent offenses as adult offenders than the control group. In contrast, when women with abuse backgrounds did become involved with the criminal justice system, their arrests tended to involve property and order offenses (such as disorderly conduct, curfew, and loitering violations; Widom, 1988, p. 17).

Given this information, taking a feminist perspective on the causes of female delinquency seems an appropriate next step. First, like boys, girls are frequently the recipients of violence and sexual abuse. But unlike boys, girls' victimization and their response to that victimization is specifically shaped by their status as young women. Perhaps because of the gender and sexual scripts found in patriarchal families, girls are much more likely than boys to be the victim of family-related sexual abuse. Men, particularly men with traditional attitudes toward women, are likely to consider their daughters or stepdaughters as their sexual property and feel justified in turning their adult sexual power against them (Armstrong, 1994; Finkelhor, 1982). In a society that idealizes inequality in male and female relationships and that venerates youth in women, girls are easily defined as sexually attractive by older men (Bell, 1970). In addition, girls' vulnerability to both physical and sexual abuse is heightened by norms that require that they stay at home where their victimizers have access to them.

Moreover, [. . .] girls' victimizers (usually men) have the ability to invoke official agencies of social control in their efforts to keep young women at home and vulnerable. That is to say, abusers traditionally have been able to use the uncritical commitment of the juvenile justice system to parental authority to force girls to obey them. Girls' complaints about abuse were, until recently, routinely ignored. For this reason, statutes that were originally placed in law to 'protect' young people have, in the case of some girls, criminalized their survival strategies. Although they run away from abusive homes, parents can employ agencies to enforce their return. If they persist in their refusal to stay at home, they are incarcerated.

Young women, a large number of whom are on the run from sexual abuse and parental neglect, are forced by the very statutes designed to protect them into the lives of escaped convicts. Unable to enroll in school or take a job to support themselves because they fear detection, young female runaways are forced into the streets. Here, they engage in panhandling, petty theft, and occasional prostitution to survive. Young women in conflict with their parents (often for legitimate reasons) may actually be forced by present laws into petty criminal activity, prostitution, and drug use.

In addition, because young girls (but not necessarily young boys) are defined as sexually desirable – more desirable than their older sisters due to the double standard of aging – their lives on the streets (and their survival strategies) take a unique shape – once again shaped by patriarchal values. It is no accident that girls on the run from abusive homes or on the streets because of profound poverty get involved in criminal activities that exploit their sexual object status. American society has defined youthful, physically perfect women as desirable. This means that girls on the streets, who have little else of value to trade, are encouraged to use this 'resource' (Campagna & Poffenberger, 1988). Sexuality becomes their main source of power and sexual services their main commodity. This also means that the criminal subculture views them from this perspective (Miller, 1986).

The previous description is clearly not the 'entire' story about female delinquency, but it illustrates a theory that starts with the assumption that experiences that differentiate boys and girls might illuminate perplexing but persistent facts, such as the fact that more female than male status offenders find their way into the juvenile justice system. However, theories that are sensitive to shared aspects of girls' and boys' lives should not be entirely neglected (see Chesney-Lind & Shelden, 1998, for a discussion of how these theories might shed light on female delinquency). Many such theories, though, were crafted without considering the ways gender shapes both boys' and girls' realities, and need to be rethought with gender in mind.

Two additional comments are important here. First, a recent attempt to salvage the theories crafted to explain boys' behavior argues that the theories are correct; girls and boys are raised very differently but if girls were raised like boys and found themselves in the same situations as boys, then they would be as delinquent as boys (Rowe et al., 1995). This seems to be a regression from the insights of Hagan and his associates. Girls and boys inhabit a gendered universe and find themselves in systems (especially families and schools) that regulate their behavior in radically different ways. These differences, in turn, have significant consequences for the lives of girls (and boys). We need to think about these differences and what they mean not only for crime but, more broadly, about the life chances of girls and boys.

In general, the socialization of boys, especially of white privileged boys, prepare them for lives of power (Connell, 1987). The socialization of girls, particularly during adolescence, is very different. Even for girls of privilege, there are dramatic and negative changes in their self-perception that are reflected in lowered achievement in girls in math and science (American Association of University Women, 1992; Orenstein, 1994). Sexual abuse and harassment are just being understood as major, rather than minor, themes in the lives of all girls. The lives of girls of color, [. . .] illustrate the additional burdens that these young women face as they attempt to contend with high levels of sexual and physical victimization in the home, and with other forms of neighborhood violence and institutional neglect (Joe & Chesney-Lind, 1995; Orenstein, 1994).

Not surprisingly, work focusing on the lives of girls and women, particularly the data on the extent of girls' and women's victimization, has caused a 'backlash' in which some suggest the numbers are inflated and meaningless (Roiphe, 1993; Wolf, 1993). Others have argued that emphasizing victimization- constructs girls and women as having no agency (Baskin & Sommers, 1993). Both perspectives (arguably one from the right and another from the left) seek to shift the focus away from the unique experiences of women back to a more familiar and less intellectually and politically threatening terrain of race and class. They also seek to deny to the starkest victims of the sex/gender system the ability to speak about their pain. To say that a person has had a set of experiences (even very violent ones) is not to reduce that person to a mindless pawn of personal history, but rather to fully illuminate the context within which that person moves and makes 'choices.'

[. . .]

1.4

Twisted sisters, ladettes, and the new penology: the social construction of 'violent girls'
by Anne Worrall

Slowly but surely a new problem population is being constructed from which the public requires protection. In the actuarial language of the new penology (Feeley & Simon 1992), a group that hitherto has been assessed as too small and too low-risk to warrant attention is now being reassessed and recategorized as high-risk and dangerous. No longer 'at risk' and 'in moral danger' from the damaging behavior of men, 'violent girls' now exist as a category within penal discourse – a category to which increasing numbers of young women can be assigned and, within which, can be subjected to the same objectives and techniques of management as young men. This process of reconstructing 'troublesome young women' as 'nasty little madams' has been barely perceptible. This is partly because the theorizing of adolescent femininity and its relationship to state intervention has a complex history with many twists and turns. But it is also because, in actuarial terms, gender is one of the most certain predictors of offending. It is therefore not easy to adjust to the realization that youth (another sound predictor), class, and race (less reliable predictors) may be displacing gender in the categorization and management of violent offending. Violence is increasingly predicted to be something engaged in by poor, young, black people of both sexes.

Some examples may serve to demonstrate this subtle shift toward gender neutrality. Rutter et al. (1998: 254) claim that the sex ratio of males to females in relation to offending in England and Wales has declined from 11:1 in the 1950s to less than 4:1 in the late 1990s (though most of that decline took place between 1950 and 1980). The ratio has also been affected by ethnicity, being even less than 4:1 for black young people and more for Asian young people. Although acknowledging that the violence committed by young women represents only a small fraction of that committed by young men, Rutter et al. argue that violence by young women has increased, especially in America and especially where girls have been exposed to gang membership (1998: 74).

It may be that girls are becoming more violent, Rutter et al. (1998: 278) argue, because they are increasingly exposed to social contextual influences where violence is a risk rather than because girls, in some general sense, are becoming more violent. Steffensmeier and Haynie (2000) similarly dispute the claim that the structural disadvantage normally associated specifically with *being a woman* (poverty, income inequality, joblessness, single parenthood [see also Pantazis 1999]) has significant effects on *juvenile* female homicide. Rather, they argue that homicides by young women (though rare) are more likely to be caused by either individual desperation (for example, killing an unwanted newborn baby) or exposure to social contexts more usually associated with homicide by young men (firearms, gangs, and drugs). Again, the argument is that being a young woman per se is not the issue.

Finally, a study of the extent of weapon carrying among school-age children in England (Balding et al. 1996) showed that, although girls were less likely (16 percent) than boys (27 percent) to carry weapons for protection (including sound alarms and sprays), the ratio was less than 2:1 and the carrying of weapons was closely related to lifestyles (drugs, drink, smoking), concerns (bullying, assault), and attitudes (especially toward protecting disposable income). So the potential for violence was predictable more by these latter factors than by gender alone. At the same time, however, the study showed that girls were most likely to carry defensive sound alarms, while boys were most likely to carry weapons with blades – a rather important difference that was overlooked by a subsequent television program (Channel Four Television 1996) arising from the study.

These examples indicate, I would suggest, that postfeminist explanations of violence by girls are taking one of two forms: a return to individually based psychological explanations (albeit informed by feminist psychotherapy, as will be discussed later) or a 'liberation hypothesis' which refutes the role of gender in women's and girls' offending. These explanations share a belief in the moral agency of women and the importance of 'empowering' them to take responsibility for their own actions (Hannah-Moffat 1999). The corollary of this 'responsibilization' is that the 'welfarization' and 'soft policing' of young women's behavior by both formal and informal social control mechanisms has now given way to the straightforward 'criminalization' of that same behavior, with increasing numbers of young women being incarcerated, not on spuriously benevolent welfare grounds, but on spuriously equitable 'justice' grounds.

Barbara Hudson foresaw this danger more than fifteen years ago:

If we rescue girls from the rigidities of notions of orthodox femininity embodied in our judgements of girls as 'beyond control,' or 'in moral danger,' we do not eliminate girls from being judged by the double standard we apply to girls' and boys' behaviour; rather we transfer judgement from a set of stereotypes connected with girls' behaviour within the family to another set connected with female delinquency. (B. Hudson 1984: 108 cited in Howe 1994: 185)

But this warning was overlooked because, at the same time, Annie Hudson (1983) had written a groundbreaking article entitled *The Welfare State and Adolescent Femininity*, which provided the theoretical underpinnings of the 'sexualization' analysis of state intervention in the lives of young women in the United Kingdom for the rest of that decade. This resulted in practitioners looking for alternatives to traditional welfare approaches without necessarily heeding Barbara Hudson's warning.

The 'sexualization' theory of welfare regulation posited that

the majority of girls do not get drawn into the complex web of the personal social services because they have committed offenses. It is more likely to be because of concerns about their perceived sexual behaviour and / or because they are seen to be 'at risk' of 'offending' against social codes of adolescent femininity. (A. Hudson 1989: 197)

According to the 'sexualization' theory, 'troublesome' girls have always provoked anxiety in those who work with them, and fear and suspicion in those who look on (Baines & Alder 1996; Brown & Pearce 1992). Chesney-Lind and Okamoto suggest that girls are 'much more emotional than boys in the treatment setting . . . have distinctly different needs . . . and elicit unique counter-transference reactions from practitioners' (2000: 20). They have been socially constructed within a range of legal, welfare, and political discourses as, on the one hand, deeply maladjusted misfits and, on the other (and more recently), dangerous folk devils, symbolic of postmodern adolescent femininity.

Although welfare concerns have always dominated professional responses to girls 'in trouble,' concerns to provide protection to girls have always been mingled with anxieties about the wildness and dangerousness of girls who are 'out of control.' 'Passionate and willful girls' (Alder 1998) have always aroused as many respectable fears as have hooligan boys (Pearson 1983; Davies 1999). In particular, bad girls who become pregnant, engage in prostitution, get drunk, are generally 'unruly' (Belknap & Holsinger 1998), 'rough' (see chapter 2), or commit acts of violence run the risk of no longer being socially constructed as children or even as troubled young women, but rather as witting threats to the moral fabric of society.

I have argued elsewhere (Worrall 2000) that, in recognition of the problems highlighted by feminist critiques of traditional approaches to adolescent female delinquency (the 'sexualization' paradigm of juvenile justice), three alternative discourses have (re)emerged in the late twentieth century: informality (in the specific form of restorative justice), just deserts, and a renewed appeal to the 'lost' innocence of childhood, as a result of the victimization of girls (predominantly by men). These alternative approaches to dealing with bad girls, which attempt to divert them from incarceration, have proved no more successful than traditional welfare interventions. Instead, I have argued that we have seen a number of indicators of a paradigm shift in the treatment of bad girls: more girls who offend are being dealt with by the criminal justice rather than by welfare systems; more bad behavior by girls is being redefined as criminal, particularly fighting; more immoral behavior by girls is being constructed as 'near criminal' (for example, so-called 'early' pregnancy and lone parenthood). As a consequence of these changing attitudes, there has been a shift away from the 'welfarization' of troublesome girls toward their criminalization.

In this chapter, I want to extend that analysis, specifically in relation to the perception that 'girls are getting more violent.' In particular, I argue here that the key concepts of the new penology – risk assessment and dangerousness – have taken on new meaning for girls. The discursive attempts, described above, to foreclose the debate about female juvenile delinquency have between them created a lacuna from which has emerged the 'violent girl' – the ungovernable, 'nasty little madam' – who can *only* be dealt with by risk assessment and management within the formal criminal justice system.

From tank girl to twisted sisters – or, cute but deadly?

In its policy proposal paper, 'Crime, Justice and Protecting the Public,' which preceded the Criminal Justice Act 1991 in England and Wales, the Conservative Government suggested that the number of girls under the age of eighteen years sentenced to custody by the courts was so small that the abolition of detention in a young offender institution for this group might be feasible in a civilized society. The 150 or so girls in custody (compared to more than seven thousand boys) could be dealt with quite adequately by the 'good, demanding and constructive community programmes for juvenile offenders who need intensive supervision.' Those few who committed very serious crimes could still be dealt with by means of section 53 (of the Children and Young Person Act 1933) detention in local authority secure accommodation.

The ascendancy of the 'just deserts' model of criminal justice, coupled with the inclusion of a supposedly antidiscriminatory clause in the 1991 Criminal Justice Act, might have resulted in fewer girls being incarcerated. The principle of proportionality in sentencing should have led to the fairer sentencing of women (since their offending behavior is generally less serious than that of men) and this trend should have been buttressed by greater access for women to community sentences. But any such optimism was short-lived. A decade later custody in young offender institutions for girls remains and has expanded and the reason, we are led to believe, is that girls are committing more crime, especially violent crime.

The 1990s saw the emergence of several moral panics in relation to juvenile delinquency (Worrall 1997). The first was 'rat boy,' the elusive persistent offender who laughed at the system. The 'discovery' that a small number of children were committing a disproportionate amount of not-so-trivial crime, especially burglary and criminal damage, led to public outrage that, because of their age, these children could not be given custodial sentences. The government's response to this was to announce the introduction of secure training units for twelve to fourteen year olds, the first of which opened in April 1998. But this concern was to prove merely a precursor to the second moral panic, which followed the murder of Jamie Bulger in 1993. After this appalling event, serious questions were asked about the retention of a system of justice for children which was based on a belief in the still developing understanding of right and wrong between the ages of ten and fourteen years (the principle of 'doli incapax') and the consequent need to protect such children from the full weight of the criminal law. Increasingly, the media demanded that so-called 'adult' offenses should be dealt with by 'adult' sentences, regardless of the age and maturity of the offender. The vexing issues of the age of criminal responsibility and doli incapax became matters of public and parliamentary debate until the latter was finally abolished in the Crime and Disorder Act 1998.

This level of media-fueled public anxiety was based on the scantiest of empirical evidence. Hagell and Newburn (1994), for example, found far fewer persistent young offenders (and virtually none of them girls) than the then Home Secretary had claimed existed. Nevertheless, it was against this backdrop that the third moral panic emerged.

In 1994 Lisa Brinkworth wrote an article in the *Sunday Times* entitled 'Sugar and spice but not at all nice.' The article claimed to have discovered 'all-girl gangs menacing the streets' and 'cocky, feminist, aggressive' super-heroines targeting vulnerable women and other girls. Moreover, this 'new breed' of criminal girl apparently 'knows' that the criminal justice system is lenient on her. She knows how to work the system, dressing smartly for court and playing up to the magistrates. The illustration for the article was 'Tank Girl' – an American cartoon fantasy heroine who turned the tables violently (and frequently to their surprise) on repressive and sadistic men. The reasons for this supposed upsurge in young female crime are, however, confused. On the one hand, Brinkworth argues that women's liberation has raised women's expectations but has not delivered in terms of careers and wealth. Consequently, frustration and anger lead to street violence. On the other hand, women are supposedly sick of feeling unsafe in the home and are now fighting back (but why then are the targets so often not men but other young women?). Either way, according to Brinkworth, the responsibility for all this lies with feminism. This is what happens when you loosen the controls on women. This is what happens when adolescent girls are allowed to think themselves equal or superior to boys. It is every mother and father's nightmare – their daughter's sexuality rampant and violent.

Brinkworth, in both this and a subsequent article (1996), was in the business of creating a third moral panic alongside those of 'rat boy' and 'child killer' (Worrall 1997). At the time there was no evidence at all to support her argument other than one or two celebrated 'nasty' incidents which were only newsworthy *because* of their rarity. Feminist analyses of violence by women had revealed that the overwhelming majority of 'violent' women were themselves victims of violence. 'Battered woman syndrome' – though a highly contentious concept – was slowly being accepted by courts as, at the least, a mitigating factor in domestic violence committed by women. Campaigning groups such as 'Women in Prison' demonstrated that violent young women (such as Josie O'Dwyer – see Carlen et al. 1985) had been abused by individual men and by the prison system from an early age. Yet this was not the kind of 'girl violence' that Brinkworth was talking about. She was clearly on a different mission – the 'search for equivalence.' Her concern was to demonstrate that 'girls do it too.' And in so doing, she set in train a particular media 'hunt' characterized by the oft-repeated themes – younger and younger girls becoming increasingly aggressive, mushrooming girl gangs, increased use of drugs and, especially, alcohol, and the wilful abandonment of gender role expectations.

In 1996, Jo Knowsley in *The Sunday Telegraph* used the manslaughter of thirteen-year-old Louise Allen by two girls of a similar age to claim the mushrooming of 'girl gangs, apeing American gangs . . . fuelled by cheap, strong wine . . . who] travel in pairs or packs, carry baseball bats, mug for money and jewellery, and stage shoplifting raids on designer shops' (see also Archer 1998). No, that was *not* what happened with poor Louise Allen (where an argument between a group of schoolgirls got disastrously out of hand), but who cares? It makes for a good, coherent news story that offers some, albeit distorted, explanation for a horrible but rare incident.

Such distorted reporting was not confined to the UK. The following year, in Canada, a fourteen-year-old south Asian woman called Reena Virk, was attacked and killed by a group of young women and one young man. According to Sheila Batacharya's account (2000) the media coverage appears to have been very similar to that surrounding the death of Louise Allen in England. The difference was that Virk was a young woman of color and 'the narrative of girl violence obscures race' in the analysis of her death. By constructing a category of 'girl violence' the media was able to proffer explanations devoid of dimensions of racism, classism, ableism, and heterosexism (Batacharya 2000). The sole relevant risk factor to be considered was that of gender.

Journalists are now warning us that 'psychologists have projected that by the year 2008, the number of girls reverting [*sic*] to violence will outnumber boys if they carry on lashing out at this rate' (Fowler 1999). This prediction is, it seems, based on a claim that the number of women sentenced for violence against the person 'has quadrupled from just a handful of cases in the 70s.' The fact that the numbers (according to Fowler's own, inaccurate, statistics) are now 460, compared with more than 11,000 crimes of violence committed by men, does not cause her to reflect on her hypothesis. In fact, although there has been an increase in violent crime committed by young people (Home Office 2000a), the gender ratio of such offenses has remained that of around one female to five males throughout the 1990s (Rutter et al. 1998). Arrest rates of girls for serious crimes of violence in the United States have also remained largely unchanged (Chesney-Lind & Brown 1998, cited in Belknap & Holsinger 1998: 43).

In August 2000, *The Guardian* reported on an eighteen-year-old girl charged with rape (Chaudhuri 2000) and asked, 'A shocking lone incident or a sign of rising woman-on-woman violence?' Again, we hear the garbled statistics about the apparent increase in violence by women; again, the attribution of bad behavior to girl gangs and alcohol misuse; again, the role of feminism in making women more aggressive yet, because of their continued powerlessness in relation to men, causing that aggression to be displaced onto other women. These are no longer fantasy Tank Girl figures; these are the girls 'next door.' In their more benign form, these are 'ladettes;' in their more sinister form, the sisters have become 'twisted.'

This shift of attitude which moves 'violent girls' from fantasy to 'next door' has been conceptualized by Shiokawa's (1999) analysis of the popularity of 'cuteness' in Japanese cartooning. 'Cute but deadly' cartoon action heroines represent, Shiokawa argues, an attempt to manage the constructed threat of powerful young women (who are not, in reality, powerful at all but can be flattered into thinking that they are):

> The repetitive formula of 'cute' action heroines indicates that 'cute' women are desirable and that being 'cute' is advantageous to women who, in reality do not possess equal ground in the male-dominant culture. 'Cute' means imperfection . . . is an achievable quality, equally available to everyone . . . if she develops fuzzy, likable flaws in her character, so as to remove the threat that her very presence poses to the general public. (Shiokawa 1999: 120)

'Nasty little madams'

Whatever promise the 'just deserts' approach might have held for young women in the early 1990s, it has, in practice, resulted in a greater criminalization of girls' bad behavior and has proved no more successful in diverting them from incarceration than traditional welfare intervention. Instead, the construction of 'violent girls' has resulted in at least two indicators of a paradigm shift in the treatment of bad girls:

More girls who offend are being dealt with by criminal justice rather than welfare systems.

There has been a disproportionate increase in the number of girls being brought to court, placed on community service and combination orders, and sentenced to Young Offender Institutions in England and Wales since 1993. Similar patterns are identifiable in Australia (Alder & Hunter 1999), Canada (Reitsma-Street 1999), and the United States (Schaffner 1999; Chesney-Lind & Okamoto 2000). In Canada and the United States there is evidence that the much criticized use of 'status offenses' to justify the incarceration of girls on welfare grounds has now been replaced by 'failure to comply' charges. The latter, which may concern breaches of noncriminal court orders (curfews, residence and association conditions) allow the courts to reclassify status offenders as delinquent and incarcerate them in penal, rather than welfare, facilities. Both Chesney-Lind and Okamoto (2000) and Schaffner (1999) suggest that increasing numbers of girls may find themselves in court following family disputes. In the UK there is anecdotal evidence that girls are being transferred from 'ordinary' children's homes to Secure Units (on 'welfare' grounds) for assaults on house-parents, which would perhaps have been tolerated in the past.

More bad behavior by girls is being redefined as criminal, particularly fighting.

Frances Heidensohn (2001) has pointed out 'that we do not have notions of "normal" uses of force and violence by women and girls,' which contrasts with our acceptance of 'rough play and fighting' among men and boys. Sibylle Artz (1998) has demonstrated that a certain level of 'hitting' among mainstream (as opposed to marginalized) schoolgirls is commonplace to settle disputes about boys and enhance reputations as 'tough girls.' Yet this violence is very different from the violence of 'hitting' among school boys (who formed a much more distinct group in her research) and invariably arose out of friendship situations. The significance of friendship for girls has been noted in many studies and, most recently in Burman et al.'s study of the experiences of violence among Glasgow girls (2000). It is this, however, which has also provoked the media constructions of 'girl gangs' – where two or three girls are gathered together, a gang is formed in the eyes of the media. The Howard League Report 'Lost Inside' found that half the girls imprisoned for 'violence' were there for fighting with other girls. Beikoff (1996) has identified another pattern among Australian girls charged with assault. The assault charge is frequently one of 'assaulting a police officer,' accompanied by a charge of 'resisting arrest,' arising out of a public order incident involving drunk and disorderly behavior. She refers to this as the 'public space trifecta' and asks whether this has replaced the 'care and control' applications of the past. What all these studies, and others, also make clear is that girls' violence is almost always borne out of experiences of violence. Burman et al. (2000) for instance, conclude that 98.5 percent of their sample of girls had witnessed at first hand some form of interpersonal violence and 41 percent had experienced someone deliberately hitting, punching, or kicking them. Only 10 percent of their samples described themselves as 'violent.' Most girls, Burman et al. argue, handle the routine experience of low-level violence and intimidation without resorting to violence themselves.

As a consequence of these changing official attitudes, however, there has been a shift away from the 'welfarization' of troublesome girls toward their criminalization. Talking to prison officers in women's prisons about the inappropriateness of imprisoning girls, the response one invariably receives these days is that they are *not* lost and bewildered souls, but 'nasty little madams.'

At risk, in danger and in prison

The plight of girls in prison in England was highlighted in 1997 by three events: a thematic review of women in prison by HM Chief Inspector of Prisons, a report by the Howard League on the imprisonment of teenage girls, and a High Court ruling that a teenage girl should not be held in an adult female prison. There are no institutions in the female prison estate designated solely as Young Offender Institutions. There are two standard Prison Service justifications for mixing young and adult offenders in the female prison estate: first, there are too few young offenders to warrant separate institutions, which would, in any case, exacerbate the problem of women being imprisoned at unreasonable distances from their homes; second (and conveniently!), adult women are regarded as having a stabilizing influence on young women (though, strangely, adult men are seen as having a corrupting influence on young men!). Setting aside the complaints of adult women that young women have a disruptive influence on their lives, reports from the Chief Inspector and Howard League present a rather different picture of girls and young women being bullied, sexually assaulted, and recruited as prostitutes and drugs couriers:

> There are serious child protection issues in mixing young prisoners with others who may include Schedule 1 offenders (women convicted of offenses of violence against children under the 1933 Children and Young Person Act) which covers a multitude of behaviours. . . . We noted, for example, women convicted of procuring being held alongside 15 and 16 year olds. (HM Inspector of Prisons 1997: 26)

The exposure of girls to an environment that is seriously damaging is explored in detail by the Howard League. In particular, the 'culture' of self-harm, or 'cutting up,' which is endemic in most women's prisons, can socialize vulnerable girls into dangerous and violent ways of expressing their distress:

> For the vast majority of the young girls we interviewed it was the first time they had come across self-mutilation and we were told by staff that it was rare a 15, 16 or 17 year old would come in self-harming. The danger is that they will copy this behavior partly as a way of creating some control in their distressed and chaotic lives and partly because it is part of the culture of prison life to which they now belong. (Howard League 1997: 33)

The special needs of adolescent women are not being addressed. Prison officers reported to the Howard League that girls in prison had disproportionate experience of sexual abuse, poor or broken relationships with parents, local authority care (between one-third and one-half of women in prison having been in care), drug or alcohol abuse, prostitution, school exclusion, and truancy. If one has any lingering doubts about the 'special needs' of girls and young women in prison, one has only to consider the statistics of offenses against prison discipline. The rate of disciplinary offending is considerably higher in all Young Offender Institutions than in adult prisons, but the rate for female young offenders is the highest (Home Office 2000b). By far the most common offense is that of 'disobedience or disrespect.' However one chooses to explain this phenomenon (as being an indicator of either very badly behaved young women or of overly controlling female prison officers), it is clear that there is a very real risk that young women who are no more than ladettes outside prison can quickly become twisted sisters inside it.

Risk, dangerousness, and justice

The history of juvenile justice has been a history of the conflict between justice and welfare concerns (Worrall 1997) and girls have tended to experience both the advantages and disadvantages of welfarism to a greater extent than boys, on the grounds that they are 'at risk,' 'in moral danger,' and 'in need of protection.' In particular, under the 'old penology' criminal girls were regarded as girls 'in need' – *individuals* requiring *individual* attention and treatment (Gelsthorpe 1989; Holsinger 2000). They were too few in number to warrant categorization and were more often seen as 'misfits' – as 'non-descript women' who could not readily be categorized (Worrall 1990). Feminist critiques of welfarism in the 1980s resulted in moves toward 'just deserts' for girls, which promised much (Elliott 1988) but delivered greater criminalization and incarceration in the 1990s. Within this general trend, there has been a barely perceptible move toward the classification of delinquent girls and, in particular, a specific category of 'violent girls' has been constructed. This has been necessary because, as Muncie points out (2000, 29), the political agenda for the New Youth Justice is no longer based on matters of guilt, innocence, deterrence, and rehabilitation, but on the actuarial principle of risk assessment and techniques of 'identifying, classifying and managing groups sorted by levels of dangerousness.' So while common sense (and official statistics) may tell us that girls – even violent ones – are neither high-risk (in terms of the predictability of their violence) or dangerous (in terms of the harm they cause), they must nevertheless be made 'auditable.' They have to be given a risk classification and be subjected to objectives and techniques of management. Kemshall (1998: 39) has suggested that 'there is the possibility that the pursuit of risk reduction may eventually outweigh the pursuit of justice.' She warns that concerns for public protection and victims' rights may eventually lead to an unacceptable (though to whom?) erosion of the rights of the offender. In the case of violent girls it could be argued that, rather than the pursuit of risk *reduction*, it is the pursuit of risk *amplification* that is outweighing justice. No one would deny that young women are capable of acts of violence but the category 'violent girls' is a social construction that serves as a mechanism 'for the colonisation of the future and for managing the uncertainty of contingency' (Kemshall 1998: 38). It is a way of managing the anxiety, fear, and suspicion that troubled and troublesome girls and young women provoke in respectable citizens. It is a form of insurance against the perceived threat of ever-increasing numbers of Myra Hindleys, Rose Wests, and Josie O'Dwyers. Yet nothing is more certain to ensure the enlargement of the next generation of such women than locking up increasing numbers of our teenage daughters.

Part 2
Engendering the victim

Introduction

Our first reading by Susan Brownmiller (1975), provides an early, and often angrily polemic, example of early feminist writing. Brownmiller's (1975) landmark text, *Against Our Will*, draws on theoretical, historical and cultural analysis and empirical research to challenge criminological assumptions regarding rape and to reconceptualise rape as a crime of gendered sexual violence. This reading is written with great passion, as a campaigning piece, and is filled with a sense of the injustice which has been perpetrated against women for centuries. Brownmiller starts by tracing the history of rape and how it has developed as a concept and a practice to aid men's desire to secure property rights for their descendants. Rape, for Brownmiller, has always been about ownership and has become, in contemporary life, one of the ways in which men repeatedly emphasise their power and dominion over women. Brownmiller's writing is typical of its time in that it sets men and women up in opposition and as essentially different from each other. She speaks of male and female logic and writes that the legal system follows the former and cannot intervene fairly to represent women's interests because it is so steeped in traditions which disadvantage and humiliate the female sex. For Brownmiller, rape is the product of a cultural system which has allowed aggressive male power to dominate society as though this were the natural order of things. Her solution is to put women at the centre of the criminal justice and legal systems so that their logic might prevail. In the meantime women are enjoined to 'fight back', both physically and ideologically, against male power and the patriarchal system which sustains it.

In the second reading however, Stanko starts from the paradox that, according to officially recorded crime statistics, men face more interpersonal violence than women and yet record far less fear of crime. Feminist criminology had already revealed that much of the violence perpetrated against women is hidden from official records, but as far as violent encounters outside the domestic setting are concerned, men appear in the statistics as more likely to be victimised. Stanko explores the gendered nature of fear and asks why it is that women, across all ages and class backgrounds, report more fear than their male peers. Echoing Brownmiller's argument that 'all men are *potentially* dangerous because it is impossible to predict with absolute precision which men will be violent, in what circumstances, and to whom' (Stevens, 2006: 46, emphasis in original), she concludes that women can be considered as 'universally vulnerable'. Women's knowledge and experiences of rape, abuse and harassment at the hands of men – whether acquaintances, intimates or strangers – leads to an ever-present threat of assault for all women. This threat limits women's lives and leads to the employment of everyday strategies to minimise their vulnerability, while men appear to continue their lives unfettered by such concerns. Stanko acknowledges that some men do report fear of crime, especially those who live in high crime areas or who are more vulnerable due to their age or minority status, but that this is not a particularly limiting factor for most men. Women's vulnerability, on the other hand, is internalised and constant and successfully serves to control women's behaviour. This is not the overt patriarchal authority which Brownmiller describes but it is no less powerful in its ability to subdue women despite its relative subtlety.

Undoubtedly Stanko's analysis highlights that women's fear of crime in both public and private domains is an 'inescapably gendered, differentially experienced, phenomenon' (Stevens, 2006: 47). However her emphasis on the sexual danger associated with men imposes a problematic uniformity upon women's experiences and neglects the relationship between men, masculinity and fear of crime (Walklate, 2001: 90). Indeed, the essentialism inherent to feminist scholarship on fear of crime and female victimisation serves to deny the differences between and within both women's and men's experiences, particularly with regard to the material and ideological circumstances surrounding, for example, the class and race of subjects. Inevitably this tendency to essentialism has attracted a range of valid and valuable criticisms (Cain, 1986; Carlen, 1985; 1990a; 1990b; 1992; Carrington, 2002; Stevens, 2006), which Stevens summarises as incorporating the recognition that 'not all survivors of sexual and domestic assault are female and not all perpetrators are male, and neither are all men perpetrators' (2006: 52).

The remainder of the readings explore how the study of criminal victimisation and the fear of crime have developed in the aftermath of this critique. While earlier writings tended to construct an image of the crime victim as predominantly female (Walklate, 2004), notwithstanding Stanko's observation on the variability of men's fear, by the late 1990s men and boys were beginning to feature more prominently in discussions around the impact of crime. The third reading by Gilchrist et al. (1998) reveals a number of important points – not only that men's and women's fear is more similar than had been previously acknowledged, but that there are significant differences in fear, and coping strategies, within gender groups and that these might be more significant than the differences between them. The insertion of male experiences into the debate around victimisation is double-edged. On the one hand Gilchrist et al's data reinforces the error of treating all men as problematic and calls for a more sensitive understanding of their experiences and behaviours. This reading of the data is in accordance with feminist insights which focus on multiple inequalities (Daly, 1997), after all, men may also be poor, black, gay and marginalised in many ways – and will be exposed to various hate crimes as a result. On the other hand, such material can be used to question feminist insights into the nature of women's experiences and their *universal* vulnerability at the hands of men. A 'backlash' (Faludi, 1991) against feminism gained some popular impact in the 1990s, especially in the USA, and used such material to diminish feminism's gains and to denigrate a feminist standpoint which privileged women's experiences and focused on women's victimisation at the hands of men (Chesney-Lind, 2006).

Indeed, so far did the backlash travel that the early twenty-first century has seen the necessary re-emergence of some of the key early feminist themes. This is reflected in the last reading in this part in which Rebecca and Russell Dobash critique the recent perspective which concludes that women are as violent as men within their personal, intimate relationships. They carefully re-examine the nature of violence within intimate relationships and re-state the assymetrical nature of violent encounters which are still more often perpetrated against women than men, and are of a different order of severity and persistence, with greater consequences for the victim when violence is male on female.

Suggestions for further reading

Brooks Gardner, C. (1990), 'Safe conduct: women, crime, and self in public places', *Social Problems*, 37(3): 311–28.

This article provides an illustrative account of women's adaptations within public space which help to engender feelings of safety and that place them as 'others' in public space, not fully comfortable or belonging in this key social sphere.

Scully, D. (1990), *Understanding Sexual Violence: A Study of Convicted Rapists*, Boston, MA: Unwin Hyman.

This book remains one of the classic texts which revealed the extent of women's victimisation at the hands of men and the accounts given by sex offenders of their actions and perceptions of female victims.

Campbell, A. (2005), 'Keeping the "lady" safe: the regulation of femininity through crime prevention literature', *Critical Criminology*, 13: 119–40.

In this article Campbell uses a post-structuralist perspective to reflect upon theorisation around gender and the body and applies these to the study of crime and social control.

2.1

Women fight back
by Susan Brownmiller

[...]

To a woman the definition of rape is fairly simple. A sexual invasion of the body by force, an incursion into the private, personal inner space without consent – in short, an internal assault from one of several avenues and by one of several methods – constitutes a deliberate violation of emotional, physical and rational integrity and is a hostile, degrading act of violence that deserves the name of rape.

Yet by tracing man's concept of rape as he defined it in his earliest laws, we now know with certainty that the criminal act he viewed with horror, and the deadly punishments he saw fit to apply, had little to do with an actual act of sexual violence that a woman's body might sustain. True, the law has come some distance since its beginnings when rape meant simply and conclusively the theft of a father's daughter's virginity, a specialized crime that damaged valuable goods before they could reach the matrimonial market, but modern legal perceptions of rape are rooted still in ancient male concepts of property.

From the earliest times, when men of one tribe freely raped women of another tribe to secure new wives, the laws of marriage and the laws of rape have been philosophically entwined, and even today it is largely impossible to separate them out. Man's historic desire to maintain sole, total and complete access to woman's vagina, as codified by his earliest laws of marriage, sprang from his need to be the sole physical instrument governing impregnation, progeny and inheritance rights. As man understood his male reality, it was perfectly lawful to capture and rape some other tribe's women, for what better way for his own tribe to increase? But it was unlawful, he felt, for the insult to be returned. The criminal act he viewed with horror and punished as rape was not sexual assault *per se*, but an act of unlawful possession, a trespass against his tribal right to control vaginal access to all women who belonged to him and his kin.

Since marriage, by law, was consummated in one manner only, by deflor-
ation of virginity with attendant ceremonial tokens, the act man came to
construe as criminal rape was the illegal destruction of virginity outside a
marriage contract of his making. Later, when he came to see his own definition as too narrow for the times, he broadened his criminal concept to cover
the ruination of his wife's chastity as well, thus extending the law's concern to
nonvirgins too. Although these legal origins have been buried in the morass of
forgotten history, as the laws of rape continued to evolve they never shook free
of their initial concept – that the violation was first and foremost a violation of
male rights of possession, based on *male* requirements of virginity, chastity
and consent to private access as the female bargain in the marriage contract
(the underpinnings, as he enforced them, of man's economic estate).

To our modern way of thinking, these theoretical origins are peculiar and
difficult to fully grasp. A huge disparity in thought – male logic versus female
logic – affects perception of rape to this very day, confounding the analytic
processes of some of the best legal minds. Today's young rapist has no
thought of capturing a wife or securing an inheritance or estate. His is an act
of impermanent conquest, not a practical approach to ownership and control. The economic advantage of rape is a forgotten concept. What remains
is the basic male-female struggle, a hit-and-run attack, a brief expression
of physical power, a conscious process of intimidation, a blunt, ugly sexual
invasion with possible lasting psychological effects on all women.

When rape is placed where it truly belongs, within the context of modern
criminal violence and not within the purview of ancient masculine codes, the
crime retains its unique dimensions, falling midway between robbery and
assault. It is, in one act, both a blow to the body and a blow to the mind, and a
'taking' of sex through the use or threat of force. Yet the differences between
rape and an assault or a robbery are as distinctive as the obvious similarities.
In a prosecutable case of assault, bodily damage to the victim is clearly evident. In a case of rape, the threat of force does not secure a tangible commodity as we understand the term, although sex traditionally has been viewed
by men as 'the female treasure'; more precisely, in rape the threat of force
obtains a highly valued sexual service through temporary access to the victim's intimate parts, and the intent is not merely to 'take,' but to humiliate
and degrade.

This, then, is the modern reality of rape as it is defined by twentieth-
century practice. It is not, however, the reality of rape as it is defined by
twentieth-century law.

In order for a sexual assault to qualify as felonious rape in an American
courtroom, there must be 'forcible penetration of the vagina by the penis,
however slight.' In other words, rape is defined by law as a heterosexual
offense that is characterized by genital copulation. It is with this hallowed,
restrictive definition, the *sine qua non* of rape prosecutions, that our argument
begins.

That forcible genital copulation is the 'worst possible' sex assault a person can sustain, that it deserves by far the severest punishment, equated in some states with the penalties for murder, while all other manner of sexual assaults are lumped together under the label of sodomy and draw lesser penalties by law, can only be seen as an outdated masculine concept that no longer applies to modern crime.

Sexual assault in our day and age is hardly restricted to forced genital copulation, nor is it exclusively a male-on-female offense. Tradition and biologic opportunity have rendered vaginal rape a particular political crime with a particular political history, but the invasion may occur through the mouth or the rectum as well. And while the penis may remain the rapist's favorite weapon, his prime instrument of vengeance, his triumphant display of power, it is not in fact his only tool. Sticks, bottles and even fingers are often substituted for the 'natural' thing. And as men may invade women through other orifices so, too, do they invade other men.

Who is to say that the sexual humiliation suffered through forced oral or rectal penetration is a lesser violation of the personal private inner space, a lesser injury to mind, spirit and sense of self?

All acts of sex forced on unwilling victims deserve to be treated in concept as equally grave offenses in the eyes of the law, for the avenue of penetration is less significant than the intent to degrade. Similarly, the gravity of the offense ought not be bound by the victim's gender. That the law must move in this direction seems clear.

A gender-free, non-activity-specific law governing all manner of sexual assaults would be but the first step toward legal reform. The law must rid itself of other, outdated masculine concepts as well.

Since man first equated rape with the ruination of his wholly owned property, the theft of his private treasure, he reflected his concern most thunderously in the punishments that his law could impose. Today in many states of the Union, a conviction for first-degree felonious rape still draws a life sentence, and before the 1972 Supreme Court ruling that abolished capital punishment, a number of Southern states set the penalty at death. A modern perception of sexual assault that views the crime strictly as an injury to the victim's bodily integrity, and not as an injury to the purity or chastity of man's estate, must normalize the penalties for such an offense and bring them in line more realistically with the penalties for aggravated assault, the crime to which a sexual assault is most closely related.

Here the law must move from its view that 'carnal knowledge' is the crux of the crime to an appreciation that the severity of the offense, and the corresponding severity of the penalty that may be imposed, might better be gauged by the severity of the objective physical injury sustained by the victim during the course of the attack. Another criterion that the law can reflect beyond objective physical injury in the imposition of penalties is the manner in which the assault was accomplished. As the current law distinguishes between the severity of an armed robbery versus an unarmed robbery so must the law distinguish between the commission of a sexual assault with a deadly weapon – in which the threat against the victim's life is manifest and self-evident – and a sexual assault committed without a weapon. The participation of two or more offenders is another useful indicator of the severity of a sexual assault, since a number of assailants by their overwhelming presence constitutes a realistic threat of bodily harm.

[. . .]

Rape, as the current law defines it, is the forcible perpetration of an act of sexual intercourse on the body of a woman not *one's wife*. The exemption from rape prosecutions granted to husbands who force their wives into acts of sexual union by physical means is as ancient as the original definition of criminal rape, which was synonymous with that quaint phrase of Biblical origin, 'unlawful carnal knowledge.' To our Biblical forefathers, any carnal knowledge outside the marriage contract was 'unlawful.' And any carnal knowledge within the marriage contract was, by definition, 'lawful.' Thus, as the law evolved, the idea that a husband could be prosecuted for raping his wife was unthinkable, for the law was conceived to protect *his* interests, not those of his wife. Sir Matthew Hale explained to his peers in the seventeenth century, 'A husband cannot be guilty of rape upon his wife for by their mutual matrimonial consent and contract the wife hath given up herself in this kind to her husband, which she cannot retract.' In other words, marriage implies consent to sexual intercourse at all times, and a husband has a lawful right to copulate with his wife against her will and by force according to the terms of their contract.

[. . .]

In the cool judgment of right-thinking women, compulsory sexual intercouse is not a husband's right in marriage, for such a 'right' gives the lie to any concept of equality and human dignity. Consent is better arrived at by husband and wife afresh each time for if women are to be what we believe we are – equal partners – then intercourse must be construed as an act of mutual desire and not as a wifely 'duty,' enforced by the permissible threat of bodily harm or of economic sanctions.

In cases of rape within a marriage, the law must take a philosophic leap of the greatest magnitude, for while the ancient concept of conjugal rights (female rights as well as male) might continue to have some validity in annulments and contested divorces – civil procedures conducted in courts of law – it must not be used as a shield to cover acts of force perpetrated by husbands on the bodies of their wives. There are those who believe that the current laws governing assault and battery are sufficient to deal with the cases of forcible rape in marriage, and those who take the more liberal stand that a sexual assault law might be applicable only to those men legally separated from their wives who return to 'claim' their marital 'right,' but either of these solutions fails to come to grips with the basic violation.

[. . .]

The concept of consent rears its formidable head in the much debated laws of statutory rape, but here consent is construed in the opposite sense – not as something that cannot be retracted, as in marriage, but as something that cannot be given. Since the thirteenth-century Statutes of Westminster, the law has sought to fix an arbitrary age below which an act of sexual intercourse with a female, with or without the use of force, is deemed a criminal offense that deserves severe punishment because the female is too young to know her own mind. Coexistent with these statutory rape laws, and somewhat contradictory to them, have been the laws governing criminal incest, sexual victimization of a child by a blood relation, where the imposition of legal penalties has been charitably lenient, to say the least – yet another indication of the theoretical concept that the child 'belongs' to the father's estate. Under current legislation, which is by no means uniform, a conviction for statutory rape may draw a life sentence in many jurisdictions, yet a conviction for incest rarely carries more than a ten-year sentence, approximately the same maximum penalty that is fixed by law for sodomy offenses.

[. . .]

'Consent' has yet another role to play in a case of sexual assault. In reviewing the act, in seeking to determine whether or not a crime was committed, the concept of consent that is debated in court hinges on whether or not the victim offered sufficient resistance to the attack, whether or not her will was truly overcome by the use of force or the threat of bodily harm. The peculiar nature of sexual crimes of violence, as much as man's peculiar historic perception of their meaning, has always clouded the law's perception of consent.

It is accepted without question that robbery victims need not prove they resisted the robber, and it is never inferred that by handing over their money, they 'consented' to the act and therefore the act was no crime. Indeed, police usually advise law-abiding citizens not to resist a robbery, but rather to wait it out patiently, report the offense to the proper authorities, and put the entire matter in the hands of the law. As a matter of fact, successful resistance to a robbery these days is considered heroic.

[. . .]

In a sexual assault physical harm is much more than a threat; it is a reality because violence is an integral part of the act. Body contact and physical intrusion are the purpose of the crime, not appropriation of a physically detached and removable item like money. Yet the nature of the crime as it is practiced does bear robbery a close resemblance, because the sexual goal for the rapist resembles the monetary goal of the robber (often both goals are accomplished during the course of one confrontation if the victim is a woman), and so, in a sex crime, a bargain between offender and victim may also be struck. In this respect, a sexual assault is closer in victim response to a robbery than it is to a simple case of assault for an assaultive event may not have a specific goal beyond the physical contest, and furthermore, people who find themselves in an assaultive situation usually defend themselves by fighting back

Under the rules of law, victims of robbery and assault are not required to prove they resisted, or that they didn't consent, or that the act was accomplished with sufficient force, or sufficient threat of force, to overcome their will, because the law presumes it highly unlikely that a person willingly gives away money, except to a charity or to a favorite cause, and the law presumes that no person willingly submits to a brutal beating and the infliction of bodily harm and permanent damage. But victims of rape and other forms of sexual assault do need to prove these evidentiary requirements – that they resisted, that they didn't consent, that their will was overcome by overwhelming force and fear – because the law has never been able to satisfactorily distinguish an act of mutually desired sexual union from an act of forced, criminal sexual aggression.

[. . .]

Currently employed standards of resistance or consent *vis-à-vis* force or the threat of force have never been able to accurately gauge a victim's terror, since terror is a psychological reaction and not an objective standard that can be read on a behavior meter six months later in court, as jury acquittal rates plainly show. For this reason, feminists have argued that the special burden of proof that devolves on a rape victim, that she resisted 'within reason,' that her eventual compliance was no indication of tacit 'consent,' is patently unfair, since such standards are not applied in court to the behavior of victims in other kinds of violent crime. A jury should be permitted to weigh the word of a victimized complainant at face value, that is what it boils down to – no more or less a right than is granted to other victims under the law.

Not only is the victim's response during the act measured and weighed, her past sexual history is scrutinized under the theory that it relates to her 'tendency to consent,' or that it reflects on her credibility, her veracity, her predisposition to tell the truth or to lie. Or so the law says. As it works out in practice, juries presented with evidence concerning a woman's past sexual history make use of such information to form a moral judgment on her character, and here all the old myths of rape are brought into play, for the feeling persists that a virtuous woman either cannot get raped or does not get into situations that leave her open to assault. Thus the questions in the jury room become 'Was she or wasn't she asking for it?'; 'If she had been a decent woman, wouldn't she have fought to the death to defend her "treasure"?'; and 'Is this bimbo worth the ruination of a man's career and reputation?'

[. . .]

A history of sexual activity with many partners may be indicative of a female's healthy interest in sex, or it may be indicative of a chronic history of victimization and exploitation in which she could not assert her own inclinations; it may be indicative of a spirit of adventure, a spirit of rebellion, a spirit of curiosity, a spirit of joy or a spirit of defeat. Whatever the reasons, and there are many, prior consensual intercourse between a rape complainant and other partners of her choosing should not be scrutinized as an indicator of purity or impurity of mind or body, not in this day and age at any rate, and it has no place in jury room deliberation as to whether or not, in the specific instance in question, an act of forcible sex took place. Prior consensual intercourse between the complainant and the *defendant* does have some relevance, and such information probably should not be barred.

[. . .]

The most bitter irony of rape, I think, has been the historic masculine fear of false accusation, a fear that has found expression in male folklore since the Biblical days of Joseph the Israelite and Potiphar's wife, that was given new life and meaning in the psychoanalytic doctrines of Sigmund Freud and his followers, and that has formed the crux of the legal defense against a rape charge, aided and abetted by that special set of evidentiary standards (consent, resistance, chastity, corroboration) designed with one collective purpose in mind: to protect the male against a scheming, lying, vindictive woman.

Fear of false accusation is not entirely without merit in any criminal case, as is the problem of misidentification, an honest mistake, but the irony, of course, is that while men successfully convinced each other and us that women cry rape with ease and glee, the reality of rape is that victimized women have always been reluctant to report the crime and seek legal justice – because of the shame of public exposure, because of that complex double standard that makes a female feel culpable, even responsible, for any act of sexual aggression committed against her, because of possible retribution from the assailant (once a woman has been raped, the threat of a return engagement understandably looms large), and because women have been presented with sufficient evidence to come to the realistic conclusion that their accounts are received with a harsh cynicism that forms the first line of male defense.

A decade ago the FBI's *Uniform Crime Reports* noted that 20 percent of all rapes reported to the police 'were determined by investigation to be unfounded.' By 1973 the figure had dropped to 15 percent, while rape remained, in the FBI's words, 'the most under-reported crime.' A 15 percent figure for false accusations is undeniably high, yet when New York City instituted a special sex crimes analysis squad and put police*women* (instead of men) in charge of interviewing complainants, the number of false charges in New York dropped dramatically to 2 percent, a figure that corresponded exactly to the rate of false reports for other violent crimes. The lesson in the mystery of the vanishing statistic is obvious. Women believe the word of other women. Men do not.

That women have been excluded by tradition and design from all

significant areas of law enforcement, from the police precinct, from the prosecutor's office, from the jury box and from the judge's bench, up to and
including the appellate and supreme court jurisdictions, has created a double
handicap for rape victims seeking justice under the laws of man's devise. And
so it is not enough that the face of the law be changed to reflect the reality; the
faces of those charged with the awesome responsibility of enforcing the law
and securing justice must change as well.

[. . .]

I am not one to throw the word 'revolutionary' around lightly, but full
integration of our cities' police departments, and by full I mean fifty-fifty,
no less, is a revolutionary goal of the utmost importance to women's rights.
And if we are to continue to have armies, as I suspect we will for some time to
come, then they, too, must be fully integrated, as well as our national guard,
our state troopers, our local sheriffs' offices, our district attorneys' offices,
our state prosecuting attorneys' offices – in short, the nation's entire lawful
power structure (and I mean power in the physical sense) must be stripped
of male dominance and control – if women are to cease being a colonized
protectorate of men.

A system of criminal justice and forceful authority that genuinely works
for the protection of women's rights, and most specifically the right not to be
sexually assaulted by men, can become an efficient mechanism in the control
of rape insofar as it brings offenders speedily to trial, presents the case for the
complainant in the best possible light, and applies just penalties upon conviction. While I would not underestimate the beneficial effects of workable sex
assault laws to 'hold the line' and provide a positive deterrent, what feminists
(and all right-thinking people) must look toward is the total eradication of
rape, and not just an effective policy of containment.

A new approach to the law and to law enforcement can take us only part
of the way. Turning over to women 50 percent of the power to enforce the
law and maintain the order will be a major step toward eliminating *machismo*.
However, the ideology of rape is aided by more than a system of lenient laws
that serve to protect offenders and is abetted by more than the fiat of total
male control over the lawful use of power. The ideology of rape is fueled by
cultural values that are perpetuated at every level of our society, and nothing
less than a frontal attack is needed to repel this cultural assault.

The theory of aggressive male domination over women as a natural right
is so deeply embedded in our cultural value system that all recent attempts to
expose it – in movies, television commercials or even in children's textbooks –
have barely managed to scratch the surface. As I see it, the problem is not that
polarized role playing (man as doer; woman as bystander) and exaggerated
portrayals of the female body as passive sex object are simply 'demeaning' to
women's dignity and self-conception, or that such portrayals fail to provide
positive role models for young girls, but that cultural sexism is a conscious
form of female degradation designed to boost the male ego by offering

'proof' of his native superiority (and of female inferiority) everywhere he looks.

Critics of the women's movement, when they are not faulting us for being slovenly, straggly-haired, construction-booted, whiny sore losers who refuse to accept our female responsibilities, often profess to see a certain inexplicable Victorian primness and anti-sexual prudery in our attitudes and responses. 'Come on, gals,' they say in essence, 'don't you know that your battle for female liberation is part of our larger battle for sexual liberation? Free yourselves from all your old hang-ups! Stop pretending that you are actually offended by those four-letter words and animal noises we grunt in your direction on the street in appreciation of your womanly charms. When we plaster your faceless naked body on the cover of our slick magazines, which sell millions of copies, we do it in sensual obeisance to your timeless beauty – which, by our estimation, ceases to be timeless at age twenty or thereabouts. If we feel the need for a little fun and go out and rent the body of a prostitute for a half hour or so, we are merely engaging in a mutual act between two consenting adults, and what's it got to do with you? When we turn our movie theaters into showcases for pornographic films and convert our bookstores to outlets for mass produced obscene smut, not only should you marvel at the wonders of our free-enterprise system, but you should applaud us for pushing back the barriers of repressive middle-class morality, and for our strenuous defense of all the civil liberties you hold so dear, because we have made obscenity the new frontier in defense of freedom of speech, that noble liberal tradition. And surely you're not against civil liberties and freedom of speech, now, are you?'

The case against pornography and the case against toleration of prostitution are central to the fight against rape, and if it angers a large part of the liberal population to be so informed, then I would question in turn the political understanding of such liberals and their true concern for the rights of women. Or to put it more gently, a feminist analysis approaches all prior assumptions, including those of the great, unquestioned liberal tradition, with a certain open-minded suspicion, for all prior traditions have worked against the cause of women and no set of values, including that of tolerant liberals, is above review or challenge. After all, the liberal *politik* has had less input from the feminist perspective than from any other modern source; it does not by its own considerable virtue embody a perfection of ideals, it has no special claim on goodness, rather, it is most receptive to those values to which it has been made sensitive by others.

[. . .]

Once we accept as basic truth that rape is not a crime of irrational, impulsive, uncontrollable lust, but is a deliberate, hostile, violent act of degradation and possession on the part of a would-be conqueror, designed to intimidate and inspire fear, we must look toward those elements in our culture that promote and propagandize these attitudes, which offer men, and in particular, impressionable, adolescent males, who form the potential raping population, the ideology and psychologic encouragement to commit their acts of aggression *without awareness, for the most part, that they have committed a punishable crime,* let alone a moral wrong. The myth of the heroic rapist that permeates false notions of masculinity, from the successful seducer to the man who 'takes what he wants when he wants it,' is inculcated in young boys from the time they first become aware that being a male means access to certain mysterious rites and privileges, including the right to buy a woman's body. When young men learn that females may be bought for a price, and that acts of sex command set prices, then how should they not also conclude that that which may be bought may also be taken without the civility of a monetary exchange?

That there *might* be a connection between prostitution and rape is certainly not a new idea. Operating from the old (and discredited) lust, drive and relief theory, men have occasionally put forward the notion that the way to control criminal rape is to ensure the ready accessibility of female bodies at a reasonable price through the legalization of prostitution, so that the male impulse might be satisfied with ease, efficiency and a minimum of bother.

[. . .]

But my horror at the idea of legalized prostitution is not that it doesn't work as a rape deterrent, but that it institutionalizes the concept that it is man's monetary right, if not his divine right, to gain access to the female body, and that sex is a female service that should not be denied the civilized male. Perpetuation of the concept that the 'powerful male impulse' must be satisfied with immediacy by a cooperative class of women, set aside and expressly licensed for this purpose, is part and parcel of the mass psychology of rape. Indeed, until the day is reached when prostitution is totally eliminated (a millennium that will not arrive until men, who create the demand, and not women who supply it, are fully prosecuted under the law), the false perception of sexual access as an adjunct of male power and privilege will continue to fuel the rapist mentality.

Pornography has been so thickly glossed over with the patina of chic these days in the name of verbal freedom and sophistication that important distinctions between freedom of political expression (a democratic necessity), honest sex education for children (a societal good) and ugly smut (the deliberate devaluation of the role of women through obscene, distorted depictions) have been hopelessly confused. Part of the problem is that those who traditionally have been the most vigorous opponents of porn are often those same people who shudder at the explicit mention of any sexual subject. Under their watchful, vigilante eyes, frank and free dissemination of educational materials relating to abortion, contraception, the act of birth, and female biology in general is also dangerous, subversive and dirty. (I am not unmindful that a frank and free discussion of rape, 'the unspeakable crime,' might well give these righteous vigilantes further cause to shudder.) Because the battle lines were falsely drawn a long time ago, before there was a vocal women's movement, the anti-pornography forces appear to be, for the most part, religious, Southern, conservative and right-wing, while the pro-porn forces are identified as Eastern, atheistic and liberal.

[. . .]

[. . .] The gut distaste that a majority of women feel when we look at pornography, a distaste that, incredibly, it is no longer fashionable to admit, comes, I think, from the gut knowledge that we and our bodies are being stripped, exposed and contorted for the purpose of ridicule to bolster that 'masculine esteem' which gets its kick and sense of power from viewing females as anonymous, panting play things, adult toys, dehumanized objects to be used, abused, broken and discarded.

This, of course, is also the philosophy of rape. It is no accident (for what else could be its purpose?) that females in the pornographic genre are depicted in two cleanly delineated roles: as virgins who are caught and 'banged' or as nymphomaniacs who are never sated. The most popular and prevalent pornographic fantasy combines the two: an innocent, untutored female is raped and 'subjected to unnatural practices' that turn her into a raving, slobbering nymphomaniac, a dependent sexual slave who can never get enough of the big, male cock.

There can be no 'equality' in porn, no female equivalent, no turning of the tables in the name of bawdy fun. Pornography, like rape, is a male invention, designed to dehumanize women, to reduce the female to an object of sexual access, not to free sensuality from moralistic or parental inhibition. The staple of porn will always be the naked female body, breasts and genitals exposed, because as man devised it, her naked body is the female's 'shame,' her private parts the private property of man, while his are the ancient, holy, universal, patriarchal instrument of his power, his rule by force over *her*.

[. . .]

But does one need scientific methodology in order to conclude that the anti-female propaganda that permeates our nation's cultural output promotes a climate in which acts of sexual hostility directed against women are not only tolerated but ideologically encouraged? A similar debate has raged for many years over whether or not the extensive glorification of violence (the gangster as hero: the loving treatment accorded bloody shoot 'em ups in movies, books and on TV) has a causal effect, a direct relationship to the rising rate of crime, particularly among youth. Interestingly enough, in this area – non-sexual and not specifically related to abuses against women – public opinion seems to be swinging to the position that explicit violence in the entertainment media does have a deleterious effect; it makes violence commonplace, numbingly routine and no longer morally shocking.

[. . .]

A law that reflects the female reality and a social system that no longer shuts women out of its enforcement and does not promote a masculine ideology of rape will go a long way toward the elimination of crimes of sexual violence, but the last line of defense shall always be our female bodies and our female minds. In making rape a *speakable* crime, not a matter of shame, the women's movement has already fired the first retaliatory shots in a war as ancient as civilization. When, just a few years ago, we began to hold our speak-outs on rape, our conferences, borrowing a church meeting hall for an afternoon, renting a high-school auditorium and some classrooms for a weekend of workshops and discussion, the world out there, the world outside of radical feminism, thought it was all very funny.

[. . .]

Within two years the world out there had stopped laughing, and the movement had progressed beyond the organizational forms of speak-outs and conferences, our internal consciousness-raising, to community outreach programs that were imaginative, original and unprecedented: rape crisis centers with a telephone hot line staffed twenty-four hours a day to provide counseling, procedural information and sisterly solidarity to recent rape victims and even to those whose assault had taken place years ago but who never had the chance to talk it out with other women and release their suppressed rage; rape legislation study groups to work up model codes based on a fresh approach to the law and to work with legislators to get new laws adopted; anti-rape projects in conjunction with the emergency ward of a city hospital, in close association with policewomen staffing newly formed sex crime analysis squads and investigative units. With pamphlets, newsletters, bumper stickers, 'Wanted' posters, combative slogans – 'STOP RAPE'; 'WAR – WOMEN AGAINST RAPE'; 'SMASH SEXISM, DISARM RAPISTS!' – and with classes in self-defense, women turned around and seized the offensive.

The wonder of all this female activity, decentralized grassroots organizations and programs that sprung up independently in places like Seattle, Indianapolis, Ann Arbor, Toronto, and Boulder, Colorado, is that none of it had been predicted, encouraged, or faintly suggested by men anywhere in their stern rules of caution, their friendly advice, their fatherly solicitude in more than five thousand years of written history. That women should *organize* to combat rape was a women's movement invention.

[. . .]

We know, or at least the statistics tell us, that no more than half of all reported rapes are the work of strangers, and in the hidden statistics, those four out of five rapes that go unreported, the percent committed by total strangers is probably lower. The man who jumps out of the alley or crawls through the window is the man who, if caught, will be called 'the rapist' by his fellow men. But the known man who presses his advantage, who uses his position of authority, who forces his attentions (fine Victorian phrase), who will not take 'No' for an answer, who assumes that sexual access is his right-of-way and physical aggression his right-on expression of masculinity, conquest and power is no less of a rapist – yet the chance that this man will be brought to justice, even under the best of circumstances, is comparatively small.

I am of the opinion that the most perfect rape laws in the land, strictly enforced by the best concerned citizens, will not be enough to stop rape. Obvious offenders will be punished, and that in itself will be a significant change, but the huge gray area of sexual exploitation, of women who are psychologically coerced into acts of intercourse they do not desire because they do not have the wherewithal to physically, or even psychologically, resist, will remain a problem beyond any possible solution of criminal justice. It would be deceitful to claim that the murky gray area of male sexual aggression and female passivity and submission can ever be made amenable to legal divination – nor should it be, in the final analysis. Nor should a feminist advocate to her sisters that the best option in a threatening, unpleasant situation is to endure the insult and later take her case to the courts.

Unfortunately for strict constructionists and those with neat, orderly minds, the male-female sexual dynamic at this stage in our human development lends itself poorly to objective arbitration. A case of rape and a case of unpleasant but not quite criminal sexual extortion in which a passive, egoless woman succumbs because it never occurred to her that she might, with effort, repel the advance (and afterward quite justifiably feels 'had') flow from the same oppressive male ideology, and the demarcation line between the two is far from clear. But these latter cases, of which there are many, reflect not only the male ideology of rape but a female paralysis of will, the result of a deliberate, powerful and destructive 'feminine' conditioning.

The psychologic edge men hold in a situation characterized by sexual aggression is far more critical to the final outcome than their larger size and heavier weight. They *know* they know how to fight, for they have been trained and encouraged to use their bodies aggressively and competitively since early childhood. Young girls, on the other hand, are taught to disdain physical combat, healthy sports competition, and winning, because such activities dangerously threaten the conventional societal view of what is appropriate, ladylike, feminine behavior.

[. . .]

It is no wonder, then, that most women confronted by physical aggression fall apart at the seams and suffer a paralysis of will. We have been trained to cry, to wheedle, to plead, to look for a male protector, but we have never been trained to fight and win.

Prohibitions against a fighting female go back to the Bible. In one of the more curious passages in Deuteronomy it is instructed that when two men are fighting and the wife of one seeks to come to his aid and 'drag her husband clear of his opponent, if she puts out her hand and catches hold of the man's genitals, you shall cut off her hand and show her no mercy.' When the patriarchs wrote the law, it would seem, they were painfully cognizant of woman's one natural advantage in combat and were determined to erase it from her memory.

[. . .]

Is it possible that there is some sort of metaphysical justice in the anatomical fact that the male sex organ, which has been misused from time immemorial as a weapon of terror against women, should have at its root an awkward place of painful vulnerability? Acutely conscious of their susceptibility to damage, men have protected their testicles throughout history with armor, supports and forbidding codes of 'clean,' above-the-belt fighting. A gentleman's agreement is understandable – among gentlemen. When women are threatened, as I learned in my self-defense class, 'Kick him in the balls, it's your best maneuver.' How strange it was to hear for the first time in my life that women could fight back, *should* fight back and make full use of a natural advantage; that it is in *our interest* to know how to do it. How strange it was to understand with the full force of unexpected revelation that male allusions to psychological defeat, particularly at the hands of a woman, were couched in phrases like emasculation, castration and ball-breaking because of that very special physical vulnerability.

Fighting back. On a multiplicity of levels, that is the activity we must engage in, together, if we – women – are to redress the imbalance and rid ourselves and men of the ideology of rape.

Rape can be eradicated, not merely controlled or avoided on an individual basis, but the approach must be long-range and cooperative, and must have the understanding and good will of many men as well as women.

My purpose in this book has been to give rape its history. Now we must deny it a future.

2.2

Typical violence, normal precaution: men, women and interpersonal violence in England, Wales, Scotland and the USA
by Elizabeth A. Stanko

Victimisation surveys note that individuals commonly fail to report criminal incidents to the police. Only about one-third of all serious crime is reported to the police in the United States and England, Wales and Scotland (Bureau of Justice Statistics, 1983; Chambers and Tombs, 1984; Hough and Mayhew, 1983 and 1985). Researchers have noted that failure to report crime involves assessments of individuals about how 'private' they feel the dispute is; the fear of reprisal for reporting the matter to police; the feeling that the police would not think the matter serious; that, even if reported, nothing could be done to resolve the matter; or that despite its statutory seriousness, the matter was not important enough to report to the police (Bureau of Justice Statistics, 1983; Hough and Mayhew, 1983 and 1985; Chambers and Tombs, 1984). As such, reporting of serious criminal events to the criminal justice system also reflects the confidence of individuals in the authority of the police to resolve disputes involving criminal matters.

At the same time as citizens' reporting of crime remains low, fear about criminal victimisation remains high. This fear about criminal victimisation, researchers suggest, focuses around issues of personal safety, particularly safety from various forms of violent personal criminal behaviour – robbery, assault or rape (Hindelang et al., 1978: Maxfield, 1984a; Skogan and Maxfield, 1981). Furthermore, criminologists speculate that this fear for one's personal safety is centred around concern about violent crime, generally associated with outside, street crime – the type of crime the police are supposedly more responsible for preventing (Rubenstein, 1973).

It is this concern about the fear of crime which has become a target for policy-makers in both the US and Great Britain (Hanmer and Stanko, 1985). In the US, for example, 45 per cent of respondents expressed concern about being alone at night on foot in their own neighbourhoods (Hindelang et al., 1978). Respondents to recent crime surveys in Scotland, England and Wales also expressed concern about personal safety outside their own home and within their own neighbourhood (Hough and Mayhew, 1983 and 1985; Chambers and Tombs, 1984; Maxfield, 1984a). This fear undermines the confidence of individuals in the police as protectors and sustainers of an orderly society. As governmental officials and law makers focus on the danger violent crime poses to a 'free' society, combating fear of crime among citizens becomes an important area for concern.

Police, government policy-makers and citizens alike conceptualise fear of crime as associated with individual citizens' concern about being outside, alone and potentially vulnerable to personal and harmful confrontation from criminal violence. As such, fear of crime affects the lives of both women and men: it is characterised as a feeling involving a diffuse sense of anxiety or unsafeness when one is alone, particularly when one is alone and walking on the street after dark, and which may affect a person's lifestyle choices and mobility.

The purpose of this chapter is to explore the role that gender – a significant variable within a gender-stratified society – plays in our understanding of criminal victimisation, men's and women's fear about it and the implications of this fear for understanding male violence to women – one process of the social control of women in a male-dominated society. While researchers acknowledge that violence among the familiar and familial – 'inside' crime – is under-reported in government sponsored victimisation surveys, they focus their analysis of the findings on 'outside' crime and fear among citizens about the violence of strangers. This focus has additional significance for understanding how criminal violence and fear about it affects men's and women's lives. Women's fear of criminal violence is reported in officially-sponsored victimisation surveys, but, as will be discussed later, not their experiences of violence. It is the growing body of knowledge about male violence, largely collected by feminist researchers, which shows that women's experiences of criminal violence continues to remain hidden (Hanmer and Saunders, 1984; Russell, 1982 and 1984; Stanko, 1985). This chapter puts forward the argument that contemporary discussions about fear of crime omit many of women's experiences of criminal violence and distort our understanding of the importance of male violence within women's everyday lives.

Fear and risk of victimisation

Who, according to national crime surveys, is most likely to be victimised by interpersonal, violent crime? When government-funded crime surveys assess risk, men, not women, have a greater likelihood of being victimised by interpersonal forms of violence. Compounding the risk are the variables of age, race, income, residence and marital status. Young, single, black, Hispanic or Asian poor men who live in urban areas have the highest likelihood of being victims of interpersonal violence and have the greatest probability of sustaining injury as a consequence of that victimisation. Hindelang et al. (1978), Skogan and Maxfield (1981), Hough and Mayhew (1983), Gottfredson (1984) and Widom and Maxfield (1984) suggest that this population is typically victimised by individuals with similar demographic characteristics. Exposure to victimisation, these authors further suggest, varies according to the lifestyle of the victim (Hindelang et al., 1978, p. 122).

Criminal violence, largely robbery and assault, is one part of male-to-male interaction, particularly for young males who are single, spend several evenings out a week and engage in social drinking (Maxfield, 1984a; Gottfredson, 1984). Male violence to men, at least as the results of crime survey data in the US and Great Britain indicate, takes on the appearance of 'exchanged' blows rather than predatory crime. Moreover, predatory crime, not exchanged blows, is most commonly associated with 'fear producing' situations (Maxfield, 1984a). While men are more likely to be robbed by strangers and assaulted by non-strangers, young men's lifestyles – socialising activities, bravado and greater mobility outside the home – seem to affect their risk of victimisation.

In contrast to men's higher risk of criminal victimisation, young and middle-aged men report feeling reasonably safe or very safe on the streets alone after dark. While fear increases with age and area of residence (Maxfield, 1984b), overall, men's reported fear is much lower than women's. Men's reported fear of personal victimisation is approximately one-third that of women's (Hindelang et al., 1978; Skogan and Maxfield, 1981; Hough and Mayhew, 1983; Maxfield, 1984a; Chambers and Tombs, 1984). So while men of all ages appear to be at greater risk of criminal victimisation than women, on the whole they report feeling safer than women. 'Young males are at risk,' states Maxfield, 'but their lower fear may be the product of either reckless disregard for their own well-being (not unknown among the young), or a self-assured confidence that neighbourhood streets hold no dangers for them' (Maxfield, 1984a, p. 13).

On the other hand, women, as a gender class, constitute a 'low risk' population with respect to interpersonal violence, at least according to the results of government-sponsored victimisation surveys. Just as with men, the risk of victimisation varies with age, income, race, residence and marital status. The demographic characteristics of women's assailants are generally similar with one major exception: women are not the targets of other women, but the targets of male assailants who may also sexually victimise them. In their analysis of the 1982 British Crime Survey data for England and Wales, Widom and Maxfield (1984) found that one in four of women's assailants were other women, and approximately one in three assaulted women were assaulted by female assailants (p. 14). The majority of women's assailants, however, on both sides of the Atlantic, are men.

Criminal violence for women takes on elements of sexual violence and, according to victimisation surveys, women's assailants are as likely to be strangers as people known to them. Rape as a crime of violence primarily affects women and women's consciousness (Gordon et al., 1980; Griffin, 1971; Beneke, 1982; Russell, 1973, 1982 and 1984; Brownmiller, 1975; Stanko, 1985). So too, rape is often the action of acquaintances, lovers, relatives, husbands or friends – men known to the raped woman. And while women are less likely to be robbed or assaulted than men, when women *are* assaulted, they are as likely to be assaulted by acquaintances or relatives as by strangers. While researchers do acknowledge that data on interpersonal violence between acquaintances or relatives tends to be under-reported by respondents, what *is* reported shows, in fact, that two-thirds of all assaults on divorced or separated women were committed by acquaintances and relatives; half of all assaults on never-married women and 40 per cent of assaults on married women were committed by relatives or acquaintances. If one were to look solely at spouse or ex-spouse assault committed in the US, 95 per cent of those assaults were committed by men on women (Bureau of Justice Statistics, 1983, p. 21). While women's assailants, as reported by official sources, include many men who are known to them, stereotypical images about criminal violence remains focused on violence occurring outside, on the street and typically from strangers.

In contrast to the 'low risk' of women to recorded criminal victimisation, women's fear of criminal victimisation – a fear which has been examined in terms of their feelings of safety while walking alone at night in their neighbourhoods – is significantly higher than men's. As noted earlier, one complicating factor for women is that interpersonal violence is commonly violence from known male assailants, creating, perhaps, a fear of known (and presumably safe) environments as well as a fear of violence in familiar (but presumably unsafe) environments – their own neighbourhoods. As with men, women's fear varies according to age, race, residence, income and marital status. Yet women's fear crosses the boundaries of all these variables. Despite their reported low level of risk of victimisation, young and old, women constitute the group most fearful of crime in the US, England, Wales and Scotland. Overall, the most significant predictor in understanding fear of crime is being female (Balkin, 1979; Hindelang et al., 1978; Dubow et al., 1979; Riger and Gordon, 1981; Maxfield, 1984a and 1984b).

Explanations of the gap between men's and women's reported fear of crime focus on issues related to gender experience and gender role expectations (Balkin, 1979; Clemente and Kleiman, 1977; Bowker, 1981; Riger and Gordon, 1981; Riger et al., 1978; Hindelang et al., 1978; Lewis and Maxfield, 1980; Maxfield, 1984a; Skogan and Maxfield, 1981). Similarly, researchers continue to speculate about the differing levels of men's and women's fear of crime. Men's fear of crime, as every researcher examining victimisation and fear recognises, does not seem to match their risk of, and experiences of, reported criminal victimisation. Since men are at greater risk, should they not also be the most fearful? Why do men, the more common recipients of reported interpersonal violence, not report being wary of dark streets at night, or of having feelings of insecurity? Is it simply a case of cognitive dissonance? Is it, as some researchers have speculated, that men are simply reluctant to report fear (Clemente and Kleiman, 1977) – a speculation squarely located in one gender expectation; men's bravado?

Perhaps men, as a gender, feel less vulnerable to interpersonal violence and more physically secure than their female counterparts. There is, however, one exception. Residing in 'high crime' neighbourhoods, Maxfield (1984b) has recently noted, may affect even young men's feelings of fear. In areas where 'crime problems are regular features of the neighbourhood environment, measures of physical vulnerability are less important in predicting differences in fear among individuals' (Maxfield, 1984b, p. 233). For young men, characteristically the least fearful group, living in 'high crime' areas may reduce their feelings of immunity from criminal victimisation.

Even in high crime areas, however, men's fear of crime remains low in comparison to women's fear. As speculated earlier, what men report as instances of interpersonal violence is related to their lifestyles. Men who wish to avoid certain forms of assault – pub fights, for example – might simply avoid violence-prone drinking spots (Gottfredson, 1984). So, too, men who wish to avoid sites of victimisation – particularly if they live in 'safe' neighbourhoods, can do so by avoiding 'dangerous' places. But to what extent is crime avoidance part of men's everyday context? It may be for those living in a 'high crime' area because other factors reflecting social and economic disadvantage might mitigate against being able to avoid victimisation. Is fear, however, a part of advantaged men's lives?

In order to advance our understanding of interpersonal violence and fear of crime, the issue of men's fear and victimisation needs to be explored through the question of 'maleness' rather than the current taken for granted-gender-neutral approach to criminal victimisation. As mentioned earlier young, minority, poor men who live in urban areas have the highest rates of interpersonal victimisation; they also share demographic characteristics with those who are most likely to victimise others. Yet many questions about male interpersonal violence still remain. The dynamics of male-to-male interpersonal violence may differ from male-to-female interpersonal violence, and for that matter, female-to-female and female-to-male interpersonal violence. To what extent is male-to-male victimisation a result of male predatory behaviour; a result of male fighting; the failure of male compromise; or a solution for men's disagreements? Might the fear-producing consequences of that victimisation differ from the way men define their victimisation? These and other questions remain as speculation in current research knowledge about men's fear of crime.

In explaining women's fear of crime. Skogan and Maxfield (1981) suggest that the fear that women and the elderly feel is a perception of their social

and physical vulnerability. To Skogan and Maxfield (1981), physical vulnerability concerns 'openness to attack, powerlessness to resist, and exposure to
significant physical and emotional consequences if attacked'; social vulnerability involves 'daily exposure to the threat of victimization and limited
means for coping with the medical and economic consequences of victimization' (pp. 77–8). Fear of criminal victimisation, then, may be a logical assessment of women's and the elderly's ability to physically defend themselves
in the face of (most commonly) male assailants, and when women and the
elderly are victimised, they are more frightened as a consequence (Skogan
and Maxfield, 1981, p. 78).

It was Griffin (1971) who linked this 'powerlessness' and 'daily exposure'
to one significant reality of women's lives: the fear of rape. As such, for
women, fear is the invisible barrier which surrounds them in all aspects of
their everyday lives. The work of Riger, Gordon, LeBailly and Heath (and
various combinations thereof) attributes women's fear of crime to their fear
of rape (Riger and Gordon, 1981, Riger et al., 1978; Gordon et al., 1980;
see also Hough and Mayhew, 1985). The authors note that women's fear is
proportionate to their subjective estimates of the risk of rape (Riger and
Gordon, 1981, p. 86). Estimates of risk do affect women's everyday strategies
to protect themselves from possible confrontation with potentially violent
men. Women's assessments of risk include their perception of risk, linked with
their perceptions of physical competence and the degree of what Riger and
Gordon term as 'women's attachments to their communities'.

According to Riger and Gordon (1981), women's strategies for avoiding
victimisation involve both social isolation – not going out at night because
they are concerned about safety – and adopting 'street savvy' – the variety of
precautionary strategies many women already adopt when they are out alone
at night. Two out of five women respondents in Riger and Gordon's study
indicated that they used isolation tactics, while three out of four reported
frequently using a variety of precautionary strategies. Moreover, the use
of these strategies will vary depending on how safe women feel their daily
context to be. Heath (1984) notes that the media contributes to women's
everyday context of safety. The media's role in disseminating information
about murder and sexual assault can effect women's fear of crime, particularly in situations where there may be acute danger. During the 'Yorkshire
Ripper's' reign of terror in the North of England, for example, women
stepped up their use of both types of protective tactic. In Dallas, Texas, in the
spring of 1985, where five women were murdered within a six-month period,
women were flocking to self-defence courses and many were reported to be
buying handguns for protection. Fear, elicited by the all-too-common serial
killers of women, immediately translates into everyday lifestyles where
women alter shopping, travel and social habits.

Throughout the work of Riger et al., however, is the undercurrent that
fear of rape is still a subjective risk, a perception, not an assessment of real

risk or real experience. While they do query the available objective data on rape victimisation (Riger and Gordon, 1981, p. 76), Riger et al. found that only 11 per cent of their 367 respondents (which included sixty-eight men) reported rape and sexual assault. Reported experiences of victimisation, then, still do not match the levels of fear reported by women. But we know that women do not always report experiences of rape and sexual assault, even to researchers (Russell 1973, 1982 and 1984; Clark and Lewis, 1977; Hanmer and Saunders, 1984).

Rather than informing us about officially recorded levels of risk of victimisation and fear of crime, women's fear of crime may alert us to the unrecorded instances of threatening and violent behaviour by males and thus give us far more information about the structure of gender and violence in a gender-stratified society. If women commonly encounter threatening and/ or violent behaviour from men who are strangers *and* from men known to them, how can they predict which man will be violent to them and in what instance? Moreover, disarmed by friendship or kinship, women's ability to protect themselves against familiar and familial interpersonal male violence is reduced. One study, for example, of women who were raped and those who avoided a rape indicates that women were more likely to avoid rape when the rapist was a stranger! (Bart and O'Brien, 1984).

The gap between women's fear of crime and the objective, official estimates of women's experiences of interpersonal violence is not an anomaly for feminists working in the area of violence to women. Even casual analysis of official data on interpersonal violence underscores what women working in rape crisis centres and refuges for battered women have heard so often: physical and sexual violence are common experiences of many women. Russell's study of 930 women in San Francisco, California, for example, found that there is a 26 per cent probability that a woman will be the victim of a completed rape at some time in her life (Russell and Howell, 1983, pp. 690–1) and that there is a 46 per cent probability that a woman will experience a completed or attempted rape in her lifetime (p. 692). She further found that 50 per cent of the women who had been attacked at least once had experienced attack from different assailants. Russell's data further shows that women's subjective estimate of their risk of rape may indeed be an objective risk, not a perception of risk.

British researchers, Hanmer and Saunders (1984), provide us with further clues as to women's experiences of threatening and violent male behaviour. Interviewing 129 women in a door-to-door survey, Hanmer and Saunders used a format similar to that of victimisation surveys, except that they asked women to describe situations of 'violence' which they had experienced, witnessed or overheard involving women in the past year. Fifty-nine per cent of these women reported at least one instance of male violence they had either experienced themselves, had witnessed or had overheard. What threatened women most was the inability to predict the outcome of a disturbing event. A 'flasher' intimidated and threatened women because of the fear of potential violence, as did men who followed women down a street. Moreover, instances of sexual harassment – 'cat calls' while walking on the street – also created feelings of insecurity. So, in addition to the probability of rape in women's lives, the probability of being sexually harassed while walking on the street or while at work is extremely high (MacKinnon 1979; Stanko 1985). These daily, commonly taken-for-granted experiences of women contribute to the hostile and intimidating atmosphere wherein women are presumably supposed to feel safe.

While women's fear remains an anomoly of perception for criminologists and policy-makers, understanding women's fear of crime – which might also be read as *women's fear of men* – entails understanding the ever-present reality of women's experiences of men's threatening and/or violent behaviour. Could not women's fear of crime be, in many ways, a recognition that women feel unsafe by virtue of their femaleness, to men by virtue of their maleness? If so, do women then expend greater time and energy making themselves feel safer? The fact that women's assailants are characteristically male, and frequently known to the women, is another factor aiding our understanding of interpersonal violence of men to women. Can women feel safe around strangers when those familiar to them have already harmed them? Russell's (1982) survey, for example, indicates that women currently in violent relationships are more afraid of sexual assault outside the home (p. 221) and thus fear the unknown more than the known violence. Another key factor for women is knowing whether outside agencies will intervene in situations of male violence: women commonly predict that those in decision-making positions in the criminal justice system will consider the victimisation event itself to be a non-criminal matter (Hanmer and Saunders, 1984; Stanko, 1985; Hanmer and Stanko, 1985; US Attorney General's Task Force on Family Violence, 1984). *In effect, women's feelings of fear may relate to their tacit understanding of the likelihood of experiencing male violence and the lack of protection they receive from those around them, and in particular, from those in positions of authority to protect them from abusive situations.*

Precaution and fear

Another way of examining the differences in men's and women's perceptions of personal safety and fear of crime is to explore the use of precautionary strategies used by individuals to increase the feeling of security. Precautionary strategies are, for women and men, mechanisms for coping with feelings of insecurity. Researchers note that in addition to the cognitive effects of fear of crime, behavioural changes might also occur for individuals afraid of victimisation (Riger and Gordon, 1981; Tyler, 1980). Assessments of personal vulnerability to criminal victimisation, Tyler (1980) found, are strongly related to crime-prevention behaviour. Precautionary strategies of individuals who fear crime, for example, might include the installation of additional locks on their property; the avoidance of certain 'high crime' areas; the 'insurance' of a companion when leaving or returning to one's home; the carrying of keys between one's hands; the self-assured walk on the outside of the pavement and the avoidance of poorly-lit spots on the street; the purchase of a watch dog, and so forth.

With respect to perceptions of personal vulnerability, Perloff (1983) notes that individuals who have been victimised tend to perceive themselves as more vulnerable than before. How victimised individuals cope with victimisation, she suggests, relates to whether they 'feel "uniquely vulnerable" (more vulnerable than others) or "universally vulnerable" (equally vulnerable as others)' (p. 41).

Do feelings of unique vulnerability and universal vulnerability vary by gender? If we read the use of precautionary strategies as one indication of universal vulnerability, most of the research indicates that women feel more universally vulnerable than men. While, on the whole, individuals who have experienced some form of victimisation have a greater tendency to change their behaviour to avoid future victimisation, many victimised men do not seem automatically to alter their behaviour to protect their *physical* safety. Preliminary evidence from this ongoing research indicates that men are more likely than women to take additional measures to protect their material possessions – their cars or their belongings – rather than their persons, even if they themselves had been physically threatened or assaulted. Moreover, physical competence and confidence seem to influence male respondents' feelings of safety. Be it bravado or be it an accurate assessment, the male respondents feel that in general they can physically match any single assailant. If the male respondents did express concern for their physical safety, they reported being wary of groups of assailants – situations where they would be physically outnumbered. Riger and Gordon (1981) have also found that men's perceived immunity to victimisation is reflected in the minimal use of precautionary strategies to avoid victimisation.

Precaution, particularly for women in structurally more vulnerable situations, may be the only way to approach living in a world which is potentially, and actually, dangerous for women. Goldstein (1984), for example, in an examination of violence within drug addicted women's worlds, notes that most women addicts in his study reported at least one experience of attempted rape or robbery that took place when they were buying drugs. As a precautionary strategy, women either employed other drug users to buy their drugs or teamed up with a male friend for protection when buying drugs (p. 13). While not all women live in such dangerous surroundings, some evidence exists that women who adopt non-traditional ('unprotected') lifestyles are more likely to be victimised than women living in traditional ('protected') lifestyles (Widom and Maxfield, 1984).

Another common strategy for women – particularly those following more traditional lifestyles – is to use 'safe' men for protection from other men. This strategy is not always successful. Firstly, it is not always possible to distinguish 'safe' from 'unsafe' men. If, however, women do find 'safe' men, it is virtually impossible for them to be protected twenty-four hours a day. And from the experience of women in supportive, loving relationships with 'safe' men who have encountered violence from male strangers, we know that these women must take time to sort out 'safe' male behaviour from that which was harmful. 'Like other victims,' states one women. 'I had problems with sex, after the rape. There was no way that Arthur could touch me that it didn't remind me of having been raped by this guy I never saw' (MacKinnon, 1983, p. 646, note 23).

It is the social context of womanness that continually reminds women of their universal vulnerability. And as additional information about sexual and/or physical abuse comes to light, we know that womanness also is likely to involve the experience of some form of male threatening and/or violent behaviour in a woman's lifetime. No doubt, for women, one typical result of an experience of victimisation is the adoption of precautionary strategies aimed at avoiding future victimisation. Whether it be sexual assault (Burgess and Holmstrom, 1974; Janoff-Bulman, 1979; Russell, 1982; Scheppele and Bart, 1983; Bart and O'Brien, 1984), physical assault (Hilberman and Munson, 1978; Walker, 1978), or sexual harassment (MacKinnon 1979; Farley 1978; Stanko 1985), women adopt precautionary strategies as a way of living in a male-dominated world.

Women and men adopt precautionary strategies very differently – regardless of whether they have been victimised or not (Riger and Gordon, 1981). Few men – if any – turn to women for protection against women, or men. It seems that women – more so than men – continually monitor the threat of danger around them from men (particularly strangers) – regardless of age, class or race. Women must observe men for potential danger, a price of subordination (Goode, 1982). As one way of explaining the continual use of self-protective strategies for women, Beneke (1982) suggests the following exercise for men:

Walk down a city street. Pay a lot of attention to your clothing; make sure your pants are zipped, shirt tucked in, buttons done. Look straight ahead. Every time a man walks past you, avert your eyes and make your face expressionless.

It is the connection between the use of precautionary strategies, gender and social control that is most useful in understanding the dynamics of 'fear of crime' and criminal victimisation. Why do women, more so than men, exercise elaborate precautionary strategies to avoid interpersonal violence in their everyday lives? Are they merely exaggerating risk or have they, as some have speculated, successfully avoided victimisation because of their precautionary strategies (Balkin, 1979)? Are women, as others speculate, 'overly afraid' (Dubow, 1979)? Is their fear a rational assessment of risk (Hough and Mayhew, 1983)? Or does the gap in women's and men's reported fear arise because of gender expectations: women are more willing to admit to being afraid (Clemente and Kleiman, 1977)? Many unanswered questions remain, but it is possible to begin to frame them within an understanding of gender and gender stratification. While we continue to ask why women, who reportedly occupy a position of low risk to interpersonal violence (Skogan and Maxfield 1981), fear dark streets and feel unsafe alone at night on the street, perhaps we should direct our inquiry to the reality of 'risk' and the long-term consequences of learning what it means to be universally vulnerable, a subordinate, in a male-dominated society.

2.3

Women and the 'fear of crime': challenging the accepted stereotype

by Elizabeth Gilchrist, Jon Bannister, Jason Ditton and Stephen Farrall

It is commonplace to assert that fear of crime has become a major social and political problem, perhaps bigger than crime itself (Hale 1993: 1–2; Bennett 1990: 14–15; Warr 1985: 238). Some results are discovered with monotonous regularity: for example, when fear of crime rates are compared with officially recorded (or unofficially self-confessed) victimizations, it is frequently discovered that women, and especially elderly women, are more fearful of crime but have less chance of being victimized than young men; and that young men, who are most likely to be victimized, are not fearful of crime at all (see e.g. Hale 1993: 15).

The resulting media privileging of gender as the primary social division (with age as the runner-up) may have begun empirical life as a relative frequency, but has now separated and become ossified as an absolute mediated stereotype. Currently, all women are reported to restrict their lives due to the perceived threat of criminal victimization, and they are portrayed as feeling unsafe walking in the street and even whilst at home. Yet, when they are mentioned at all, men are portrayed as less fearful and even offhand about the threat of criminal victimization.

This article tries to rescue women – and men – from the condescension of stereotypography, and by illustrating the very real presence of – contrarily – fearless women and fearful men, attempts to tease out the conditions under which some women avoid fear, and the conditions under which some men are enveloped by it. If, by so doing, we begin to understand why some women are not fearful, we might understand why some are; if we start to learn why some men are fearful, we might see more clearly why most men are not.

The worried woman

The major stereotypical emphasis is on fearful women, and many explanations for their presence have been advanced. It has been suggested that, for example, women have an 'irrational' response to an objectively lower crime threat, that women are more vulnerable to attack than men are, that women are less able to defend themselves and less able to cope with victimization (Riger et al. 1978: 277, 278, 282). Susan Smith has suggested that women's responsibility for and thus concern about their children fuels their fear of crime (Smith 1989: 62). Alternatively, it has been suggested that women have less control over their personal space and over public space than do men and so fear more (Brooks Gardner 1990: 315, 316, 324; Pain 1991: 423; Pain 1993: 62–6), that women do suffer more low level victimization (in the sense that they suffer routine sexual harassment) which would explain higher fear levels (Stanko 1990), that women fear sexual assault and rape which is not generally a threat for men (Riger et al. 1978: 278; Warr 1985: 248), and unusual and serious crimes, which are rare and which often involve female victims are over-reported and exaggerated in the media (Ditton and Duffy 1982; Winkel and Vrij 1990: 264).

Some have argued that women are socialized into fear of public space, a fear of strangers and a fear of men, and they are also socialized into a dependence on known men (brothers, fathers, partners) and also socialized into a position of responsibility for offences against them as a form of 'contributory negligence' (Burt and Estep 1981; Sacco 1990: 500–1). More recently Warr has suggested that females may report exaggerated fears of some offences such as burglary as they assume that this will be a precursor to more serious assaults, such as rape (Warr 1984).

Many of the early assertions regarding women's seemingly unjustifiably high fear of crime have been challenged by feminist and realist researchers. It has been suggested that women are not hysterically overreacting to a 'non-existent' threat when they report high levels of fear of crime. Rather, they are responding sensibly to the reality of their everyday lives (Hale 1993: 15–17). Feminist writers have suggested that women routinely face the threat of physical and sexual violence, on the street, at work and at home (Junger 1987: 382; Stanko 1990: 176). It has been suggested that the majority of women suffer regular low level victimization from men, in the form of sexist and sexual comments, and innuendo and unnecessary minor physical violations, and that their high fear levels merely reflect this reality (Junger 1987: 360, 381). Others have suggested that the treatment of female victims of violence (which focuses blame on the female victim) and the advice given to women as to how to avoid victimization (which focuses prevention of victimization on women's behaviour and the manner in which women present themselves in public) reinforces the fear of attack (Stanko 1990: 179–82).

Whilst this body of work has developed a challenge to the assumed irrationality of the hysterically fearful female, it has not questioned the underlying stereotypes that women are fearful and men are not. An exception is the work of Newburn and Stanko who directly challenge this assumption of homogeneity within gender groups. They write that 'the realists continue to

talk of men and women as if they (too) were largely homogenous categories
. . . such assumptions about social cohesion are perhaps overly optimistic'
(Newburn and Stanko 1994: 159), and later 'the underlying philosophy [of
realist victimology] that "crime is a problem for the working-class, ethnic
minorities, for all the most vulnerable members of capitalist societies" – is
too simplistic to allow for a properly realistic understanding of the scope of
victimization' (Young, quoted in Newburn and Stanko 1994: 159).

Newburn and Stanko further argue that 'little is known about men's
experience of victimization' and state that 'in the study of the fear of crime, of
which gender is the most significant feature, there is considerable discussion
of the disparity between women's and men's reported levels of fear. In much
of the literature it is seemingly quite unproblematically assumed that men are
reticent to disclose vulnerability' (p. 160).

Conversely, they claim that 'a proportion of men are significantly affected
by crime' and 'the effects of violent crime are severe for a high proportion of
men as well as women', and King adds that there are 'striking similarities
between the reactions of male victims and those reported for women who
have been sexually assaulted' (King 1992: 10). Research carried out by
Stanko and Hobdell, which used qualitative interviews to explore the relationship between victimization, masculinity and the process of coping with
victimization, indicated that in their study of male victims of assault, many
'reported fear, phobias, disruption to sleep and social patterns, hypervigi-
lance, aggressiveness, personality change and a considerably heightened
sense of vulnerability'; reactions which share some features with the reactions
of female victims (Stanko and Hobdell 1993).

Yet others suggest that while there are similarities in men's and women's
reactions to certain crimes, this is not necessarily true of worry about crime
and this is not constant across all types of offence. For example, Pain suggests
that 'whereas men and women worry equally about property crime, women
are far more worried than men about personal crime' (Pain 1993: 57; see also
MORI 1994). Equally, it is beginning to become apparent that men are as
fearful, if not slightly more so, of car crime than are women (Mirrlees-Black
et al. 1996:51).

We can no longer assume that men and women are different yet intern-
ally homogenous groups. As Stanko and Hobdell (1990) conclude: 'No
longer is it appropriate to dismiss men as "naturally" reticent'. Similarly it is
inappropriate to portray women as irrationally fearful.

Methods

A short (quantitative) interview with an initial sample of 168 individuals was
used to place respondents into one of four categories (produced by two
dimensions – fear and risk – described as high or low), 64 selected respondents (16 from each of the four fear/risk groups) were interviewed about their

feelings about crime. Responses from the (stereo)typical groups (i.e., high fear women and low fear men) were compared to those given by members of the atypical groups (i.e. high fear men and low fear women). Initially, concentration was on attitudes to four offences: housebreaking, assault, vandalism and car crime. Overall similarities and differences between the gender groups were considered and all responses examined to see whether men talk about crime similarly to each other and differently from women, despite different (quantitatively reported) fear levels; and to see whether all women talk similarly about crime, again despite different fear levels. These concerns were schematically distilled into three questions: one, do men and women talk about fear of crime differently? Two, do men and women give the same weight to the (fear-inducing or fear-reducing) cues to which they refer? Three, is the difference based not on gender, but on fear level?

Results

Fearful men and women

It is immediately noticeable, first, that the fearful (of both genders) cite 'vicarious victimization' (i.e., indirect experience of victimization, from friends, neighbours or the media) as a source of fear. [Of housebreaking it was said, for example:] 'just there's a lot of break-ins round here', 'you just hear about people getting broken into all the time', and, [you] 'see so much on television' were commonly described media through which fear was delivered.

Secondly, and also distinguishing the fearful from the fearless was apprehension about 'perceptually contemporaneous offences' (Warr, 1984: 699): serious victimizations that might immediately follow minor ones. Direct fear of specific types of assault, for example, sexual assault, was not mentioned, although some did mention the fear of weapons being used in a possible assault as a reason for them to worry. For the fearful, perceptually contemporaneous offending occurring with a burglary was also a source of fear, and this was so more often for women than men [y]et fearful men did mention it [too]. It seemed that men and women had different beliefs about offences which might co-occur: women being more likely to think that a more serious offence, like assault, would happen during a burglary; for men, it was just their routines (or the contents of their houses) that would be left in disarray. Both men and women did mention the idea of vandalism co-occurring with burglary. Although this was mentioned more by women than men, when it was mentioned by men, it was tempered by the fact that this type of event was seen as very unusual and unlikely, and so not a cause for concern. There were two explanations mentioned only by high fear men. One was the inconvenience and financial loss which would result from vandalism, and which would not by covered by insurance, and the other was they would worry about vandalism if it were 'personal' or meaningful, and perhaps indicative of a threat of violence.

A third distinguishing feature of the talk of the fearful was a sense of constant awareness of risk. A number of both men and women mentioned that they were 'aware of', or 'concerned about', assault, rather than being fearful of it (although in the earlier quantitative interview, they had claimed to be 'highly' fearful of it, see Farrall et al., 1997). The comments of one of the high fear males illustrate this point:

> It's just the thought of it I'm always conscious of space, as soon as people come very close to me . . . if someone comes up to me, in the street . . . and they ask for the time, I may go towards my watch, but I'll never look at the watch . . . I'll keep my eye on the person. (male, 64, outlying affluent)

Four, this tended to be intensified (particularly for the fear of assault) 'in particular places' (unfamiliar, dark, quiet) and/or 'at particular times' (after dark, at night even in summer). Both groups also mentioned fear of assault connected to 'specific types of people': strangers, and junkies, but women mentioned more types more often than men, and for them, the list also included: alcoholics, drug dealers, and groups of youths. Familiarity with an area was often the only thing that reduced fear, but this was more true for men than for women. Feeling personally vulnerable was used to explain worry about assault. More women than men felt this.

Lack of domestic rather than personal security also informed worry, and both fearful men and fearful women talked of worrying about burglary if they had to leave their house empty. Good security was a factor which reduced this worry, as was having good neighbours, or a dog. Not perceiving one's house as an attractive target also reduced fear. The fearful like comforting commercial security devices and good neighbours. One of the high fear females worried because she had to leave her flat empty, and because she thought housebreaking was common in her area, but was somewhat reassured by the security devices she had installed and because she perceived that her neighbours would have a deterrent effect on potential housebreakers. A key element of this fourth feature that distinguishes the fearful from the fearless is the over-estimation of risk.

A fifth source of worry for the fearful might be termed 'altruistic' or 'referred' worry (i.e., worry for someone other than oneself). In terms of assault, fearful men worried for women, and fearful women worried for their children. These differences are clear in the following examples, the first is a high fear male and the second a high fear female:

> Oh, yeah, I do worry about Jane going out, yeah . . . well because she is my wife basically . . . I mean there's probably just as little chance of her

being attacked as me, but the very fact that she's my wife, you know, you do worry about it. (male, 26, inner city affluent)

I worry about the boys, maybe if they are going to a concert in town or something, you worry about them coming home, there's so much badness now. (female, 58, inner city poor)

Sixth was 'contagious' worry: a factor mentioned only by women and which referred to the effect of other people's worry on their own fear levels. This may be related to vicarious victimization, and lead, in turn, to more precautionary behaviour. A number of women claimed that their partner's worry had increased their worry for themselves. This high fear female illustrates this feeling:

My husband would rather that I drove round there . . . which is always like a minute [on foot] whereas I would rather walk and there are sort of shortcuts that go from [inner city affluent area] through the flats just down there, I've been kind of warned not to go. (female, 30s, inner city affluent)

Seven, matching their keenness on domestic security precautions, most of the fearful mentioned the various personal precautions that they took. Only men mentioned carrying some sort of weapon to protect themselves, but both men and women did talk about taking other precautions to avoid getting into a situation where they could be assaulted. It seemed that, while many of the factors referred to by fearful people are common to men and women, some are used more by men and others more by women. High fear men reported less vulnerability, were less affected by the media and worried altruistically (for women) more than did high fear women. High fear women worried for their children, reported more vulnerability, were more affected by the media, feared a wider group of strangers than did high fear men, and were affected by their partner's fears for them.

Fearless men and women

Fearless men and women also tended to worry about assault in specific places, but from a shorter list of specific groups of people (only strangers, junkies) and at fewer specific times (after dark only). They were also less worried about the areas that they lived in (although often these were the same areas that the fearful worried about). Fearless men and women mentioned familiarity with their area as a factor reducing their worry about assault, as did use of precautions.

A second distinguishing feature of the fearless (when compared with the fearful) was their relative under-estimation of risk. This seemed to reflect a failure to absorb personally the 'vicarious victimizations' that concerned the fearful. Two of the relatively fearless seemed almost dismissive of the prospect of assault, for example, even though the first had had personal experience of it. Both fearless men and fearless women talked about not feeling vulnerable and claimed that this reduced their worry. However, for men this was not feeling personally vulnerable, whereas for women this tended to mean not feeling that they were vulnerable due to their lifestyle. This difference is obvious from the following quotes, the first from a low fear male and the second from a low fear female:

> Well I think it's because I'm about 6 feet ye know I mean I'm . . . I can look after myself, so I don't feel worried. (male, 30, inner city poor)

> I don't tend to go out much by myself so I'm always with other people . . . I think that significantly reduces the chance of being assaulted . . . I honestly don't think I worry at all to be honest, about being assaulted. (female, 16, outlying affluent)

Relative under-estimation of risk was consistently referred to by a number of fearless men. Assault, for example, was thought unlikely, housebreaking, too, was seen as unlikely (or the fact that it was only occasionally seen as likely) was something which the fearless referred to when explaining their low worry levels. Lack of experience of victimization, whether direct or indirect, and positive feelings about the area in which they lived – whether or not they felt safe there, were also used to explain their lack of worry. However, lack of vicarious victimization, and the idea that housebreaking was rare, was used more often by men than by women. Similarly, both low fear men and low fear women referred to their lack of experience of vandalism, both personally, and in their area, to explain their lack of worry. The fearless did mention vandalism during housebreaking, however the men used this as a factor which reduced their worry as it was unlikely, and 'you do not hear of much happening', while the women suggested this could increase their worry as they would be upset at the destruction.

A third feeling mentioned by low fear men (but not by low fear women) was that they could handle a situation of, for example, threatened assault and so did not worry. Indeed, a couple of the men who had been assaulted were annoyed that they had not handled it better rather than fearful because of it, as this low fear male explained:

> I don't worry about it . . . I used to do martial arts and that . . . I think I could defend myself . . . if somebody did attack me, I think I know how to handle myself. (male, 21, inner city affluent)

Men and women who reported low fear of assault talked similarly about it, only fearing specific people, places and times and reporting that they had low fear due to taking precautions or not feeling vulnerable. However, for women, this lack of vulnerability arose from their lifestyles (not being out alone in places seen as dangerous) and for men, this lack of vulnerability was derived from a perception that assault was unlikely coupled to the feeling that they could cope with any threatened assault that might occur.

Only one of the fearless woman specifically mentioned the threat of rape and did so by saying that it was at the back of her mind but she kept reminding herself to remain calm and confident believing that by acting in this way she would avoid any such experience.

Fourth, in terms of housebreaking, many low fear men and low fear women suggested that the precautions they had taken (and the security measures installed) reduced their worry about it. Access to social support whether formal or informal was used more by women than by men to explain lack of worry, although men did occasionally refer to it. This could also relate to low worry about vandalism – the good security they had and the lack of people hanging around, were both reasons for the fearless not to worry. The low fear men and women also were conscious of car crime, but talked about it less than the high fear respondents. A number of the low fear men did refer to taking precautions to avoid car crime as a reason not to worry about it, and the fact that the effects of car crime would only be a hassle or an irritation was referred to by a number of the men and by one woman who referred to car crime.

The fifth explanation given to explain why they didn't worry about housebreaking, was the idea that their house was not a target. This explanation was used more by men than by women. There were a number of explanations given by low fear men which were not used by women: not worrying as the person knew the offenders and he or his friends would retaliate; not worrying for self but worrying because of the effect it would have on one's family; and not worrying at the idea of encountering a burglar as the burglar would be more scared than the 'victim'.

Seeing the offender as weak rather than strong was a persisting, and sixth theme. Thinking about vandals, if respondents believed that the perpetrators were either non-threatening locals or children, then any vandalism was seen as less threatening. Further, if vandalism was perceived as random and impersonal, then it was also seen as less worrying. It was interesting that men suggested vandalism was so unlikely as to be nothing to worry about, while the women thought the impact of such a thing would be so bad as to make it something to worry about. The meaning of vandalism and who was doing it, was also important, but, overall, vandalism was not an offence which provoked much fear for these relatively fearless respondents.

Implications

It seems that men and women refer to similar factors when talking about worry and crime, but there are great differences between low fear and high fear men and great differences between high fear women and low fear women. There are perhaps more similarities than differences between both high fear men and high fear women, and between low fear men and low fear women.

The fearful appear to have gathered more knowledge of victimization (whether direct or indirect); they appear to think that they have a higher risk of being victimized and see themselves as more vulnerable than the fearless. The fearful seemed to think their security measures were poor and they appeared to link more minor offences with more serious ones and so worried about the minor offences. For example, the high fear men talked about worrying about vandalism if it were meaningful (i.e. if there was a threat of attack) and the high fear women talked about worrying about vandalism if it occurred during a housebreaking, and of worrying about housebreaking due to the possibility of encountering a housebreaker, and then because there would be a risk of attack.

Although women seem to talk similarly to men who have similar fear levels, they refer to a wider range of situations, people and factors which inform their fears, apart from talking about car crime, where the men are more expansive. Also, both groups of men appeared to refer to more factors which reduced their worry. For example, both groups of men referred to familiarity with their area as a factor which reduced their worry about assault, but only the low fear women talked about this feature.

In general, the explanations given for worry about crime followed an expected pattern. That is, people who report high worry explain this by referring to their experiences of victimization and to the fact that they consider victimization likely. However, some of the explanations are somewhat counter-intuitive. For example, some of those who reported low worry thought that it was highly likely that they would be victimized, but did not worry as there was no point in worrying about a fact of life – about something they could not avoid. Other explanations, such as vicarious victimization, either informed or reduced worry depending on how other factors were employed. For example, people who thought victimization was likely, who considered themselves vulnerable either through personal characteristics or membership of a vulnerable group, explained that media stories about victimization informed their worry.

However, people who thought victimization unlikely and considered themselves not to be at risk as they were neither an attractive target, nor a member of a vulnerable group, mentioned media stories, but did not refer to them as a factor which increased worry.

Conclusions

What does this mean in terms of the large body of research into and recent literature on fear of crime? This exploration of men and women talking about their feelings about crime provides support for Newburn and Stanko's (1994: 160) suggestion that although it has been assumed that men are reticent to disclose their fears about crime, this is not the case and perhaps merely reflects the previous methodologies employed. Similarly, this paper supports and expands upon the work of King (1992: 10), and Stanko and Hobdell (1993), who reported striking similarities between men's and women's experiences of, and reactions to victimization. Our data suggest there are striking similarities between men and women's fears about crime; in the steps they take to avoid crime and in the overall impact of crime in their everyday lives.

This research also provides some support for Maxfield's (1987) suggestion that men's worries about crime are 'altruistic', but, in addition, our data suggest that some women's fears are also 'altruistic'. The difference between the genders seemed to arise from the focus of those worries. That is, men reported worrying about women and women reported worrying about children. The data also supported a hypothesis proposed by Warr (1985: 245–7) that there may be differences in offences which would be perceived as occurring contemporaneously, and this could explain otherwise inexplicable differences in fear levels.

It further appears that women and men report different beliefs about certain crimes. For example, some women thought they would be likely to encounter a burglar, and so face the threat of assault, during a burglary and so reported worrying about it. However, some men thought that certain acts of vandalism might be connected to a threat of assault, and so worried more.

In general, our data provide prima facie evidence that men and women cannot be treated as independent, homogenous groups. There appear to be as many variations within gender groups as similarities between them. Equally, there are as many similarities across gender groups as differences between them.

What does this mean for future research into fear of crime? One way ahead is to develop more sensitive and probing tools for measuring worries about crime so that we can be more alert to the ways in which people understand their own victimization, the factors which people use to explain their awareness of crime, and the cues to which people refer when estimating their risk of victimization and vulnerability to crime.

What is clear is that we can no longer ignore men's vulnerabilities, nor can we consider worry about crime as relating solely to women. It is an issue for a broad range of people, and needs, in the future, to be addressed from this perspective. But there is more to it even than this. The challenge is not to develop more precise quantitative instrumentation, but more sensitive qualitative understanding. We now know that some women are not fearful, and that some men are fearful: yet we are some way from knowing why this should be, and we are a long way from knowing whether or not fear (or, fearlessness) encompasses shared meanings.

2.4
Women's violence to men in intimate relationships: working on the puzzle
by Russell P. Dobash and
R. Emerson Dobash

Introduction

Violence against women by an intimate male partner is now recognized
throughout most of the world as a significant social problem. It has been
identified by many countries, the United Nations and the European Union as
an issue of human rights (United Nations 1995, Kelly 1997). In the past two
decades, significant changes in policies and practices have occurred worldwide, but particularly in the United States, Britain, Canada and Australia
(Dobash and Dobash 1979; 1992; Schechter 1982; Heise 1994; Stubbs 1994;
Mullender 1996; Schneider 2002). The majority of changes have been in
the areas of community support, public policy, social services and civil and
criminal law and law enforcement.

The pragmatic experience of most community advocates and professionals dealing with violence between intimates on a regular basis and the
research findings of most social scientists studying this phenomenon agree
that 'intimate partner violence' is overwhelmingly an issue of male violence
against a female partner. However, the findings of some social scientists,
particularly in the United States, appear to support the notion that the
phenomenon is equally likely to be women's violence against a male partner,
and some even claim that women are more likely than men to be violent to
their intimate partner.

[. . .]

In order to examine women's violence, we present findings from a study
that included 95 couples in which men and women reported separately upon
the violence in their relationship. This included both men's violence against
women partners and women's violence against male partners in terms of the
nature, frequency, severity and physical and emotional consequences. A
close examination of women's violence is especially important because there
is a need to reflect on both men's and women's violent behaviour in order to

consider the veracity of these contradictory findings. To date, there has been very little in-depth research about women's violence to male partners and it is difficult, if not impossible, to consider this debate without such knowledge. But why bother about the apparent contradictions in findings from research? For those making and implementing policies and expending public and private resources, the apparent contradiction about the very nature of this problem has real consequences for what might be done for those who are its victims and those who are its perpetrators.

[. . .]

Intimate partner violence: studies of couples

In an extensive review of the literature, Margolin (1987) concluded that there was little overall agreement between couples about men's and women's violence, and that women are more likely than men to acknowledge their own violence. Women were also more likely to experience considerably more violence and women's initiation of violence was often appropriately defined as 'protective reactive' responses – a term initially used by Gelles (1997). She noted that 'Spouses may have different definitions and thresh-olds as to what they view as violent, may ascribe self-serving labels and interpretations to behaviours, or, simply falsify reports' (Margolin 1987: 77). One significant finding of Margolin's own research was that it was impossible to make sense of her results without a consideration of the mean-ings attached to the violence of men and women. She noted that, 'While [violent acts] appear behaviourally specific, their meanings are open to question' (Margolin 1987: 82). As an example of this problem, she cites a couple that reported kicking each other – clearly an act of violence – yet, in her subsequent in-depth interviews, she discovered that this was a playful activity that they engaged in when in bed. She concluded that assessments of violence should include a consideration of the severity of injuries, the percep-tions of the victims and the intentions of the attackers: 'A woman's hardest punches, which might be laughed at by her husband, would count as "husband abuse" based on actions alone' (Margolin 1987: 83).

A study of intimate partner violence reported by couples

In order to consider the claims of equivalence in the perpetration of violence by men and by women, we present findings from in-depth interviews with couples that were part of a larger study of criminal justice intervention in intimate partner violence (Dobash et al. 2000). The wider study included a sample of 122 men and 134 women, drawn from cases dealt with in two different courts. The sample used here is based on 190 interviews with 95 men and 95 women. In-depth interviews were conducted separately with men and women. A context-specific method was used and both quantitative and qualitative data were gathered. While men's violence was the main focus of the study, women's violence and aggression were also examined. Using the quantitative and qualitative data from the interviews, we examined the prevalence and incidents of men's violence and women's violence, the detailed nature of the physical and sexual acts involved, and of the injuries inflicted. Focusing on women's violence, we consider the nature of women's violence, of men's reactions and the issue of self-defence. Little is known about the specific nature and context of women's violence and yet this is essential if the claim of equivalence between men and women is to be assessed.

It should be noted that while the focus of this paper is on women's violence to a male partner, the sample is drawn from men who have used violence against a woman partner. As such, women's violence is being examined in the context of men's violence. While it might be useful to study only women who have been arrested for using nonlethal violence against a male partner, this is such a rare occurrence that it would be difficult to obtain an adequate sample. The main concern is to consider men's accounts and women's accounts of violent 'acts', 'events', injuries and consequences, as well as their contexts, meanings and interpretations. Both quantitative and qualitative results are presented. 'Violence' is conceptualized as malevolent physical or sexual 'acts', used in a purposive manner and intended to inflict physical and/or psychological harm. Such acts usually, although not always, have harmful consequences for the victim, particularly physical injuries. In addition, the wider 'constellation of abuse' includes acts that are not physical per se but are meant to frighten, intimidate and coerce. Intimidating and coercive 'acts' are measured and/or assessed separately and reported separately from physical/sexual 'acts', in order that they are not conflated. It should be stressed that coercive and intimidating acts may have important and negative consequences for victims but, as discussed earlier, it is important that they are not collapsed into one category and referred to as though there is no difference between them.

Men's and women's perpetration of violence and injuries to an intimate partner

Violent events: couples' reports of men's violence

The couples were asked how often the man had been violent to the woman during the previous year. It was difficult for respondents to give a precise number of violent events, particularly if there had been many such events. As such, respondents were asked to indicate how many events occurred in a usual month and this was used to arrive at an annual estimate. [M]en generally reported perpetrating significantly fewer violent events against their woman partner than were reported by the women themselves. Of the sample, no direct physical violence was reported in the interviews by 21.1 per cent of women and 30.5 per cent of men. Of those reporting violence in the interviews, 47.4 per cent of women and 55.8 per cent of men reported one to four violent events, 17.9 per cent of women and 9.5 per cent of men reported five to nine violent events, and 13.7 per cent of women and 4.2 per cent of men reported ten or more incidents of violence perpetrated by the man.

Couples' reports of women's violence

The couples were also asked how often the woman had been violent to the man during the year prior to the interview. Most had little difficulty in giving a precise number of violent events, because the number of incidents perpetrated by women against men was usually few or none. Just under half of the men and women agreed that there had been no physical violence perpetrated by the woman against the man (46.3 per cent of women and 40.0 per cent of men reported NO violence by the woman). Of those reporting violence by the woman: 44.2 per cent of women and 50.6 per cent of men reported one to four events; 4.2 per cent of women and 7.4 per cent of men reported five to nine events; and 5.3 per cent of women and 2.1 per cent of men reported ten or more events perpetrated by the woman.

Violent 'acts'

The couples were also asked to specify the different types of violent 'acts' that made up the physical or sexual violence within these 'events'. Both men and women reported a much wider range of violent physical and sexual 'acts' committed by men against women than vice versa. For the purposes of comparing men's violence and women's violence, we include only those physical 'acts' committed by both men and women. While this allows for direct comparisons of men's and women's violence, it omits some of the 'high-end' violence that was perpetrated only by men against women, including sexual assault. We include ten comparisons of physical 'acts' perpetrated by men and women against their partner.

[W]hether reported by men or by women and whether the differences between them are great or small, many more men perpetrate every type of violent or threatening 'acts' than do women. Secondly, sometimes a larger percentage of women than men report their own violence (e.g. slap, push – shove and kick body), while men never report more of their own violence than is reported by their female partners. Thirdly, some 'acts' are perpetrated by a large percentage of men but are rarely perpetrated by women (e.g. choke, damage property and threaten to hit). Fourthly, men and women tend to agree more about women's violence than about men's violence. The rarity of women's 'threats to hit' men would seem to be indicative of an absence of the overall 'constellation of abuse' so familiar in men's abusive behaviour.

[A]bout 40 per cent of women reported that their male partner had 'demanded sex' from them and nearly 20 per cent indicated that their partner had 'forced' them to have sex on at least one occasion. By comparison, far fewer men reported having committed such acts against their woman partner, with about 15 per cent saying that they had 'demanded sex' and about 3 per cent saying that they had 'forced sex' on their woman partner. None of the men or women in the study reported sexual coercion or violence perpetrated by women.

Perceived seriousness of men's and women's violence

Women and men were also asked about their perceptions of the seriousness of their partner's violence to them. The overall pattern is one in which men and women generally agree that men's violence is 'serious' or 'very serious' and that women's violence is 'not serious' or 'slightly serious'. The vast majority of both women (82.0 per cent) and men (66.1 per cent) describe men's violence as either 'serious' or 'very serious', whereas only 36.0 per cent of women and 28.5 per cent of men describe women's violence similarly.

Contextualizing women's violence against male partners

Evidence from this study provides information about the prevalence of violence and injuries among couples and the perceived seriousness of men's and women's violence. While the main pattern is one of men's violence to women, nonetheless the evidence suggests that some women do commit violence against male partners. Here, we examine women's violence by considering more fully its nature, context and consequences, as well as how men and women view women's violence.

Nature of women's violence

During the lengthy interviews in which violent events were discussed in detail, women were usually more willing to speak at length about their own violence than were men.

The following comments illustrate this violence.

How serious would you say your violence was? Well I suppose the fact that I stabbed him made it pretty serious. I was arrested for attempted murder but, I mean, he gets arrested for a 'domestic' and I get arrested for 'attempted murder'. It was dropped to 'assault', right enough, and I got eighteen months probation. (woman.1082)

That time he had cracked my cheekbone, I went for him with a knife. After he done it [abused her], I just went for him. (woman.1160)

Reports of *serious* violence by women were not the norm. Accordingly, the majority of men's and women's reports show a restricted range of 'acts' and types of injuries perpetrated by women, as revealed in the comments of both men and women.

> *Have you ever been violent to him?* Oh, I've kind of thrown things, and things like that, but no punching and kicking or that kind of thing. (woman.1041)

> Well, apart from throwing that cup, which I don't see as being violent because I got it worse that time. (woman.1064)

Men's reactions to women's violence against them

Men and women reacted very differently to the violence they experienced. In order to understand better men's reactions to women's violence, it is important to set them in the context of women's reactions to men's violence. The 95 women indicated that they reacted to the violence perpetrated against them in ways that illustrate the impact and importance of these events in their lives. Here, we report only a few. Most women said they were usually 'frightened' (79 per cent), felt 'helpless' (60 per cent), 'alone' (65 per cent) and 'trapped' (57 per cent). They felt 'abused' (65 per cent) but were also 'bitter' (82 per cent) and 'angry' (80 per cent).

Men's reactions to women's violence against them usually did not reflect the negative consequences similar to those reported by women. Of the men who described their response to the violence of their woman partner, the largest proportion said they were 'not bothered' (26 per cent), followed by those who felt that the woman was justified' (20 per cent) and those who 'ridiculed her' (17 per cent) or were 'impressed' (3 per cent) that she had managed to respond. Others felt 'angry' (14 per cent) or 'surprised' (6 per cent) and there were a variety of 'other' reactions (8 per cent). Only a few of the men felt 'victimized' (6 per cent).

Men often described women's violence toward them as insignificant:

> *Has her violence toward you been serious?* No, never. *Not at all?* No. (man.123)

> *Do you feel concerned about her violent behaviour?* No, not really. (man.116)

Men sometimes viewed women's violent/aggressive acts as comical or ludicrous.

> Like we've had an argument and I've had the clothes flung at me and a

cup smashed over my head. You know, she does that to me and I end up laughing and it makes her worse. (man.036)

What would you do or say [when she hit you]? If she hit us, I would say, 'is that the best you can do?' She'd hit me again and I'd say something like, 'Oh [Betty], for God's sake, just pack it in'. *So, you'd make fun of her?* I would just laugh at her, you know, just laugh at her [saying] 'you're mental'! (man.055)

Some men found it impossible to contemplate women's violence. It was only men who could and should use violence, not women.

What do you think about her being violent to you? Well, I think she's not got the right to do that. I'm a man, she's a woman! (man.008)

Has [she] ever been violent to you? No, because she's a woman, I'm a man. Basically, my wife's 98lbs. (man.041)

A few men even expressed a form of 'admiration' of the woman's violent reaction to their abuse. For them, the violence seemed to be the only meaningful expression of her objections to his violence toward her. While women repeatedly expressed their rejection of and anger about his violence to her, for some men these actions were 'invisible' or inconsequential. Women may have reacted in these ways for many years; it was only when she acted 'like a man' that he appeared to notice her objections. Ironically, the woman's response to the man's repeated abuse might serve to expurgate his guilt.

How do you feel about the violence? Good. *How's that?* The fact that she's getting her aggression back out on me what I used to do to her. (man.038)

It did me good. I was quite pleased she did it because I knew she was starting to stand up for herself. (man.089)

Both the quantitative and qualitative evidence suggest that men's reactions to and interpretations of the violence they experienced differ from those expressed by women about men's violence. The fear, bewilderment and helplessness expressed by the women were not apparent in the responses of the men. Unlike the women, few of the men reacted to the violence in ways that suggested it had seriously affected their sense of well-being or the routines of their daily life. Rather, in those relationships in which women's violence occurred, men were often unconcerned and viewed it as relatively inconsequential and of no lasting effect. Although a few men were affected in a negative fashion and did experience serious injuries, this was not the norm for most of the men in the study.

Self-defence

The issue of self-defence in intimate partner violence has been a subject of considerable debate. As recognized in law, the concept of self-defence and its corollary, provocation, incorporate contextual and situational elements (Polk 1997). In order to define an act as 'self-defence', it is necessary to consider the context in which the 'act' occurred, including the interaction between the individuals involved.

In this study, men and women were asked about the use of violence in 'self-defence'. The responses are highly gendered and illustrate the complexity of this issue. Men generally did not use the term 'self-defence' to describe their violence toward women. When discussing the violent event that led to their arrest and conviction, only six of the 95 men indicated that they hit their partner because 'she hit him first', but even they did not describe this as 'self-defence'. By contrast, women often used the term 'self defence' or 'self-protection' to describe their violence to men.

Men and women were asked whether women's use of violence was 'always' in self-defence Focusing only on responses from individuals where women had used violence, 75 per cent of these women said their violence was 'always' in self-defence and 54 per cent of men agreed. The different terms used by respondents to describe what might be seen as 'reactions' in response to particular 'acts' of violence (e.g. raise an arm to deflect a blow, push against the chest in order to facilitate running from the room to escape further blows, etc.) raise questions about how such acts might be defined by the men and women involved, as well as by researchers. Are these acts of 'self-protection' and/or 'self-defence', or acts of 'violence'? Acts of 'self-protection' might include such things as 'putting one's arms up to deflect an oncoming blow', while an act of 'self defence' might include the 'return of a blow'. Surely, these are not acts of malevolent violence. This is a complex issue, as reflected in some of the comments made by men and women about women's violence.

> *Was she ever violent when you were arguing?* No, not really. She would usually try and protect herself. (man.089)

> *Did [she] ever try to stop you being violent to her?* She'd pick up something, like a glass for instance and warn me. She's kicked me out of the house and I couldn't get back in because of the [my] violence. (man.041)

These quotes demonstrate some of the complications of this issue. In the literature, it is often implied that women's reactions to men's violence do not include elements of retaliation and/or revenge. In this study, it was clear that women did at times respond to their abusive male partner out of 'reactive anger' about a specific attack against her or as a result of the cumulative effect of many attacks over a prolonged period of abuse.

Have you ever been violent to him? Only sort of in self-defence. *So you have retaliated if you have been hurt?* Yes. *Have you ever hurt him in any way or has he been bruised as a result of what you have done?* The first time it happened, I picked up a shoe and smacked him across the face with it and his nose went a bit 'squifff' for a while, but then things went back to normal [him hitting her]. (woman.1081)

Women's use of violence, whether in self-protection, self-defence or retaliation, sometimes resulted in an escalation of the man's violence toward her.

Have you ever been violent to him? A couple of times I've sort of slapped him back, but I mean I don't get anywhere so I didn't bother. *When you've slapped him back, how did he respond?* I get it all the more, that's why I don't bother. (woman.1126)

How did he respond to your violence? I think the fact that I tried defending myself made him ten times worse. (woman.1066)

Conclusions and implications for legislation, policies and interventions

What are the policy implications of these findings? These findings indicate that the problem of intimate partner violence is primarily one of men's violence to women partners and not the obverse. A recent review of existing policies on domestic violence in England and Wales includes a comprehensive list of 'detailed recommendations on key policy areas' (Harwin 2000). The general principles underlying a national strategy should include: promoting the protection of women and children at risk of violence; prevention through public awareness, education and the law; and the provision of effective services. The 'framework for action' includes a host of specific recommendations across a broad spectrum, including: specialist refuge and advocacy services, civil law, criminal law, law enforcement, divorce and court proceedings, child protection services, social services, welfare benefits and related issues, housing, immigration laws and education (Harwin 2000: 382–91). These efforts are overwhelmingly directed at the problem of men's violence to women.

The findings reported here are in line with this overall orientation to policy. They support the general trend of policies and interventions relating to intimate partner violence that are almost wholly designed to deal with the serious problem of men's violence directed at women (Dobash 2003). While any and all conflict and negative encounters between couples is regrettable, policies and interventions, particularly those of criminal justice, are not developed to provide wide-scale responses to such encounters; nor are public resources spent upon them. This is not to say that conflicts, heated arguments, name-calling or a one-off push or shove are unimportant but, rather, that great care must be taken in the definition and measurement of any such behaviour before it is labelled as 'violence' and before public policies and interventions are directed at it (Gordon 2000: 750).

Even so, what about the perennial question of women's violence to male partners? If such violence occurs with the same frequency and ferocity as men's violence and has a similar impact on the victims, then responding to the needs of male victims should be identical to those for women victims. Accordingly, laws, social services, health care, education and the like would all need to expend similar resources in assisting the equal numbers of male victims of violence to escape to shelters where they might be safe, to obtain protection orders so that they might be safe, and to access public housing for themselves and their children in order that they might be safe. A follow-up study of men who identified themselves as victims of domestic violence in the Scottish Crime Survey 2000 was conducted in order to examine the nature and veracity of these reports and to consider the need for services for such 'abused' men (Gadd, et al 2002). The findings revealed that one-quarter of the men had not experienced violence from their partner but had misunderstood the meaning of the term 'domestic violence' and were referring, instead, to crimes in the domestic dwelling (e.g. non-domestic assaults and property crimes). The follow-up showed that some of the men were also assailants and very few defined themselves as 'victims'. Of those men who did experience some form of violence from their female partner, they were less likely than women to be repeat victims, to have been seriously injured and to report feeling fearful in their own home. Based on these findings, the researchers concluded that there was no need for a special agency or refuge provision for men (Gadd, et al 2002). In the United States, more women are being brought into the criminal justice system because of 'domestic violence', primarily because of dual arrests of both the man and the woman (Miller 2001). This may suggest the occurrence of violence by both women and men and the need for victim services for both. However, a closer examination of these cases suggested that the majority of the women were rarely the 'primary' perpetrator, were often the victims of violence from their male partner, and that men's and women's need for services were rarely equivalent (Hamberger and Potente 1994; Miller 2001).

If women's violence is not equivalent to that of men and does not require identical policies and interventions, then how do we conceive of women's violence and what is to be done by way of intervention and prevention? According to the findings of this and other research, when women's violence against a male partner does occur, it is usually, although not always, in the context of men's violence to the woman (Swan and Snow 2002). However, as already stated, this violence is rarely identical or truly reciprocal. The type and level of violence, the nature and number of injuries, the perceived seriousness of the violence and the sense of safety and well-being are not the same for men and women. For the most part, women's violence is reactive and self-protective and is often in self-defence.

As mentioned earlier, it has been suggested that one strategy for reducing intimate partner violence is to propose that woman never use violence against a male partner, regardless of the circumstances, because this may result in the escalation of the man's violence against the woman (Straus 1993). It is neither possible nor reasonable to make 'fixed' recommendations about the nature of how any woman should respond to violence against her, because it is impossible to know the relevant circumstances within a given event or relationship. It would be similar to recommending in advance that a woman who is being raped should never 'fight back' or 'always fight back'. Perhaps a more positive strategy for preventing or reducing women's violence, and one in keeping with the findings of this study, is to eliminate men's violence against women partners.

Finally, what is to be done about the very small number of women who may initiate severe, persistent, repeat physical and sexual violence against a male partner in a context of no violence from the man? We have yet to see any evidence that would enable us to consider this issue. Identification of this putative group would require the same kind of intensive studies that have been done on men's violence, using both qualitative and quantitative data to provide a holistic picture of the violence and the context, consequences, motives and intentions associated with it. What is required is research methods that provide a more adequate representation of this violence and the contexts in which it occurs, rather than conceptual and operationalist abstractions that are once removed from such real-life events. Even if this were to be found, all extant evidence would predict that the numbers would be very small. As such, priority should continue to be given to policies that seek to effectively intervene to end violence against women in intimate relationships.

Part 3

Gender and social control

Introduction

Criminal law, conviction and imprisonment do not comprise the primary means of governing the behaviour of women and girls. Rather, their social control has been accomplished through more subtle but nevertheless wide-ranging and no less effective means. The female sex is often viewed as in need of protection and guidance, and where the state has intervened it has been its welfare arms which have encircled and restrained women and girls – especially regarding the control of their sexuality and sexual expression (Lees, 1986), defining the limits of acceptable behaviour and strongly condemning and punishing any trans-gressions. The first reading highlights how the dangers associated with girls' sexuality have proved a key factor in adjudicating the state's disciplinary regula-tion of female behaviour. Annie Hudson addresses the unique and particular needs and experiences of troublesome young women. She demonstrates how young women's relationships with statutory criminal justice and welfare agencies have over time been subject to a complex fabric of control and subordination that is inextricably connected to their perceived sexuality, emotionality and their ability to fulfil normative expectations of appropriate female conduct. Hudson's analysis provides a clear warning that the problem-atic, as opposed to criminal, behaviour of girls can both directly and indirectly lead to them being embroiled in the criminal justice system

Gender differentials in offenders' treatment within the criminal justice sys-tem have proved a complex focus of criminological concern. In particular, the contradictory hypotheses that female offenders are subjected to chivalry or treated as doubly deviant have provided rich sources of empirical enquiry in the study of sentencing processes and outcomes. The former proposes that female offenders receive more lenient treatment on the basis of their gender, while the latter that female offenders receive harsher treatment because they have not only violated the criminal law but also assumptions about what is appropriate and acceptable behaviour for women. The conclusions of a pleth-ora of empirical studies addressing these hypotheses have proved contradictory and ambiguous (Carlen, 1983; Daly, 1994; Eaton, 1986; Edwards, 1984; Farrington and Morris, 1983; Gelsthorpe, 2001; Hood, 1992). However it is clear that men and women are treated differently in the sentencing process (Gelsthorpe and McIvor, 2007) and, as Worrall (1990) asserts, sentencing outcomes for female defendants are inextricably linked to their perceived domestic, sexual and pathological qualities.

The second reading is derived from Hedderman and Gelsthorpes's 1997 study *Understanding the Sentencing of Women* which sought to investigate whether 'sex differences in sentencing statistics simply reflect differences in the type and number of offences for which male and female offenders are convicted or something more?' (1997: 1). In this reading Gelsthorpe and Loucks outline the findings from individual and group interviews with 197 magistrates to illustrate the complexity of sentencing decisions which they argue are linked to but go 'well beyond a simple male/female offender distinction' (p. 43). The reading outlines the complex interplay of factors that combine to construct defendants as either 'troubled' or 'troublesome' offenders. They conclude that female defendants are more likely to be viewed as 'troubled' offenders who require help, as opposed to punishment, in order to address offending behaviour which is strongly rooted in need. By contrast, male defendants are more likely to be viewed as 'troublesome' offenders motivated by greed, and as such in need of punishment both for their own sake and for the purposes of deterrence.

The understanding and leniency forthcoming for women characterised as 'troubled' offenders does not extend to those women adjudged to have atypical domestic circumstances, less than conventional lifestyles or those who refuse to or are unable to conform to traditional gender roles (Carlen, 1983). As Cook perceptively observes justice for women has 'more to do with *who* they are than *what* they have done' (1997: 82, emphasis in original). Of course, cultural norms and conventions make few concessions to diversity, and a range of cultural, social and legal factors have interacted to promote discriminatory criminal justice processes and the criminalisation of black minority ethnic groups (Gelsthorpe and McIvor, 2007; Phillips and Bowling, 2007). Notwithstanding findings from self-report studies that black and white people have an equal likelihood of involvement in crime (Sharp and Budd, 2005), black people are disproportionately likely to be 'stopped and searched', arrested, remanded to custody, imprisoned and subject to longer prison terms (Gelsthorpe and McIvor, 2007; Home Office, 2006; Phillips and Bowling, 2007).

In the third reading, Chigwada-Bailey reflects on the particular difficulties and disadvantages faced by black women in their interactions with the criminal justice system. She argues that the prevalent and stereotypical constructions of black women as a 'suitable enemy' (p. 133–34) within British culture have contrived to make them 'uniquely vulnerable' (p. 73) to unequal and discriminatory treatment within the criminal justice process. Utilising a range of shocking examples and case studies, Chigwada-Bailey powerfully illustrates the discriminatory and racist tendencies integral to the law, policing practices, the court system and prison culture, which in combination serve to oppress black, working-class women of both British and foreign nationalities. She concludes that justice for all will only be forthcoming when the British criminal justice system recognises 'other cultures as different, not inferior' (p. 142), and utilises this knowledge to enact justice which is class, race and gender sensitive.

Debates regarding gender and social control have increasingly become dominated by the inexorable rise in female incarceration across western jurisdictions (Gelsthorpe and McIvor, 2007; Heidensohn and Gelsthorpe, 2007). In marked contrast to the Home Office's prediction that by the end of the twentieth century 'fewer or no women at all being given prison sentences' (1970: 1), female imprisonment has increased steadily since the mid-1970s (Gelsthorpe and Morris, 2002: 278). Indeed, the period between 1994 and 2004 witnessed a 150 per cent increase in the woman's prison population in England and Wales (Gelsthorpe, 2007), far outstripping the smaller proportionate increase in male imprisonment (Gelsthorpe and McIvor, 2007: 335). Explanations for this phenomenon are based on the nature and seriousness of women's crime; changes in sentencing patterns; moves towards the more 'equal' treatment of men and women; changes in the 'type' of woman sentenced to custody; increases in the length of women's prison sentences; the imprisonment of more foreign-national women for drugs offences and the reform of prisons have not proved entirely adequate (Gelsthorpe, 2007; Gelsthorpe and Morris, 2002). Rather, the relentless growth in female imprisonment appears to reflect the fact that more women are being sentenced to custody and that the average sentence imposed is longer (Deakin and Spencer, 2003; Gelsthorpe and McIvor, 2007; Hedderman, 2004; Heidensohn and Morris, 2007).

The final reading addresses this 'new punitiveness' towards female offenders. Gelsthorpe and Morris identify a 'penal paradox' in the propensity towards the imprisonment of women when there is substantial evidence that the nature and severity of their offending has not significantly changed and remains deeply rooted in individual, social and economic adversity. Highlighting the male-centric nature of criminal justice processes and interventions – currently designed for, and orientated to, the needs and offending experiences of men – they advocate a need for further research to establish the causal factors underlying women' resort to crime. Furthermore, while welcoming and acknowledging the value of the gender-sensitive policy recommendations forwarded to deal with the inappropriate imprisonment of women, Gelsthorpe and Morris note that the relative severity of women's offending and the low risk of harm and reconviction they present provide more than adequate justification for reducing female imprisonment. Thus, contrary to the tenets of the 'new punitiveness', they persuasively conclude that recourse to imprisonment should be reduced for all, and that social and criminal justice polices should strive to address the individual, social and structural factors which 'line the pathways to crime for both men and women' (p. 124).

Suggestions for further reading

Ballinger, A. (2000), *Dead Woman Walking: Executed Women in England and Wales 1900–1955*. Aldershot, Vermont and Sydney: Ashgate.
    Ballinger provides a detailed and sensitive account of the cases relating to the last 15 women hanged in England and Wales, powerfully demonstrating how their refusal or inability to conform to dominant discourses of femininity contributed to their sentencing and punishment.
Heidensohn, F. (1996), *Women and Crime*, 2nd edn. Basingstoke: Macmillan.
    In this text Heidensohn explores women's criminal behaviour and mounts a persuasive case for locating it with regard to the informal social control mechanisms which regulate and discipline the behaviour of women and girls.
McIvor, G. (ed.) (2004), *Women Who Offend*, Research Highlights in Social Work 44. London: Jessica Kingsley.
    This is a wide-ranging edited collection which provides insights with regard to contemporary theoretical, empirical and policy debates relating to women's offending, how it is and how it should be responded to by policy-makers, the courts and criminal justice practitioners.

3.1

'Troublesome girls': towards alternative definitions and policies
by Annie Hudson

> She is a very promiscuous girl and, if all that she tells the other girls is to be believed, *then no young man is safe*. (Residential Social Worker, my emphasis)

Embedded at the heart of contemporary British welfare practice with adolescent girls is an almost psychic fear of a predatory female sexuality. The irony of this should be obvious: it is men who rape and the sexual abuse of children is almost entirely perpetrated by men. Yet, perhaps highest on the professional agenda is the assumption (and concomitant practices) that girls in trouble fundamentally have problems with *their* sexuality. Whilst welfare professionals frequently legitimate their intervention with girls as 'for their protection', the quote from the social worker above (made in a report for a case conference) prizes open the complexity of the 'welfare as protector' discourse. It suggests that, hidden beneath, lies an almost inarticulated but profound fear of the young woman who is sexually active, sexually explicit, and who is not actually possessed by any one male. This conceptualization of adolescent girls as 'property' (of men, of the family, of the dominant social order) will be a key thread to much of this discussion. It helps explain why some girls are defined as 'troublesome'; it is also a crucial component of any attempt to conceptualize different welfare strategies for responding to their needs.

This chapter focuses on girls who are seen, often very generally and vaguely, as manifesting some kind of social or emotional trouble. The apparently loose concept of 'troublesome girls' allows for a discussion of girls who are not necessarily delinquent (in the sense of committing criminal offences). Statistics (DHSS, 1986) suggest that the majority of girls do not get drawn into the complex web of the British personal social services because they have committed offences. It is more likely to be because of concerns about their perceived sexual behaviour and/or because they are seen to be 'at risk' of 'offending' against social codes of adolescent femininity.

Work with girls in trouble has, in terms of explicit policy, been marginalized and rendered almost invisible. Because girls do not so publicly resist the normative order (McRobbie and Garber, 1976) because there is not much political capital to be gained by developing strategies for responding differently to their modes of rule-breaking, and because it has been assumed that girls' deviant behaviour will be dealt with normally from within the boundaries of the family, policies have been ad hoc, framed in vague and diffuse language and lacking in imagination. This, of course, does not mean that the net result has had any less of an impact upon the experience of girls deemed to require state intervention, whether controlling or apparently benign. In fact, the reverse has often been true; the assumption that extant policies and practice are 'in their best interests' adeptly conceals a complex fabric of control and subordination (for example, see Casburn, 1979; Campbell, 1981).
[. . .]

Redrafting the agenda: whose troubles, whose definitions?

The somewhat skewed triangular relationship between adolescent girls, their families and welfare professionals forms the axis around which definitions, policies and practices have evolved. In prizing open some of the implicit assumptions and ideologies embedded in such definitions, we can begin to redraft a somewhat different agenda for policy and practice.

Social historians such as Weeks (1981) have suggested that the 1880s were a particularly significant moment when the dichotomy between the private/decent and the public/unrespectable was firmly established. But whilst women and girls are supposed to keep to the former area, men are free to travel between the two without fear of social sanction. Moreover, in their zeal to protect working-class girls from prostitution, late nineteenth-century reformers created new objects for control. Simultaneously they also established an explanatory code that portrays girls as passive and in need of protection, but also as potentially socially dangerous if they do not conform to codes of sexual respectability and domesticity. Such codes are clearly still firmly entrenched (Hutter and Williams, 1981). But it is girls from specific social groups who are particularly vulnerable to state intervention. Working-class and black girls have to walk a particularly shaky tightrope between demonstrating both their respectability and their sexual attractiveness. Black girls for example may be perceived as contesting not only codes of femininity but also white norms; they may thus be on the receiving end of a double dose of disapproval. One residential social worker commented about a Rastafarian girl in a report in my study: 'Her hair is the one thing which she resents us criticizing and it is this which spoils her otherwise attractive appearance.'

The overt moral tone of the late Victorian era was gradually eroded by the ascendancy and increasing attachment to psychoanalytic paradigms which meant that an apparently plausible veneer of scientism could occlude latent values. Girls who got into trouble (criminal or otherwise) could be confidently defined as 'neurotic', 'hysteria prone' and so on. Such scientism continues to legitimize welfare professionals' assessments not just about current behaviour but, more significantly, about anticipated future behaviour. Such persistence in maintaining the validity and viability of 'the tutelary complex' (Donzelot, 1979) in such a full-blown form is perhaps particularly striking when we consider that welfare's management of boys in trouble has increasingly been subjected to scepticism about the capacity (let alone the morality) of making judgments about future conduct.

Discussions elsewhere (Campbell, 1981; Casburn, 1979; Gelsthorpe, 1981; Hudson, A., 1983) provide substantive accounts of the dominant ideologies influencing the careers of adolescent girls through the welfare and justice systems.

Four key precepts form the kernel of the discussion that follows and provide the basis for the alternative practices suggested in the final section:

1 girls as the 'property' of the family: is the home so safe?
2 adolescent female sexuality as a barometer of 'womanhood': the need to problematize gender relations;
3 'troublesome girls' as victims of psychological inadequacies: reclaiming emotionality;
4 normalizing girls' troublesome behaviour: collective similarities and differences.

Girls as the 'property' of the family: is the home so safe?

There is more than a note of truth in the assumption that girls' troubles are often related to family problems and their position in the family. However, such 'family problems' have been viewed in an apolitical way: the power dynamics between parents and daughters (most crucially those between fathers and daughters), and those between women and men in the family have been completely obscured by traditional commentators. Yet it is the family which is one of the key sources of the social control of women (Barrett and McIntosh, 1982; Segal, 1983). The under-reporting of child sexual abuse together with the blaming of mothers for such abuse is obviously one of the most blatant ways in which the politics of family life is pushed aside as 'irrelevant' (Ward, 1984). Moreover, whilst the Cleveland child sexual abuse 'crisis' provoked an enhanced consciousness of the extensiveness of child sexual abuse, the terms in which that debate is developing suggest that there continues to be a reluctance both to acknowledge that child sexual abuse occurs in otherwise seemingly 'normal' families and that it is predominantly a crime perpetrated by adult men towards children whom they know and are supposed to protect. (For an excellent discussion of the Cleveland 'crisis', see Campbell, 1988.) Child sexual abuse is thus a powerful mechanism by which girls and young women are maintained within the institution of the family. Physical violence and threats from abusers that disclosure will lead to 'breaking up the family' added to girls' internalized feelings that they are guilty and responsible for the crimes of adult men ensure that the costs of disclosure of abuse frequently seem greater than the benefits.

However, in other more subtle ways, girls are subjected to an unspoken but relentless subordination. For daughters, like their mothers, are essentially seen as the 'property' of 'the family'. Adolescent girls are controlled by the idea that they 'belong' to the home, unlike their brothers whose rights to be 'on the street' are unquestioned. Girls are expected to act like 'little housewives' and to service the family (and particularly their fathers and brothers) both emotionally and materially (Griffin, 1985). Such beliefs affect families as much as welfare professionals. When the family's regulation of girls seems to be breaking down parents can easily construe that their daughters are 'beyond their control' and demand that 'something is done'; over a quarter of the cases in my study fell into this category. What is perhaps of equal significance is that it was usually the mother who was most active in expressing such concerns to welfare agencies. This reflects, I suggest, the role of mothers as 'emotional housekeepers' which demands that they nurture and cosset the family's emotional life. If conflicts arise, they are expected to act to resolve and smooth them over.

Like their daughters, mothers are in a double bind; they are vested with a duty and responsibility to be concerned about their daughters' behaviour, to be worried if they do not return at night or when they seem depressed. But they also frequently get blamed when things go wrong inside the family. Given the lack of emotional support from fathers in many families it is perhaps not surprising that some mothers turn to welfare agencies for help and support. Blaming mothers for their daughters' problems leaves unchallenged the inequitable division of emotional labour in families.

It is important to point out here that girls themselves (unlike the majority of boys who are referred to the personal social services) often request to be taken into care. The emotional (and sometimes physical) struggle for survival at home becomes too much for some girls to cope with. They have few accessible or legitimate 'escape' routes and so care may be viewed as a preferable, if not ideal, alternative. Sometimes therefore welfare agencies do need to offer girls a refuge from the family; such provision, however, needs to be based around different assumptions and methods of practice than residential care is at present.

The constant sexualizing of the 'troublesome' behaviour of girls by welfare professionals has meant that they have often avoided looking at a further contradiction of familialism: the extensiveness of sexual abuse of girls in their families. In a fifth of the cases I studied the girl had been sexually abused by her father or stepfather, but in only a small percentage had this been a factor influencing the decision to take her into care. It was normally only much later that the abuse had come to light.

In refusing to recognize the deeply entrenched power inequalities between male and female members of families, social workers have thus colluded with the assumption that 'the home is a safe place' (Hudson, A., 1985). When girls are 'signalling' that they are being abused (for example by constantly running away or by taking overdoses) their behaviour is reinterpreted as evidence of their 'uncontrollability' and of their pathology, rather than as a manifestation of the results of their father's abuse of power and trust. Moreover, in tacitly accepting a variety of myths, for example that girls are 'seductive', social workers have thereby reinforced the moral and emotional guilt felt by girls who have been sexually abused.

The girl as property of the family ideology is carried on into the workings of welfare establishments. For not only are girls' residential establishments often based around the objective of re-establishing femininity (Ackland, 1982), but if girls in care do become pregnant then this is often viewed in a positive light. It is as if pregnancy symbolically represents a girl's return to 'the family' and her apparent acceptance of traditional femininity. This is somewhat ironic given that fears of unmarried teenage motherhood are usually high on the list of the perceived risks of adolescent girls becoming 'beyond control'.

When girls reject or refuse to take on their responsibilities as 'dutiful daughters' they are viewed as problematic and 'disloyal'; in short, they are not 'good little girls'. As long as welfare policies collude with such definitions there will be little possibility of diminishing the unequal power differentials in families; as long as they remain, adolescent girls are the losers.

Adolescent female sexuality as a barometer of 'womanhood': the need to problematize gender relations

The development of a more critical and feminist influenced analysis of young women's deviance (see, for example, Casburn, 1979; Heidensohn, 1985[a]; Smart, 1976) has demonstrated how girls who appear before the juvenile court for criminal offences are subject to a 'double penalty'. They are punished both for the offence itself and for the 'social' crime of contravening normative expectations of 'appropriate' female conduct via 'promiscuity', 'wayward' behaviour, 'unfeminine' dress and so on. Similarly, my study found that the most common cause of anxiety at the point of referral was that the girl was 'beyond control' and/or at risk morally. The centrality of sexuality in welfare's definitions of 'troublesome' girls reflects three key taken-for-granted assumptions.

First, it is assumed that girls' sexuality, once 'unleashed' is uncontrollable and not bound by any sense of self-responsibility or self-control. As Bland

(1983) has argued, the instincts of women have traditionally been viewed as focused on her reproductive capacity, on her potential for maternity. The prostitute or the adolescent girl whose behaviour is interpreted as potentially like that of a prostitute is seen as representative of an active female sexuality, of a sexuality which may threaten the girls interest and capacity to be a 'good wife' and mother and therefore her future 'womanliness'.

Secondly, a girl's apparent sexual behaviour is seen as a barometer for testing her capacity to learn the appropriate codes of social (but particularly sexual) conduct with men (Lees, 1986). One of the contradictions of the double standard revealed time and time again [. . .] is that it implies that boys need to have access to different sexual experiences; yet the girls who presumably are supposed to 'meet' such needs are stigmatized and punished.

As long as boys' sexual behaviour is heterosexual their sexuality remains unproblematic; it is 'natural' and thus does not merit attention. But my own research highlighted how a girl's sexual 'reputation' is often a determining factor in shaping her career through the personal social services. In over a quarter of the cases examined, social workers acknowledged that their decision making was a function of what other people (particularly the police and parents) were alleging. Moreover, once an opinion had been formed, it was easy for the label of 'promiscuity' or 'being on the game' to stick, with all the negative connotations that such labels imply. Labels based on shifting and unsubstantiated opinions are particularly hard to shed; as one social worker commented about one of her young female clients: 'Once (she) had developed a 'reputation' (for sexual activity), it became very easy to say that she was actually involved in prostitution.' Once created, such reputations, with all their attendant anxieties, seem to have pushed many of the social workers in my study (if sometimes quite reluctantly) to regard many of their adolescent female clients as in need of the 'protective' care and attention of a residential placement. This was despite the fact that many social workers acknowledged that care is hardly an effective contraceptive.

There was also evidence that the police similarly act on a girl's 'reputation' in this way. They were involved in almost half of the referrals in my study and in more than half of these they obtained place of safety orders (these give police or social workers the power to remove children and young people). Police involvement in these situations was only very rarely because a girl had committed a criminal offence. Moreover, there were disproportionately more police place of safety orders taken on girls living in an area with a significant Afro-Caribbean population and also with a local 'reputation' as a 'red-light district'. The other area studied was comparable in terms of many indices of social disadvantage but did not have such a reputation; the Afro-Caribbean population was also much smaller. This suggests that the level of police (and possibly social work) control may increase according to the social composition and 'reputation' of the neighbourhood. Although as yet not empirically tested, it would seem that certain groups of black adolescent girls (most particularly Afro-Caribbean girls) are especially vulnerable to perceptions by the police and possibly social workers that their behaviour warrants special scrutiny and policing. The research also highlighted other ways in which racist stereotypes can affect police and welfare practice. One social worker said of her white adolescent female client, who had run away from home and was detained by the police on a place of safety order: 'People think that as she has got black boyfriends, she must be promiscuous, she must be on the game, or she is being used'. The association in some people's eyes between black men and 'unrespectable' sexuality suggests that the fears of racial miscegenation which were so prevalent in the 1950s and 1960s in the UK (Gilroy, 1987) continue to have purchase on the relationship between working-class white girls and welfare agencies. In short, white girls' relationships with black male youth may conjure up images of the potential 'descent of white womanhood' (Gilroy, 1987: 80) and thereby further 'legitimate' the intensification of state intervention.

Whilst it is increasingly accepted that girls (like adult women) are informally disciplined through concepts of acceptable sexuality, what is undoubtedly more contentious is what should be done. It would be naive to suggest that girls are not vulnerable to male sexual exploitation but balancing 'here and now' realities with visions of what the future could and should be like poses acute problems. To date the problem has always been framed as a problem of and for women; male power and responsibility barely enter the discussion. Bringing gender relations onto the agenda allows us instead to see cultural definitions of male sexuality as problematic.

We must take seriously girls' rights as well as their responsibilities and the risks to which they are subject. One such right must surely be to informed contraceptive advice and practice; there is, moreover, as yet little evidence that AIDS health education programmes are altering young male heterosexual practices. Another right should be to an adequate understanding of gender and familial relations. Finally, there are issues concerning girls' rights to choose their sexual identity. Social work agencies should be more conscious of the extent to which policy and practice is predicated upon an assumption of heterosexuality as both the norm and as the most 'desirable' form of sexual expression. The option of lesbianism is almost invariably closed off in discussions between welfare professionals and adolescent girls. If it is part of the discussion it is invariably cloaked with negative connotations. Some girls may want to choose lesbianism as their preferred sexual identity; to deny them this as an option is once more to misrecognize and render invisible the real needs of individual girls.

We need also to unlatch the association of adolescent female sexuality from its connotation of potentially sullying a girl's prospects of a 'happy and satisfying' womanhood. There is no reason why either having had several or no sexual partners in adolescence should prejudice a girl's enjoyment of adult life. Her enjoyment and satisfaction as an adult woman is much more likely to be related to other factors such as decent housing, employment, and adequate child-care provision.

At a more concrete level, the influence of girls' reputations in the decision-making processes affecting them should be critically monitored. Welfare professionals need to take a much stronger stand, vis-à-vis the police, their own organizations and girls' families, in seeking out actual evidence of the risks which a girl is alleged to be under. Similarly, court reports and case conference discussions should be more thoroughly scrutinized as a way of beginning to minimize the power of the 'give a dog a bad name' process that clearly operates against the interests of many girls.

'Troublesome girls' as victims of psychological inadequacies: reclaiming emotionality

The dominance of psychopathological paradigms in welfare professionals' assessments of the needs of adolescent girls has been emphasized elsewhere (Hudson, B., 1984b; Campbell, 1981). The persistence, in my study, of such explanations as 'bizarre family relationships', 'missing out on affection' and 'insufficient parental control' testifies to the continued adherence to a family pathology model.

I would not want to contest unequivocally the notion that girls manifest some of the social contradictions of adolescent femininity in emotional ways; many girls referred to welfare agencies often do feel depressed, suicidal and have very poor self-images. But the assumption that emotional expression is intrinsically negative and that emotional responses are unaffected by social and material processes has to be challenged. Perhaps it is rather the lack of overt emotionality amongst boys and men which should be problematized. The rational, masculinist British culture generally denigrates emotional expression as a sign of weakness; moreover, whilst British culture rewards men for certain forms of emotionality (aggression is the most obvious example), it punishes girls for the same kind of behaviour.

The emotionality of 'troublesome girls' is usually problematized and even feared. Certainly, many social workers take for granted the assumption that girls are 'more difficult to work with'; their apparent mood swings, non-rationality, outbursts of aggression and internalization of emotional discontents often act to make welfare professionals feel impotent, uncertain of their skills and at a loss for what to do. So when girls step outside the bounds of expectation that they should be self-controlled and passive, it is not wholly surprising that they meet with panic, disapproval, and assessments that they need 'treatment'. For, after all, they are implicitly challenging normative codes of emotional conduct. Two shifts in thinking are required. First, adolescent girls' emotional responses need to be seen as a form of resistance or struggle against 'the inner hold' of their oppressive circumstances. Their responses should be legitimated as not 'unnatural' but as quite rational ways of surviving. To psychopathologize their emotions is to perpetuate the belief (one that is often internalized by girls themselves) that their troubles are their fault. Secondly, emotionality as a means of social communication and expression should be seen not as a sign of a deficient personality but rather as a positive resource. It is only by affirming girls' emotional responses as a comprehensible and positive means of coping with their experience of social injustice that they are likely to begin to feel any sense of autonomy in their lives. As long as they are effectively told that their emotional responses are 'crazy' their confidence in their right to express themselves will be undermined.

Normalizing girls' troublesome behaviour: collective similarities and differences

It has become obvious that the dominant definitions and assumptions of troublesome girls are essentially social constructs. What is also striking is how many of these 'troubles' are experienced, in some way or other, by the majority of adolescent girls. Certainly one of the most constant characteristics of my personal contact with girls 'in trouble' is how very many of their dilemmas, problems and needs connect with my own memories of growing up 'to be a woman'.

This leads to the central imperative, in addressing alternative definitions and policies for 'troublesome girls', of developing a framework which normalizes their behaviour. Linked to this is the parallel urgency to analyse and act towards girls' troubles from a perspective which actively acknowledges the cultural, ideological and material pressures on adolescent girls, and most particularly those which black and working-class girls face. The bifurcation of adolescent girls into the 'respectable and decent' and the 'promiscuous and dangerous' creates socially constructed categories which are both rigid and ambiguous. They deny the fact that most girls experience the need to demonstrate respectability and sexual attractiveness. Such a dichotomizing of young women also denies that girls might be interested in things other than the opposite sex, such as work, politics, music, female friends, social adventure and excitement.

My own experience of working with adolescent girls has consistently highlighted how they are invariably extremely aware (in both a personal and political sense) of many of the contradictions of adolescent femininity. Whilst some girls cope with such contradictions and injustices in an overtly rebellious and public way, others internalize them as 'their fault'. Still other girls accept their 'lot' apparently stoically and fatalistically but recognizing, at the same time, that there are personal costs (for example, 'tolerating' violence from boyfriends because 'I love him'). Girls who have particularly restricted access to society's material and social 'goodies' (employment, education, decent housing and so on) perhaps have less to lose by their active resistance than their more privileged counterparts.

The principle of defining girls' needs, problems and resources in collective terms could facilitate a depathologizing of their particular predicaments, whether those be as survivors of sexual abuse, arguments with parents or delinquency. It could also encourage a recognition of the possibility of girls providing more effective support to one another than huge armies of professional 'helpers'. The concern with collective consciousness raising in the contemporary women's movement evolved out of the need to enable women to name more publicly what were previously private experiences. Certainly, welfare agencies could learn much from the work of feminist groups such as Women's Aid and Rape Crisis Centres in asserting the possibility of the support and concrete action that can emerge out of challenging traditional maxims about how people are best 'helped' (Pahl, 1985).

Alternative approaches to welfare practice with adolescent girls must thus be based upon an active acknowledgement both of their socially constructed similarities and of the differences mediated by class, race and sexual identity. The hegemony of casework in social work has inhibited the possibility of recognizing similarities which, whilst mediated through individuals, are none the less socially and culturally constructed. There are, however, certain inherent dangers in shifting from an individualistic paradigm to one which places 'blame' on external social forces. Very few radical perspectives on social relations have explored the ways in which social circumstances distort and appropriate the individual's needs and capacities. In contrast, feminists have politicized subjectivity and highlighted the reciprocal relationship between individual identity and the material world (see, for example, the work of Eichenbaum and Orbach, 1984). Girls' apparently personal troubles should be viewed through a perspective which recognizes that girls' experiences are both unique and linked inextricably to their status as young women.

[. . .]

3.2
Justice in the making: key influences on decision-making
by Lorraine Gelsthorpe and Nancy Loucks

Magistrates are supposed to have a certain degree of intelligence – certainly stipendiaries are – and an ability to assess human beings and the manner in which they give their evidence and the way that they come over and behave themselves, and conduct themselves. Stipe. at one of the sample courts (M)

There's still something of the defence for sex, I'm afraid. And you really wonder how the innocent-looking young lady in front of you, who's obviously been told by her solicitor to look as helpless as possible, could possibly have undertaken the violent elements that are there. Mag. 3, Hallam court (M)

In this part of the study 189 lay and eight stipendiary magistrates were interviewed either in groups or individually. From these discussions it emerged that magistrates saw offenders broadly in terms of whether they were primarily 'troubled' or 'troublesome'; and the group an offender fell into was determined by factors such as motive for the offence, degree of provocation, relationship to victim, abuse of drugs or alcohol, and mental state. It was also affected by the way an offender behaved in court, by the way magistrates perceived other courtroom 'players' and the information they provided, and by magistrates' awareness of how their decisions might be seen by others. Together these factors shaped magistrates' views of an appropriate sentence.

Images of offenders: troubled or troublesome?

Think of them as greedy, needy or dotty. Group 3, Shelley court (F)

One explanation which magistrates gave for differences in the sentences given to men and women was that their motives were rarely similar. In their opinion, a 'typical' shop theft committed by a female defendant differed considerably from the 'typical' thefts which men committed:

> . . . *the women feed the family whereas the men, although they have to support their family, don't.* Mag. 13, Byron court (F)

'Troubled' offenders include those who steal items from shops which they, or particularly their children, need (mainly food, or sometimes clothing or shoes, but nothing very extravagant). This definition stretches to women (specifically) who steal tins of salmon, for example, as a treat for the family which they otherwise could not afford. Indeed, magistrates described this as the most typical scenario they dealt with when sentencing women convicted of shop theft. In contrast, those interviewed portrayed men as stealing out of greed rather than need:

> . . . *a shoplifting woman would probably be a single mother without enough money. A shoplifting man would very rarely be a single father without enough money and kids yapping around – they would be lads out on the town wanting to get a snappy pair of jeans . . .* Mag. 12, Shelley court (F)

Rather than food or shoes, men were characterised as stealing alcohol or CDs and videos to sell. Magistrates commonly referred to women as stealing to feed their children where men stole to support drug habits. Even offences relating to prostitution could often fall into this 'survival' category. Some magistrates viewed it as something which was legally an offence, but which did little harm.

To some extent, fraud against the Department of Social Security was also seen as being for 'survival'. Magistrates generally sympathised with women who 'did a couple of cleaning jobs on the side every once in a while' and 'didn't realise' that they were doing something wrong, or had become dependent on the extra income. Men were invariably seen as much more deliberate and profit-driven.

Although this was exceptional, women could be 'troublesome' rather than 'troubled'. Magistrates expressed least tolerance for women shoplifters whose offences were planned and/or done for profit – in other words, those whose offences were closer to the stereotype of the male shoplifter. They said that such women tended to work in groups and 'stole to order'. Some women were even believed to use their children either as a distraction or trained them to take the goods themselves (though magistrates thought that this was relatively infrequent).

Surprisingly perhaps, some violent offences were viewed by magistrates with a degree of understanding.[. . .]

One magistrate explained that where women commit violent offences, they tend to commit offences against people they know (an abusive partner, perhaps, or a neighbour or friend), with some identifiable cause. Men, on the other hand, are apt to be involved in offences against strangers, such as in pub brawls. These too may have an identifiable cause, but such causes tend to be unrelated to the victims of the offence. Examples those interviewed gave included expressions of frustration because of offenders' redundancy or continued unemployment, or their consumption of alcohol or drugs.[. . .]

Factors relating to family background, such as a history of abuse during childhood, met with a mixed reception. Forty-six individual magistrates and 10 groups who mentioned such factors said they would take them into consideration. Fifteen individuals and three groups specifically said they would not; and nine individual and 10 groups of magistrates had no clear view on this matter.

While a small number of magistrates (four out of the eight who mentioned it) believed that male and female co-defendants would be regarded as equally culpable, others (three individuals and one group) commented that they were inclined to believe that a woman invariably played a lesser role or was perhaps coerced into committing an offence rather than sharing equal responsibility:

If a man and a woman come up together, there will be a tendency, unless you were told otherwise, [to assume] that the man was influencing the woman, that the man was the ringleader. This happens with juveniles, that a younger juvenile is influenced by the older juvenile . . . I think that is ingrained, a man and a woman together that you are expecting the man to be dominant. Mag. 10, Byron (M)

. . . there is a tendency to feel that women are more victims than men in that they are more vulnerable, the pressures of their various partners, and that they are following rather than instigating. Mag. 14, Byron (F)

Ten individual magistrates and two groups also mentioned that they believed male offenders used women in crimes – to steal pension books or pass stolen cheques for example – in the belief that, if caught, they would be dealt with more leniently. Interestingly, one magistrate commented that male offenders would never admit to being led by a woman, with the result that, at most, female co-defendants would share equal blame and probably much less. This in turn may produce disparity in the sentencing of men and women facing the same charge.

Magistrates expressed a general lack of tolerance of addiction to drugs or alcohol, which they viewed as self-inflicted problems. In addition only one group distinguished between binge drinking (which few would dispute is a matter of choice) and addiction (which is treated by the medical profession as an illness). Although magistrates said that they quite frequently recommended drug or alcohol programmes (16 individual magistrates and four groups mentioned this specifically), to some extent they viewed such programmes as an 'easy option'. Two magistrates also said that they would refer defendants to such programmes only once, after which they considered a more punitive response appropriate.

Magistrates very rarely viewed intoxication as a mitigating factor. Only one magistrate mentioned this possibility, whereas eight individuals and four groups were clear that it would *not* mitigate. In fact, eight individual magistrates and six groups thought that intoxication could well have an aggravating effect on sentence.

Drugs-related crime was generally viewed very seriously by the magistrates. Only possession of drugs for one's own consumption (with no other connected offences) was thought to warrant anything other than a very severe response. Few magistrates reported having any direct experience of sentencing women for dealing in drugs or even for possession. The main exception seemed to be women who resorted to prostitution to feed a drugs habit. This tended to be viewed as 'hurting no-one but themselves'. In contrast, men were characterised as likely to resort to burglary to feed a drug habit. If women were involved in selling drugs at all, then the magistrates believed that men were usually behind it (e.g., as pimps or suppliers).

Proof of some form of mental illness, on the other hand, was an acceptable form of mitigation. A further factor mentioned was 'hormonal problems' for older women. Male magistrates in particular tended to mention 'the Change' as an explanation of offending, especially shop theft. Only one female magistrate introduced this idea among the six individuals and four groups who mentioned it. Again, this perceived 'illness' generated sympathy rather than censure.

Magistrates' impression that most of those charged with not having a TV licence are women is confirmed by the sentencing statistics. All those interviewed described this offence as deserving of compassion. Magistrates believed that these women were doing their best in a bad situation: they could not afford their licence, or their husbands would not give them the money for it. Single mothers were particularly vulnerable as they relied heavily on the television to occupy their children. Magistrates also recognised that where women lived with partners, they were the ones who were most likely to answer the door while their children were watching the television (and thus they were the ones charged with having no TV licence).

In contrast there were a few particular offences which individual magistrates and groups said they could not understand and offenders with whom they could never empathise. The most commonly mentioned of these was having no motor insurance (mentioned by four individuals and three groups) – an almost entirely male offence in the view of those whom we interviewed. Despite earlier references to other magistrates finding some violent offences 'understandable', one group of magistrates and one stipendiary magistrate mentioned that they found violence of any sort anathema. Finally, three magistrates who had been burgled themselves mentioned burglary (one magistrate in particular blamed the death of his mother on the burglary of her house). All such offences were those usually committed by men.

The offender at court: body language and appearance

When we're interviewing applicants to become magistrates . . . we say 'Have you any prejudices?' . . . And the stock answer is 'no.' Well that's a nonsense, isn't it? We've all got prejudices of some sort. We all have. And it's how we handle the prejudices. And so, in the days of punk, when they came into court with red hair and . . . earrings and all this sort of thing, then you'd find some magistrate with shock horror, you know 'Fancy coming to court dressed like that', and you would say 'Well, are you prejudiced . . . enough to [have] it affect your sentence?' Chairman of the Bench at one of the sample courts (M)

You know that there are certain types of people that appeal to you and certain types that don't. I have a particular problem with tattoos. I have this home-spun theory that tattoos and crime go hand in hand. I mean, I would say that 90% of the defendants that we see have a visible tattoo. I don't know what it is – it's something they put in the dye or what, but – and usually the worse the tattoos, the more I think, 'Oh, no . . .' Mag. 5, Hallam court (F)

Magistrates were divided regarding the relevance of a defendant's appearance in court. On the one hand, just over a quarter of the 33 individual magistrates and 19 groups of magistrates who discussed appearance commented that appearances were deceptive and should be ignored. On the other hand, two-thirds (22 out of 33 individual magistrates, and 12 groups out of 19) claimed that a person's appearance indicated his or her attitude to the court and court procedure, so it was seen as 'human nature' for magistrates to take this into account (though they said it should not affect the eventual sentence). Similarly, body language was seen as a key tool by most magistrates, helping them to decide not only who had respect for the court, but who was telling the truth and who was remorseful. People who appeared to be nervous or tearful generally gained the sympathy of the magistrates – again, this tended to be female offenders – as long as the magistrates believed that the behaviour was genuine:

> *. . . I think it is just a feeling that they are either genuine or not – this is where the wiles of women play a part. You can be easily swayed into believing a woman is really contrite.* Mag. 5, Shelley court (M)

While many said that first impressions were often misleading and should not be relied upon, three individuals and one group specifically commented on how difficult it was to make a decision without the defendant in front of them:

> *. . . it would be just like putting all the information into a machine and churning out the answer if . . . we weren't there and there wasn't a person standing in front of us.* Mag. 6, Milton court (F)

One magistrate voiced and then disagreed with the idea that more attractive defendants seem more believable than others. However, we note here evidence to the contrary in studies of jury decision-making (e.g. Efran 1974). Interestingly, six female magistrates accused their male colleagues of being too quick to believe any female defendants who appeared before them – but whether this was directly related to the perceived attractiveness of defendants it was hard to tell.

Magistrates generally described themselves as being more understanding with first offenders. They recognised that people in court for the first time were likely to be nervous and unsure. If they were upset or cried, magistrates were likely to accept it as genuine. Repeat offenders, on the other hand, were viewed very differently. If they dressed up and behaved politely (addressing the magistrates and Clerk as 'Sir' or 'Ma'am'), it was seen to be a con. If they dressed down, wore a hat or put their hands in their pockets, or reacted arrogantly, they were deemed by some magistrates to have no respect for the court. Indeed, magistrates believed that many repeat offenders deliberately defied the authority of the court by wearing hats, chewing gum, or 'playing up' to their friends at the back of the court – behaviour which prompted a negative response from the magistrates:

> *. . . something inside of me says 'Right, well,' you know, 'we're going to teach you a lesson, sunshine', and you tend to be more punitive.* Group 1, Milton court (F)

Even without a defendant's record in front of them, magistrates said they could tell the more experienced defendants from the first offenders. They gave examples of people who walked straight to the dock and let themselves in, perhaps giving their name, address and date of birth before the clerks asked for it, compared to those who had to be told where to go and when to stand and sit.

When we asked about the sentencing of women, the vast majority of the magistrates said that they rarely saw them in court (although, Criminal

Statistics show that one in every six adult offenders sentenced by magistrates are female). As a result, magistrates perceived women to be less criminal, less experienced, and less likely to return to court than men. However, three individual magistrates and one group dissented from this view, arguing that for a woman to be brought to court was in itself an indication of the seriousness of her conduct.

Related to the experience of defendants and their consequent behaviour was their credibility. Magistrates were apt to believe what first offenders told them. First offenders not only generally inspired greater sympathy from magistrates, but they were inclined to attribute a first offender's body language to nervousness rather than to furtiveness or dishonesty. More experienced defendants who averted their eyes or who seemed unsure of what they were saying were assessed as likely to be lying:

People have mannerisms that you get the feel through . . . you take people not at face value, but they'll say something and you've got the feeling whether they're actually telling the truth or not – facial expressions, the way they stand. Group 2b, Shelley court (M)

On the other hand, as one magistrate suggested, people who argued their case too fervently were less believable than those who were more matter-of-fact in their presentation. Defendants and witnesses who used the same terminology or phrases in their testimony were thought likely to have collaborated with each other.

[. . .]

Generally, female defendants were perceived to be deferential and respectful. They were not only more likely to cry than men, but they were widely perceived to be less threatening in their behaviour and appearance, and so more deserving of compassion. Once again, however, there were exceptions. A male magistrate from Shelley court (Mag. 4) was keen to distinguish between 'nice ladies' and 'ladies that are far short of being ladies'. Such a stance reflects an expectation of higher morality on the part of women. The claim '*I expect women to know better*' (Mag. 1, Byron court (F)) was not uncommon in informal discussion with magistrates, though formal questioning on this point produced a rather more guarded response.

Previous researchers and those responsible for the training of magistrates within the Judicial Studies Board consider cultural background to be a strong influence on how a person uses body language, as well as its meaning and interpretation, but this was mentioned by only a quarter of individual magistrates and a third of the groups. In the context of the courtroom, cultural differences in eye contact and body posture may sway a magistrate's opinion about whether a defendant is respectful, believable, deceitful or remorseful. A small number of magistrates considered that minority ethnic group males could be perceived as arrogant in court. As the magistrates put it:

. . . you have to be very careful because West Indians, for example, come bouncing into court – they are very loose-limbed – and you can almost interpret that as arrogance and rudeness and so on, but it is not – it is just their way of behaving . . . and Asians tend to be rather arrogant looking. Mag. 5, Shelley court (M)

Well, insolence is insolence . . . and let's be honest, there's far more insolence . . . with ethnic minorities. Group 1, Shelley court (M)

. . . some of the Asians may not look you in the face, which doesn't mean to say that they are not telling the truth, because they would revere you, whereas the West Indians would look you in the face and swear that black was white . . . Mag. 14, Byron court (F)

Two individual magistrates and one group also commented that the interpretation of body language was especially difficult if a defendant or witness was using an interpreter.

Eleven of the 30 individuals and eight out of 10 groups who discussed Human Awareness training or specific training on ethnic issues had received significant input (i.e., beyond learning which name was the surname for Asian defendants or witnesses). Nineteen individual magistrates and two groups, on the other hand, claimed that they had received no training whatsoever in this area. Magistrates had mixed views as to whether any special training regarding ethnicity and cultural factors was necessary, but many believed that they could rely as much on what their family and friends told them about body language as on such training from the courts. Others (four individual magistrates and 4 groups) said they relied on 'life experience' to make them aware of cultural differences in behaviour. A number of Justices (four individuals and two groups) added that they 'bend over backwards' to be fair to ethnic minorities, specifically because the magistrates do not wish to appear biased against them.

A magistrate at Byron court, who described herself as West Indian, reported that she was very frustrated with the ignorance of her colleagues about ethnic and cultural differences. A West Indian magistrate at Milton court commented that his colleagues may not think that culture and ethnicity have a bearing on their decisions, but that they invariably do. Magistrates at Hallam court were most inclined to brush away concern about ethnic minority issues because they saw such defendants in court so rarely. Interestingly, we noted that a book in their coffee room (*Black People in the Magistrates' Courts* – produced by the Justices' Clerks' Society) warned that this was not an acceptable excuse.

[. . .]

JUSTICE IN THE MAKING   121

Dealing with the troubled and troublesome: help or punishment?

The magistrates' impressions of defendants as 'troubled' or 'troublesome', whether based on the offence itself or on other factors, appeared to influence the outcome of both bail and sentencing decisions. 'Troubled' offenders were seen by magistrates to need help more than punishment, whereas 'trouble-some' offenders were seen to deserve punishment both for their own sake, and to deter others.

'Help' was interpreted in many different forms. Probation was seen to be the most common source of 'help' for offenders, despite the fact that almost all the magistrates acknowledged that probation orders are intended to encompass other sentencing objectives, including punishment. Magistrates often classified female offenders as being in need of help: with running the household, with organising finances, and [. . .] with controlling their emotions:

> . . . probation is the best thing, because they're not really naughty, they just need help and support . . . Whereas perhaps with men, people see it more as a straight financial choice, and so hurting them financially with a fine is what's required. Mag. 11, Shelley court (F)

In contrast, men were only seen as needing help when they had the responsibility of raising children on their own (which virtually never happened). Men who were unemployed, for example, were seen as 'layabouts', whereas women who were unemployed were 'doing all they could' to take care of their children.

Other types of punishments could also be seen as 'doing the offender a favour' both because they were noncustodial and because of their intrinsic characteristics. Community Service Orders (CSOs) were one of these, where offenders were seen as being encouraged to do something constructive with their lives. Three individual magistrates commented that a CSO could lead to job opportunities in the future. However, as Barker (1993) also found, Community Service Orders were seen as an option for women only if there were care facilities for the children and if the woman could do something suitable (again, usually a care role). A number of magistrates (4 individual magistrates and 2 groups) commented that they almost never sentenced a female offender to a CSO.

Magistrates perceived their use of custody for women as a sentence of last resort, employed either because the crime was so serious that prison was the only option, or because they felt forced into it by the legislation, such as for non-payment of fines. In contrast, men were open to any sort of penalty, though tended to be given probation orders if their offence involved the use of drugs or alcohol, or involved motor vehicles. Male offenders reached the custody threshold much faster than women, either because of the motivation for the offence (e.g. it was inspired by 'greed' rather than 'need'), or because they had relatively limited mitigation compared to women (e.g. no direct responsibility for child care, at least in the view of the magistrates). We should acknowledge, however, that magistrates declared that custody was a rare option for both men and women.

Only a few magistrates (4 individuals and one group) believed that prison could help either male or female offenders in addition to punishing them, either through training or education, or by restricting access to drugs, alcohol, or people who were bad influences on their behaviour. Similarly, 'protection' was one of the grounds for remanding someone in custody. This could be protection from others who would try to avenge a crime or, in some cases, to help *prevent* someone from committing suicide. Prevention of suicide is included on Bail Forms as an exception to the Bail Act 1976 – in other words, as a justification for denying bail.

Conclusion

What emerges from the interviews with magistrates is a complexity that goes well beyond a simple male/female offender distinction, but appears to be closely tied to it. Magistrates generally seemed to make distinctions between offenders depending on whether they could understand the offence as a matter of survival, see it as a result of provocation or coercion, or attribute it to illness rather than irresponsibility.

How magistrates perceived defendants in the courtroom is influenced by considerations other than the simple 'facts of the case'. Appearance and demeanour, the novice status of first-timers or 'know it all' status of experienced offenders, the 'believability' of defendants, expressions and perceptions of remorse, and the reading or misreading of cues about ethnicity and culture all seemed to play a part in shaping magistrates' perceptions of the offenders before them. Such factors cut across simple sex differences, but we can surmise that the relative inexperience of female defendants and their concomitant 'nervousness' might lead magistrates to view them as more 'believable' than others – a point which reiterates the findings of Hedderman (1990) in earlier research. Additionally, women's relative inexperience in offending might be reflected in their behaviour in court – showing deference and remorse – thus leading the magistrates to view them more sympathetically than some of the male defendants who were experienced offenders, well-rehearsed in courtroom procedures and thus seemingly less remorseful.

A distinction between 'troubled' and 'troublesome' offenders was, thus based on the perceived motivation for the offence and the demeanour of defendants in court. In turn, magistrates may make different decisions for bail and certainly choose different options for sentencing. They appeared to favour the use of probation orders or discharges for women – the 'troubled' offenders – as a means of assisting rather than just punishing them. Only occasionally did magistrates believe that male offenders merited assistance, and sometimes 'assistance' for men came in the form of CSOs or custody. Even allowing for the fact that women were more likely to be first offenders or less frequent offenders than men, and were more likely to behave respectfully in court, on the basis of these interviews it would seem that magistrates are less inclined to sympathise with men and to impose a sentence intended to address their underlying problems and needs. [. . .]

3.3
Black women and the criminal justice system
by Ruth Chigwada-Bailey

[. . .]

Background

Since the early 1990s the female prison population of all ethnic origins has increased sharply, and this has been most pronounced for black and 'Chinese /others'. Although Africans and Caribbeans make up only 2 per cent of the total population of England and Wales, they account for 19 per cent of the female prison population. This disproportionate number is striking, fuelling the myth that the black community are more dangerous than their white counterparts, yet there is no substantiating evidence that black people are more prone to commit serious crimes than white people. The statistics give weight, therefore, to the widely held perception that those from the black community and other ethnic minorities are not treated fairly within the penal system and that this is caused by direct and indirect or institutional racism (Bowling and Phillips 2002; Chigwada-Bailey 1997).

The rise in prison figures is partly due to the 1990s introduction of more punitive sentencing policies and an increased tendency to use custodial sentences, and to use them for longer periods. Under the 1991 Criminal Justice Act aggravating and mitigating circumstances were restricted and linked to the offence itself and not to the offender. In consequence not only an increasing number of women with children were imprisoned, but so also were those with addictions, mental illness and histories of physical and sexual abuse. This meant that women committing crimes out of need were as readily imprisoned as those committing them out of greed. The insensitivity of this sentencing system which valued formal justice – dealing with all offenders alike – above substantive justice – doing what is appropriate for the individual case – impacted on men as well as women. However, because of the circumstances typically surrounding women's criminality, women were disproportionately affected, and women's imprisonment grew at a faster rate than men's (Hudson 2002). Black women, above all, suffered a triple disadvantage – they were poor, they were black and they were female.

Mainstream criminology

Within critical criminology literature, race, class and gender have each been given exclusive attention. What has been conspicuously absent has been the investigation of their various intersections – the set of configurations that are more than the sum of the individual parts. Each of these factors, on their own and in combination, shapes or structures the life course of an individual (Groves and Frank 1993). In other words, race, class and gender function to enhance or limit access to economic and political power, which in turn shapes the choices people have at their disposal. As a generality, men have more choices than women, whites have more choices than minorities and the wealthy have more choices than the poor. If you combine these factors it is obvious that wealthy white males have access to the greatest number of choices in their life course, while the poor, black and other minority women would appear to have the fewest. There is a compelling argument that those with the greater number of choices should be held more accountable for their behaviour (Groves and Frank 1993). In reality, criminal justice and legal practices tend to hold the powerless more accountable because, as we shall discuss, the impact of custodial sentencing on them is frequently more devastating.

Critical criminologists have also argued that those with economic power also have access to political power, and thus to the ability to influence the scope and shape of the law (Quinney 1980; Reiman 1979). This means that values found in law will generally be most consistent with the interests of the upper class. Since race, class and gender have a strong impact on economic power, the dominant race, class and gender will be more likely than other groups to control the political and legal process. Crime, which is a political phenomenon, will reflect this in that the less powerful a person is in terms of race, class and gender, the more likely that person is to be subjected to the controlling power of the law and the more likely it is that behaviours common to those disempowered groups will be treated as criminal. This becomes clear when we look at the issue of stereotyping.

It is important to remember that race, class and gender effects are not simply 'additive forces' (Anderson and Collins 1995). If, for example, some-one is a lower class, black woman, she does not experience the simple negative additive effects of being 'female', 'black' and 'lower class'. Rather, her experiences are an outcome of how these forces intersect with each other through the social and economic structures. In other words the effect is contextual, not mathematical (Anderson and Collins 1995).

[. . .]

Black women as suspects

The prevalent assumption that black people are more likely to commit crimes than white people is misplaced. African-Caribbean women are stereotyped as strong, over-excitable and dominant. Asian women, by contrast, are seen as 'passive' and 'hysterical', subject to oppressive practices within the family (see Chigwada 1991). Such stereotyping has permeated the legal system, affecting the ways in which both police and courts respond to black women. Kennedy (1992), for example, mentions the trial of a Ugandan woman for grievous bodily harm to her husband – she poured hot cooking fat over him. It came to light that although she had called the police repeatedly, her violent husband was never arrested. It was suggested in court that she was not telling the truth about making previous complaints. There was no record of the complaints and it was put to her in cross-examination that she was exaggerating her husband's brutality. It was a prosecution witness, a neighbour, who inadvertently came to her aid. He complained in the witness box about the number of times he had been awakened, first by her screams and then by police mistakenly ringing his doorbell when they came in to answer her calls.

The highly publicised case of Joy Gardner, a black woman of Jamaican origin who died in 1993 in London, lends support to the view that authorities can see black women as potentially violent. Joy Gardner had overstayed her visa and was visited by the Alien Deportation Group (Chigwada-Bailey 1997). Her wrists were handcuffed to a leather strap around her waist, another belt was strapped around her thighs and a third around her ankles. As she lay on the floor, 13 feet of adhesive tape were wound around her head and face. Mrs Gardner collapsed and died in hospital a few hours later. Until her tragic death the use of body belts, surgical tape and the existence of a special deportation squad were unknown to the general public. It subsequently came to light that two other African women had been deported in this way.

The alarming conclusion that underlies these events is that the treatment she received was considered to meet the legal requirements of being 'reasonable in all circumstances' (Chigwada-Bailey 1997). Some politicians used the events to hammer home their anti-black, anti-refugee message. Teresa Gorman, Conservative MP for Billericay, said of Mrs Gardner: 'She had been bumming on the Social Services for five years . . . she cost the taxpayer an enormous amount . . . If she had gone quietly none of this would have happened' (see Chigwada-Bailey 1997).

Penal outcomes depend on constructions of culpability – on how much offenders are held to blame for their crimes. There are no hard-and-fast distinctions between being a victim and being an offender, but rather there is a continuum of blameworthiness which has important criminal justice implications. Black men and women are at one end of the continuum and considered as wholly to blame for their crimes. They fit the stereotype of 'suitable enemy' rather than 'ideal victim' (see Daly 1994). White women are at the end other end of the continuum with white men in between. This means for white women the line between being a victim and being an offender is somewhat blurred and can be crossed (Hudson 1988).

Black women, who are perceived as independent and unconventional, as defiant rather than fearful, with a succession of partners and with children in care, are held more blameworthy than white women who have committed similar offences. What counts as mitigating circumstances differs markedly for white and black mothers. For example, a study of probation reports found that when officers asked white mothers about the fathers of their children, the point of the question was to ascertain whether the fathers were supportive economically and in other ways (Hudson 1988). When black mothers were asked the same questions, the point was to find out if the children were from different fathers, or whether the women had a record of promiscuity and unstable relationships. In other words with white women the point at issue was the adequacy of the father's performance of his role. With black women the point at issue was the mother's sexual lifestyle (Green 1991). These stereotype-led differences meant that for the white woman being a mother was likely to be a mitigating factor, whereas for a black woman it was used as proof of her fecklessness, and thus became an aggravating factor.

This distortion of perception is also reflected in attitudes to foreign nationals who account for an increasing proportion of the female prison population. The fact that their crimes are committed out of extreme poverty and as a way of supporting their children is unlikely to be seen as reducing their culpability. They are likely to be judged not as women who are going to extreme lengths to support their families, but as women who have left their families and who have neglected their responsibilities to their dependants.

It is significant that drug barons are targeting mothers who have no criminal records and women in Caribbean hospitals who need money for medical treatment. These women are nearly all single parents and sole providers for their children and elderly relatives. The majority have never travelled out of their countries before. A number of studies have looked at the extent to which women participate in the illicit drug economy and Green (1991) notes that although 80 per cent of couriers are men, virtually all journalistic and pressure group interest in couriers has been on women. The couriers, she says, who are 'poor, foreign, visible and vulnerable', have thus been reconstructed as traffickers who are 'wealthy, powerful, manipulative and dangerous'.

In June 1999 more than three-quarters (77%) of sentenced female prisoners who were foreign nationals were held for drug offences. Of this number a staggering 10 per cent were Jamaican passport holders, almost all proven or suspected mules. Women caught trying to smuggle drugs inside their bodies can expect a sentence of between 4 and 6 years, but sentences of up to 15 years are not unusual (Green 1991).

What makes these women take such huge risks – risks not only of long prison sentences, but of death through cocaine leakage into their bodies? What makes them risk leaving their children destitute? In the main it seems to be poverty and naivety. They are paid between £150 and £1500 per trip, but if they change their minds before departure they are threatened with death and locked up before being taken directly to the airport (Gordon 1985). Most women are unaware not only of the length of sentence they face in Britain if they are caught, but of the physical dangers they face. In 2001, 8 so-called 'mules' died after cocaine packets burst in their stomachs and 31 others were rushed to hospital after their packages began to leak.

Black women and the police

The experience that black women have of policing is quite often bound up with Britain's immigration and nationality laws. These laws have undergone considerable refinement and expansion in the post-war period but, as Paul Gordon (1985) argued, they have not been concerned simply with controlling who has right of entry to Britain: 'Immigration control has increasingly entailed the growth of controls and surveillance of those [black people] already here.' To this end the police and immigration services have been given ever-increasing resources, both in terms of personnel and technology, and these have resulted in the police stopping and questioning black people about their nationality, as well as conducting controversial passport raids on black communities.

Gordon argues that all black people are seen as immigrants. A typical authoritative view, he says, is summed up in the comment 'the only way to tell an illegal black from a legal one is to suspect the lot'. As a result many black people do not report crimes to the police for fear of their complaint being turned into an immigration enquiry. A case reported in *The Guardian* supports this view (17 March 1995). A 29-year-old black man of Nigerian parentage born in the UK went to a police station in South London in July 1993 to report the theft of his fiancée's car radio. He was arrested and detained for more than three hours while police questioned him about his immigration status. Police then took him in handcuffs to his home where he showed them his passport and birth certificate. He was taken back to the police station, fingerprinted and detained for another one and a half hours. He was not believed when he told police officers that he was born in this country. He later sued for false imprisonment, assault and discrimination under the Race Relations Act. He won an undisclosed but 'substantial' out-of-court settlement.

The problem of the use and abuse of immigration powers in relation to black women was also highlighted by a case reported in 'Campaign Against Racism and Fascism' in which an East African woman who stopped to ask a policewoman for directions was held at the police station until her passport could be produced (cited in Chigwada 1986). In another case a black woman was taken to the police station by police officers who had come to her flat to look for her partner. After the police had searched the house and found nothing, they took the woman with them to the police station 'to answer questions about a forged passport'. When she pointed out that the picture on the forgery bore no resemblance to her, the officers said: 'We know you black people, you disguise yourselves.' The police used family responsibilities to force a 'confession' out of her. She was further victimised in that she was not told of her rights and was not seen by a solicitor. On the second day of the hearing the passport charge was dropped (Chigwada-Bailey 1989).

Police and abuse of mental health powers

Section 136 of the Mental Health Act 1983 covers situations where a person's behaviour is causing a nuisance or offence. Incidents leading to the use of the section are usually reported to the police by members of the public and routinely involve minor offences. The provision reads:

> If a constable finds in a public place to which the public have access a person who appears to him to be suffering from mental disorder and to be in immediate need of care or control, the constable may, if he thinks it necessary to do so in the interests of that person or for the protection of other persons, remove that person to a place of safety. Somebody removed under section 136 can be detained at a 'place of safety' for up to 72 hours.

The intention behind the provisions is to ensure that 'mentally disordered' people are examined by a registered medical practitioner and interviewed by an approved social worker so as to make arrangements for their care. The appropriateness of police involvement in medical issues and the use of police vans instead of ambulances has been questioned by organisations such as MIND. The statutory definition of 'place of safety' includes a police station.

However the procedure followed in London – where the section is most frequently used – give the police greater power with which to detain and refer people, as a result of which both men and women tend to be admitted to hospital for three days following police detention, and are rarely assessed by social workers. Studies have shown that young African-Caribbean people born in Britain were admitted at four times the rate for whites (Littlewood and Lipsedge 1979; see also Dunn and Fahy (1990) on differences in admissions between black and white women). Dr S.P. Sashidhartam commented: 'The crisis in British psychiatry is not about large numbers of black people breaking down with any given psychiatric diagnosis, but how such individuals are being inducted into the mental health services and being labelled as having serious mental illness' (*The Guardian*, 4 November 1989).

The possibility that high rates of police admissions may be partly affected by conscious or unconscious racist attitudes has been a cause of concern among psychiatrists. Writing about their clinical experiences in the East End of London, Littlewood and Lipsedge (1979) suggest the police behaved 'in an overtly racist manner as an alternative to arrest, selectively picking out mentally healthy black people and taking them to psychiatric hospitals under Section 136'.

It could be that because cultural difference means that black women tend to speak loudly and gesticulate more frequently, their behaviour can be mis-interpreted as 'crazy' or in need of psychiatric attention. Certainly more women are detained under Section 136 than for criminal charges – this may be instead of being charged, of course – and the loss of rights and ramifica-tions of this are serious. Under Section 136 there is no right to see a solic-itor and any children may be taken into the care of the local authority. If employed, an individual's job may also be in jeopardy. Not only that, but if a woman is not diagnosed as in need of hospital treatment but released after the 72 hours allowed by the Act, she has no redress in law unless she can prove that the police acted 'in bad faith or without reasonable care'.

During a series of interviews with black women I found they had extremely negative views about their treatment at the hands of the police. They felt they were viewed as suffering from some kind of paranoia, just because they were black. Lorraine, who was pregnant at the time of her arrest, said:

> The police pushed me about and took me to the police station with my brother's girlfriend, who was also pregnant. While in the police cell, the police went back to my flat, broke the door and searched the flat. There was no need for that . . . they could have asked me for the keys. They found nothing but took my filofax, babyclothes and photographs. It was wrong for them to do that. I should have been present. I did not know about all this until the next day. They would not treat a pregnant white woman like that. (Chigwada-Bailey 1989, pp. 100–101)

Police officers have been known to take no action if the person responds well to them and behaves respectfully. The way a woman is dressed also seems to matter. Police officers in Elaine Player's (1989[b], p.47) research stated: 'They would be more likely to arrest a woman who behaved aggressively or who was verbally abusive or obstructive than a woman who was trying to be helpful or appeared to regret what she had done.'

The way the police treat and speak to black women may contribute to the way black women respond to them.

Black women and the courts

Historically British law has been made or determined mainly by socially dominant white males, and the great majority of people in senior positions within the judicial institutions are still white men. Apart from setting out criminal offences the law in effect defines acceptable behaviour in areas such as marriage, sexual relations, domestic relationships, care of children, and so on. It sets the parameters of what is 'normal' and 'proper'. This 'man-made' law sets the context within which courts respond to women, and to particular groups of women such as black women, mothers, victims of domestic violence, prostitutes and lesbians. The largely middle- or upper-class judges and magistrates then administer the law. Kennedy (1992) maintains that the law mirrors society and continues to reflect the subordination of women while the construction of defendants as white and British, or perhaps nowadays European, reinforces and perpetuates racism.

There has been no direct focus as yet on black women's experience of sentencing practices. There are certain clues, however, which suggest there is a need for concern. Women in general who, because of their behaviour or lifestyle, or even their dress or hairstyle, do not appear to conform to the stereotypical norm, may receive different sentences from those who do. This also applies to women whose sexuality or racial origins appear to challenge the courts' definition of 'normal' or 'acceptable'. This is supported by Hedderman and Hough's (1994) research which suggests that in general women may receive more lenient sentences than men unless they transgress the boundaries of stereotypical acceptability, when the converse may be true. Black women would be particularly vulnerable to this aspect of discrimination.

Certainly black women are more frequently refused bail than white, and this may partly be because of not having what is perceived to be a stable family background. There appears to be a general assumption that ethnic minority women will 'disappear into their own subculture' which it will then be difficult for the police to penetrate (Chigwada-Bailey 1997). In addition, poverty within the black community often means that it is difficult to obtain financial sureties or a security. Such considerations mean that black women who should be on bail may find it being refused.

Another problem area for black defendants in general is the difficulty in deciding whether to have a white lawyer whom they believe is less likely to lose the sympathy of the court, or a black lawyer who understands their own culture. Black women wanting to change their lawyers may also experience difficulties. In the interviews I conducted with a range of black women it is, of course, difficult to know how much of the dissatisfaction stemmed from the solicitor being unhelpful, and how much was due to disappointment with the outcome of a case, or indeed how much was due to the inherent mistrust between black women and criminal justice agencies.

All the women I spoke to were convinced that judges and magistrates were racist. For example, Edith said: 'I feel you are found guilty the minute they see your colour. I don't think they should go through the procedure of hearing the case when they have made up their minds the minute they saw you.'

Many women talked about judges that were known by the black community to be anti-black. 'I have been in trouble with the law a few times,' said Anthea. 'Where I live every black person knows about this judge in the Crown Court. He is definitely anti-black and dishes out long sentences to blacks.'

During an interview Judge Pickles tried to put the other perspective: 'A Rastafarian standing in front of you with dreadlocks can look rather intimidating,' he said. 'If we could understand their minds better, we might be able to better understand what they are doing and why they are doing it. There is no deliberate racism but there may be unconscious bias because we don't know enough about the people' (*The Voice*, 11 September 1990).

All the women interviewed felt aggrieved and were dissatisfied with the sentences they were given. After discussing them with other women in prison they realised that white women get shorter sentences compared to black. This remark from Dawn summarises the feelings of many of them:

> Courts are not fair. I had one and a half kilo of cocaine and was given ten years and have done four years so far. Since I have been in prison I have found that some white women, although they had more cocaine on them, got lesser sentences. One white woman here had six kilos and was given five years. I feel it's unfair as it's my first offence.

It is difficult to say how much of this apparent disparity in sentencing was due to legitimate considerations – such as the seriousness of the offence, the offender's past criminal record and the exact circumstances of the offence – and how much was due to extra legal variables like being black, being a woman and being working class.

Black women in prison

Up to a third of women in prison in England and Wales are drug couriers or 'mules' from other countries who will be deported after serving their prison sentence. In addition to the problems usually associated with imprisonment, such women have to face the difficulties of coping with a different culture, with a language they may not speak, or speak very inadequately, with isolation and lack of family contact as well as acute anxiety about the welfare of children who are either in care or in poverty-stricken conditions in their home country.

Some of these women prisoners lack adequate clothing, having been arrested at ports of entry with only one set of clothes and unsuitable shoes. Penny Green notes:

> The vast majority of foreign national couriers arrive in Britain with an expectation of staying only five or so days – they bring enough clothes only for these few days, and if they arrive in summer they have no clothing adequate for the British winters ahead. Those they have with them are then all they have when they find themselves in prison for six to ten years: One Nigerian woman interviewed burst into tears as she lifted her blouse to show she had no underwear at all, her plastic sandals were totally inadequate for the British climate. (Green 1991, p.54)

Discrimination in custody also includes a paucity of basic information in their own language and a lack of even the most basic interpreting services, poor catering for special diets and a failure to access education classes because of the cultural problems they present. Many black women are in prison for sentences of less than 12 months. Had they been men, certainly white men, this group of offenders would have been targeted for community service or probation.

All women in prison experience difficulties, but for black women there are additional burdens which they encounter on remand as well as during their sentence and on their release. Many feel acutely the bias with which they are viewed by prison officers. 'We [black women] are . . . mad and we commit crime and we sponge off the system . . . Black women are not even allowed the patronising treatment of being seen as "fragile little creatures" that must be protected. We are supposed to be able to cope in whatever situations arise' (Black Women in Prison 1985). In prison black women are often viewed as so violent they have to be dealt with by male officers (Chigwada-Bailey 1997).

The *Race Relations Manual* for prison officers states that racist behaviour or abuse is a serious, disciplinary matter. Launching the manual in 1991, Angela Rumbold, Home Office minister with responsibility for prisons, said:

> We all know that discrimination does still occur in our prisons, against both prisoners and staff. Some is overt, perhaps racial abuse of prisoners or harassment of ethnic minority officers. While some is unintentional, like stereotyping which leads to false assumptions about a person's behaviour . . . I . . . firmly believe that prisoners . . . regardless of colour, race or religion, should be treated with equality, humanity and respect. (NACRO 1991)

The minister emphasised race and colour without mentioning gender, as if racial discrimination is not sometimes, as argued throughout this chapter, likened to gender or class discrimination. To this list of discrimination, must be added yet another – religious discrimination – since the Home Office has consistently refused to recognise Rastafarianism as a religion; thus adding to the institutionalised discrimination already experienced by black women Rastafarians.

Genders and Player (1989) found that the prevailing perception among most prison officers was that Asians are 'clean' and 'hardworking' and 'no trouble' while blacks are 'arrogant', 'hostile to authority' and have 'chips on their shoulders'. Race relations officers could also experience difficulties with their colleagues. One was referred to as the 'Sambo Samaritan'.

This experience of multi-faceted discrimination expressed by black prisoners was confirmed by a report put out by the Oxford University Centre for Criminological Research which found a wide gap between the actual number of racial incidents recorded by the prison service, which was low, and the high number of complaints reported to them. The researchers concluded that black prisoners were indeed subjected to victimisation by prisoners and staff, unfairly treated over access to facilities and education, and subjected to racial abuse, harassment, unfair discipline, bullying and assault (Genders and Player 1989).

One south east London probation officer noted that although black women who served long sentences for drug offences were 'almost all dignified, respectful and unworldly . . . [they] tend to get all the shit jobs in the prison, like working in the kitchens from 6.0 am to 5.0 pm, but they don't complain because it keeps them occupied. They prefer it because they don't have time to think about their families' (cited in Chigwada-Bailey 1997).

Conclusion

Feminist penologists have rightly been critical of the construction of equality that is inscribed in law and criminal justice, but this does not mean they are opposed to an ideal of equality. The thrust of feminist critique in and beyond criminal justice is that to treat people equally has in the past been taken to mean to treat them the same (see Carlen 1990[b]; Eaton 1986; Hudson 1998). In law, as in other institutions within liberal societies, this means treating women the same as men, and treating black women the same as white women.

According to Hudson (2002), Equality versus Difference has been the big debate among feminist theorists in so-called 'second wave' feminism, and takes as its point of departure the realisation that rights and other bedrock concepts of law are constructed from a male view of the world. The political–legal structure of modern societies is based on a masculine imagery. The cultural complex of which law is part is based on constructions of subjectivity based on masculine philosophies. It is based on masculine desires, masculine imaginings of the life they would lead, and masculine fears about the structures and other subjectivities that are likely to obstruct the fulfilment of their desires and ambitions (see Hudson 2002). Any further gains for women can only be achieved through interposing a feminine imagery, which can develop its own ideas about the rights, freedoms, rules and protections women need to fulfil their hopes and to permit their development as free, authentic females (Cornell 1995; Irigaray 1994). The feminine imagery would need to include race and class to represent all women.

The reasonable behaviour, the reasonable person of the law, is not just a male person but a white, middle-class male person, constantly reproduced through legal thinking and legal practice (Lloyd 1994; Naffine 1990). The yardstick for a reasonable woman's behaviour for the court is a white, middle-class female. The reasonable woman yardstick has to be cultural and class sensitive if 'justice' is to prevail. This is about acknowledging other cultures as different, not inferior.

In this chapter I have tried to demonstrate how race, gender and class interlink in a way specific and unique to black women, contributing to their over-representation in prison. Apart from obvious and blatant racism, there is a more insidious and subtle racism that reaches right into the heart of the British criminal justice system. Not only is there a need for black people to be properly represented within the legal profession itself, but the institutional racism that pervades British criminology also needs to be clearly identified and recognised. At the moment nearly all research into the workings of the legal system is done by the Home Office. We need more independent criminologists who can conduct independent research, and we need ethnic criminologists to be included into the mainstream. Unless the criminal justice system is class, race and gender blind, and seen to be so, it will continue to be a tool not for justice but of oppression.

3.4
Women's imprisonment in England and Wales: a penal paradox
by Lorraine Gelsthorpe and Allison Morris

[. . .]

Increasing penality

Increasing reliance on the use of imprisonment has been described by Smith and Stewart (1998: 106) as 'the most notable penal development of the mid 1990s' and England is generally seen as following the American lead in this, Increasing levels of the fear of crime have created a climate in which 'protection', 'incapacitation' and 'risk management' are Government priorities (Home Office, 1999). Crime increased markedly in England and Wales throughout the years of a Conservative government (1979 to 1997) and discourse on crime both then and since has been dominated by the need for ever tougher and punitive sanctions. Prison populations spiralled.

Almost 6000 adult women were received into prison under sentence of immediate imprisonment in 2000 (Home Office, 2001a: Table 1.1). Indeed, receptions into prison under sentence have increased steadily since the mid-1970s: as noted above, the number has more than doubled between 1990 and 2000 (Home Office, 2001a: Table 1.10). The rate of increase for receptions under sentence of immediate imprisonment has also been much higher for female prisoners than for male prisoners over the past 10 years [. . .].

Indeed, it is projected that this increase will continue (White, 1999). England and Wales now reflect the trend in women's imprisonment apparent in other jurisdictions (Chesney-Lind, 1997; Cook and Davies, 2000; Cameron, 2001). [. . .]

Pathways to crime

[. . .] [W]omen commit relatively few offences, although they are now committing more offences that 10 years ago. There has, however, been a slight change in the nature of women's offending, mainly with respect to offences involving drugs (although, as noted, these mostly involve possession of Class B drugs). Research suggests that the sentencing of women, including the decision to sentence women to imprisonment, is not straightforward. There is some evidence of increased punitiveness because a greater proportion of women are being sentenced to imprisonment and more women are being received into prison for short periods. However, the 'type' of women imprisoned remains much the same as 10 years ago: most are criminally unsophisticated, serving their first custodial sentence, and have been received into prison for property offences. A key question, therefore, is how we can account for this increase and the apparent lack of significant change in the female offending population.

[. . .]

Without doubt, the criminal justice system of England and Wales has experienced huge changes over the past 20 years, with numerous pieces of legislation relating to sentencing. Some elements of this legislation are viewed as quite punitive (see, for example, Cavadino and Dignan's (2002) commentary on the reinvigoration of 'law and order' approaches within the 1993 Criminal Justice Act, the Criminal Justice and Public Order Act 1994, the Crime (Sentences) Act 1997 and the 1998 Crime and Disorder Act). Other elements of this legislation are viewed as 'liberal', but are frequently subverted or resisted by the judiciary and magistracy (see, for example, the discussion by Dunbar and Langdon, 1998; Cavadino et al., 1999). However, on the published data available, there is little evidence of an increased punitiveness *solely* towards women. The penal climate did change from the mid-1980s, but it seems likely that the increase in women's imprisonment is partly explained by changes in sentencing policy which affected both women and men. At the same time, this increasing penality highlights a gap between what is done (sentences imposed) and what we know about the social and economic situation of women who are at risk of offending – the pathways to crime. And it is to this issue that we now return.

A high and increasing prison population is not the only legacy of the Conservative era. It also produced high unemployment, benefit cuts, reductions in services (for example, in health, social services and housing) and increasing gaps between the 'haves' and the 'have-nots' (Walker and Walker, 1987, 1997; Townsend et al., 1992; Morris, 1994; Alcock et al., 2000). 'Social exclusion' is the term that has been introduced to refer to those in these categories (Jones Finer and Nellis, 1998) and it is difficult to avoid connecting these broad social and penal consequences. Also characteristic of this time was what has been called 'the feminization of poverty (Glendinning and Millar, 1992). By the late 1990s, nine out of 10 lone parent families were headed by a woman and many women rely on benefits or on low pay in the part-time work sector (Office for National Statistics, 1999). Indeed, Smith and Stewart (1998) suggest that the financial and other circumstances of offenders have got worse over the last 30 years or so leading to the (somewhat cynical) comment that imprisonment has become an effective way of managing the unemployed. This point can be readily extended to cover the management of women who are socially and economically marginalized.

Precisely why some women commit crimes can be approached on two different levels. First, from a description of the broad features of women's structural positions and lifestyles in society, it is possible to see that many are vulnerable to financial difficulties and to the stresses and strains that go along with child-care responsibilities, domestic violence and high levels of childhood victimization. Indeed, one might refer to these vulnerabilities as 'indirect' pathways towards crime. Certainly, research on female offenders indicates that a high number of them experience a wide range of social problems (Rumgay, 1996). Second, as we will show later, there are links between some of these broad social and structural problems and more immediate 'criminogenic factors'.

Walmsley et al. (1992) reported that, although some of the needs of male and female prisoners were similar, female prisoners were also likely to have particular needs in relation to child-care responsibilities (often they were single parents), drug and/or alcohol abuse (often directly linked to their offending), limited qualifications, lack of work skills or experience, low income and histories of abuse. These early indications of women's needs were confirmed in a subsequent study of the specific needs of female prisoners (Morris et al., 1995) and in Her Majesty's Chief Inspector of Prisons' thematic review of women in prison (Her Majesty's Inspectorate of Prisons for England and Wales, 1997; 14–16). Mair and May's (1997) study of offenders on probation also confirms the picture of female offenders as having distinctive needs which relate to their general poverty and deprivation.

A key question, from all of this research, is the extent to which these social characteristics can be said to be offending-related. Recent research on criminogenic factors points towards the importance of: poor cognitive skills, anti-social attitudes and feelings, strong ties to and identification with anti-social/criminal models, weak social ties, difficulty with self-management, dependency on drugs and alcohol, adverse social or family circumstances, unemployment and literacy problems (McGuire, 1995, Mair and May, 1997). These general claims of crime causation may be perceived to be gender-neutral rather than gender-specific. Elaine Player (1989[a]) cautions that women's criminality should not be perceived as a homogenous and specialist area of criminology and that social factors and processes of interaction apply equally to men and women. However, in our view, there has been too little recent research specifically on women's offending to make this claim and the possibility of different contributory factors in women's offending needs to receive more research attention.

There are numerous reviews of early theories of women's crime (for example, Smart, 1976; Leonard, 1983; Morris 1987; Naffine, 1987; Heiden-sohn, 1996) which point out that theories have often been based on studies of men, that images of female offenders have been distorted or that women's crime is a form of 'acting out'. While it is not relevant to describe these studies in detail here, it is relevant to mention that our knowledge of female offenders has been beset with myths, muddles and misconceptions which often reflect ideological concerns rather than objective evidence. Equally, it is tempting to assume that the social and individual characteristics of female offenders, whether imprisoned or on probation, are predictive of offending. But, of course, prediction is not straightforward. Many of the studies of female offenders show 'associations' between the particular needs and circumstances of female offenders (low self-esteem, accommodation and financial problems and so on) and their routes into crime, but this is not the same thing as showing 'causal mechanisms'.

One of the problems here is that classification and risk prediction instruments have been designed and validated exclusively in relation to male offenders. The HM Prison Service review of the literature on female offenders (Howden-Windell and Clark, 1999) helps a little in this regard by sifting through the evidence to indicate which factors can be said to be more predictive of offending and reoffending than other factors. They concluded that:

- the criminogenic factors associated with male offenders are clearly relevant for female offenders too, but their level of importance and the nature of the association may differ;
- additional criminogenic needs exist in female offenders, although their exact relationship to recidivism is not known;
- different criminogenic factors may be relevant for adult female offenders and for juvenile female offenders.

Notwithstanding the difficulties of prediction studies, and the fact that there have been too few comparisons with women in the general population to help sort out which factors might be predictive of offending (that is, which factors indicate the precise *causes* of crime) we can, at the very least, argue that all the social and individual factors which characterize women on probation and in prison may be *sources* of crime (that is to say, these circumstances contribute to crime). Crime is one response, but there may be other responses too, As Cook (1997) indicates, crime may be chosen for a variety of complex reasons, which include:

- an act of desperation: for example, the offence may be the only way for those in debt 'to keep their heads above water';
- taking a chance: for example, the offence may be the result of an impulsive response to illegitimate opportunities which are presented;

- nothing to lose: for example, the offence may be the product of disillusionment and social exclusion;
- a rational economic choice: for example, the offence may be a response to the fact that the woman is not able to perceive a legitimate way of gaining the same benefits;
- a means of asserting economic or emotional independence: for example, an abused woman may 'see' no other option to gaining her 'freedom' than to kill her abusive partner; and
- a narrowing of options for employment.

It is for these reasons then that one can argue that criminal justice practice needs to focus not just on the immediate lead-up to the crime of an individual female offender (the psychological processes involved) but on the broad social and individual factors which may contribute to and which, so to speak, put women on the pathway to crime. These *sources* of crime need to be tackled as well as any immediate psychological motivation (arising from *particular* stresses or reasons). Indeed, it may be argued that the need to address underlying issues is fundamental to any attempts to reduce crime. As Rumgay (1996) has argued, the backgrounds and circumstances of women's lives are inseparable from their involvement in crime. Far from being irrelevant to an understanding of women's offending, personal difficulties and welfare problems are inextricable from it.

Resolving the paradox

It would be unfair to suggest that there has been no action at all to address the broad range of social problems which fuel connections between individuals, their communities and crime. The Social Exclusion Unit, for instance, has produced an impressive array of reports and policy analyses, and has spawned policy action teams across Whitehall looking at a range of social and urban decay problems and renewal initiatives. Nevertheless, the Social Exclusion Unit seems to have ignored as many social problems as it has addressed (Walker, 2000). Similarly, the Labour Party's flagship legislation on crime, the Crime and Disorder Act 1998, was widely expected to be 'tough on crime, tough on the causes of crime' though a common conclusion is that it focuses more on being tough on crime than on the socially deprived contexts from which crime emerges (Muncie, 1999).

A further sign of energy and hope is the 1999 Crime Reduction Programme (Home Office, 1999), one strand of which reflects the 1998 Effective Practice Initiative sponsored jointly by the Home Office Probation Unit, Her Majesty's Inspectorate of Probation, the Association of Chief Officers of Probation and the Central Policy Committee and which revolves around the development of national programmes for community-based supervision of offenders. While recognized as a positive, constructive response to crime, again, there are criticisms that some of these programmes are narrow in focus: for example, their starting point reflects a psychological and cognitive basis rather than a social basis; and even where they are persuasive, attempts to improve offenders' reasoning skills may not be enough to keep them away from crime (Rex, 1999). But the main point here is that for all the positive effect of such interventions, they do not come close to addressing the problems that offenders (male *or* female) encounter in their everyday lives in the real world.

There has been no shortage of alternative proposals to deal with female offenders in a way which would reduce the use of imprisonment and reflect more closely what we know about women's pathways into crime. In order to draw attention to the increase in the number of women in prison in the last decade, the Prison Reform Trust recently commissioned an independent enquiry by Professor Dorothy Wedderburn and others. The resulting report *Justice for Women: The Need for Reform* (Prison Reform Trust, 2000) not only rehearsed some of the many sound points outlined by Carlen and Tchaikovsky (1996) and Carlen (1998), but also developed the theme that it is important to recognize the backgrounds of women in prison and the wider consequences of custodial sentences for them.

Report after report has questioned the treatment of women in prison and the sentencing policy and practice which has led to women being there. What seems particularly valuable in the Wedderburn Report is the way in which it recognizes that criminal justice policy 'should be consistent with the whole spectrum of criminal justice and social policy objectives' (Prison Reform Trust, 2000: 78, Para. 7.3), thus ensuring that sentencing policy does not militate against attempts to reduce structural social exclusion. Recommendations for increased diversion from court on the grounds that women generally commit offences of relatively low seriousness, and for a co-ordinated network of Women's Supervision, Rehabilitation and Support Centres (Recommendation 4.ii) which would facilitate a reduction in the use of imprisonment and which, at the same time, would serve to address women's needs for support and social integration go some way to direct attention away from the 'prisoncentricity' which has come to dominate sentencing policy. Other recommendations include the setting up of a national system of geographically dispersed custodial units to replace present prison arrangements, the repeal of Part 1 of the Crime (Sentences) Act 1997 (which concerns minimum limits on sentences for certain offences), the reintroduction of unit fines (so as to reflect the fact that women, as a group, are relatively poor and that fines should be imposed according to means) and a requirement that sentencers take into account the distinctive position of female offenders (for instance, their economic position, their mental health, their childhood or recent experiences of physical or sexual abuse, or their responsibilities towards children, partners, parents or other family or household members). Combined, these recommendations (and others) stem from an understanding of the lower seriousness of women's offending, their comparatively lower likelihood of reoffending and the strong evidence that the lives of female offenders are characterized by individual and social problems.

Welcome as such proposals are, there is also the need to question whether or not such moves are enough, and whether or not initiatives which promulgate new policies for women but not for men run the risk of creating as many discrepancies as they resolve. Also, circumvention of conventional sentencing values through legislative changes and the provision of alternatives do not amount to a challenge to the normative framework for sentencing. The recent report of a review of the sentencing framework (Home Office, 2001[b]) may hold out some promise of reform through its recommendation (not for the first time by a government committee) that imprisonment should only be used when no other sentence is adequate to meet the seriousness of the offence, taking into account the offender's previous criminal history. On the other hand, its emphasis is on crime reduction rather than on cutting the prison population. And there is nothing in the recommendations to suggest a radical shift in philosophy of an order which would lead to considerable reductions in the use of imprisonment. The latest additions to the existing panoply of high tariff alternatives to custody (in the Crime and Disorder Act 1998) along with the tougher breach conditions introduced in the Criminal Justice and Courts Services Act 2000 and the flexible approach to custody suggested by the Review may simply have the same result as many previous alternatives to custody: increases in the prison population (Pease, 1985; Bottoms, 1987).

At the same time, while claims that women commit less serious crimes and pose fewer risks than men are grounded in incontrovertible evidence which legitimates calls for the differential treatment of men and women, there is some difficulty in applying this same logic of differentiation on the basis of women's *social* backgrounds. While there is a need for more research in this area, few would dismiss indications of social hardship among men in prison. In 1991, the Prison Reform Trust carried out a survey of men in prison which revealed high levels of unemployment, problems with literacy, problems with housing and high levels of experience in local authority care. Indeed, their 'identikit prisoner' would have experienced a good number of social and economic deprivations (Prison Reform Trust, 1991). This strengthens the argument that the use of imprisonment for such men is also often inappropriate. To argue the case for women as opposed to women *and* men on these grounds, therefore, invites criticism of unfairness towards men. It is preferable to let the case for a reduction in the use of imprisonment for women stand on the grounds of the *seriousness of their offending and their risk to others*, while at the same time addressing the social problems which line the pathways to crime for both women and men.

Part 4
Engendering masculinity
Introduction

The 1990s saw criminology engage overtly with the concept of masculinity and especially its problematic and criminogenic characteristics. Campbell's chapter, taken from her 1993 work *Goliath: Britain's Dangerous Places* explores a troubled and troublesome masculinity. The book from which this chapter is taken is a journalistic account of the riots which swept through a number of predominantly white, suburban, yet economically deprived, housing estates in England and Wales in 1991. Through a retelling of the events which lay behind these disturbances, she reveals a level of destruction of self and community which is perpetrated by men and boys. She compares this very male reaction to the attitudes and behaviours of the females resident within the same neighbourhoods. They too are similarly deprived, poorly educated and housed, and lacking social and economic opportunities, yet they attempt to build community, family and collectivity at the same time as their male peers reject their endeavours and the positive examples which they set. As Campbell posits, in a later chapter: 'the difference with what men and women do with their troubles and with their anger shapes their strategies of survival and solidarity on the one hand, danger and destruction on the other' (1993: 303)

Campbell's work, while understanding of the troubles of economically marginalised males still sets them up in opposition to their female peers. The emerging emphasis on 'masculinities' which materialised at around the same time as Campbell's work (Connell, 1992; 1995; Messerschmidt, 1993) puts forward a more subtle and nuanced consideration of what it is to be male. This perspective argues that masculinity can be achieved in a various ways, although these are constrained by cultural stereotypes and limited by dimensions such as race, class and sexuality. In our second reading, Messerschmidt, like Connell (1987), rejects the suggestion that there are 'natural' differences between the sexes. Rather he argues that there is no one-dimensional and fixed view of either masculinity or femininity and that both sexes use the resources at their disposal to construct gendered ways of being.

Men and women assert gendered identities in many ways, adapting to the limitations imposed by dominant ideas of gender and constrained in their opportunities to act by class position, ideas of race and of sexuality. Thus the 'making of masculinity' (and likewise femininity) is achieved on a daily basis through the ways in which men interact with those individuals who surround them and the institutions with which they come into contact. This remains as true for the powerful as the powerless male and as a result the policing of males and females is as gendered as the criminal acts which each commits.

In the third reading, Richard Collier critiques the work of Messerschmidt and those who have subsequently employed the concept of hegemonic masculinity to understand the question of why men commit more crime than women. Messerschmidt's work has, he acknowledges, gained considerable support since its publication but he argues that it still cannot answer the question as to why some men accomplish their masculinity through criminal and illegitimate activities and why many others do not. Collier then examines an alternative perspective which seeks to explore male criminality through individual biography and life-history. He references the work of Jefferson and Hollway which inserts a psycho-social perspective into an exploration of criminality and also of fear. This approach explores the individual's investment in different social discourses and practices, together with the contradictory experiences and attitudes displayed by individual males who are struggling to make sense of an uncertain, changing world which sends out different signals as to what is acceptable and what is illegitimate. As an example, in this much more messy and confusing world, aggression and dominance are celebrated in certain organisations and life-worlds but are condemned in others. Jefferson employs these methods to study the American boxer, Mike Tyson, who is encouraged to cultivate a violent and destructive persona in order to become a professional success but who then is denigrated and despised when this becomes uncontrolled and spills into his private relationships. But where, Collier argues, does this focus on the individual psyche and experience leave us in a discipline which ultimately seeks to bring about positive change and a reduction in crime? Ultimately Collier argues that neither approach can capture the complex and changing multiplicities of the commission of crime and suggests that 'the masculine turn' in criminology may have drawn to an end.

The last reading in this part was written by Pat Carlen in 1994. Although it appears out of synch with the previous readings – in that it pre-dates some and is informed by work on the social control of women – it raises some key points which theorists of gender in general, and masculinity in particular, would do well to heed. Carlen addresses the thorny issue of theory formation with regard to gender, crime and social control. She grapples with the relative importance of gender and other constituents of unequal power relations – class and race – to the social control of law-breaking women. She provides an overview of the extant theorisation of the social control of women through ideologies of femininity, economic systems, and family and welfare institutions. Carlen observes that, while such theories provide important insights, they fail to provide a theory of women's criminal careers which explains them in 'the fullness of *all* their contradictions and specificities' (p. 185, emphasis in original). Rejecting the approach of postmodernism which brings the very category of 'woman' into question, Carlen is strongly of the opinion that it is possible to make theoretical statements about gender and crime, and asserts that post-structuralist theorisation – which recognises the impact of existing inequalities but denies that such inequalities will have the same applicability in all circumstances and to all individuals – may provide a means to address the diverse and evolving meanings of crime and social control in a variety of contexts and circumstances. Carlen's work demonstrates that 'engendering' criminology remains vital if it is to continue to provide insights into the behaviours of both male and female, and if it is to help to bring about social justice for all.

Suggestions for further reading

Adkins, L. (2004) 'Gender and the post-structural social', in B.L. Marshall and A. Witz (eds), *Engendering the Social*, Maidenhead: Open University Press, pp. 139–54.
    Adkins argues that a gendered narrative which privileges the masculine experience remains a feature of contemporary theorising within sociology, and that while this differs from past exclusions of the female, is equally limiting in its consequences.
Jefferson, T. (2002), 'Subordinating hegemonic masculinity', *Theoretical Criminology*, 6(2): 63–88.
    In this article Jefferson explores and critiques the use of Connell's concept of hegemonic masculinity and argues for the development of a more psycho-social theory of masculinity.
Stanko, E.A. and Hobdell, K. (1993), 'Assault on men, masculinity and male victimisation', *British Journal of Criminology*, 33(3): 400–14.
    Stanko and Hobdell's article reveals the absence of literature on men's fear which has taken the invulnerability of men for granted. Their interviews with men who have been violently victimised illustrates the limitations placed on men's ability to express their fears and thereby to deal adequately with their victimisation.

4.1
Boys will be boys
by Beatrix Campbell

The scale of the pyrotechnics during the riots was, to the places where violence, joyriding, burglary and fires were everyday events, all that seemed to
distinguish the riots from the travails of daily life. The riots did not represent
revolt, they were simply larger displays of what these neighbourhoods had to
put up with much of the time. The tempo of the policing – passive and then
explosive – was also just another thing they had to put with from the men in
their lives. What none of these neighbourhoods believed was either that they
were *supported* by politicians or the police or that they were *represented* by the
riots or the rioters.

A conversation with a group of boys and girls in Ely revealed the confu-
sions and crisis of confidence that the riots created in their communities.
The teenagers were there, some of them had taken part, but did they know
what they meant? As displays of force the riots had followed a familiar
format – they were about being hard – but as displays of dissent they seemed
to be meaningless. The girls in this conversation watched the riots, the boys
joined in:

'Since the riots we've had more police. You feel you are being watched
for everything you do.'

'The riots gave Ely a bad name – it was unfair.'

'I was throwing stones at the coppers because it was fun and everyone
else was doing it.'

'*Did you want to hit the police?*'

'I didn't care.'

'You can't stop it, can you? People won't listen to you.'

'They'd call you a sap if you didn't do it.'

'I was throwing stones at the police because everybody was doing it. If it's
happening it's worth doing it because you wouldn't want to be called a sap,
would you?'

'*What does fighting achieve?*'

'Nothing really, it shows who is the hardest, so you get more respect.'
'*Who from?*'
'Other boys.'
'*Girls?*'
'They don't really matter.'

The legal definition of 'riot' in the Public Order Act is a *collective* disturbance for a *common purpose*. The riots of 1991 were something else: they were a cacophony of dissenting voices – dissenting from each other. What they showed was what divided the communities, not what bonded them. The protagonists were young men whose response to the world they lived in was pestering and predatory. The *places* they firebombed were not icons of public pain and punishment – there were no Bastilles; they were mainly public service buildings or small shops. The flames carried no message except beautiful menace. In a relatively unarmed country, fire had become a ubiquitous weapon. To the fire-raisers it carried mesmerising potency. The motif for media representations of Meadowell's most notorious night became a flaming landscape. The fire-raisers' work was mighty, it transcended the boundaries of Meadowell, and made this place which had no signpost into a place that suddenly did not need one. Its horizon was a sunset where the landscape entered the heavens and expanded into space.

Another tactic was to knock out the street lights or to blow out the power supply. Controlling darkness and light like this implied omniscience. The flame-throwers were like Icarus, boys flying, and that night in Meadowell they could do anything.

'Fire-setters aren't communicators. It's easier to strike a match than talk to someone. It is a very extreme response, of course, and we see it among people who don't think about consequences,' says Andrew Mutley, who works with fire-raisers at Newton Ayecliffe children's centre. Fire has changed its place in British life, with the demise of the cooking range and the open fire in the sitting-room. 'It is in nature, like wind and water, but in modern British culture people don't have access to it, they don't learn about it,' he adds. 'They don't learn that it can be positive. You can cook on it, sing around it, be warmed by it. At one time it was a domestic event. Now people don't have fireplaces.' For fire-setters, however, 'it is the most exciting tool at their disposal.'

'The police and these young men are very close to one another,' reckoned a professional in the criminal justice system who worked with both. She was, of course, referring to their shared predilection for masculine company and mastery, and their compulsion to take control, to overcome.

It was also true that many of the young men arrested in the riots tended to be 'known' – they were familiar to the police because they were already caught up in the criminal justice system. They appeared in court, usually recognisable as the accused not just because they were familiar, or because they were standing in the dock, but because they were the skinny, pale lads who looked, as they used to say, like 'ninepenny rabbits'.

One young man had a formidable record. He had been a burglar; he had stolen cars; he had beaten a man accused of being a grass with a baseball bat. Beautiful, with a blond crop and a thin, statuesque body, he had had a career in burglary characterised by a boldness that was hardly efficient – he kept getting caught. He made no effort to hide himself during the riots in the West End of Newcastle. Indeed, they were a great show. The police had provoked and the lads did their duty.

The West End was this lad's patch. Most of his offences had happened within a mile or so of where he lived. He was on his way home to Scotswood from an offenders' attendance centre in town when he saw a notice attached to the lamppost outside his local pub, the Bobby Shafto, announcing the riot that evening. He was spotted looking at the notice, but any attempt to pin the poster on him foundered – he could not write.

Around teatime he returned to the pub and found a stolen white Vauxhall Nova parked outside, with a group of lads standing round it. It was waiting to be played with. He started it up with a little piece of metal and drove it down to Benwell and back again. The white Nova ended up incinerated. He was part of the group of lads who tried to smash a hole in the post office shutters, who then kicked a door in and shot up to the flat above. People across the road saw these boys throwing petrol bombs at the post office, at the window of the flat above, and then at the stairs as they rushed out and back into the crowd.

He had been released from custody not long before the riots. On most days, his life was lived within a one-mile radius. He went the couple of miles into the city only when his mother took him to buy clothes or when he was due at an attendance centre – an alternative to custody. He never went to the cinema – 'I don't like it' – and he never went to any cafés – 'I don't know any.' He heard about the Meadowell riot when he was at home with his mother, like thousands of other listeners who tune in nightly to Alan Robson's popular local radio show, *Night Owls*. 'My ma said they were daft. I said nowt.' Did he think they were daft? 'In a way, aye, in a way no. Burning everything down was a bad idea. But they did it for their mates, the two lads that died.' He was tried and convicted on charges of firebombing the post office – one of Scotswood's most important economic resources.

When Elswick was set alight the night before Scotswood, he was there. 'All the kids were talking about it so we went up. It was daft because they wouldn't let the fire engines past to put the fires out. They were at the fire engines, not the police – but they should have let the fire engines through because it's their job. Then we just went back to Scotswood. I went to the Bobby Shafto, as I usually do, sniffing glue with my mates. My mam knew about the glue. She tried to keep me out of it, she kept watching me.'

After he had first seen the notice outside the Bobby Shafto, 'I was talking to my mates for half an hour, then I went home. My mam is always in – she makes the tea. I had a bath, got changed, went back to the Bobby. Around six o'clock loads of people were getting into hoistie cars [stolen cars] and the white van that was full of kids from Benwell was there. About eight o'clock they were flinging the car about and the police started coming.'

When people started throwing the petrol bombs stored behind the kebab shop opposite the post office, he joined them. 'I was high as a kite on glue. It was daftness. Everyone was shouting to the busies [police] "black cunts" because of their uniforms and because of the way they treat us.'

He was throwing petrol bombs into the road 'so that the police couldn't get past, because they would just have kicked us all over.' But there were other people who wanted the police to get through, weren't there? 'Aye, all the women. The old people didn't like it either, and half the young lasses were shouting and bawling at us.' Did he take any notice? 'No, they were just shouting in case they got hurt or their houses got hurt. They were just being scared.'

His route to the riot had begun a few years earlier when he was fourteen years old. He was not very good at reading and writing. 'I packed in school. Teachers asked us to read in front of the class. I cannot. It just showed me up.' Was that why he stopped going to school, because he felt daft? 'Aye.'

'I'd leave the house about nine o'clock, when my mam thought I was going to school – I never told her I wasn't. I'd go down to the park at Scotswood Dene with my mates. We messed about.'

Messing about was a frugal sport. 'We were banging into glue. We didn't talk much.' So who does this young man talk to? 'Just my mam.' What about? 'All sorts.' He tells her things he tells no one else, not secrets especially, just anything. 'I don't know if my mates would be interested.' When he wasn't going to school he was at the dene or 'hanging around the school at the back where everybody went for a smoke – we didn't go in. My mam found out when the school board woman came after about eight months. My mam said I had to go to school! Then she took me to school. I felt shown up. My mates were just laughing. I didn't go back.'

Then he became a burglar, and he had a habit. 'We were all bored. We wanted some glue and one of the lads mentioned burgling a house. It was near where we lived. We kicked the front door in and took the video. One of my mates sold it for about £100, so we all got £33 each.' That lasted for about two days. 'We just kept burgling. I liked it – till we started getting caught. I liked the money.' Hanging around the pub connected the boys to a network of fences who would sell their stolen goods. The lads sat on the front steps of the pub and did business in the back. Passers-by were often the inhabitants of houses they had penetrated and whose property they had pinched. Sometimes these people were still paying off the instalments on items the lads had long since forgotten.

Burgling was a boy's thing. 'It's not a lasses' thing: they go shoplifting.' He kept getting caught. His mother was furious and that bothered him. He loved her, but she was no match for a laugh, for a rave, for his mates. 'I couldn't do anything about it. Me and my mates just had a good laugh, just pinching cars and having a laugh. I got out of my head really. We got glue from the paper shop. I liked the illusions, just seeing things, like trees moving in front of you when they weren't really there.'

When he and his mates began stealing cars he started driving them up the Armstrong Road. 'People used to laugh. I'd have preferred it if they didn't watch, in case I crashed.' It was the burgling and the joyriding that drove the neighbourhood crazy. 'People think we're rogues.' Did he care? 'Sometimes, because you could be walking along the street and they could be saying, "He's a house burglar." ' He had beaten up people who had given information to the police. 'Sometimes I think they're just cunts, sometimes I think they're doing people favours to stop people taking property.'

His own property consists of a bedroom with a bed, a wardrobe, a television his mother bought him and a 'ghetto blaster' his father bought him for Christmas. He liked driving cars and doing handbrake turns around Armstrong Road, but he did not care to keep one, have one for himself. 'Didn't matter, I just wanted to have a go in a car.'

He had been locked up four times and spent another four months in cells after the riots. Nothing much made any difference to him. He rarely kept appointments, rarely put in his community service hours or went to his attendance centre sessions. Not unusually for young men, the only thing that began to get to him was a girl. 'Don't know what I'll do but I've got engaged. I'll settle down in my own house, not burgling.' He liked her. 'She's good to be with.' Why did she like him? 'I don't know. She just says I've got to stop burgling. She says it's people just the same as us we've been taking things off. I've seen people whose houses we've burgled and I've seen what they've been like, just upset, going mad.'

This is a young man who is a glue sniffer and petrol bomber, a burglar and a joyrider who takes tea with his mother and tidies his room. He costs his community a fortune. But he has lived his life in an era which disinvested in the social skills he might otherwise have acquired – literacy, work and cooperation. He was capable of deadly dangerousness. He and the lads like him made the difference between a poor place and an impossible one – hundreds of households in his neighbourhood decided that the only way to survive was to leave.

The criminal justice system saw some of what he did and locked him up from time to time.

In the aftermath of the riots and the incremental political panic over neighbourhood crime, a parliamentary consensus in favour of locking up these young men was cemented in 1993.

Lock-up made little difference to this young man. It made a difference to his home – he wasn't there. It made a difference to his community – it gave it a rest. But it made no difference to him. Except that it was just one damn thing after another.

'I feel young men get no respect from anybody,' said one Juvenile Justice worker, who worked with adolescent offenders for many years in a professional culture committed to keeping them out of custody. 'The police treat them like shit, the system treats them like shit. They have no status in society, no respect, and they don't give it to anybody either. Locking them up, beating them up – I've never understood how you can help a person be more caring by treating them in a brutal way.

'I'm not sure they think about what they do, and that's what we try to get them to do: think about it. But this society treats children very badly. They're punished but they get no service. If they go to court and get a supervision order – which means they stay in the community – they will hardly be seen by the system or by social services until they do something else. They go back to court, they get punished, but they get no service. Most of the young men we see in Juvenile Justice have poor standards of education. The kids are blamed, but the education department isn't called into court to explain itself.'

And so it was with this young man. Nothing made a difference, except now and again his mother and his girlfriend. They were the ones who made him get up in the morning and keep appointments and think about something else other than having hallucinations, cars, and breaking and entering.

They, of course, could be seen as accomplices rather than as the one resource that might restore him to a community so hurt by him that it does not want him. The community itself was seen as an accomplice by a criminal justice system that knew, as much as any and more than most, how bad he was, but also knew as little as any about what to do with him. 'Lock him up' was its answer, sometimes. 'Blame the parents' was its rhetoric. 'What do you expect, where he comes from!' The criminal justice system relied on his mother to get him to court and keep him out of trouble. However, she was treated like a problem rather than a resource. Their neighbourhood, too, was seen to be part of the problem, not part of the solution. When the community tried to secure police cooperation in its campaign against crime, the police walked away. 'They burgle from each other,' said the police. That attitude gave them permission to give up.

The men and boys arraigned in Cardiff's riot trials would, in the olden days of the Fifties and Sixties, when their parents were their age, have been wrought in the image of what used to be known as 'the working man'. They might have gone mad on Friday nights, got girls pregnant, got drunk, got into fights, but they would have stayed on the right side of respectability because they earned enough to live and stay legal.

One generation later the men's relationship to the world had changed: instead of being defined by work, it came to be defined increasingly by crime.

With alternative sources of employment abolished, scavenging, stealing or redistributing stolen goods were hardly surprising sources of income. One man in his early twenties lost his job after he was arrested during the Ely riot. He was in the streets because he lived there. His presence implied no endorsement of the events, he hated the violence. 'The police should have acted as soon as the crowd built up, but they let it grow, then they got agitated and wanted arrests. I'm absolutely against violence – I grew up with it. My mother is a school dinner lady; she knows I didn't do anything because my father used to be violent to her and I've got a great hatred for him. He knocked her teeth out, he broke her jaw. I used to jump on his back when I was a kid to try to stop him. I'd wake up and hear it, and I used to go out in the street. I wouldn't want any child to go through that. The police came once or twice, but they'd just put him in the cell for the night and then he'd come home. I'd never fight, I'd always talk rather than fight.'

He voted Labour, hated Tories. 'I've lived all my adult life through the Tories and they've done nothing for us.' He thought 'loadsamoney' meant earning £250 or £300 a week, regarded community leaders as posh people, and described himself as 'a pauper'.

Apart from minor motoring offences he had never been in trouble with the law but he lived in constant tension with it. 'I've never stolen in my life. Mind you, I have taken parts off stolen cars to make a bit of money. That's stealing I suppose – stealing by finding.' He was being modest about himself as a mover in Ely's informal economy, but was actually part of the chain in a massive trade in stolen goods, the videos, televisions, hi-fi systems, keyboards, car wheels, car seats, bikes, trainers, clothes, stolen cigarettes and drugs: anything useful that could be taken from one place and put in another.

There is a significant trade in small supplies of cannabis, amphetamine and cocaine, sold by young unemployed people who would no more fit the fantasy of a 'dealer' than they would fit the image of a 'worker'. They earned a little, and would hang about at home or in other people's homes. Drugs or drink were as significant a part of their lives as anyone else's. Drugs, drink and video technology domesticated the social life of the young poor.

'The action is in people's homes,' said this receiver. 'You have a smoke and watch a video. People would rather stay at home. They're at home getting block-up, getting stoned. Ely's main problem is money. The council isn't bothered about the place, but then it's short of money. About eighty per cent of the youngsters haven't got jobs. If they have, then the wages are so crap that they can't afford to live.'

Clean, legal, decent families now had their grip on respectability, however precarious a grip it might have been, severed by their boys' behaviour. Post-war full employment tended to make transgression sporadic rather than structural but the effect of the economic crisis on these places, and the criminalisation of young men, contaminated entire families and their neighbourhoods. The parents of one young man, yet again supporting him through a court appearance, were reminded of their boy's exile from their own society. 'The judge said, "You will not go to Ely to intimidate these good people", but we live here! We've lived here all our lives,' said his mother.

His family was close and calm but there was little they felt they could do to keep him from the lawless culture of his peers. 'I can't say a lot about the police because my son has been in trouble,' said his mother, 'and if one is in trouble they condemn the whole family. A lady across the road called me over one day, though, when she heard about our trouble, and said, "You hold your head up high, don't take any notice!" Her son had been beaten by the police once and they'd never been in trouble before.'

Her son, a rather serene young man, pretty, who looked like a pale Prince, had worked as a hairdresser, a butcher and then a builder's labourer. He had been made redundant more than once and had already been imprisoned for a series of car offences. He had been arrested when police were moving up streets close to the riot in Ely – he was watching the spectacle with friends. Several of them later made statements repudiating police evidence that he had thrown a stone at a police officer, but none was prepared to appear in court. When he was arrested he was found to have three truncheon bruises across his chest.

'Three times I've been beaten up when I've been arrested,' said the son. 'When the police see us in the street they say "We'll get you." The other day they arrested me and said, "This is one of many: we're waiting for you." So I've got to look out all the time. I'll be standing on the corner, they'll go past and stick two fingers up and if I did anything they'd arrest me. Most of the kids I know have been beaten up when they've been locked up.' Though he had been arrested mainly for car offences, he and his comrades were also using the cars for burglaries off the estate, usually from sports shops and clothing stores in neighbouring towns which they would relieve of their leather jackets, tracksuits, jumpers, 'all the dear stuff that the kids wear.' They would sell it for half the shop price.

His parents' hold on respectability had been attacked not only by the boy's offences, but by police behaviour. 'The police officers are as bad as the boys,' said his mother. 'We were down the road and we heard one of them shout at a boy who is well known for joyriding, "What time are you going out joyriding?" They get a kick out of it as well. They came to arrest my son once for stealing a car radio. They kicked the door in at seven o'clock in the morning. The officer was so wound-up he was kicking the door and dragging my son out. I said why didn't he let the lad get dressed, I didn't want him going out in his boxer shorts. But the policeman went to his car radio and asked for assistance!

'If a police officer comes to the door about my son I invite him in and talk to him decently. But this behaviour makes you turn away from the police. To be honest, I have no respect for them now. I know this is getting to be a bad place, there's such a lot of crime nowadays and the police have to put up with a lot, but all they seem to do is lash out and think later.' It was no use to her that the police behaved just like the boys.

The young men above were imprisoned on charges of violent disorder arising from the riots. They and their peers – including the police – were caught up in popular cultures that chiselled masculinity as brittle, impregnable and volcanic. This insulation is confirmed by friends of some of the rioters.

'This police–criminals thing is massive,' said a Meadowell youth worker. 'They both need each other to get their kicks.' The dominant culture among the young men of the estate provided the kicks. 'There's a glorification of the criminal thing, and there's not a lot of pressure to pull out of it. Age barriers don't matter. The thirteen-year-olds and eighteen-year-olds might be in the same peer group. They might include people up to thirty years old. Maybe that's something to do with the men on this estate not growing up.' So it was more important for the lads to be among the lads, whatever their age, than among their chronological peers, whatever their gender.

[. . .]

The lads got into trouble and the lasses got pregnant. The one was on the run, the other was trying to make relationships. The one was killing cars, the other was kissing a baby. According to a youth worker who had, himself, been one of the lads, their culture was about 'proving themselves by having bottle, being good drivers, getting into places, looking for fights all the time, being a bit crazier than everybody else, being able to get control of other people.'

Another community worker reckoned that 'by the time the lasses have kids the lads are twiddling their thumbs. They just walk away from it. I've seen it happen for years. They never take responsibility, and then they start having relationships with younger lasses of thirteen or fifteen as if they want to extend their own childhood. Lasses are just bodies to be shagged. Then of course the lads get in trouble: they're racing around in cars, or doing odd "jobs" to finance the booze or the drugs. The lasses have the bairns. The relationship with the lad has broken down, but the relationship with his mother will remain. It's amazing. The responsibility bypasses the son, who does nothing, but his mother will be helpful, passing on a cot, or some clothes. Often the lasses will still go to see his mother, and go round for Sunday dinner. You go into houses to meet the women and you just know that they are coping with *difficult people* – the men go underground. As they get older they don't even meet each other any more. They don't go out, they're these figures who you must not wake.'

The conventional wisdom that the police and the criminals mirror each other implies more than the obvious – that the territory they share is crime – it is concerned with the way both live their masculinity. For the police, their identity as a gender is secured by their employment as enforcers: the institution endorses an identity in its power, its preoccupations, its uniform, its exclusivity. The criminals' empathy with the police, and their envy of police officers, are not so much about an institution as an informal illicit regime of force.

Among unemployed men – so the argument goes – poverty produces an identity crisis; their unemployment leaves them without a role. Is it a wonder, we sigh, that they turn to crime? However, these conversations with men about riots and crime tell us a different story, one that shows how unemployment *reveals a mode of masculinity* whereas the commonsense notion has been that it *causes a crisis of masculinity*. We know that unemployment and poverty produce a human and economic crisis for both men and women, but that is perceived as an economic crisis for a woman and an identity crisis, a gender crisis, for a man. Yet the masculine trauma lies not so much with poverty as with its assignment to the world of women. Archetypal proletarian employment, no less than the City, the Church, Parliament or the police, has been characterised by sex segregation. Masculinity established its identity by enforcing difference, by the exclusion of women. Unemployment denies that difference its institutional framework. The social space men inhabit becomes solely local and domestic, and that is the space they share with women. Difference is reasserted in a refusal to cooperate in the creation of a democratic domesticity.

In employment, men's exit from the domestic domain was excused – they had to go *out* to work. In unemployment they have no alibi, their existence is domesticated. But their resistance is evident in their emotional and physical itinerancy. As workers, their flight from fatherhood was mediated by their pay packet: men's quest to purge women from the world of work, and their struggle to gain privilege for their own pay packet, at the expense of women, was expressed symbolically in the notions of the 'breadwinner' and the 'family wage'. In unemployment, men's flight from fatherhood has no hiding place, they have children and then leave someone else to look after them. What they all seem to insist upon, however, is that someone other than themselves take care of *them*, too, that someone should take them in. Nothing in the culture these men make encourages them to take care of themselves, to create a domestic domain. Being a man means being not-a-woman. So, unable and unwilling to make homes of their own, they become cuckoos moving between their mothers and other women.

But while the young women are at least trying to *make* life, the lads who are their contemporaries are often living like the Sicilians in Tomasi di Lampedusa's novel, *The Leopard*. They are the ones who 'never want to improve for the simple reason that they think themselves perfect; their vanity is stronger than their misery.'

4.2

Structured action and gendered crime
by James W. Messerschmidt

[. . .]

To structure a comprehensive feminist theory of gendered crime, we must bring men into the framework. However, we should do this not by treating men as the normal subjects, but by articulating the gendered content of men's behavior and of crime. This approach requires a different theoretical lens – one that focuses on a sociology of masculinity – to comprehend why men are involved disproportionately in crime and why they commit different types of crime. [. . .]

First, it is essential to make the relevant theoretical links among class, gender, and race without surrendering to some type of separate systems approach (e.g., capitalism plus patriarchy). Second, it is crucial to construct a theory of crime that recognizes that illegal behavior, like legal behavior, personifies synchronously both social practice and social structure. Indeed, social structures do not exist autonomously from humans; rather, they arise and endure through social practice. Social structures originate, are reproduced, and change through social practice. In short, we can only speak of *structured action*: social structures can be understood only as constituting practice; social structures, in turn, permit and preclude social action.

Individuals exist within the basic structures of society, structures that circumscribe present experience and set limits on future action (Giddens, 1976; 1981). Thus, as we engage in social action, we simultaneously help create the social structures that facilitate/limit social practice. This chapter, then, examines how social action is linked to social structures, identifies specifically how gendered social structures enable and constrain actors in their everyday activity, and analyzes how this relates to crime committed by men.

Appropriate, then, is a theory that conceptualizes how gender, race, and class relations arise within the same ongoing practices (Acker, 1989: 239). For to understand crime by men, we must comprehend how class, race, and gender relations are part of all social existence rather than viewing each relation as outside, and at times encroaching upon, the other two. Crime operates subtly through a complex series of class, race, and gender practices and, as such, is always more than a single activity. Consequently, rather than identifying systems (such as capitalism and patriarchy) and then attempting to interconnect them, we must begin, as Joan Acker (p. 239) suggests, with 'the assumption that social relations are constituted through processes in which the linkages are inbuilt.' That is, social actors maintain and change social structures within any particular interaction, and those social structures simultaneously enable and constrain social action.

I begin by identifying the major social structures in contemporary Western industrialized societies, and then turn to the importance of social action in comprehending crime by men.

Social structures

Social structures, defined here as regular and patterned forms of interaction over time that constrain and channel behavior in specific ways, 'only exist as the reproduced conduct of situated actors' (Giddens, 1976: 127) and construct social relations of relatively durable quality yet of obvious historical variability. Class, race, and gender relations are each constituted by a variety of social structures and, therefore, structured action. Divisions of labor and power are examples of social structures extant in each of the three social relations. Social actors perpetuate and transform these divisions of labor and power within the same interaction and these structures simultaneously constrain and enable social action. The result, as depicted in Figure 4.2.1, is the ongoing social construction of class, race, and gender relations.

Following the important work of Bob Connell (1987) and the insights advanced by radical and socialist feminists, I propose three specific social

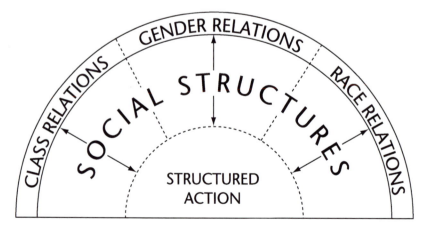

Figure 4.2.1 Social relations, social structures, and structured action

structures underlying relations between women and men: the gender division of labor, gender relations of power, and sexuality.

The gender division of labor

[. . .]
The gender division of labor, a well-known and critical social structural feature of all Western industrialized societies, refers to the fact that the nature of labor performed for species survival is different for men and women. Historically, in Western industrialized societies labor has been divided by gender for (1) housework, (2) child care, (3) unpaid versus paid work, and (4) within the paid labor market and individual workplaces. However, this gender division of labor is not simply attached to an alleged gender-neutral class structure. Rather, like race, gender divisions are a fundamental feature of all forms of production.

The form and character of the gender division of labor have undergone fundamental historical transformation. Although gathering/hunting societies maintained highly egalitarian gender divisions of labor, a pronounced masculine-dominated gender division of labor first appeared in horticultural societies (Draper, 1975; Messerschmidt, 1986). In sixteenth- and seventeenth-century Europe, production was organized on the basis of the household unit to which all members contributed. [. . .]

Nevertheless, by no means were women the social equals of men [. . .].

With the onset of industrialization in mid-1800s England, some types of production were removed from the home and organized on a large scale. [. . .] Thus, the productive resources of the household unit left the home and entered the wage-labor market. And with this change, the gender division of labor became more entrenched. As Hartmann (1979: 217) has shown, in the paid-labor market the dominant position of men was maintained through gendered job segregation:

> Women's jobs were lower paid, considered less skilled, and often involved less exercise of authority or control. Men acted to enforce job segregation in the labor market; they utilized trade union associations and strengthened the domestic division of labor which required women to do housework, childcare, and related chores. Women's subordinate position in the labor market reinforced their subordinate position in the family, and that in turn reinforced their labor market position.

[. . .]
By 1840, however, the wage labor of the working-class family outside the home began to change, as men working in factories lobbied for an eight-hour day for working children under the age of thirteen and for a ban on employment of children under the age of nine. The exploitation of children was viewed by men as undercutting their own wages (p. 28). Ironically, one

negative effect of subsequent child-labor laws concerned parental difficulties with child care: problems with the training and supervision of working-class children (Hartmann, 1979: 217–218).

Married women who worked in the paid labor force were accused of deserting their children to 'steal men's jobs,' and single women in the paid labor force were criticized for growing up without the proper domestic feminine socialization it was argued they needed to be competent wives and mothers (Seccombe, 1986: 66–67). Moreover, widespread employment of women constituted a direct threat 'to the job security and wage levels of skilled tradesmen' (p. 67). Consequently, working-class men and the upper classes began to recommend that women, in addition to children, be removed from wage labor in the factories. Unions controlled by men fought for and won 'protective legislation' for women, limiting the number of hours they could work. Moreover, men denied women training for skilled work and eventually drove them out of trade unions (Hartmann, 1979: 226).

Consequently, for the upper layers of the white working class, a 'family wage' developed that was barely sufficient to allow women to remain at home, raise the children, and maintain the family. In this way, rather than having all family members working in the labor force, men appropriated both the position of breadwinner in the labor market and the labor of women in the home. This is not to imply that men operated entirely consciously to subjugate women. Rather, operating within a particularized masculine-dominated gender division of labor, white working-class men strongly resisted the destruction of the patriarchal household unit and attempted to ameliorate the oppressive nature of the wage-labor system on 'their women.' In addition, although many women resisted the family-wage system, many others viewed the workplace as a desperate and dangerous place for them and for their children. Thus, along with their husbands, these women supported the family-wage system.

[. . .]

As seen through the lens of a theory of structured action, the family-wage system validated the husband/father as the sole breadwinner with all but sufficient earnings to maintain his wife and children who did not earn wages outside the home. The family-wage system was supportive of the class division of labor in that it helped guarantee a more stable and healthy work force as well as a reserve army of labor ready to be drawn into the paid-labor force.

Yet it also maintained, albeit in restructured form, masculine domination of the gender division of labor. This rearranged gender division of labor constituted the social construction of a new type of white-adult masculinity – full-time work in the paid-labor force as the sole breadwinner – and white-adult femininity, the full-time mother/housewife. As Jessie Bernard (1982: 207) points out, hegemonic masculinity became associated with being a 'good provider': 'The good provider had to achieve, to win, to succeed, to dominate. He was a bread*winner*.'

This of course differed by race and class. African American men were largely excluded from labor unions, and so worked either for low wages at menial jobs or were unemployed. This is one of the reasons why so many African American married women worked in wage-labor domestic and service jobs (Ferguson, 1991: 86). Consequently, African American men were without the resources to construct a 'breadwinner/good provider' form of masculinity and African-American women shaped a femininity centered on more than their own domesticity and child rearing.

Middle-class, white men, not only expected to be breadwinners/good providers, also developed masculinities centered on expertise, technical knowledge, rationality, and calculation (the 'bureaucrat' and the 'business-man' emerged as social types). White working-class masculinities were organized around holding a steady job, bringing pay home reliably, skill and endurance in paid labor, and a combative solidarity among wage earners (Connell, 1992: 12; Seccombe, 1986; 62). Accordingly, the family-wage system simultaneously formed practices that reproduced class, gender, and race divisions of labor, thereby constructing whiteness as a class-specific gendered phenomenon.

Separation of the center of production from the household unit to the public workplace enhanced white masculine dominance. For the first time in history, white women were thrust 'to the margins of economic activity' (Young, 1981: 59). Moreover, women's work in the home was devalued, causing women to become even more economcally dependent on men for survival (Andersen, 1988: 151) [. . .].

Yet class, race, and gender relations were simultaneously reproduced at the site of domestic labor. Paralleling the changes in the division of labor, the number of women employed as domestic servants expanded rapidly. Most white middle-class women were in the position to hire primarily women of color to perform much of the domestic tasks of cleaning house, laundering and ironing clothes, scrubbing floors, and caring for infants and children (Palmer, 1990). [. . .]

Glenn (1992: 32) shows that from the late 1800s to around the 1920s, African American, Mexican American, and Japanese American women were drawn into domestic service work by a 'combination of economic need, restricted opportunities, and educational and employment tracking systems.' White middle-class women justified employing women of color by arguing that they were especially suited for domestic service. As Glenn (p. 14) states:

These racial justifications ranged from the argument that Black and Mexican women were incapable of governing their own lives and thus were dependent on whites – making white employment of them an act of benevolence – to the argument that Asian servants were naturally quiet, subordinate, and accustomed to a lower standard of living. Whatever the specific content of the racial characterizations, it defined the proper place of these groups as in service: they belonged there, just as it was the dominant groups place to be served.

In short, within the context of a family-wage system, throughout everyday interaction, social actors simultaneously produced class, race, and gender divisions of labor in both the market and the home. The outcome was not only the ongoing social construction of class, race, and gender relations, but specific configurations of race/class masculinities and femininities.

The family-wage system stabilized materially and ideologically until World War II (1941). However, with the economic developments of the postwar period, the family-wage system and the breadwinner power of white men have significantly diminished (although the notion that paid work equals masculinity persists). Periodic inflation, unstable wages, heightened individual expectations, and material accumulation generated by advertising have compelled working-class and most middle-class families to rely on two wage earners to maintain the standard of living previously underwritten by the single breadwinner (Burstyn, 1983: 62). In addition, the ever-increasing search for new areas of investment and development has resulted in the expansion of service and clerical jobs. Again, ironically, these developments created conditions that encouraged many women to move out of the home and into wage labor to meet the demands of capital.

Outside the home, however, working women have been segregated (for the most part) into 'female jobs' – clerical, service, nursing, teaching, and cleaning of all kinds. And these jobs are simultaneously racialized: white women are preferred in public positions, such as waitress, hairdresser, and dental assistant, while women of color are preferred in 'dirty back-room jobs as maids, janitors/cleaners, kitchen workers, and nurse's aids' (Glenn, 1992: 20). Thus the gender and race divisions of labor have been restructured in the labor market so that women generally do the same type of work they do in the home.

Gendered job segregation maintains a reduced status for women and channels them generally into low-wage positions. Today, women earn approximately two-thirds what men earn, a differential wage that aids in defining women's work as secondary to men's work. Moreover, although more and more women work as wage laborers, they continue to do the major share of unpaid labor in the home (Ferguson, 1991; Folbre, 1982). Consequently, men (primarily white men) continue to benefit from higher wages in the labor market and from the work women do in the home. [. . .]

More importantly, however, new forms of masculinity and femininity emerged concurrently with these changing structural conditions. Regarding the former, Barbara Ehrenreich (1989: 217–218) has shown that by the mid-seventies 'the old notion that a working wife was a sure sign of male inadequacy was hard to find in any class.' Although the notion of men as primary wage earners and the connection of paid work to masculinity persists, hegemonic masculinity is no longer based on being the sole bread-winner. Thus, although the gender division of labor is reproduced in the paid-labor market, new constructions of masculinity and femininity are emerging from the identical ongoing practices.

[. . .]

Gender relations of power

[. . .]

A manifestation of gender relations of power is the obvious structural fact that men control the economic, religious, political, and military institutions of authority and coercion in society. In addition to such large-scale institutional power, gender power organizes advantage and inequality within smaller social groups and institutions (e.g., the family, peer group, and workplace), thereby providing men the legitimate authority to impose a definition on specific situations (Connell, 1987: 107). Because in gender relations the interests of men more often prevail over the interests of women, in most (but clearly not all) situations, men are able to impose authority, control, and coercion over women. Such power provides the means with which to arrange social life to the advantage of men, thus paving the way for greater legitimate and illegitimate opportunities. [. . .]

[. . .] Although material resources may clearly enhance masculine power, they are often unnecessary at the interpersonal level for the actual realization of that power. Indeed, a woman may have far superior material resources than an unemployed man, yet he nevertheless may exercise interpersonal power in the form of, for example, rape. That exercise of power is more than merely an individual embodiment; it is structural by being profoundly embedded in power inequalities: 'Far from being a deviation from the social order, it is in a significant sense an enforcement of it' (Connell, 1987: 107). Thus, authority and control become defining characteristics not only of gender relations, but of the social construction of masculinities as well.

Power among men is likewise unequally distributed since some groups of men (in terms of class, race, and sexual preference, for instance) have greater authority and, therefore, more power than others (Connell, 1987: 109). In other words, the capacity to exercise power is always a reflection of one's position in social relations. For example, in colonial America, 'white men as husbands had control over their wives and as fathers control over their child-ren's marriages and access to family property, but Afro-American male slaves had no such patriarchal rights' (Ferguson, 1991: 113). [. . .]

[. . .] [C]lass, race, and gender relations of power are produced simul-taneously within the same ongoing practices and, accordingly, not only does the exercise of power over women differ among men, but also among men themselves. Heterosexual men exercise greater power than gay men, upper-class men greater power than working-class men, and white men greater power than men of color. Power, then, is a relationship that structures social interaction not only between men and women, but among men as well. As the chapters that follow will show, this differing degree of power among men significantly impacts the varieties of masculinities constructed and, consequently, crimes committed by men.

Nevertheless, power is not absolute but a contested terrain of social practice that is historically variable (Connell, 1987: 108–111). As Kathy Davis (cited in Segal, 1990: 261) has argued, power is never simply a matter of 'haves' and 'have nots':

> Such a conception can only lead to an over-estimation of the power of the powerful, closing our eyes to the chinks in the armour of the powerful as well as the myriad ways that the less powerful have to exercise control over their lives, even in situations where stable, institutionalised power relations are in operation.

At any point in space and time, gender relations of power promote and constrain the social action of both men and women, and conflict and resistance is pervasive. Notwithstanding, the social structure of gendered power is basic to understanding not only why men engage in more crime than women but also why men engage in different types and degrees of crime.

Sexuality

In addition to the social divisions of labor and power, sexuality is a major social structural feature of gender relations and, therefore, of the social construction of masculinity. Over the last fifteen years, an important and sophisticated historical scholarship has demonstrated three salient features of sexuality. First, sexuality is socially constructed and not biologically ordained. Beginning with Michel Foucault's *The History of Sexuality* (1978) and continuing with the important works of Jeffrey Weeks (1981, 1986) and Gayle Rubin (1984), research has consistently shown that forms of sexuality are constructed in historically specific social practices. Accordingly, sexuality varies not only from society to society but within societies themselves. Sexuality is not, therefore, a biological constant but a product of human agency.

Second, historically, certain sexual practices have been restricted. Plummer (1984) has shown that most societies define who are 'appropriate' partners – for example, in terms of gender, class, race, age, and species – and restrict the human organs that may be used, the orifices entered, what is touched, with what frequency, and so on. These definitions and restrictions provide the permissions, prohibitions, limits, and possibilities with which erotica and desire are constructed (Weeks, 1986: 27). For instance, in some New Guinea societies, homosexual activities are obligatory for all men and homosexual acts are considered utterly masculine; yet such men and their society do not view them as homosexuals (Rubin, 1984: 285). [. . .]

Third, the result of the foregoing is that in Western industrialized societies, a hierarchical system of sexual value exists, with marital-reproductive heterosexuals alone at the top, followed closely by unmarried heterosexuals, those who prefer solitary sexuality, lesbians and gay men, prostitutes, transvestites, and sado-masochists (Rubin, 1984: 279). Thus, heterosexuality is deemed normative and carries 'injunctions to love and marry the right kind of person, to find such-and-such a kind of masculinity or femininity desirable' (Connell, 1987: 112). [. . .]

The result is that 'deviant' sexual identities are ridiculed, policed, and repressed; not surprisingly, heterosexuality becomes a fundamental indication of 'maleness.' However, it is not simply heterosexuality, but a particular type of heterosexuality. Hegemonic masculinity is currently established through an alleged uncontrollable and insatiable sexual appetite for women, which results in a 'naturally' coercive 'male' sexuality. [. . .]

Yet while normative heterosexuality structures hegemonic masculinity as well as specific forms of sexual incitement and inequalities between sexualities, simultaneously it is organized on the basis of gendered relations of power. For example, female sexuality has historically been limited by (1) economic and social dependence on men, (2) the power of men to define sexuality, (3) the limitations of marriage, (4) the burdens of reproduction, and (5) the endemic fact of violence by men against women (Weeks, 1986: 39). The 'male' insatiable sex drive empowers men, shapes women as objects of heterosexual desire, and delineates lesbianism as mysterious, incomprehensible, and pathological (Smart, 1989[b]: 30). As Connell (1987: 113) argues:

A heterosexual woman is sexualized as an object in a way that a heterosexual man is not. The fashion industry, the cosmetics industry, and the content of the mass media are tangible proof of this. For instance, the glamour shots on the covers on women's magazines and men's magazines are pictures of women in both cases; the difference is in the way the models are dressed and posed. Broadly speaking, the erotic reciprocity in hegemonic heterosexuality is based on unequal exchange.

For many women, economic survival entails learning to present themselves as sexual beings. As Alison Jaggar (1983: 308–309) points out:

[. . .] much of women's paid work is sexualized; and, in the end, the best chance of economic security for most women remains the sale of their sexuality in marriage . . .

[. . .] Consequently, while sexuality is clearly a domain of extensive exploration and pleasure for women today, it remains simultaneously a site where gendered oppression may occur – violence, brutality, and coercion – and a site of considerable gendered repression of women's desire and sexual pleasure. Thus, normative heterosexuality helps legitimize the ideology that women are dependent on men for their sexual and economic well-being and simultaneously denigrates women's relationships with other women.

Because normative heterosexuality likewise is based on power relations, not only between sexualities but also between men and women, it defines masculinity through difference from, and desire for, women. Normative heterosexuality therefore is not only a major structural feature for understanding gender, but for understanding masculinities and crimes committed by men as well.

Structured action

[. . .]

[. . .] [C]omprehension of these social structures is only part of the gender equation. As stated earlier in this chapter, it is essential to theorize structure and action as one and the same. Giddens (1981: 171) similarly argues that a social structure consists of 'both the medium and outcome of the social practices it recursively organizes.' In other words, social structures are 'both constituted *by* human agency and yet at the same time are the very *medium* of this constitution' (Giddens, 1976: 121). In this sense, structure is not external to the agent, nor is it simply and solely constraining. Rather, structure is implicated in social action and social action is implicated in structure, so that structure both constrains and enables social action.

To understand why men engage in more and different types of crimes than women and in differing amounts and forms among themselves, we need an adequate account of social action. We can begin by recognizing that in society all individuals engage in purposive behavior and monitor their own action reflexively. That is, we comprehend our actions and we modify them according to (among other things) our interpretation of other people's responses. Social action is creative, inventive, and novel, but it never occurs separately from, or external to, social structures. Social structures are constituted by social action and, in turn, provide resources and power from which individuals construct 'strategies of action' (Swidler, 1986: 227). Social structures organize the way individuals think about their circumstances and generate methods for dealing with them.

[. . .]

Gender as situated accomplishment

In a series of articles, West, Zimmerman, and Fenstermaker (West and Zimmerman, 1987; Fenstermaker, West, and Zimmerman, 1991; West and Fenstermaker, 1993) distinguish 'sex' (one's birth classification), 'sex category' (the social identification as a woman or man), and 'gender' (social action validating that identification). They agree with Goffman and Kessler and McKenna that we attribute the 'correct' sex to individuals when they display the appropriate social signs of a sex category. We attempt to adorn ourselves in a culturally appropriate 'female' or 'male' fashion and daily, in every interaction, we engage in gender attribution – we identify and categorize people in an appropriate sex category while we simultaneously categorize ourselves for others.

Nevertheless, the concepts of gender display and gender attribution are not wholly sufficient in and of themselves. West, Zimmerman, and Fenstermaker argue correctly that *gender* entails much more than simply the social signs of a sex category. Rather, it involves a 'situated accomplishment,' that is, 'the activity of managing situated conduct in light of normative conceptions, attitudes, and activities appropriate to one's sex category' (West and Zimmerman, 1987: 127). Thus, while sex category refers to social identification as a woman or man, gender is the processual corroboration of that identification and is accomplished in social interaction; we coordinate our activities to 'do' gender in situational ways.

Crucial to the conceptualization of gender as a situated accomplishment is the notion of 'accountability': 'the possibility of describing activities, states of affairs, and descriptions themselves in serious and consequential ways – for example, as "manly" or "womanly" behaviors' (Fenstermaker, West, and Zimmerman, 1991: 294). Because individuals realize their behavior is accountable to others, they construct their actions in relation to how they might be interpreted by others in the particular social context in which they occur. Since sex category is always pertinent, an 'individual involved in virtually any course of action may be held accountable for her/his execution of that action *as a woman or a man*' (p. 294). Because we believe there are but two natural sexes, we attempt to become one of them.

Moreover, we expect others to attribute a particular sex category to us – a sex category that corresponds to our 'essential nature' – and we satisfy the ongoing task of accountability by demonstrating that we are a 'male' or a 'female' by means of concocted behaviors that may be interpreted accordingly. We configure our behaviors so we are seen unquestionably by others in particular social situations as expressing our 'essential natures' – we do masculinity or femininity. As Fenstermaker, West, and Zimmerman (p. 294) conclude, 'doing gender involves the management of conduct by sexually categorized human beings who are accountable to local conceptions of appropriately gendered conduct.'

In this view, then, masculinity is accomplished, it is not something done to men or something settled beforehand. And masculinity is never static, never a finished product. Rather, men construct masculinities in specific social situations (although not in circumstances of their own choosing); in so doing, men reproduce (and sometimes change) social structures. [. . .]

Behavior by men is obviously considerably more complex than that suggested by the idea of a universal masculinity that is preformed and embedded in the individual prior to social action. [. . .] In contrast, what is being suggested here is that men 'come to be involved in a *self-regulating process*' as they monitor their own and others' gendered conduct (West and Zimmerman, 1987: 142). The accomplishment of gender 'involves not only the appropriation of gender ideals (by the valuation of those ideals as proper ways of being and behaving) but also *gender identities* that are important to individuals and that they strive to maintain' (p. 142). [. . .]

Masculinity personifies the construction of personal history up to a specific point in time and exemplifies the unification of self-regulated practices. These practices do not, however, occur in a vacuum. Rather, they are influenced by the gender ideals we have come to accept as normal and proper and by the social structural constraints we experience. Because men reproduce masculine ideals in structured specific practices, there are a variety of ways of 'doing masculinity' (and femininity). Although masculinity is always individual and personal, specific forms of masculinity are available, encouraged, and permitted, depending upon one's class, race, and sexual preference. Masculinity must be viewed as structured action – what men do under specific constraints and varying degrees of power. As Connell (1987: 222) perceptively notes, we are 'not monads closed off from others' but experience ourselves as 'having shared pasts and sharing the present.'

In this way, then, social relations (which are constituted by social structures) place each of us in a common relationship to others – we share structural space. Consequently, common or shared blocks of knowledge evolve through interaction, in which particular masculine ideals and activities play a part. Through interaction, masculinity becomes institutionalized, and men draw on such existing, but previously created, masculine ways of thinking and acting to construct a masculine identity in any particular situation. The specific criteria of masculine identities are embedded in the recurrent practices whereby social relations are structured (Giddens, 1989: 285).

Thus, a sociology of masculinity must first recognize that men are positioned differently throughout society and, therefore, share with other men the construction of masculinities peculiar to their position in society. Further, a sociology of masculinity must acknowledge that socially organized power relations among and between men are historically constructed on the basis of class, race, and sexual orientation. In other words, while there is a complex interlocking of masculinities, these masculinities are quite clearly unequal.

Hegemonic and subordinated masculinities

Several pro-feminist men have begun to employ Antonio Gramsci's notion of 'hegemony' to distinguish between 'hegemonic masculinity' and 'subordinated masculinities' (Carrigan et al., 1987; Connell, 1987; Frank, 1987). [. . .]

Simply defined, in any culture, hegemonic masculinity is the idealized form of masculinity in a given historical setting. It is culturally honored, glorified, and extolled, and this 'exaltation stabilizes a structure of dominance and oppression in the gender order as a whole' (Connell, 1990: 94). In contemporary Western industrialized societies, hegemonic masculinity is defined through work in the paid-labor market, the subordination of women, heterosexism, and the driven and uncontrollable sexuality of men. Refined still further, hegemonic masculinity emphasizes practices toward authority, control, competitive individualism, independence, aggressiveness, and the capacity for violence (Connell, 1990, 1992; Segal, 1990). Hegemonic masculinity is substantially different from the notion of a 'male sex role,' because it allows us to move beyond universal and, therefore, categorical formulations of what constitutes 'male' behavior. With it, we are able to explain power relations among men based on a hierarchy of masculinities and see how such masculinities are socially constructed.

The concepts 'hegemonic' and 'subordinated' masculinities also permit investigation of the way men experience their everyday world from a particular position in society and how they relate to and attempt to construct differently (or in fact reject) the cultural ideals of hegemonic masculinity. Because 'most men benefit from the subordination of women, and hegemonic masculinity is the cultural expression of this ascendancy,' most men engage in practices that attempt to sustain hegemonic masculinity (Connell, 1987: 185). Indeed, most men help maintain hegemonic masculinity (and consequently the subordination of women) by means of the practices that reflect their particular positions in society. Thus, the cultural ideals of hegemonic masculinity need not correspond to the actual personalities of most men (pp. 184–185). [. . .]

Structured action and gendered crime

[. . .] Masculinities are constructed through practices that maintain certain types of relationships between men and women and among men (Morgan, 1992: 67). Specific forms of masculinity are constructed in specific situations, and practices within social settings produce, reproduce, and alter types of masculinity. Thus, we 'do gender' (West and Zimmerman, 1987) in response to the socially structured circumstances in which we live and within different social milieux diverse forms of masculinity arise, depending upon prevalent structural potentials and constraints. Because masculinity is a behavioral response to the particular conditions and situations in which men participate, different types of masculinity exist in the school, the youth group, the street, the family, and the workplace. In other words, men do masculinity according to the social situation in which they find themselves.

[. . .]

When men enter a setting, they undertake social practices that demonstrate they are 'manly.' The only way others can judge their 'essential nature' as men is through their behavior and appearance. Thus, men use the resources at their disposal to communicate gender to others. For many men, crime may serve as a suitable *resource* for 'doing gender' – for separating them from all that is feminine. Because types of criminality are possible only when particular social conditions present themselves, when other masculine resources are unavailable, particular types of crime can provide an alternative resource for accomplishing gender and, therefore, affirming a particular type of masculinity. For, although men are always doing masculinity, the significance of gender accomplishment is socially situated and, thus, an intermittent matter. That is, certain occasions present themselves as more intimidating for showing and affirming masculinity. As Coleman (1990: 196) states, 'Such an occasion is where a man's "masculinity" risks being called into question.' The taken-for-granted 'essential nature' of a man or boy can be questioned, undermined, and threatened in certain contexts, those situations where he lacks resources for masculine accomplishment.

In such predicaments, sex category is particularly salient; it is, as David Morgan (1992: 47) puts it, 'more or less explicitly put on the line,' and doing masculinity necessitates extra effort, generating a distinct type of masculinity. Under such conditions, performance as a member of one's sex category is subjected to extra evaluation and crime is more likely to result. Crime, therefore, may be invoked as a practice through which masculinities (and men and women) are differentiated from one another. Moreover, crime is a resource that may be summoned when men lack other resources to accomplish gender.

[. . .]

Crime by men is not simply an extension of the 'male sex role.' Rather, crime by men is a form of social practice invoked as a resource, when other resources are unavailable, for accomplishing masculinity. By analyzing masculinities, then, we can begin to understand the socially constructed differences among men and thus explain why men engage in different forms of crime.

[. . .]

4.3
Masculinities and crime: rethinking the 'man question'?
by Richard Collier

Introduction

The relationship between men, masculinities, and crime has, over the past decade, assumed an increasing prominence within criminology. Indeed, it is arguably a now well-established feature of the criminological landscape; if not the 'very stuff' of the discipline then at least a visible presence in both mainstream journal and criminological textbook (Carlen and Jefferson 1996; Jones 2001; Maguire et al. 1997; Walklate 1995). The issue of how the gender of men – understood as their masculinity or, more recently, masculin*ities* – might connect to crime has been described as a 'new direction' and 'new frontier' (Maguire et al 1997) for criminology to discover. It has been acclaimed as something without which 'there will be no progress,' the study of which is 'vital' (Heidensohn 1995: 80–1: see also Walklate 1995: 160–84). This question of how masculinity connects to crime, criminality, and understandings of social (dis)order has not only become a pressing issue within academic criminology, however. It has also informed a range of concerns and debates bearing directly on the substance and direction of criminal justice policy and practice. For both academic criminologists, those working with male offenders in the diverse fields and contexts of criminal justice and for governments themselves in seeking to develop gender-relevant policies, the integration of a sensitivity to 'the masculinity of crime' has been increasingly foregrounded within debates about criminality and criminal justice. The core assumption throughout has been that there is some analytic gain to be made for criminology by seeking to 'take masculinity seriously.' It is an assumption that, in this essay, I wish to question many aspects of.

[. . .]

Masulinities and Crime presents a rich account of men's crime as a way of "doing" gender (see also Messerschmidt 2000, 1997) and has been rightly heralded as an "extremely important" (Hood-Williams 2001: 53) "significant advance" (Jefferson 1996a: 340) in theorizing masculinity and crime. It has, without question, made a major contribution to the criminological debate on masculinities. As an attempt to integrate the complexities of race, class, gender, and sexuality, and to take structural patterns of inequality seriously, it paved the way for further studies adopting a broadly similar approach in viewing crime as a way of accomplishing masculinity (see, for example, the Australian-based studies of interpersonal male violence by Polk 1994a, 1994b; and, in the UK context, the account of urban disorder by Campbell 1993). Nonetheless, as soon became clear, there are a number of problems with Messerschmidt's approach.

Assessment

Perhaps of greatest significance, not least in view of the fact that the theory is attempting to develop a politically useful engagement with the gender of crime, critics noted a marked failure in Messerschmidt's account to theorize the subjectivity of *individual* men. That is, the question of why some men 'turn to' crime and others do not; 'as is now widely recognized most crime is committed by *highly specific sub-groups of the category "men"* ' (Hood-Williams 2001: 43, original emphasis), men who are themselves often the principal victims of crime (Collier 1998; Hall 2002; Jefferson 1992; Walklate 1995). What is not asked is 'why only *particular* men from a given class or race background (usually only a minority) come to identify with the crime option, while others identify with other resources to accomplish their masculinity' (Jefferson 1996 b: 341). If masculinities are 'offered up' for all men within a sociocultural, structural location, why do men choose one, and not another, masculine identity? And who, in any case, is doing the 'offering up' (Walklate 1995: 180)? It can be argued that most men, regardless of their socio-economic group, 'do' a masculine gender without resorting to (at least certain) crimes. Yet it is difficult to see in structured action theory any account of *why* this should be the case (Jefferson 1994a, '1996b, 1997a); nor, importantly how individual life-history and biography impact on any such 'choice' (see below). In the reproduction of the normative hegemonic masculine ideal, therefore, we find a certain rigidity in how men are seen to accomplish the attributes of dominant masculinity. Structure, in effect, constrains practice to such a degree that, at the very least, it is difficult to see where the contestation and resistance central to Connell's original thesis fit in here.

The above issue relates to the way in which Messerschmidt deploys a particular notion of the masculine social subject; a man conceptualized as a reflexively rational, self-interested being and whose social action, we have seen, relates in a distinctly deterministic way to the cultural norms of hegemonic masculinity (whatever these may be: Collier 1998; Hood-Williams 2001; Jefferson 1994a, 1997a). Yet what is not explained is precisely what it *is* in hegemonic masculinity that causes crime (or, at least, some crimes). Nor, importantly, why the criminal*ized* are nearly always poor and overly black. The idea that 'most crime' is committed by men is 'a highly generalized notion which puts together disparate practices and invites us to treat them as if they were similar' (Hood-Williams 2001: 43). Men, for Messerschmidt and those who have broadly followed his analysis, are seen as 'doing' their gender (masculinity) through engaging in crimes as diverse as burglary, rape, the sexual abuse of children, the taking of motor vehicles without consent, corporate crime, football hooliganism, state terrorism, traffic offences, road rage, violence toward others, and so on (each, it is to be remembered, the subject matter of recent analyses). To account for such diversity in terms of men 'accomplishing' a gender identity is asking a great deal of the concept of masculinity, however. Is it the case that *all* crime is to be explained in this way? Or is it only to be those crimes which are violent and/or destructive which bespeak their origins in masculinity? Men, we have seen, dominate nearly all crimes, though some crimes appear to escape being gendered *as* masculine in ways in which others do not (which begs rather different questions about structure, discourse, and power). Masculinity is depicted as both primary and underlying *cause* (or source) of a social effect (crime); and, simultaneously, as something which itself *results from* (after all, it is accomplished through) recourse *to* crime. As Walklate observes, 'not only does this reflect a failure to resolve fully the tendency towards universalism, it can also be read as tautological' (Walklate 1995: 181).

Hegemonic masculinity appears, ultimately, an unambiguously positive attribute for men in the sense that it is, for a host of (unexplored) psychological imperatives, something which is desired, to be achieved, to be accomplished. Yet leaving aside the fact that the qualities presently associated with manhood are not necessarily considered negative (or positive) in all cultural contexts, and that crime itself does not *necessarily* require strength, toughness, aggression, violence, and so forth, critics have taken issue with Messerschmidt's underlying assumption that the experience of being masculine is itself premised on the domination of women and children. The cultural valorization of hegemonic masculinity certainly correlates strongly with – if it is not inherently interlinked to – various destructive, violent ways of 'being a man.' Yet, Hearn suggests, what is really depicted as negative about men here is itself, in effect, a description of culturally masculine traits (Hearn 1996: 207). These, certainly, conjure up powerful images about men and crime and speak to an empirical reality inasmuch as, as we have seen, most crime is almost unimaginable without the presence of men (Jefferson 1992: 10). However they remain, ultimately, popular ideologies of what constitutes the ideal or actual characteristics of being a man at particular historical moments and cultural contexts (Hearn 1996). Messerschmidt's account seems to open up an analysis of the diversity of masculinities. Yet it would appear to do so in such a way as to simultaneously *hold in place* a normative masculine gender to which is then assigned a range of (usually undesirable/negative) characteristics. As such it imposes: 'an a priori theoretical/conceptual frame on the psychological complexity of men's behavior. What continues to be evaded . . . are the ways in which each act of aggression or kindness, sensitivity or independence, self-sacrifice or selfishness is itself encoded at particular moments and locations as a "masculine" or "feminine" attribute' (Collier 1998: 22).

The fact that the political, cultural, and ethical qualities of the 'acceptable masculine' may be far removed from this hegemonic form within late modern gender regimes – or that they are, at the very least, more psychologically complex than this model would allow (Wetherell and Edley 1999: see further below) – is an issue which tends to be effaced in Messerschmidt's account. And, notwithstanding the continued 'salience' of the accomplishing masculinity thesis for criminology (Goodey 2000: 489), it is this issue of the complexity and multi-layered nature of the masculine social subject with which a 'third stage' in thinking about masculinities has been primarily concerned (Jefferson 1996a: also Hood-Williams 2001).

Later developments: the (masculine) psycho-social subject

In the work of Tony Jefferson, either writing alone (1994a, 1996a, 1996b, 1996c, 1997a, 1997b, 1998) or with Wendy Hollway (Hollway and Jefferson 1996, 1997, 1998, 2000), a concerted effort has been made to move thinking about masculinity and crime onto a 'different level' (Jefferson 1996b). Jefferson's work constitutes, first and foremost, an attempt to explore the tensions between the *social* and *psychic* processes which inform men's experience of masculinity. It is presented as an explicit challenge to etiological criminology to take the 'psychic dimensions of subjectivity' seriously (Jefferson 1994a). It is not possible to do justice here to either the complexity of the substantive analyses which have been produced on this topic (for example, in relation to the boxer Mike Tyson, on date rape, sexual harassment, and the fear of crime: Jefferson 1996b, 1997b, 1998; Hollway and Jefferson 1996, 1997, 1998); nor the complex groundings of this work within contemporary psychoanalysis (on which see further Adams 1996; Chodorow 1994; Elliot 1994, 1996; Hood-Williams 1997; Hood-Williams and Cealey Harrison 1998). It is possible, however, to trace briefly some of the key characteristics of this development in the masculinities and crime literature with a view to establishing how it differs from, as well as what it shares with, Messerschmidt's account.

The psycho-social approach is based on a fusing of aspects of poststructuralist and psychoanalytic theory. From the former it is the concept of discourse, rather than that of social structure, which is utilized (cf. Pease 1999). In contrast to traditional psychoanalysis, what is placed center-stage is an attempt to engage with the presentational forms of 'masculine' performances, identities, corporeal enactments, and so forth (cf. Butler 1990, 1993; also Bell and Valentine 1995; Gatens 1996; Grosz 1990, 1994; Grosz and Probyn 1995). At the same time, the approach rejects the idea of the unitary rational subject which Jefferson argues is implicit within Messerschmidt's determinist structured action model, as above. The focus of analysis shifts, in contrast, to the way in which a non-unitary and 'inherently contradictory' subject comes [himself] to invest – whether consciously and unconsciously – in what are seen as empowering social discourses around masculinity (Jefferson 1996b, 1998). Jefferson's subsequent work in this area has been made up, accordingly, of a series of analyses which have sought, in different ways but utilizing a broadly similar theoretical framework, to develop a *social* understanding of the masculine *psyche* which might, it is argued, then shed some light on the relationship between men, masculinities and crime (Jefferson 1996b: 341–2).

Assessment

By engaging with the notion of a dynamic unconscious this perspective recognizes, Jefferson suggests, the complexity of male subjectivity in such a way as to 'prize open' the possibility 'of making sense of the contradictions and difficulties that particular men experience in becoming masculine' (Jefferson 1994a: 28–9). That is, by integrating questions of individual biography and life-history (Hollway and Jefferson 1997; 2000), and addressing the lived experience and contradictions of 'being masculine,' a handle is given on the important question, noted above, of why some men do, and others do not, engage in certain crimes: 'Placing the individual's biography within social structural forces [in this way] recognizes the *reality*, and not simply the theoretical *rhetoric*, of relative power and powerlessness experienced by different men throughout their lives' (Goodey 2000: 489, my emphasis).

It is no longer an overarching, all-encompassing social structure or gender norm which is seen as accounting for the crimes of men. It is within the complex interaction between the social realm and the individual psyche that the disposition or motivation of particular men toward particular actions is located (see, e.g., the readings of Mike Tyson: Jefferson 1998, 1997a, 1996b, 1996c). Crime is depicted, in effect, as the product of a range of biographically contingent anxieties and desires; the 'choice' to commit crime is, like the fear of crime itself, not necessarily exercised or experienced rationally or logically. The psyche is, rather, understood as constantly defending itself against unconscious and powerful anxieties and desires producing psychological defenses which 'are not only produced but are necessary. Necessary, but not without contradictions' (Walkerdine 1995: 327).

This would appear to be a great advance politically on the (always, already) empowered masculine subject implicit in Messerschmidt's work. Jefferson does not ignore the all-too-real social costs of men's crimes, be it for women, children, or other men, but seeks, rather, to 'appreciate' the contradictory nature of social experience; for example, the coexistence of feelings of empowerment and powerlessness on the part of men (see, by way of illustration, the readings of domestic violence produced by Gadd 2002). What then emerges, it is suggested, is the possibility of developing a progressive politics of change which might recognize how the psychodynamic dimensions of social experience can be pervaded as much by emotional ambivalence and contradiction as any straightforward hegemonic masculine identification (Connell 1995; Goodey 1997, 2000; Jackson 1990; Thurston 1996; see further Hollway and Jefferson 1997; Edley and Wetherell 1997; and cf. Messerschmidt 2000). As such, this is an argument which would appear to resonate with themes in existing accounts of male offenders themselves (Graef 1992), as well as having clear implications for criminal justice policy; for example, in questioning many assumptions underlying the cognitive-behavioral frameworks which have, to date, tended to underpin many govern-mental strategies in dealing with male offenders across a range of spheres (see further Gadd 2000; on the fear of crime, Hollway and Jefferson 2000).

Notwithstanding what some have seen as the clear advantages of this approach over and above structured action theory, however, such a 'merging' of poststructuralist and psychoanalytic theory has not escaped criticism. The charge that this is an approach which (to put it mildly) sits uneasily with the sociological moorings of criminology is one which advocates of the psychosocial approach might easily dismiss. The very *point*, indeed, is that sociogenic criminology has failed to engage with the 'inner life' of a complex male subject. The well-established broader critique of psychoanalysis, how-ever, remains pertinent in this context. The relation of these accounts to *other* psychoanalytic traditions, non-psychoanalytic psychology or, indeed, the idea that there might be multiple psychological mechanisms of subjective 'positioning' is, at best, uncertain. Leaving aside the question of whether the particular strand of Kleinian psychoanalysis and object relations theory invoked in Jefferson's work is itself premised on an unduly mechanistic model of personality formation, the argument remains that, although psy-choanalysis (of whatever form) might offer a rich story for describing the emergence of fantasies of sexual difference, these remain, at the end of the day, just that: stories. It is difficult to see, for example, how the kinds of readings produced by Jefferson of individual men (say, Mike Tyson) can ever be tested or proven in any meaningful way. Is what we are left with, ultim-ately, no more than a reflection of the researcher's own projection (no more, or less, plausible than any other reading) (Frosh 1994, 1997)? Or are we reduced, effectively, to an 'all is discourse' position which, in disavowing an outer reality, embraces a wholly semiotic account in which 'with so much emphasis on the signifier, the signified tends to vanish' (Connell 1995: 50–1)? Is it only the trained psychologist, counselor, or academic expert who is able to ascertain what is 'really' behind an individual's actions? It is open to question whether the linear 'third-stage' thinking presented by Jefferson is not equally as androcentric as the social structure theory it claims to super-sede in the way in which it betrays a profoundly positivistic notion of pro-gression (from first, to second, to third stage . . .) in depicting what is, ultimately, a 'grand theory' of the crimes of men (cf. Smart 1990). As Hood-

Williams (2001) notes, it is very difficult to maintain simultaneously that, on the one hand, psychoanalysis is just one of many 'discourses of subjectification' whereby gendered identities become attached to individuals; and, on the other hand, to maintain that the claims it is making are grounded in real, historically specific, and *irreducible* psychological processes which result from the contingent dynamics of (in this case) pre-Oedipal attachment.

The implications in terms of policy and practice are similarly uncertain. Even *if* it is accepted that it is psychoanalysis, and not some other approach, that is necessary to theorize the subject, it remains unclear how theorizing subjectivity at the level of the individual can ever be an effective strategy in facilitating social change in a broader sense (for example, in reducing the incidence of crime in general, or in relation to certain crimes). The potential policy implications are, taking on the methodological difficulties and logic of the approach to their conclusion, arguably so far-reaching as to appear unmanageable. By what criteria is one offender to be chosen for intervention or analysis over and above another? Both offender and prosecutor, prison inmate and officer, policeman and young offender, government minister and 'hooligan,' criminology student and teacher each appear locked, albeit in different ways, in a complex matrix of defenses and projections, splitting, and introjections. Given that this always-defended masculine subject is constituted in a complex interaction with other individuals, at what point does it become necessary to engage with the accounts of others in order to obtain anything like a 'complete' picture of an individual, and with a view to 'appreciating' their biography? Or is it the case that what we are left with here is, ultimately, simply a call to engage with a gendered (masculine) culture and a certain form of (hegemonic) masculinity – something which is not dissimilar, in effect, to that found within structured action theory?

The limits of masculinity

Although 'certainly provisional' in nature (Hood-Williams 2001: 54), it has been from outside of the discipline of criminology (or, at the very least, on its fringes) that a rather different set of questions about the relationship between men and crime has emerged. Coming from the interface of feminist, queer, materialist, and postmodern theory, within this recent sociological scholarship (work depicted as potentially 'gate-crash[ing] . . . the criminological party', Groombridge 1999: 532) there has occurred a growing questioning of the concept of masculinity which has involved (amongst other things) a reappraisal of what it means to speak of, perform, or (in Messerschmidt's account) 'do' a masculine gender (Collier 1998; Hearn 1996; MacInnes 1998; McMahon 1999; Pease 1999). Such a development can be seen, on one level, as part of a broader concern within the social sciences to develop a self-reflective 'science of the subject' (Hood-Williams 2001: 54); to take seriously, that is, how a particular social experience (let us say, of being a

man) might be 'offered to thought in the form of a problem requiring attention' (Rose and Valverde 1998: 545; cf. Smart 1989a: ch. 1; see also Rose
1994). And such a questioning of the analytic status of masculinity can be
seen to chime in certain respects with the broadly Foucauldian-inspired
engagement with the role of mechanisms, arenas, functionaries, forms of reasoning, and so forth in late modern societies which is itself a tradition well
represented within contemporary criminological thought (Rose and Valverde
1998: 546; cf. Naffine 1997; Rose 1999, 1994, 1989, 1987). Nonetheless,
what we have here is a development which does raise important questions
about what criminology is seeking to achieve in 'taking masculinity seriously.'

Both the structured action and psychosocial perspectives discussed above
do engage, in different ways, with this question of how *ideas* of masculinity
become problematized at particular historical moments and contexts. Yet both
approaches stand in an uneasy relation, as we have seen, to some essentialist
conceptualizations of masculinity itself – whether it is in the tendency of structured action theory to depict a mechanistic relation between masculinity, culture, and crime or in the psychosocial grounding of gender difference in
irreducible psychic processes. It is open to question, ultimately, just how
adequate the concept of masculinity is when seeking to explain, understand, or
otherwise account for the crimes of men. The general use of masculinity in this
context has been seen as premised on 'heterosexist' and heterosexual assumptions (Groombridge 1999: also Collier 1998), as 'an ethnocentric or even a
Eurocentric notion,' a product of a particular historical moment which is, in
some cultural contexts, at best 'irrelevant or misleading' (Hearn, 1996: 209;
cf., e.g., Connell 1995: 30–4; Gilmour 1993; Mangan and Walvin 1987; also
MacInnes 1998; Pease 1999). And it has been depicted as analytically impre-
cise; 'it is as if this concept exemplifies [a] field of concern and even, possibly,
distils the aggregation of activity of men in the social world into one neat word'
(Hearn 1996: 202; see, by way of response, to these charges Connell 2002).
Criminological conceptualizations of masculinity have themselves, as Judith
Allen suggested back in 1989 (predating the largely male-dominated current
masculinity turn), tended to perpetuate a 'stranglehold grip of Cartesian-style
dualisms by trading in uneven oppositions around the mind and the body, the
real and the romantic, the scientific and the fantastic' (Murphy 1996: 57; note
also Cousins 1980). Both the structured action and psychosocial perspectives,
in 'categoriz[ing] . . . a vast range of activities and treat[ing] . . . them as if they
were all subject to the same laws' (Smart 1990: 77; in effect, laws of gender),
can be seen to be framed by, and as seeking to develop, a criminological project
premised on giving 'primacy to one form of explanation rather than another'
(Smart 1990: 77). Yet it is this very kind of thinking for which, some critics
have suggested, the time has '[itself] now passed' (Hood-Williams 2001: 53;
also Collier 1998; Groombridge 1999).

Beyond this issue of conceptual ambiguity, the *political* consequences of
focusing an analysis of men, gender, and change on the concept of masculinity

have been called into question. Both the psychosocial readings and structured action accounts are clearly concerned with social practice and questions of politics and power. Yet both, we have seen, tend to presume the existence of normative masculine practices, cultures or identities; things which exist to be accomplished (in Messerschmidt's account) or performed (in Jefferson's more poststructuralist approach). Whether embedded within and reproduced through the interaction of social structure and practice, or else discursively constituted via the contingencies of psyche and society, masculinity continues to be deployed as 'a reference point' against which a range of behavior and identities might be evaluated (Hearn 1996: 203). In each approach, however, while aspects of men's practices may be criticized, the focus of analysis is on the gender category masculinity; it is this which is to be challenged, transcended, or 'changed.' What remains open to question in such a line of thinking, McMahon (1999) suggests, is the extent to which this argument depicts men's gender as something which 'floats free' from what men *do*. That is, male personality appears 'a reification . . . of men's practices (and, of course, the practices of women that support them). [This] reification is then employed to explain these same practices' (McMahon 1993: 689). What is then effaced, McMahon (1999, 1993) argues, is the question of whether men should change their behavior, of men's social *power* relative to women, and of men's individual and collective *interest* in maintaining present gender relations (compare, on the issue of freeing men of the responsibility for seeking to change, Frosh 1994; MacInnes 1998). As a material practice gender cannot be detached from increasingly global(ized) struggles around power and interest (Marchland and Runyan 2000). And 'changing men,' as Connell has long argued (1995, 1987), cannot be reduced to such individual or collective projects of self-actualization.

This is an argument which recasts the question of what criminology is ultimately trying to achieve in 'taking masculinity seriously.' I do not wish to argue that the concept of masculinity has proved ineffective in reconceptualizing the 'problem of men' in relation to crime. It is increasingly rare, at the level of academic criminology at least, to find a collapsing of the politics of crime into familiar questions of class, capital, and/or race in such a way that the 'question of gender' is totally effaced. In the very act of naming men, the subject matter of criminology has (to varying degrees) been transformed. A question remains, however. What, ultimately, is the aim of criminology's masculinity turn? Is it to 'complete' an understanding of crime (Walklate 1995: 180), to provide, as it were, an ultimate Truth, the final piece of the (modernist) jigsaw? Is it to make mainstream criminology aware of feminism and gender perspectives, reeducating (presumably male?) criminologists to the inequalities of sex/gender? If so, then it is to misread Connell's (1987) original point about the ways in which *all* men are empowered by hegemonic masculinity:

How can we expect democratic reform of gender relations from an institution that is dominated by those who benefit from the present gender order? What kind of reform process could possibly transform the gendered character of the state, without being trapped by the politics of social control in which the state is enmeshed? (Connell 1993: xvi)

Notwithstanding the (re)discovery of masculinity by criminology, the masculinity *of* criminology remains profoundly suspect (cf. Rock 1988, 1994). And in such a context, and bearing in mind the disciplinary research imperative to seek out new subject matters, new disciplinary terrains – to boldly go where no criminologist has gone before – whether the discipline of criminology will ever adequately address the sexed specificity of crime in the way that some of the protagonists within the masculinity debate hope is perhaps open to question – certainly for as long as criminology itself remains trapped in ways of thinking which make it so difficult to 'see' the interconnections between men, gender, and power in the first place (Collier 1998: ch. 1; see also Naffine 1997; Young 1996).

What of the future? By the mid-1990s masculinity and crime was a topic being described within Anglo-American criminology as an area in which 'much more . . . work needs to be done' (Walklate 1995: 181), a 'barely started project' (Jefferson 1996b: 342; see also *Masculinity and Crime* (Messerschmidt 1993b)). Less than a decade on it may well be that the ebb and flow of academic fashion – and commissioning editors' perceptions of commercially viable topics – has moved on. It is surely significant, however, that the vast majority of criminological scholarship, of whatever political or theoretical hue, continues to feminize a consciousness of 'gender issues' via the routine association of sex/gender with aspects of the still-pervasive 'woman question' – albeit that it might increasingly be doing so in an ostensibly pro-feminist form. 'Gender' continues to be about women. It is all too rarely about questions of men and what men *do*. Far from rendering contingent the historically specific male subject of criminological discourse, whether it is in terms of methodological prescriptions or epistemological assumptions which surround tackling the 'man question,' men arguably remain the unexplored, desexed norm of criminology. A range of cultural discourses are, certainly, problematizing the relationship between men and crime in far reaching ways. They are doing so, however, in such a way that, behind a purportedly progressive rhetoric of equity, issues of power and material interest continue to be systematically marginalized and depoliticized.

To address issues of gender and power in relation to the production of criminological knowledge is not to deny that certain groups of men, rather than men in general, can be seen to benefit (all too clearly) from present social arrangements (Hall 2002). For as long as the 'man question' is silenced at the point of criminological knowledge production, however, then notwithstanding the growing cultural salience of a desire to speak about the 'maleness' of crime, perhaps what we will continue to be left with is, regardless of approach adopted, just the same old story of 'boys' doing [criminological] business' (Newburn and Stanko 1994).

4.4
Gender, class, racism, and criminal justice: against global and gender-centric theories, for poststructuralist perspectives
by Pat Carlen

The title and contents of this paper were provoked by two questions: (1) How important is gender in the theorization of the penal control of lawbreaking women? and (2) How best can the other (non-gendered or more-than-gendered) constituents of unequal power relationships (especially class and racism) be theorized in relation to the gendered constituents? To structure and deconstruct discussion of these two questions, the paper is divided into three parts. The first briefly outlines the main empirical findings, the dominant substantive concepts and the major modes of formal theorizing that have informed recent work on the control of women by the criminal justice and penal systems. The second suggests that poststructuralist perspectives might productively inform new analyses of the relationships between lawbreaking, class, gender, racism and criminal justice in different societies and at different historical conjunctures, and the third addresses some criticisms that feminists have made of poststructuralisms.

Women and criminal justice

During the past fifteen years there has been a much more sustained focus upon the control of women by the criminal justice system than there had been prior to the mid-1970s. Study after study has argued, first, that women's crimes are committed in different circumstances to men's and that women's crimes are usually the crimes of the powerless, and second, that the response to women's lawbreaking is constituted within typifications of femininity and womanhood, which further add to women's oppression. In other words, the emphasis has been upon lawbreaking, women's economic and political powerlessness and their ideological and physical coercion. Dominant constructs informing the analyses of the control of women, therefore, have been those relating to (1) control via ideologies of femininity; (2) control via the economic systems and ideological structures of patriarchy; and (3) control via the politico-economic institutions of family, marriage and welfare. A fourth type of 'control theory' (Hirschi 1969) has been invoked to explain not only women's regulation but also the relatively low rates of women's lawbreaking (Heidensohn 1985 [b]) as well as the actual conditioning of their crimes and punishments (Carlen 1988).

Control via ideologies of femininity

Much of the work that has privileged ideologies of femininity (and masculinity) in explaining the differential social controls imposed on women and men has been of an empirical exposé kind. In unravelling the discourses within which women are controlled as such, ethnographers and deconstructive analysis have also contended that ideologies of femininity are dominant in shaping the regulatory discourses and practices constitutive of the informal control of women in general (Hutter and Williams 1981); the disciplinary regulation of female adolescents in particular (Hudson 1984; Cain 1989); and the discourses and practices of psychiatry (Chesler 1972); the courts (Edwards 1984; Allen 1987); probation (Worrall 1990); and the women's prisons (Carlen 1983).

Most theorists have employed more than one theory to inform analysis of empirical data relating to the social control of women, though it has been a criticism of gender-centric theories that they underplay (or cannot explain) the relationships between gender, class and racism as empirical factors constitutive (albeit in different combinations) of women's experiences and women's consciousness (see, e.g., Rice 1990). Such a criticism, however, involves a realism that assumes that all theories should have a one-to-one relationship, or at least a verisimilitude, with the empirical object. This is not a theoretical tenet that I hold (see Lacan 1977: 171; Ulmer 1985: 88; and below).

Control via economic systems and the ideology of patriarchy

Although several feminist writers on the social control of women have argued that the values and logic of law (both criminal and civil) operate in the interests of men (Smart 1976, 1984; MacKinnon 1983; Dahl 1987; Fineman and Thomadsen 1991), only Messerschmidt (1986) has attempted to develop a theory that posits both the class and the sexual divisions of labor as being equally important factors in lawbreaking. But Messerschmidt's analysis relates only to crime *causation*, not crime *control*, and based upon Hartmann's (1981) definition of patriarchy as 'a set of social relations of power in which the male gender appropriates the labor power of women and controls their sexuality (Messerschmidt 1986: x),' Messerschmidt employs the term patriarchy merely as a descriptive category rather than an explanatory concept. Nonetheless, Messerschmidt's book does have the virtue of insisting upon the mutuality of patriarchal and class relations in *crime* production, though it is unlikely that useful knowledge of the political effects of class and gender phenomena can be gained via their conflation in the process of theoretical production (see Cousins 1978).

My own reluctance to invoke a universalizable concept of patriarchy as providing more than part explanation of the official response to lawbreaking women is that, unmodified by regional analysis, it would imply that the effects of gender relations on criminal law are homogeneous, global and always-already in the interests of men (cf., Cousins 1980). Apart from the fact that such a position would imply that the (male) state has an omniscient feedback mechanism that functions in the interests of all men regardless of race and class, such a position would preempt any possibilities for penal politics and change. It would also be a barrier to the development of regional theories that might wish to privilege (or problematize) either class relations or racism as explanatory (or as yet untheorized) formulations in analyzing the operations of the criminal law.

One substantive area of study, in which analyses of specific instances of patriarchal domination have been productive, is in the deconstruction of judicial logic in cases of female rape victims and domestic homicides by women. For when in these cases the meanings of women's actions have to be judged in order that 'consent' (in the case of rape) or guilty intent (in the case of homicide) can be imputed, there is considerable evidence that English courts tend to render women's experience null and void as they compute culpability according to what they think the normal male would do in similar circumstances (see, e.g., Adler 1987). Likewise, women who fetch a knife in order to protect themselves against violent husbands are seen as acting with guilty premeditation. Yet it could be argued that they are merely acting as *reasonable women* (with prior experience of their powerlessness to confront male violence effectively without a weapon) might be expected to act. However, though these specific instances of patriarchal judicial reasoning provide useful evidence of one system of gender discrimination in the administration of criminal law, it cannot be argued from them that the logic of the criminal courts is essentially and universally predicated on *all* men's experience, equally in the interests of *all* men or even that it uniformaly disadvantages female defendants (see, e.g., Allen 1987). Moreover, in the cases of black women, a white man's judicial reasoning may well be more influenced by racial stereotypes about 'black promiscuity' or 'black violence' than by patriarchal stereotypes about how 'normal' (i.e., moral) women could be expected to behave if only they were to behave like reasonable men!

Control via family and welfare institutions

The strength of the best studies that analyze the social control of women within the interrelationships of the politico-economic institutions of family, marriage and welfare lies firstly in their historical specificity. Secondly, it inheres in a thoroughgoing materialism that, in prioritizing analysis of the political, ideological and economic conditions in which women's physical and economic control is accomplished, at the same time is also able to facilitate explanation of the modes of control wherein their *subjective* coercion is achieved. A good example of this type of study is that of Ehrenreich and English, which was published in 1978 and entitled *For Her Own Good*, Subtitled '159 Years of the Experts' Advice to Women,' the book shows how nineteenth- and early twentieth-century experts controlled women (and taught middle-class 'ladies' how to control working-class 'housewives') via an attractive mix of rationalist and romanticist discourses that both objectified women's sexuality in the service of men and denied them their independence for the 'good of the family.' Thus, although Ehrenreich and English do indeed use the term 'patriarchy' to refer to the historical phenomenon of male domination in every area of economic, cultural and political life, they do not invoke it as a teleology. Instead, they analyze changing historical discourses to explain just why patriarchy took the form it did in the nineteenth and early twentieth centuries.

Explaining control via control theory

In 1985, when I began the research project that was eventually published as *Women, Crime and Poverty* (Carlen 1988), I set out to investigate why contemporary English women's criminal careers take the form that they do take within (1) a society characterized by increasing inequalities of wealth and income (Bull and Wilding 1983) and (2) a criminal justice system that systematically employs a differential sentencing logic based on class, gender and racial stereotypes (Box 1987). The major problem with which I had to contend at the outset of the research was a recognition that on the whole British women are a law-abiding lot, accounting in 1985 for approximately only 13 percent of all serious crime (Central Statistical Office 1987) and constituting a mere 3 to 4 percent of the total daily prison population (Home Office 1985). So, whatever experiences I was likely to posit as being part cause of some women's crimes were likely to have been shared by many more women who had never been convicted of lawbreaking. It seemed, therefore, that as far as gender differences in lawbreaking were concerned I should be posing questions more about women's *conformity* than about their relatively rare criminal activities, and it was at this point that I decided to employ 'control theory' (Hirschi 1969; Kornhauser 1978; Rosenbaum 1981) in my analyses of the ethnographic data.

Instead of posing the question 'Why do people break the law?' control theory asks, 'Why do people conform?' It replies that people are more likely to conform when they perceive that they have a vested interest in so doing, when they have more to gain than lose by lawbreaking. This perspective has the capacity to explain the lawbreaking of both rich and poor, though economic factors are not posited as being the only determinants of how people calculate the rewards expected from either lawbreaking or conformity. Nor need positive calculation be a prerequisite to lawbreaking. A drift into crime, accompanied by the concomitant rewards of friendship, financial gain and excitement, can engender the alternative 'controls' that gradually commit the woman lawbreaker to a way of life more satisfying (initially, at least) than that offered by conventional labor and marriage markets and/or meager, and often uncertain, welfare payments.

The relative rarity of women's (detected) crime led me to use control theory as a formal orientation to research about women's careers. However, empirical evidence of relationships between class, gender, race and criminal justice suggested an urgent need to develop alternative conceptualizations, ones that explain the form of *some* women's lawbreaking and judicial and penal regulation while at the same time denying that women's experiences of crime, courts and custody have a necessary and unitary existence. Denial of *'women's* lawbreaking' as a unitary object necessitated a denial that *women's* lawbreaking could possibly be in a symmetrical relationship with any posited (but impossible) *'women's* conformity.' In other words, an inversion of a control theory explaining why the majority of women appear to be law abiding would only partly explain why some other women go on to commit crime in the first place. And it would be even less useful in explaining (1) why a few of all women lawbreakers go on to become recidivist criminals and prisoners and (2) why recidivist women criminals and female prisoners are disproportionately poor, black and with backgrounds involving childhood institutionalization (Carlen 1987).

It seemed, therefore, that what I should aim to achieve by analyzing the accounts of the women's criminal careers was an indication of at what stages (if any) race or class (and possibly age) had become more important than gender in the conditioning and occasioning of their lawbreaking, prosecution and imprisonment. I failed. In explaining the criminal careers of 39 women, more than a quarter of whom had at least one parent of Asian or Caribbean origin and who had also expressed awareness of being victimized by white racism, I erased the effects of racism on *black* women's criminal careers in the service of a more generalizable theory of *poor* women's criminal careers. I succumbed to the temptation of globalism. Yet if I had kept in mind a post-structuralist notion of the variability of meanings both within and between cultures I might have produced a theory that explained women's criminal careers in the fullness of *all* their contradictions and specificities. For as I myself had claimed: 'By taking seriously women's own accounts of their criminal careers, there is first a refusal to reduce those lives to a sociology that erases the uniqueness of individual female experience; and, secondly, a commitment to deconstructing those careers into the elemental economic, ideological and political components which many of them share, albeit in the different combination that renders each unique' (Carlen 1988: 72). The tensions between the generalizing and abstractionist tendencies of theoretical production and the political and policy concerns that need both to recognize and deny the specificities of individuals' shared experiences can, in my view, be best confronted by a poststructuralism that works on the contradiction that the already known has to be both recognized (in the service of politics) and denied (in the service of theory production).

Poststructuralist perspectives

In view of my strictures against global theorizing, it may now seem perverse to attempt to argue for the possibilities of poststructural perspectives (on the relationships between economy, gender and race as constituents of crime discourses) that might be used cross-culturally and/or cross-nationally. Yet I think that from a poststructuralist perspective questions can be posed that could be used across a variety of cultural, economic and political contexts to call into question the official meanings of women in the criminal justice system as lawbreakers, convicts and prisoners. But first, some further discussion of poststructuralisms, global theories, and gender-centric theories is in order.

Poststructuralisms

Poststructuralisms are many, though they all share a 'dissatisfaction with the subject as a "programmed individual"' (Grbich 1991: 63). The poststructuralism that I am advocating both recognizes and denies structuralism. In relation to inequalities, the effectivity of the structures of social process and consciousness sociologically grouped (and often conflated) under the signs of 'class,' 'gender' and 'race' are recognized. But they are then denied any necessary unitary being in theories, subjectivities or practices. Such a poststructuralism is structuralist insofar as it attributes a nominalist reality to the concepts of 'class,' 'gender' and 'race' and then poststructuralist in that it adopts the methodological protocol of Bachelard (1940) that systems of thought must say 'no' to their own conventions and conditions of existence. It is structuralist insofar as it takes comfort from Saussurian linguistics, which demonstrate that individual words themselves have no essential meaning but acquire meaning only via syntagma, which through differentiation assign the value of a specific sign (Saussure 1974), and then becomes poststructuralist by raising the specter of otherness (Lacan 1977) or the desire for (and knowledge of) meanings that lie beyond the text (or context) but which also make possible (via 'difference' – Derrida 1976) the construction and simultaneous deconstruction) of the text (context, theoretical object) itself. In other words, the poststructuralist perspective on inequality for which I am arguing is one that will allow recognition of the value (i.e., effectivity) of existing inequalities at the same time as denying that they always and already have perennial applicability to any specific society, social formation or individual subjectivity. Such a perspective will of course strive against both globalism and the advance privileging of any one structure of inequality in the deconstruction of specific, local or individual configurations of inequalities.

Globalism

By global theories I mean those that generalize from abstract theorizing that *may* be relevant to one group of women to account for the lawbreaking of all women. 'Women's liberation leads to an increase in women's lawbreaking' is maybe the most notorious example of this kind of sociological globalism – though the biological type has also been well documented. Another brand of globalism can occur when a theorist develops a substantive theory to explain the situation of people of overlapping cultures within one nation purely in terms relevant to those of the dominant culture. Thus, as I have argued above, *Women, Crime and Poverty* is an example of globalism: although a quarter of the women in the study were black, the formalized substantive theory developed on the basis of the ethnography applied primarily to white women and, insofar as it applied to black women, only did so by putting their different histories as black women under an erasure.

Gender-centrism

Gender-centrism is often related to globalism, and in using the term I refer to academic work that either implies that concepts such as gender, class race and racism must be set in hierarchies with gender *always* being the most important in terms of explanation or characterization of sets of relationships or that all theory should be 'gendered.' My reservation about the first version is rooted in campaigning and policy concerns. For if in explaining a set of relationships one starts from the assumption that, for instance, either patriarchal relations or a universal male violence must always-already provide the key to them, it may become very difficult indeed to use that theory to inform campaigning action aimed at decreasing the levels of oppression being suffered by women in a variety of very differently balanced material and ideological circumstances. This is not to assert that there is no need for studies and theories that privilege gender questions as the most important. It is to warn against conceptual conflation and/or conceptual imperialism, both of which might result in a theoretical closure.

The second version of gender-centrism involves a realism that assumes that all theories should have a one-to-one relationship or at least a verisimilitude with the empirical object. As I said, this is not a theoretical tenet that I hold. The task of theory is to produce new knowledge and not mirror the old. Moreover (and almost conversely), I believe that theoretical production still must *initially* essentialise certain relationships as objects of knowledge that are not reducible to each other (Fuss 1989). The empirically recognized relationships of class, gender and race are, in my opinion, pre-eminent amongst those that should initially be recognized separately, then have the basis of their power revealed through analytic deconstruction, and finally have the necessity for those relationships denied in theory production. This is not to argue that material relationships are not experienced as being simultaneously class dominated, gendered, racially or culturally specific or racist; it is to argue that it is quite permissible for a theorist initially to essentialise one dimension of multidimensional discourses and theorize it separately. Thereafter, the empirical/political meanings of the discourses have to be calculated according to the historical and prevailing material, ideological and political conditions in which they are constituted. Theories of class, racism and gender are non-assimilable and non-reducible both to each other (cf., Cain 1986) and empirical sets of relationships, and the ways in which they can be used either to produce new knowledge or reduce injustices will usually be matters of political calculation.

What then has a poststructuralism to offer? At this stage a quotation from Weedon (1987: 22) well summarizes what I see to be poststructuralism's most important tenets:

Neither social reality nor the 'natural' world has fixed intrinsic meanings which language reflects or expresses. Different languages and different discourses within the same language divide up the world and give it meaning in different ways which cannot be reduced to one another through translation or by an appeal to universally shared concepts of reflecting a fixed reality. For example, the meanings of femininity and masculinity vary from culture to culture and language to language. They even vary between discourses within a particular language, between different feminist discourses for instance, and are subject to historical change.

It is with such a poststructuralist perspective in mind that I have thought it possible to pose the following three interrelated questions, which might be just one way of productively interrogating the varying meanings of crime across a range of cultures and political contexts:

1   Why does a specific criminal justice discourse take the form that it does?
2   Which cultural, racial, class and other knowledges are constitutive of and/or silenced by a specific criminal justice discourse?
3   Which masculinities and femininities are constitutive of (recognized) and/or silenced (denied) by a specific criminal justice discourse?

Conclusion . . . and beginning again

But what about the problems, the contradictions, the relativisms, the questions of agency, histories, essentialisms, translations, loss of meanings, and so on? The problems are endless. I'll now conclude by addressing just three of them.

Deconstruction and the disappearing women

Two related anxieties raised by feminists about post-structuralist analysis are (1) whether women's *histories* of oppression, resistance, etc., are made to disappear in the shifting semantics of deconstructionism and (2) whether the category 'women' is erased out of all meaningful existence, making it impossible to talk of 'women' at all. Yet there is nothing in poststructuralisms to necessitate the denial of history, and Riley (1988: 1,2,5) has succinctly summarized its importance to one poststructuralist perspective: ' "Women" is historically, discursively constructed, and always relatively to other categories which themselves change. . . . It's not that our identity is to be dissipated into airy indeterminacy, extinction . . . it is to be referred to the more substantial realms of discursive historical formation.'

And why should a poststructuralism that both seeks to recognize discourses (for purposes of the analysis of their knowledge/power effects) and deny them (the necessity of the relationships preconditional to those knowledge/power effects) to be at odds with any feminism that, as Riley describes it, assumes that 'both a concentration on and a refusal of the identity of "women" are essential to feminism' (Riley 1988: 1)? The greater problem in my view lies with feminisms that in striving to retain the rich diversity of women's individual autobiographies argue against the possibility of making any theoretical statements at all about women (white or black) as a group.

Individualism and systemicity

While some feminists fear that poststructuralisms erase the category of women via deconstruction, other feminists, conversely, are against theory per se. They claim that theory, in imposing limiting categories to universalism *some* meanings, also erases or silences others. Poststructuralists would agree. Yet, just as new knowledge can be created only out of the old already known knowledge (i.e., ideology), so too is deconstructionism dependent at least upon a *nominal* essentialism. As Diana Fuss (1989: 5) has written: 'It is Locke's distinction between nominal and real essence which allows us to work with the category of "women" as a linguistic rather than a natural kind, and for this reason Locke's category of nominal essence is especially useful for anti-essentialist feminists who want to hold on to the notion of women as a group without submitting to the idea that it is "nature" that categorizes them as such.' A poststructuralist perspective must engage in a nominalist essentialism in order to fully recognize that which it has to deny. In so doing it can also celebrate the range of women's individual experiences and subjectivities before deconstructing them into the constitutive ideological, economic and political discourses that many of them share in the different combinations that render them each unique.

The question of human agency

A constant criticism of poststructuralisms is that they are deterministic and allow space neither for individual agency and responsibility nor for political struggle. If individuals are created in discourses, how can they be accountable for their actions or indeed ever get to change things? The charge of determinism is ill founded. Subject-positions are pre-given, but they also constantly change as different sets of subjects choose how to occupy them. The choices, however, are made under specific economic, political and ideological conditions that are not of the subjects' choosing. Arguments about degrees of culpability are tasks for political jurisprudence. The job of analytic deconstruction is to unravel the combinations of discourses and economic conditions within which crime and criminal justice discourses (including political jurisprudence) take a variety of forms. And this is precisely why I am *against* the tendency towards theoretical closure inherent in global gender-centric theories about the social control of women and the always-already unfinished interrogation of the 'classes,' 'genders' and 'racisms' so central to present understandings of inequalities and criminal justices.

Part 5
International perspectives

Early feminist criminology ignored cultural differences in its essentialising notions of what it is to be female, and conversely, what it is to be male. Black and minority feminists (Davis, 1981; hooks, 1981) first took on the universal notion of 'woman' in the early 1980s, arguing that western feminism was forged from a particular ethnocentric position and that it did not encompass the experiences and disadvantages faced by the minority ethnic female. Their work led to an acknowledgement that 'feminine' ideals can be differently constructed and experienced across varied cultural perspectives and that 'femininities', and ultimately 'masculinities', must be studied in all their different manifestations. As these writers revealed, the fact that these were differences not previously noted or explored was due to the cultural dominance of white society and its racism in not recognising or valuing the diversity of experience which was present. Criminology has been slow to take up the challenges presented by such writers and, where it has, much of the work which explored diversity and difference has been based on cultural differences within western societies. Truly international comparative literature in this area has been thin on the ground. Nevertheless, it is currently growing in range and depth as global networks of academics are encouraged, new technology makes the study of other cultures and societies easier to achieve and the movement of people across the globe means monocultural outlooks are increasingly outdated and irrelevant. Furthermore, within criminology the study of transnational criminal networks is becoming more important as these become more active and take advantage of the illegitimate opportunities which globalisation brings.

The readings in this part are all based on international perspectives, some intentionally comparative and cross-cultural and others based around issues with a more global focus. They reveal a number of important issues. First, they demonstrate the universal vulnerability of women to crimes against their gender, which is a dominant feature of women's lives across the globe. Notwithstanding the message of earlier readings that it is in the intersections of class, race and gender that criminology must focus in order to reveal the truth of victimisation and disadvantage, these readings show that women are victimised as women across class and ethnic lines. However, they again reiterate that this vulnerability is increased as poverty and racism impact on women's lives in various ways.

In addressing the punishment of women across a range of western industrial nations Snider's article keys us into a range of debates regarding 'governance' (Foucault, 1991; Rose, 1999; 2000), 'the new punitiveness' (Pratt et al., 2005), 'carceral clawback' (Carlen, 2002b) and the 'criminology of the other' (Garland, 2001) which have significant resonance within the contemporary landscape of criminology. Concerned to disentangle how criminological knowledge might be complicit in the surge in punishment characteristic of the modern industrialised state, Snider suggests that valuable insights of feminist and critical criminology have often been ignored or reconstructed by state authorities for their own purposes. Thus the criminological knowledge which is 'heard' by neoliberal states constructs the female offender as 'the voluntary, predatory, violent, self-seeking woman' (p. 206) a policy construct which remains unchallenged by criminological 'truths' constituted by feminist criminology and the resistance of female offenders themselves. Snider concludes that, from the perspective of a pessimistic present, the future of criminology and the female offender is uncertain.

The second reading reveals the increasing feminisation of poverty across the globe as welfare systems are withdrawn and increasing inequalities in society are shouldered, to a great extent, by women. Radford and Tsutsumi reveal the personal abuse and degradation that women suffer at the hands of men, comparing the dangers of intimate and dating relationships in the UK and Japan. This reading also points to the ongoing and, arguably, increasing tendency to demonise the 'other', which is now a feature of a global society with extensive networks of migration. In the third reading, Poynting and his colleagues write of the impact this has had on young Muslim men living in Australia and the ways in which their lives are caricatured and denigrated by the dominant culture. They are seen as doubly dangerous on account of their maleness and their identification as Muslim, which renders them outside the acceptable values of Australian society yet powerful in their common identity at one and the same time. In this reading, gender takes on a particular significance as the media portray man's power to rape as a tool by which this marginal group assert their cultural difference and hatred of other ways of being. This strange reversal of logic nevertheless echoes previous exhortations to fear the 'black male' in white society.

It is perhaps in Jamieson's work that the arguments presented in this part come together. Her article suggests a blueprint for further work which exhorts us to forsake simple reductionist arguments and to see how violence and inhumanity can reside within any gender or social group. Jamieson demonstrates how the process of 'othering', in this case in Bosnia-Herzegovina and

Rwanda, can have devastating consequences. In attempting to understand the motivations and dynamics which inform genocide, she reveals how forms of exclusion can become so institutionalised as to lead to murder on a massive scale which engenders inclusivity for one group with terrible consequences for others. Thus the included strike out at the excluded, demonstrating a capacity for violence which engulfs the dominant population. This institutionalised violence against an 'out' group requires the active participation of the entire 'in' group, thus women and children are included as perpetrators as well as victims. Jamieson's work is often uncomfortable to read and stretches our capacity to understand some of the worst aspects of human behaviour, but in doing so she suggests a new way of understanding exclusionary processes in society and an added imperative to work towards an inclusive, and thereby safer, society.

Suggestions for further reading

Chesney-Lind, M. (2006), 'Patriarchy, crime, and justice: feminist criminology in an era of backlash', *Feminist Criminology*, 1(1): 6–26.
    In this article Chesney-Lind provides a much needed update on the terrain within which feminism and criminology currently operate.
Evans, J. (2003), 'Vigilance and vigilantes: thinking psychoanalytically about anti-paedophile action', *Theoretical Criminology*, 7: 163–89.
    This article provides a thought-provoking account of the dramatic reaction of one group of women to a campaign to 'out' and to isolate the sex offender in the community. Issues of governance, popular punitiveness and contemporary fears are explored in ways which cause us to question concepts such as innocence and victimisation.
Goodey, J. (2004), 'Sex trafficking in women from Central and East European countries. Promoting a victim-centred and woman-centred approach to criminal justice intervention', *Feminist Review*, 76: 26–45.
    In this article Goodey explores the trafficking of women and their commodification as items of economic value to be bought and sold for profit, and outlines recommendations regarding criminal justice responses to victims of sex trafficking.
Rafter, N. and Heidensohn, F. (eds) (1995), *International Feminist Perspectives in Criminology*. Buckingham: Open University Press.
    This edited collection comprises an early attempt to provide some insights with regard to international developments in feminist thinking in criminology.

5.1

Constituting the punishable woman: *atavistic man incarcerates postmodern woman*
by Laureen Snider

[. . .]

Expertise and the female offender or 'après moi, le déluge'

Feminist criminology has constituted several distinct female offenders, using diverse and discordant discourses originating in equally diverse methodological practices and epistemological assumptions. The theoretical questions dominating these investigations have been called the generalizability question – can (male) stream theories of crime be extended to cover female criminals; and the gender ratio issue – why do so few women, relative to men, commit crimes (Daly and Chesney-Lind 1988). Both questions have been addressed by traditional as well as self-identified feminist criminologists, and both assume that crime is a fact rather than a social construction, one whose salient characteristics can be known and measured objectively through scientific, value-free methodologies (Cain 1990; Smart 1995; Naffine 1996). Thus it is not surprising that the literature which addresses these two questions is the most relentlessly quantitative component of feminist criminology, though feminist criminologists have been more likely than their male counterparts to add qualitative components (such as interviews or case studies), seeking to 'comprehend women's crime on its own terms' (Daly and Chesney-Lind 1988: 122). Both questions also take male crime rates, conditions and male-based theories as the norm against which women must be compared – as Naffine (and others) have pointed out, in these literatures only women have a gender (1996: 36–7).

Rather than rehashing the history of feminist criminology, the important issue here is the punishable woman constituted by these knowledge claims. Studies claiming to assess which theories generated by all-male samples explain women's crimes and which do not, when applied to anomie/strain, labelling and social control/social bonds, have produced inconclusive, contradictory results (see, for example, Smith and Paternoster 1987). For our purposes, this body of work demonstrates, more than anything else, the depth and pervasiveness of gender bias residing in past and present-day mainstream positivist criminology. Masquerading as gender neutrality and hidden under the guise of science women, if present at all, are still 'at best, a complicating factor – in the male story – of crime' (Naffine 1996: 25). Crime is judged differently as well: rebellion by male subjects is romantic independence, in females it indicates pathology or promiscuousness; legal conformity by males indicates a well adjusted, appropriately bonded individual, legal conformity in women indicates their passivity, lack of independence or 'over-socialization' (Hagan 1991).

Thus the most important implications of this work are epistemological rather than substantive: *feminist criminology has constituted the fallible expert*. By questioning claims of objectivity made by the authorized knowers of traditional criminology, by showing that the emperors have no clothes, feminist criminology has contributed to the fragmentation of the field. But it has also legitimized dissent, in the academic community and beyond, providing tools of resistance. Destabilizing the cult of expertise has been significant in constituting the resistant female offender, providing her with the languages and the legitimacy to dispute the truth claims made about her.

The gender/ratio question, on the other hand, played a direct role in constituting the female offender on behalf of authority. Asking why so few women are labelled criminal has directed attention to systems of criminal justice, and led, predictably in cultures obsessed by punishment, to questions of equality. Were women receiving equal treatment – meaning, were they punished as much as men? – or were they, horror of horror, the recipients of 'lenience'? This question, known as the chivalry hypothesis, generated endless studies testing whether police or judicial authorities were arresting women less, dropping charges more, or sanctioning female defendants less severely. Evidence from the 1970s indicated that some women – white, older, familied caregivers – were indeed the beneficiaries of 'lenience' in some jurisdictions for some offences (Steffensmeier 1978, 1980, 1983; Moulds 1980; Nagel and Hagan 1983; Farrington and Morris 1983; Kruttschnitt 1981, 1984; Daly 1987, 1989; Morris 1987). Girls, however, received longer custodial sentences, for sexual acting-out that was ignored or admired in boys (Chesney-Lind 1981, 1987, 1988); black and aboriginal women never received less than the mandated quota of punishment (and often got longer sentences served in harsher conditions) (Kruttschnitt 1981; Spohn et al. 1987). In any event 'lenience', once it was called into existence as a knowledge category by criminology, quickly disappeared. In the United States and other Anglo-American countries it was gone by 1990 (Naffine 1989; Carrington 1993; Daly 1994; Chesney-Lind 1994; Chesney-Lind and Pollock 1994; Boritch 1997). The result, in policy terms, has been ever higher rates of incarceration for women and girls, 'equality with a vengeance' (Smart 1995: 42).

Two points here: first, it is significant that lenience arguments were only, ever, always heard as arguments for increasing the punishment of women, never for infusing mercy into the treatment of men. Punishing up, not 'leni-encing' down; equal opportunity oppression not equal opportunity clem-ency. This fact must direct our attention to how arguments are heard, how expert knowledge claims are interpreted, the cultural context in which they are received. Second, the institutional sites where women were subjected to more intensive surveillance, discipline and punishment than men, many of them outside criminal justice venues (McRobbie 1978; Hudson 1984; Nava 1984), were never deemed problematic. New, blatantly unequal initiatives aimed specifically at women continue to mount – note, for example, recent campaigns to criminalize pregnant women who smoke, drink alcohol, or give birth to babies addicted to crack cocaine (Tong 1996). These asymmetries are generally accepted by the authorized knowers of criminology, partly because the discourse of 'healthy babies' legitimates punishment, partly because studies making the claims have the sheen of science backed by the 'objectivity' of numbers, and partly because subjecting women to ever more intensive disciplinary procedures is compatible with dominant cultural scripts. Only the weak discourse of 'difference' is available to those seeking to legitimate judicial or legal 'lenience', defined as the extraction of fewer pounds of flesh per defendant than law and judicial discretion allow (Bagley and Merlo 1995).

While the generalizability question and the gender ratio issue have dom-inated the quantitatively oriented sectors of traditional and feminist crimin-ology, the issue of victimization has become central elsewhere. 'Victimization is at the heart of . . . [female] lawbreaking and this . . . best explains women's involvement in crime' (Chesney-Lind and Faith 2000: 27). The claim that female offending arises from female victimization has been extensively documented, debated, discussed throughout feminist criminology (Carlen 1983; Comack 1996). Offenders have been studied as victims of physical, sexual and emotional abuse, sexism, racism, heterosexism and classism.

When used in the context of female punishment or allied with concepts of the therapeutic prison (see next section), the discourse of offender-as-victim has had pathologizing, individualizing and disempowering effects (Balfour 2000; Frigon 1996, 2000; Kendall 2000; Pollack 2000). And it is a claim that has generated massive resistance, fuelling anti-feminist backlash. However, victimization discourses originating in feminist knowledge claims are now widely employed by the female offender and inmate, and by all manner of advocacy groups. Because the extent and nature of female victim-ization has been extensively documented, publicized in popular media, circu-lated through schools and therapy networks, it has gained acceptance far beyond academe and well outside feminist circles. Experts, prison reformers, psychologists and social workers now see the female offender through this lens and so, sometimes, does the offender herself. Victim discourse can be a useful tool in the kitbag of resistance. Or it may be used as an empowering device by demonized women to explain particular acts to themselves, and/or to those who control their fate. To retain self esteem, reaffirm identities tried on earlier in life, or resist degrading identities imposed by authority figures, familial, peer or judicial: in all these ways the victimization script has proved pivotal in the constitution of the resilient, resistant female offender.

Expertise and the female inmate

The female inmate constituted by the intersection of power and knowledge in feminist criminology has been, on the whole, the Woman in Trouble (Comack 1996), the needy but not the punishable offender. In the accounts of liberal and socialist feminism (as opposed to Foucauldian, discussed below), women's abuse experiences structure their lives and their offending. Other frequent claims are that prisons, particularly repressive maximum security prisons, are unnecessary for female offenders because most of their crimes are non-violent, that female inmates need healing and empowerment, and that punishment and healing are incompatible, if not diametrically opposed (for example, Faith 1992). The female inmate is portrayed as doubly disadvantaged, incarcerated because she has transgressed against both domesticity and law. In Carlen's phrase (1983), she is 'outwith' gender norms, family norms and work norms, deemed a failure as wife/partner, mother, daughter and worker. She is poor, a factor particularly stressed in socialist feminist accounts; she is also, in every Anglo-American country, disproportionately likely to be a woman of colour, a black African-American in the United States, of Caribbean origin in the United Kingdom, or aboriginal in Canada, New Zealand and Australia.

Once incarcerated she is more likely than her male counterpart to serve time in a locale many kilometres away from friends and family, fewer job, training and educational programmes will be available to her, and she will be housed in inferior conditions at excessive security levels. She will probably be forcibly separated from her children, if she has children, and she will be seen by herself and others as failing or abandoning them, a stigma differentially applied to women (one that is applied whether or not the woman had custody prior to incarceration). Health care, particularly reproductive and sexual care, will be poor, even in those countries that provide universal health services to all citizens (Heidensohn 1985[b]; Eaton 1986; Carlen 1988; Worrall 1990; Faith 1993; 1999; Shaw 1993; Bertrand 1999; Faith 1999; Jackson 1999; Owen 1999). (In the United States, the only developed country that does not, the comparison is less stark because no poor people have decent health care.) The only way that women are better off than male prisoners – 'and it is a significant one – is that incarcerated women appear to be far less likely [in US prisons] . . . to be raped by fellow prisoners' (Belknap 2001: 195).

A comparative study of 24 prisons for women in Canada, Denmark,

England, Finland, Germany, Norway, Scotland and the United States, between 1991 and 1996, showed that conditions are not getting better (Bertrand 1999). Despite promises and reforms, conditions for women in most countries and jurisdictions have not improved and, in some cases, have deteriorated. Even more significant is the fact that some feminist-inspired reforms are a component in this decline. 'Prison laws are sexist, male and gendered' (Bertrand 1999: 57) and, where prisoner lawsuits are allowed, female inmates are less likely to participate in or benefit from them (Belknap 2001). Bertrand also claims that reforms such as mixed gender living units, co-corrections and annual vacations with family 'go sour when applied to women' (1999: 56). On co-corrections Smykla and Williams agree with Bertrand. Their meta-analysis shows that co-corrections offer women 'few if any economic, educational, vocational and social advantages', benefiting only 'male prisoners and system maintenance' (1996: 61). Home leaves with family are problematic because, after a few months inside, there is no family left, no partner or mother holding the fort, tending the home fires, looking after the children, waiting anxiously for return of the loved one. Like many other reforms, home leave assumes a particularly male and middle class model of family life – a model increasingly invalid for everyone in the atomized individualistic postmodern world. Mixed gender living units often make life inside easier for male inmates, but harder for women. Even long-sought, much-heralded programmes such as decarceration were found to feature 'infantilizing discipline and supervision' (Bertrand 1999: 57). Mother and child programmes are criticized for domesticating women, projecting a 'pronatalist and eugenic ideology' (pp. 57–8) which instrumentalizes mothers by validating 'the model of the "good woman" who . . . is the biological mother caring all day for her young child' (Bertrand 1999: 57).

This picture of 'good intentions gone wrong' is reinforced in Foucauldian accounts of female penality, albeit in different language. Here the emphasis is on showing how sex stereotypes frame accounts of women's crime, how gender is socially constructed and how bodies are 'sexed' (Cook and Davies 1999: 62–3). In these accounts the author (the authorized knower of the text) is likely to focus more attention on other authorized knowers, typically the social workers, psychiatrists and magistrates of the criminal justice system, than on the offender. Worrall, for example, asks how professionals and experts in the United Kingdom were authorized to define certain women as requiring treatment, management, control and punishment, and identifies the discourses of domesticity, sexuality and pathology as key (1990: 32). Carrington (1990, 1993) examines how women and girls are constructed through social work and psychiatric discourses in Australia, while the masculinizing of criminality directs law's attention on to aboriginal boys.

Similarly in Canada, looking at federal incarceration, Hannah-Moffat (2001) examines the connection between punishment regimes and expert human sciences, outlining the relations of power that emerge from pastoral, maternal, disciplinary and empowerment strategies of governance. While scientific rationalities and techniques are linked to punishment in important ways, she argues that non-scientific, amateur or lay knowledges have been overlooked. Her genealogy of Canada's Prison for Women highlights the historical importance of spiritual and maternal rationalities that 'naturalize [d] the exercise of power' (2001: 22), through non-expert female reformers, who used gender-based knowledge claims to create woman-centred regimes. Even when feminists and aboriginal women were invited to participate in the policy process (as in *Creating Choices*, the 1990 Royal Commission Report on female imprisonment), the results were, to say the least, disappointing. Feminist-inspired reforms designed to empower female inmates, Hannah-Moffat reports, have been translated by the Correctional Service of Canada into 'responsibilizing strategies' extending disciplinary control. And the pivotal concept of 'inmate needs', which was supposed to guide penal policy in a humane and liberating direction, has been heard through discourses of risk. Thus, high need equals high risk equals maximum security confinement for the inmate – in the guise of meeting inmate needs and 'empowering' her.

In the United Kingdom Bosworth (1999) paid particular attention to inmate resistance in female prisons, interviewing 52 female inmates in three different institutions. She argues that, although identity and self-esteem were eroded by confinement, inmates were able to exercise (individual) agency through resistance. Resistance was accomplished in different ways by different inmates, but primarily through personal identity. By defining themselves through their spirituality, sexual orientation, race, class, education or even – a much older identity, through valorizing their role as a mother – women fought what they saw as demoralizing or degrading prison-issue concepts of themselves, their motivation and their offence. Resisting through identity had a significant advantage: it did not invite the retribution and punishment from prison authorities, which would have followed from more overt and/or more collective forms of resistance.

What, then, are the punishment claims animating these literatures? How have they constituted the female offender, and to what effect? She is clearly a woman of entitlement, one whose crimes have to be understood in relation to her victimization (albeit in a manner determined by penal authorities). Because she has been victimized, she is a subject who 'deserves' better treatment than she has received. She is entitled to demand more programmes, more healing, less punishment. As one (disgruntled) staff member at what was then Canada's Prison for Women put it, inmates now have 'attitude' (personal communication, 1999).

An excellent (though unaccountably overlooked) piece by Heidensohn (1994) makes this point well, contrasting the female prisoner today with her counterpart in the 1960s. Without oversimplifying the complex and plural responses inmates make to confinement, Heidensohn points out that 'some groups of women . . . have been transformed, or transformed themselves, stimulated . . . by modern feminism and by the research enquiries . . . directed at them (1994: 19). To illustrate she draws on her own experiences as a researcher in the Borstals of Britain in the late 1960s, when neither the female inmates nor staff had any idea why she was interviewing them or what she was looking for. The inmates had no ready reference points, no way to make sense of her – they defined themselves through the offence for which they were convicted or as 'damaged goods' (1994: 27), not as women and certainly not as victims of oppression. In her terms she, and they, were 'innocent'. How different this is from the inmate (and staff!) encountered by the Task Force studying Canada's Prison for Women in the 1990s (the aforementioned *Creating Choices*) (Shaw 1993; Hayman 2000; Hannah-Moffat 2001), or from Bosworth's British prisoners (1999), women who evaluated their choices and resisted through signifiers such as spirituality, sexuality or racial identity. Female offenders and inmates have found a voice.

The female offender/inmate today, then, is a very different subject from the woman of the 1960s (who is, undoubtedly, more different still from the elusive nineteenth-century subject). Feminism has altered, and continues to alter, the framework of meanings through which offenders see, interpret and know themselves, and the framework through which they interpret the attitudes, policies, programmes and agents of criminal justice. The consensus of 'right-minded reformers' on the offender's nature, her sins and her place in authority structures from the state to the family, has been broken. 'Our' claims on the punishment the offender deserves or 'needs', are increasingly likely to be challenged by the subject of whom we write. Her input, in turn, is likely to be fed back into new claims by authorized knowers, particularly in critical criminologies, the disciplinary branches least resistant, philosophically and epistemologically, to these voices. A feedback loop or spiral has been created, resistance is now (re) inscribed into patterns of governance (O'Malley 1996).

The atavistic woman of policy discourse

The previous two sections have examined the female offender and inmate constituted by authorized experts in (primarily) feminist criminology. As we have seen, this subject is the Woman in Trouble (Comack 1996), the caregiver, the impoverished, aboriginal, and/or victimized woman. It is most emphatically not the predatory, rational, calculating Female Criminal, the violent gang girl or the irresponsible, out-or-control Bad Mother/Child Abuser. Yet it is this offender who has increasingly become the woman of policy discourse, the woman who justifies the surge of punitiveness reflected in incarceration rates. Looking at the punishable woman constituted by feminist criminology, then, highlights the ever-widening gap between knowledge claims in criminology and official policy (Feeley and Simon 1994; Simon and Feeley 1995).

That incarceration rates have soared in the last two decades is not in dispute, it has been documented again and again (Immarigeon and Chesney-Lind 1992; Owen 1999; Belknap 2001: 166–8). Most recently, an august National Policy White Paper issued by *The Criminologist*, the self-described Official Newsletter of the American Society of Criminology, the very temple of authorized knowers at the heart of mainstream criminology, described and denounced the excessive use of incarceration in the United States (Austin et al. 2001). From fewer than 500,000 inmates in 1980, the number of incarcerated men and women has risen to 'nearly two million' in 2000 and 'numbers continue to rise'. 'Approximately one third of all Black males will experience state prison in their lifetime' (2001: 14). And, while the total number of incarcerated males increased 303 per cent from 1980–99, it increased 576 per cent for females. 'The increase in the number of women in these facilities has outpaced the increase for men each year since 1995' (Austin et al. 2001: 15). Between 1986 and 1991, African-American women's incarceration rates for drug offences rose by 828 per cent, that of Hispanic women by 328 per cent, that of white women by 241 per cent – a fact these authors call a 'war on black women' (Chesney-Lind and Faith 2000:25–6). Indeed, the increase in female incarceration has been commonly attributed to the War on Drugs and to Three Strikes laws, since there is no corresponding increase in women's crime rates which explains it. 'The proportion of women imprisoned for violent crimes has actually decreased' (Belknap 2001: 167, citing Immarigeon and Chesney-Lind 1992).

Similar, albeit less dramatic, increases have occurred in Australia, Canada, the United Kingdom and many European countries. In Australia, for example, from 1982 to 1998, the prison population increased 102 per cent; women made up 5.3 per cent of the total prison population in 1988; 5.7 per cent in 1998 (Carcach and Grant 1999). In Canada since 1977, the total number of women charged per year has increased 54 per cent (Finn et al. 1999). In 1997, aboriginal people made up 4 per cent of the Canadian population overall, but 22 per cent of female prison inmates and 41 per cent of those held in maximum security facilities (Jackson 1999). In the United Kingdom the number of women prisoners increased 100 per cent from 1993 to 1998, compared to a 45 per cent increase for men. Almost 50 per cent of this increase can be attributed to more women being convicted of drug offences, although the most common crime for women is shoplifting (British Home Office 1999). In 1970 there were fewer than 1,000 female prisoners in England and Wales; in 2001 the number stood at 4,045. In 2001, from June to September alone, the number of women in prison rose 7 per cent, leading officials to announce the conversion of a third formerly male prison to cope with the increase (*Guardian Weekly*, 29 November – 5 December, 2001: 7).

These figures illustrate how totally the discourses of atavistic (wo) man have triumphed over postmodern woman at the level of policy. They force us to ask why the discourses produced by authorized knowers that legitimate less punitive treatment for female offenders are either not heard (as in many American states) (Immarigeon and Chesney-Lind 1992), or heard in ways that authorize expanded surveillance, repression and control (as in Canada and Australia, for example) (George 1999; Hannah-Moffat 2001). Part of the answer lies in the triumph of discourses of equality, and the apparent determination of some policy makers and officials to use this idea, this set of knowledge claims, to bring women (back) into line, to ensure that female offenders, in particular, do not 'get away with anything'. This trend is made possible, exacerbated and justified by many kinds of sentencing 'reform': mandatory minimum sentences eliminating judicial discretion, for example, make it impossible to bend rules to exercise mercy, thereby enshrining vengeance as policy (Schichor and Sechrest 1996). The boomerang effect of equal treatment laws, another sentencing 'reform', has lengthened prison sentences for women, destroyed 'early' parole, and authorized women's inclusion on chain gangs (Daly and Chesney-Lind 1988; Smart 1989 [b]). 'Zero tolerance' laws on spousal assault have produced more female offenders, as women get charged with contempt of court for their unwillingness to testify against their partners, or are counter-charged (with assault) for self defence (Snider 1994, 1998; Comack et al. 2000). Such developments underline the perils of good intentions: in a culture of punitiveness reforms will be heard in ways that reinforce rather than challenge dominant cultural themes; they will strengthen hegemonic not counter-hegemonic practices and beliefs.

Linking specific knowledge claims to cultures of punishment is not easy. Traditional and critical criminologies simultaneously feed into, constitute and (in the case of some critical/feminist claims) challenge agendas of punishment. There are no linear causal links, the process is complex and over-determined, an intricate and massive series of feedback spirals and loops. However it is possible to identify some of the knowledge claims of traditional, right realist criminology in the atavistic, predatory, violent woman of policy discourse. She is a direct relative of the violent, self-maximizing, voluntary underclass criminal, raised on welfare by a single mother, lacking in self control, unable to defer gratification (Murray 1984, 1988; Wilson 1975; Wilson and Herrnstein 1985; Gottfredson and Hirschi 1990). Ironically, as was so often the case in the past, the evil woman criminology's authorized knowers have constituted is in large part an accidental creation, an add-on. The intended target of the studies and claims that legitimated preventive detention, zero tolerance laws and similar punitive measures, was not woman but man, specifically the young, urban, disenfranchised, economically marginalized, black American male, the classic Other. Feminist-inspired doctrines of equality, along with the popularity and salience of feminist work in academic disciplines, made it inevitable that 'the criminal woman' would receive equal scrutiny. Anti-feminist backlash made it probable that officials of criminal justice and their political masters would act quickly on any differences that appeared to benefit woman, or to 'let her off easy'. Add in therapeutic knowledge claims from 'psy' disciplines, claims which rationalize incarceration as humanitarian intervention (for 'her own good'), claims which resonate with dominant cultural themes valorizing health and individual responsibility, and the drug addicted, demonized female criminal was born.

Nor is the reception and evaluation of knowledge claims an equal opportunity game (Snider 2000). To understand why and how the claims of one set of authorized knowers, (for example, those of right realist criminology) 'grow legs' and hop off the computer screens of experts on to the legislative agendas of politicians, while other claims (for example those of feminist criminology) atrophy and die, one must examine relations of power. What groups benefit from each set of knowledge claims, gaining moral, economic and/or political capital? What groups lose? The mechanisms of power are important too. Once legitimated inside the academy, knowledge claims must be distributed, publicized and accepted by other elites, in the judiciary, industry, media. What groups own, control or otherwise dominate these distribution networks, particularly mass and elite media? While it is too simplistic to suggest that the knowledge claims of counter-hegemonic feminist criminology were not heard because the female subject they constitute is a woman entitled to demand an equal share of a society's social, economic and political resources, it is equally simplistic to pretend that this is irrelevant. Academics may ignore the ideological, political and economic consequences of claims. We may prefer to assume that the logic, internal consistency, methodological rigour and intellectual validity of their/our arguments are all that counts in securing their acceptance in the outside world, but elites in other institutional sectors are less obtuse. Senior civil servants in policy elites, for example, are paid to be cognisant of all the benefits and costs of particular ways of seeing and acting, and to pass these insights on to their political masters.

However the most basic questions ask how such a culture was produced, and why it goes from strength to strength. Many of these answers lie in external factors beyond the scope of this paper, outside criminal justice and its authorized knowers. Rising levels of immiseration and inequality (Cossman and Fudge 2001; Schrecker 2001), rising fear of crime (Sacco 1995, 2000; Cayley 1998), the triumph of commodification and individualism (Bauman 1997; Morrison 1995) – three defining characteristics of the neo-liberal state – are all significant. When modern states remove the economic cushions offered by social safety nets, and processes of globalization (presented as 'irresistible' market forces) threaten the stability and security of citizens, more desperate societies and more fearful, vulnerable individuals are created (Snider 1998). And when 'citizenship' is reduced to an unending, meaningless struggle for more and more commodities, to market participation and nothing else, cultures of civility decline. There is simply no public space left, no reason to conform or cooperate (Morrison 1995). Under such circumstances cultures of punitiveness and desperation, which pit individual against individual, with no quarter for the 'flawed consumers' who cannot keep up, thrive and grow (Bauman 1997).

Conclusion

This article has examined the knowledge claims that have constituted women's punishment and the female offender. When second-wave feminism first made its way into criminology in the 1970s, scholars reclaimed women's crime and incarceration, taking it away from traditional (male) criminology. By constituting female offenders as women first, offenders second, feminist criminology highlighted the reactive and trivial nature of female crime, drawing attention to the poverty and abuse histories that typify women in custody, emphasizing the differences between women and male offenders. This perspective, meant to legitimate less punishment, instead legitimated different sorts of punishment, usually disguised in the language of 'special needs'. In policy terms it justified setting up different types of institutions for women – even, perhaps, the problematic, high-surveillance, therapeutic regimes to 'serve' the needy and victimized offender so constituted. But even the most conservative versions of feminist criminology never constituted an offender who required more incarceration, punitiveness and repression. This Subject, the voluntary, predatory, violent, self-seeking woman of policy discourse who merits such treatment, is not 'ours'. She is the female criminal of the neo-liberal state. That is the first conclusion.

Second, as we have seen, the discourses and knowledge claims of feminist criminology have played a part in constituting a different, stronger, more resistant female offender and inmate, one with the language and habits of mind to oppose penal and criminal justice authorities. Women's offending has been tied to women's victimization, and the Resistant Subject has emerged. By showing how gender blind and culturally specific universalistic, science-based knowledge claims are, feminist criminology has helped to destabilize expertise, making challenges to scientific knowledge claims easier, thereby constituting the Fallible Expert. Both of these are important, noteworthy developments. However, since much of the institutional and ideological power remains in the hands of judges, wardens and parole officers, this empowerment is more about resistance than transformation, and more about the politics of identity than of redistribution. In redistributive terms – entitlement to health care, day care for children, welfare, or a job that pays enough to live on – the female offender in today's neo-liberal state is worse off when she gets out than she was in 1979 (Cossman and Fudge 2001; Ehrenreich 2001, Schrecker 2001). Neither the Resistant Subject nor the weakened-because-fallible Expert has succeeded in challenging the punitive, cost-cutting agendas of the neo-liberal state.

One final comment: feminist criminology today has reached an absurd and ironic impasse. We now have one group of authorized knowers busy using knowledge to construct new programmes and disciplinary regimes to 'help' the female offender they know, and another group busy deconstructing the efforts of the first. On one side of this divide, feminist criminologists, often originating in disciplines such as psychiatry, psychology or social work, are developing 'successful gender-responsive programming' for female offenders and inmates (Bloom 2000: 1–2). They are studying how to make prison programmes more 'effective', overcome programme failure, and 'meet women's needs' – defined in terms of drug free status, non-recidivism, responsible employees, mothers or wives (Teplin et al. 1996; Bloom and Steinhart 1993; Brennan and Austin 1997; Rice et al. 1999; Reed 1987; Koons et al. 1997; and many more). And, in the opposite corner, critical and Foucauldian academics are deconstructing the knowledge claims, agendas, rationalities and techniques of the first group, valorizing as resistance the very behaviours their colleagues see as programme failure. The body and mind of the female Subject is somewhere in the middle, claimed by both groups. Where does this leave authorized knowers and their claims to expertise? More significantly, where does it leave the female offender? How does it constitute her, and what are the impacts of this fragmentation on her ability to resist and, perhaps, go beyond resistance? At this stage in the intellectual saga of modernism, it is not clear where authorized knowers or female offenders are headed.

5.2

Globalization and violence against women – inequalities in risks, responsibilities and blame in the UK and Japan

by Lorraine Radford and Kaname Tsutsumi

Increased opportunities for targeting women

Globalization has influenced the scope and the nature of violence against women. Globalization has brought different and more opportunities for violence from men to women in the UK and Japan, making poor women and girls especially vulnerable to entrapment, exploitation, abuse and enslavement. Violence against women has never been limited to the poor or underprivileged. Well-publicized media coverage of celebrity violence to partners highlights what the feminist anti-violence movement has known for some time, that rich, famous or powerful men can be just as abusive and prone to violence as men who are poor. Women from all socio-economic groups, religions and cultures suffer sexual and domestic violence although the experience of abuse is often prolonged if a woman is isolated or lacks the resources needed to get away (Dominy & Radford, 1996; Mooney, 2000). Cuts in welfare services in rich and poor nations have aggravated the feminization of poverty leaving women more vulnerable to abuser entrapment and with fewer options to support themselves outside an abusive relationship.

Economic globalization has brought an unequal distribution of resources, concentrating them in rich regions so that the world has been divided into rich 'core' areas of wealth and capital and the poor 'periphery.' These divisions can be found within nations and between nations across the globe. The Japanese sociologist Harutoshi Funabashi (1992) used the concepts of 'benefit zones' and 'victimization zones' to refer to the uneven distribution of resources and environmental risks between Japan and poor regions such as the Philippines and Thailand. Funabashi argues up to about 1992, when the 'bubble economy' burst, Japan's economic success was built upon the development of a 'separate-dependent ecosystem,' where benefits and resources flowed into Japan from poor nations and associated risks were transported out. As a 'one way consumption society' Japan occupied a 'benefit zone' that drew resources from the world's poorer peripheral regions, or 'victimization zones,' that carried the social and environmental costs of consumption.

With globalization the boundaries between entrapment and slavery have become more blurred. The sale of women into sexual slavery or for marriage has been made easier by information technology and the shrinking of space and time associated with globalization. Human trafficking into prostitution and sexual slavery is big business, bringing profits in the region of $7 billion per year in 1998, and it is growing worldwide (Kelly & Regan, 2000, p. 16). It is also less risky than trafficking drugs as the penalties in most countries are lower. Kelly and Regan (2000) have used the concept of a 'continuum of control' to refer to the degrees of force, coercion and trickery used to get women into the sex trade. The continuum of control ranges from imprisonment to abduction to slavery through to debt bondage, deception and threats, but women are also procured through friendship and strategies that use love (Brown, 2000). There is no doubt that domestic violence contributes to the trafficking of women into the sex trade. Trafficked women are not always unaware of the risks they may face. Hope of a better life may outweigh the risks. This fudging of the boundaries between coercion, love and no options makes it easier to blame women for 'trapping themselves' in sexual slavery.

Matchmaking via the web likewise offers women from poor nations marriage and the promise of a better life. There is as yet no research to indicate how trickery, enticement, entrapment, force and choice operate when women participate in matchmaking. New technology has made it easier for men to entrap or to trick women and children into abusive relationships. Even though the internet is still an 'elite club' (extending to less than 7% of the world's population with almost 90% of its users living in rich industrialized nations; Carr, 2001, p. 22) the free flow of information and images over the internet has vastly expanded the opportunities for woman abuse. The anonymity of the internet creates a smokescreen for abusers, reducing their risks of being caught and allowing them to target and groom vulnerable women and children or to access or offload pornography using video equipment and digital cameras without ever having to visit a sex shop. Internet pornography is big business giving opportunities for organized crime and for home abusers to financially profit from their crimes. Because much of it is illegal it is impossible to accurately estimate the extent of pornographic violence worldwide. There are few statistics and those that exist concentrate on areas where the problem has been acknowledged. Research and police reports however suggest a rapid expansion of pornographic materials on the internet in the past 7–8 years. Carr (2001) pooled some of this material to present to the 2nd World Congress Against the Commercial Sexual Exploitation of

Children held in Japan in 2001. In 1996 a survey by an American market research company estimated the sales of adult pornography on the internet as being US$52 million per year (ECPAT, 2001). This was then the equivalent of one tenth of all e-business done. A google search for child pornography in 2001 brought up 425,000 hits (ECPAT, 2001). None of the 12 seizures of child pornographic images made by the police Obscene Publications Squad in the UK in 1996 involved seizures of images on computers while there were 41,000 images seized from computers in 1999 (Carr, 2001, p. 17). Sales of printed pornographic images in high street magazines such as Playboy and Penthouse are declining as 'customers' shift their attention towards the net. Playboy sales in 2000 dropped by 12%, while Penthouse sales fell from 3.5 million in 1980 to 850,000 in 2001 (Carr, 2001). Japan has a concentration of pornography, especially child pornography. Over 3000 pornography websites have been found in Japan and 73% of the world's child pornography is said to have been produced there (Carr, 2001, p. 23). The net now offers the possibility for 'virtual violence' using body 'morphing' and computerized graphics portraying violent and sexualized abuse. Morphing techniques are so advanced it can be difficult to distinguish real from virtual violence.

The developments in communication technologies have increased abusers' scope to groom, monitor and stalk women and children. SMS (short message services) and mobile phones have played a major part in the Japanese problem of enjo kosai, so-called 'compensated dating,' where young girls are lured into commercial sexual exploitation and abuse by adults rather than pushed into it by poverty (Moriyama, 2001). Enjo kosai involves men subscribing to a telephone chat club and paying to get a private phone call with a woman or a girl. The man then asks to meet the woman or girl for a date and agrees a price that can include a payment for sexual services. The Japanese press has reported cases of enjo kosai inappropriately, castigating schoolgirls for 'choosing' to sell sex for cash to buy designer fashion wear. Far less attention has been given to the men who think it is OK to buy sexual services from children. In 1999 a new law was introduced to help reduce the problem of prostitution and the commercial sexual exploitation of children in Japan. The 666 cases of child prostitution via dating services filed for prosecution from January to November 2002 are probably the tip of an iceberg of sexual crime (ECPAT, 2003).

Globalization has indeed made the world a 'smaller place' as it has allowed the rapid transport of human beings, resources and information. It has opened up the sex trade and increased the scope for violent men to evade the risks associated with crime control policies on violence against women at home by enabling them to entice, entrap or force women in the 'periphery' into abuse and exploitation. Poor areas are the supply areas for trafficked and match made women and for women who go into the sex trade. Blame and responsibility for managing the risks of victimization are unevenly spread and disproportionately borne by women and girls in the peripheral areas of victimization zones, where they lack rights to protection from violence. Even in Japan however where the scope to export risk is greatest, the majority of men who abuse women and girls, abuse those they know and live with (Prime Minister's Office, 1999). Violence against women is still very much a 'home grown' crime.

The growing awareness of risk

The world has become a more dangerous place for women but we are also now more aware of violence and, arguably, less likely to accept it. In this section we look at fear of crime and domestic violence and continue with the argument that managing the risk of violent crime is a responsibility disproportionately carried by women.

Feminist activism has done much to uncover violence against women. Recent feminist activity on violence against women emerged in the UK in the 1970s when refuges first opened their doors to women experiencing domestic violence. These quickly filled to overcrowding. By the mid-1970s, a network of refuges had been established in the UK and the Women's Aid movement was born. Feminist activists early on campaigned for policies that would enable women to separate from violent men – law reform, women's welfare benefits, housing provision and emergency protection. Efforts have lately shifted on to the recognition of domestic violence as a crime like any other.

In Japan violence against women similarly came to the fore when counseling centers and shelters opened in the 1980s and 1990s to give help to sex workers and trafficked women. Japanese women started to come to these centers to get advice about domestic violence. The numbers of Japanese women who asked for advice about domestic violence at the Asian Women's Center (which one of the authors and her feminist friends founded in 1997) were 49 in 1988, 88 in 1999, 202 in 2000, 341 in 2001 and 748 in 2002. The globalization of human rights discourses also helped to highlight the problem of violence against women. After the United Nations Fourth World Conference on Women in Beijing in 1995, Japanese women exposed to international movements against violence against women, started to speak out and share experiences. In 2000 violence against women became part of the government's gender equality strategy. A new law on domestic violence was introduced which became active in 2001. Recorded crimes of domestic violence against women have since then sky-rocketed. Two hundred and thirty-three protection orders were granted in the four months between October 2001 to February 2002 (Cabinet Office, 2002, p. 27). Reports of indecent assaults have also grown dramatically from 1875 in 1989 to 3649 in 1997, although rape reports have stayed nearly the same (Prime Minister's Office, 1999, Chap. 3). There is a huge undercounting of these crimes. It is estimated that less than 1% of Japanese women who experience domestic violence contact the police (Cabinet Office, 2002, p. 25).

Since the early 1980s, similar trends have existed in crimes of violence against women reported to the police in the UK, although the victim accounts in the British Crime Survey have been showing a decline now since 1996 (Simmons & Dodd, 2003). It does appear that women are less likely to tolerate domestic violence from their partners and more are coming forward to report these crimes, but nonetheless it remains a huge problem.

The media has helped to inform women of help that is available. There has been increased coverage of violence against women in newspapers and by television stations in the UK and Japan. In the UK in 2003 the BBC ran a week long series on violence against women that was designed to raise awareness and challenge attitudes. Despite the widespread coverage of domestic violence, research on fear of crime shows women's growing fears about 'stranger danger' rather than violence from known men (Simmons & Dodd, 2003). Dangerous men tend to be strangers, opportunistic rapists, paedophiles and child molesters, only rarely are they portrayed in the media as the 'family man' or 'father.' This affects the actions women take to ensure their personal safety. Advice for women on safety has proliferated in the UK since the 1980s ranging from advice on how to drive safely to where to walk when venturing out alone. Women's perceptions of victimization zones are more likely to be geographically situated outside the home – unsafe places to walk, especially at night. It is only very recently that we have seen a limited amount of guidance for women on how to be safe from domestic violence and still the emphasis is on what to do if you are abused, rather than on how you could prevent it. Domestic violence is apparently inevitable. There has been a proliferation of advice for parents and children, similarly focusing on stranger-danger and the risks for children outside of the home. There is hardly any safety advice for men, even though young men are the group most likely to experience a violent crime (Simmons & Dodd, 2003). Responsibility for crime control falls disproportionately upon women, as it is women who carry responsibility for their safety. Blame is diverted from the abusive man at home on to dangerous strangers and back on to women who 'fail' to protect themselves and their children.

In Japan, media facilitated moral panics about rising crime have centered on the de-traditionalization of the family and the lack of discipline of youth. Bullying, abuse to parents, refusal to go to school and child abuse are examples of recent moral panics covered by the Japanese press (Goodman, 2002). The family, once viewed as the support strut for Japan's economic strength, is now viewed as being at the root of all its social ills. Women and children disproportionately carry the blame for this moral decline. Prominent members of the Japanese government have excused male violence on the grounds that women's reluctance to marry and reproduce has left Japanese men frustrated by their 'overwhelming' sexual urges. Gang rapists have been almost congratulated for acting 'normally' and being 'virile' (Seichi Ota, 2003). The Chief Cabinet Secretary Yasuro Fukuda was reported to have similarly 'justified' a gang rape by university students on the grounds that the victim's dress provoked the attack:

> It is wrong for women to dress mostly naked. Men are black panthers, so leniency can be thinkable for the rapists. (Yasuro Fukuda, *Japan Today*, Wednesday July 9 2003)

The anti-feminist backlash in the UK and in Japan has exerted a powerful countervailing influence on attitudes about the causes and acceptability of violence, especially in times of economic uncertainty. In the next section we argue that in the UK the anti feminist backlash has sustained opportunities for men's violence by hijacking the rhetorical plea for 'equality' in the family. Attitudes about 'equality' have raced ahead of many people's experiences, especially women's. More women are reporting domestic violence to the police but research in the UK shows beliefs in the acceptability of violence against women persist. Recent research on young people and domestic violence found a third of all the boys questioned and one in five girls expressed views that suggested their acceptance of domestic violence (Mullender et al., 2002, p. 70).

Risk and crime in the family

Feminist global activism has brought a sharing of the techniques of crime control across the globe, most flowing from the USA into the UK and elsewhere. Information on homicide reduction, curricula for perpetrator re-education and risk assessment and management techniques have been widely disseminated and franchised. There is no doubt that this global activism and the sharing of ideas and strategies have brought some significant advances in policy and practice (see, e.g., Hanmer & Itzin, 2000). One example of this shared experience is the SARA, the Spousal Assault Risk Assessment guide which is used in interviews with victims of domestic violence by agencies such as the police. The SARA assesses risk to a victim with reference to 'risk indicators' drawn from research on domestic fatalities. The SARA, developed in the USA, is fast becoming the major tool in risk management for domestic violence for the police and probation service in the UK.

While risk management has been viewed suspiciously by criminologists as being strongly associated with the rationing of resources (Young, 2002), feminist collaborative activities on risk and violence against women have been motivated more by the much broader strategic aims of 'uncovering' violence and getting it 'taken seriously' by agencies like the police and courts. A whole area of work has developed in relation to 'screening' for domestic violence in health care settings and in screening and risk assessment for cases in the family courts (Hester, Pearson, & Radford, 1997). Risk assessment in feminist activism is about getting better resources for victims of crime and a greater sharing of responsibility to prevent men's violence. This offers both promises and pitfalls. On the one hand risk management offers an opportunity for feminist activists to open up a dialogue with key agencies such as the police and probation about basic standards of service response, albeit limited to the women most at risk of being killed. The allocation of resources to meet this responsibility might however invoke rationing strategies and deny protection for the majority. With reference to the SARA for example, an over-emphasis upon severe and repeat victimization might result in a poorer first response for women who are assessed not to be at risk of lethal violence or repeat assaults. Engagement with this limited discourse on risk management could divert energies away from the broader matter of gendered violence and meeting women's human rights.

Sociologists and policy makers in the UK have optimistically viewed the de-traditionalization of the family and the increased involvement of women in paid work as a potential liberation for women. It is assumed this will bring a change in attitudes and behavior as men take on more care work and responsibilities are equalized (Giddens, 1994). In the UK the equality goal has brought an enhancement of fathers' rights and (notionally also) their responsibilities on separation and divorce. In the late 1990s in the UK father deprivation became the root of many ills in society. The victimized modern man was caricatured as deprived of his children, emasculated and downtrodden by the woman who financially drained him for alimony. Men lost their breadwinner function and children became highly prized emotional capital that both men and women could fight for in the courts (Smart, Neale, & Wade, 2001). Legal concepts such as 'parental responsibility' now tie separated women to an ongoing relationship with the biological fathers of their children. In practice this means men have gained control over women's parenting after separation without seriously being required to make much commitment to the financial or practical care and support of children. Men's involvement with children is optional, on a take-it-or-leave-it basis. For women motherhood, once embarked upon, becomes a duty, nature's intent, a life plan to which we are expected to aspire. As Carol Smart once put it, fathers 'care about' children while mothers 'care for' them (Smart, 1989[a]).

The building of fathers' rights and responsibilities has given violent men a free rein to abuse women and children after separation. As domestic violence has been gaining recognition as a crime, men denied access to ex-partners by domestic violence law have sought it instead through their children. The state's failure to challenge violent fathers has forced mothers to take risks with their own and with their children's safety. Resistance by mothers or children to the father's attentions is not taken by the courts as evidence of reasonable fears but as the woman's churlish failure to sign up to the equality compact. Maternal resistance to a violent father's contact with children is viewed by courts as maternal hostility, parental alienation or, worse still, as her mental illness (Radford, Sayer, & AMICA, 1999). In the UK the government is presently investing in further support for 'equal parenting' by funding child visitation/contact services. We do not want in any way to suggest that child contact services are not a worthwhile investment for children's wellbeing. We accept the view that children have a right to know their parents. It could also be argued though that the right needs to be thought through carefully so that the child's right to safety is not compromised. A recent survey in England by Women's Aid found a worrying trend for courts to ignore the safety of women and children. Eighteen children were found to have been ordered by courts to have contact visits with parents who had been convicted (under S1 of the Protection of Children Act 1999) of an offence of violence against children (Saunders & Barron, 2003, p. 46). Women's services (Saunders, 2002), children's services (Children Act Sub-Committee, 1999) and eminent child psychiatrists (Sturge & Glaser, 2000) have all said that contact centers do not always benefit all children. It may sometimes be in the interests of a child to have time to recover and not to have an ongoing visiting relationship with an abusive father.

In the UK the re-thinking of fatherhood has pushed responsibility for managing violence and protecting children on to victimized women. Blame shifting has taken a different path in Japan. In Japan, the male breadwinner/dependant wife model of welfare began to change later than in the UK, when women entered paid employment in the 1980s. Japanese women now stay single for longer, marry later and have fewer children than women in other industrialized countries (apart from Italy). Divorce rates are also rising so women are more likely to exit unhappy relationships than ever before. A growing number of men are having a hard time finding partners. One in five men aged 35–39 in Japan is unmarried (Kokuritsu Shakai Hosho Kenkyusho [National Institute of Population and Social Security], 2003). We showed earlier that this trend for women to avoid marriage has been linked by the media and politicians to the frustration of Japanese men's 'natural' overwhelming sexual 'urges' and their 'need' to export abuse via sex tourism, woman trafficking, bride sales and match making.

The assumption that Japanese society was previously non-violent but has recently degenerated (mostly because of women's flight from marriage) needs to be challenged. The rapid exit of older Japanese women into places of safety and refuges indicates that domestic violence has long existed in Japanese families but, up to now, it has been a 'hidden' crime and part of 'normal' family life. The sex trade grew in Japan in the context of this traditional patriarchal family and ballooning economic growth. Japanese men were able to express their success through violent sexuality and the commodification of women's bodies. Economic recession has left men less able to express their 'success' by commodifying women. Economic slowdown has brought increased victim blaming and calls for a return to 'old family values.'

Moral panics over the family in Japan have situated most blame ultimately on women and mothers (Goodman, 2002) and have done little to challenge this Japanese version of hegemonic masculinity (Connell, 1995), where 'successful men' have a high capacity for sexual violence. The equal fatherhood movement has had less impact on violence against women in Japan because the care of children is still seen mostly as the sole responsibility of women. Eighty-nine percent of Japanese men continue to work after the birth of a child with no change at all to their working hours or to their leave. Forty-four percent of women either quit work of take leave following the birth of a child (Goodman, 2002). Fathers have shown little interest in seeking time to care for their children and children have not become emotional capital. A recent government advertising campaign tried to convince Japanese fathers of the benefits of caring but this has been widely criticized by men's rights groups because of the long working hours many are expected to have.

In this section we have argued that government policies on domestic violence crime control and on gender equality in the family have had contradictory results. Feminist activists in the UK have supported crime control and risk management as part of the strategy to have domestic violence recognized as a crime. But gender equality measures aimed at involving fathers more in care have failed most women and put abused women at greater risk of post-separation violence. Japanese feminists might treat warily the government slogan that 'real men care for children.'

Risk, justice and women's rights

Much of this paper has been about blame shifting and responsibility for managing violence and risk. Risks and capacities for risk management are distributed unequally and socially excluded women and children continue to bear the brunt of men's violence. Blame shifting has inevitably taken different routes in the UK and Japan because the social, political and cultural contexts in which this repositioning of blame occurs differs. In UK law, social policy and the media, representations of fatherhood have undergone radical reconstruction in recent years (Collier, 1995). One challenge for feminist activism in the UK is the marrying up of 'dangerous men' with 'fathers' so that men who are fathers take on responsibilities to provide care for children in the context of relationships with women that are truly equal and not abusive. In Japan, feminists face the challenge of turning around a victim blaming culture by pushing on to men some of the responsibility for violence and the commodification of women's bodies. This will not happen without men and women working together to challenge men's behavior and to deconstruct and expose the violence in the hegemonic masculinity of 'successful men.'

Privileges are not lightly abandoned. Sociologists of risk and modernity have argued that a 'boomerang effect' can limit the extent to which the rich can offload risks on to the poor (Beck, 1992). Transported risks such as environmental pollution caused by waste products ultimately boomerang back to effect the health of the rich. The boomerang effect does not really exist in relation to the transportation of the risks associated with acts of violence against women because third world women are the most 'disposable' people (Bales, 2000). Disposability allows 'first world' men to enjoy the benefits of violence, enforcing their expectations on women to perform sexuality, femininity and motherhood without worrying about the costs of violence – arrest, stigmatization, owing responsibility through partnership or fatherhood. The creation of a boomerang effect for some of these crimes would be a major advance in women's human rights as it would make 'third world' women less vulnerable because their abuse would carry costs. We have seen some progress made to date through the international police collaboration to establish baseline data on trafficking and prostitution and the creation of legal sanctions to internationally target perpetrators who travel overseas for child abuse and sex tourism. A boomerang effect could be enhanced by deconstructing victim blaming, improving access to justice for migrant, minority, poor and young women and targeting responsibility on to perpetrators. This could help to control and limit men's violence. The emphasis on risk and responsibility holds a limited promise for feminist anti-violence activism because the overriding emphasis is on containment rather than the elimination of the injustice of violence and abuse. We need to be aware of these limitations and keep sight of the broader project for global justice and women's rights.

5.3

'You deserve it because you are Australian': the moral panic over 'ethnic gang rape'

by S. Poynting, G. Noble, P. Tabar and J. Collins

[. . .]

'Caucasian women the targets'

[. . .]

On 29 July 2001, the *Sun-Herald* had a front-page story which headlined, '70 girls attacked by rape gangs' (a fallacious figure) which was sub-headed 'Caucasian women the targets', and in which it repeated the phraseology that the alleged perpetrators 'are all of Middle Eastern extraction' and remarked that 'their alleged victims have all been Caucasian' (Kidman 2001:1). 'Police are concerned that the acts may become culturally institutionalised', it recorded. The following day, 2GB radio talkback host Philip Clark (2001) referred to pack rapes by 'Middle Eastern gangs' around Bankstown, canvassed the belief that the crimes were racially based, and suggested that members of the 'Arabic community' could be harbouring the criminals.

We see here the ideological themes which emerged during the 'ethnic crime gang' moral panic in 1998 (Collins et al. 2000): the observation that the alleged perpetrators share a particular appearance or ethnic background; attribution of causation of criminality to the supposedly shared culture of the offenders; and apportionment of responsibility for the crimes to entire ethnic communities. In addition, in these instances it is asserted by police, media and then politicians, that the victimisation is on the basis of race:

> Police said they were 'keeping an open mind' on possible links between Tuesday's attack and similar incidents in which teenage girls and women have been targeted by middle eastern [sic] men for being Caucasian.

[. . .]

'There are suburbs in which the streets are not safe and young Caucasian women are at risk of rape', editorialised the *Telegraph*, which explained that the crime was associated with a lack of assimilation or integration into 'our' Australian society. 'Many of the members of these gangs declare they don't regard themselves as Australians even though they were born here, and this challenges the comfortable image of the society we have built' (*Daily Telegraph* 6/8/01:20). On commercial radio station 2GB, Alan Jones (26/7/02), following the further trials a year later, also attributed the crimes to immigrants' failure to integrate. Refusing to resile from what he reiterated was the truth, that gang rapists were raping girls for racial reasons, he continued, as if these claims were logically and inextricably linked, that if Lebanese Muslims wanted to live [in Australia] solely as Lebanese Muslims, then 'Australia is not going to take it'.

An opinion column in the *Daily Telegraph* remarked on the racism raging on radio talkback shows, and observed how the untrammelled racial vilification was linking the gang rapes with asylum-seekers. From being of Middle Eastern 'extraction' or appearance, or being 'Lebanese', the gang rapists were now being ideologically identified as 'Muslims'.

[. . .]

Alan Jones (30/7/01, excerpted in *Media Watch* 2002), referred to 'attacks against ordinary Australian girls carried out by out of control Lebanese Muslim gangs who hold us and our police service in contempt'. He commented, 'Now they are showering their contempt for Australia and our police on these young girls', and described this as 'the first signs of an Islamic hatred towards the community that welcomed them' (Fickling 2002).

[. . .]

Tabloid columnist Miranda Devine weighed in with a breathless argument, reprised a year later by Janet Albrechtsen (2002), that it was *multiculturalism* which caused the rapes. 'How many girls and young women have been sacrificed because no-one wanted to offend ethnic sensibilities?', she asked rhetorically (Devine 2001:15). Heaping hyperbole on the rhetoric, she wrote that it was no less than war being fought, in:

> a home-grown form of systematic ethnic cleansing by a group of men said to be of 'Middle Eastern' extraction . . . [T]hey wage war on those they feel do belong. And make no mistake. It is a war, and one in which our laws are impotent.

Very similar claims were made in an anonymous, racist pamphlet handed out to school students at Bankstown railway station and a number of other sites in Sydney around September 2002, and bearing the name, postal address and website of the Australia First Party. Subheaded, 'Don't Be a Victim of Multiculturalism Gone Mad!', the leaflet asserted that misogynist Muslim culture caused the sexual assaults. Referring to the rapists (the convicted 'leader' of whom is pictured), it asks, 'Why Do They Do It?', and answers (falsely), 'They

Quote From The Koran'. There follow three purported quotations from the Koran in English, which are summarised (again patently falsely) as follows:

In other words, women can be taken by men as they will; men can control and dominate women and use violence against them; women who assert their physical beauty could be open to punishment. The victims of the gang attacks were so chosen!

[. . .]
In the second half of 2001, the *City Star*, the local paper of Penrith in the outer west of Sydney was 'besieged by letters from angry, white males about "ethnic crime", especially rape'. The editor, Chris Hutchins, recounts to Andrew West, 'They would say these rapists were not real men . . . Send them out here and we'll show them what a real man does – all that stuff' (West 2001).

The tabloids and talkback demanded tougher sentences and Premier Carr (and, of course, the Opposition) promised tougher sentences. They reviled judges as soft and out of touch and they called for appeals on the sentencing, and the Director of Public Prosecutions indeed appealed against the 'ridiculously lenient sentences' (Morris 2001:4). [. . .]

Opposition Leader John Brogden, for his part, promised compulsory minimum sentencing should he be elected. He concurred on air with Alan Jones (2GB 18/7/02) in his criticism of Lebanese Muslim leaders for denying the racial aspects of the gang rapes, and (in this context) offered amendments to the *Crimes Act* for hate and racially motivated crimes.

Nicholas Cowdery, the NSW Director of Public Prosecutions, was critical of both the Premier and the Opposition Leader for encouraging racism:

There is an element of racism in the community, and the politicians prey on these mindsets and make statements which are sympathetic with the prejudices of the people they wish to vote for them (Gerard 2002:5).

One Nation MP David Oldfield called for a ban on the immigration of Muslims following the gang rape convictions:

What we have seen with the latest offenders is just the tip of the iceberg, these people are not alone. There are others like them. Those 14 men did not come to the conclusion that Western women are 'sluts' and 'whores' by themselves, they were indoctrinated with these beliefs by Islamic leaders . . . The socially primitive nature of Islamic society is evident . . . in the way they treat their women and, surely now, in the way they treat ours . . . such backward practices are not acceptable to Australian society (*The Torch* 24/7/02).

Two converse interesting ideological manoeuvres being effected here are the 'othering' of the perpetrators and the 'whitening' of the victims. The suspected and later convicted rapists were often referred to as 'Muslim' in contexts where this identity was contrasted with Australiannness. They were repeatedly described as 'Lebanese', notwithstanding their Australian nationality, residency and country of upbringing. By contrast, the seven victims of the rapes, invariably described as 'Australian', included two girls of Italian and one of Greek background. The victims were often collectively designated as 'Caucasian', and sometimes as 'white', despite the fact that one was of Aboriginal parentage (Fickling 2002).

'The rapists mentioned race first'

[. . .]

It should be stressed at the outset of this discussion that the mostly untested allegations of a few racist remarks do not remotely demonstrate the race-based motivation that was inferred or even assumed with such irresponsible abandon. Moreover, given the horrific humiliation and damage of the rapes, it is interesting that the relatively minor aspect of these comments should be so seized upon and emphasised – by certain media and populist politicians as a major aggravating factor of the crimes, with implications about their causality. Likewise, it is noteworthy that procedural shortcomings identified in this particular moral panic both in the processes of charge-bargaining and in ignoring victims' impact statements – processes which had been in place for a considerable time – should have surfaced and arisen to such prominence in these very instances, laden as they were with racial overtones.

Neither, furthermore, do the convictions and the backgrounds of the offenders demonstrate culpability on the part of communities from which they come, and of which they are unfairly held to be representative. Still less can they be taken as evidence of endemic cultural wrongs and inadequacies of particular ethnicities and/or religions which are ideologically taken to be causes of the crimes under discussion. All of these ideological elements pervaded the moral panic about the 'ethnic' gang rapes.

[. . .]

The issue of motivation goes to the heart of the characterisation of the rapes in question by a number of commentators, intent on attributing a measure of responsibility to the Lebanese community of the perpetrators, as racist hate crime. According to Byers (1999, cited in White & Perrone 2002: 163), a hate crime:

is a prejudice-based criminal offence *motivated* by the victim's membership within a particular social group. This could include, but may not be limited to, crimes *motivated* by the victim's real or perceived race, ethnicity, national origin or sexual orientation (emphasis added).

The evidence that some of the gang rapes in Sydney in 2000 involved abusive reference to the ethnicity of the victims, does not demonstrate such motivation. As columnist PP McGuinness surprisingly observes, '. . . gang rape is not the product of religious or ethnic factors'. He compares the recent sexual assaults with an infamous case in Sydney in 1886, the 'Mount Rennie Outrage'. Nine youths were sentenced to hanging for the offence; all had 'typical Anglo and Celtic names'. McGuinness concedes that, 'It is relevant that the perpetrators of the recent cases of gang rape had common identifiers', and also refers to the alleged race-based insults so emphasised in the recent moral panic:

> Any girl who is targeted by a bunch of thugs of any origin will be described by epithets which somehow make her inferior, and therefore fair game unlike their own women, who are protected by tribal or group loyalties (McGuinness 2002:11).

In the first of the series of trials prominently reported by the media in August 2001, four youths, two of whom were brothers, submitted pleas of guilty: three men accepting two counts each of aggravated sexual assault and the fourth man pleading guilty to detaining advantage. They further admitted a number of other sexually related crimes, which were to be considered in sentencing them. In September 2000 they had offered a ride in their car to two young women waiting at a railway station, then taken them to a house in western Sydney where they were threatened with a knife and forced to have sex a number of times (Temple 2001:3). An effect of their pleading guilty, in addition to guaranteeing their conviction, is that the victims were spared the trauma of having to confront their attackers in court and to relive their experiences in a harrowing and drawn-out trial, and they also avoided the often humiliating and painful process that cross-examination can take in such cases. To encourage this preferable course, which also delivers savings of court time and expense for the State, sentences are routinely discounted for such pleas. This became one issue in the moral panic which ensued.

Another issue was also a matter of routine in the process of 'charge bargaining'. In order to secure a plea of guilty and obtain a definite conviction with minimal delay and cost to the State and (the cynical might argue, not so crucially, from the State's point of view) less suffering to the victims, lesser or fewer charges are usually proffered: ones which both prosecution and defence agree would be likely to be sustained in the event of a defended trial. Moreover, an agreed statement of 'facts' of the case is commonly in such instances negotiated between prosecution and defence, to go before the judge in determining sentence. Again, this avoids questioning and cross-examining defendants, victims and other witnesses in the process of an expensive and protracted trial which would also cause further pain for the victims.

A third issue in the subsequent moral panic was the length of custodial sentence initially determined, which fell within the usual range for such offences: a norm which came under sudden, strident and unrelenting attack in the media from commentators, journalists and politicians. The type of corrective institution – the prisoners were minors – also became a issue, albeit a subsidiary one, linked to the general ideology about judicial leniency.

Finally, there was a significant media campaign to have the names of the convicted released to the public: something normally precluded by law in the case of minors except where a judicial determination is made that it is in the public interest. (This very exception had been provided for as the result of previous moral panic and law and order auctioneering).

[. . .]

Unholy trinity: power, thuggery and silence

One case of comparison will suffice to show that the media furore about the process of charge bargaining and the overlooking of the victims' impact statements was determined by relations of racism and class. This case in Sydney's inner west came to light in October 2000, at much the same time as the group sexual assaults in south-western Sydney, and went to trial in 2001. It involved at least 75 sexual assaults over a four-month period – 50 on one victim and 25 on another – often 'in front of "spectators" ' (Connolly 2000) who 'stood by and cheered them on and laughed as the victims screamed' (Overington 2001). The perpetrators were teenage males from the same religious background, and police stated to the court that the practices of violence, humiliation and bullying were endemic to the subculture of these young men. The group sexual assaults involved elements of torture – a description Justice Finnane used about the rapes discussed above (Wockner 2002) – tying up and beating were part of the ritual violence.

As in the case we have been concerned with here, charge bargaining took place, which shaped the course and outcome of the trials. The offenders agreed to plead guilty to lesser charges and the prosecution 'agreed to accept the pleas and drop more serious charges of sexual assault', in return for the guilty pleas which 'saved the victim the stress and trauma of having to give evidence . . .'. (Walker 2001). In one instance, 'two counts of aggravated sexual assault' were reduced to one count of intimidation' (*Sydney Morning Herald* 2001b:2). In all, 'Twelve other charges were dropped in exchange for the guilty pleas' on the basis of this agreement. One other youth had already accepted the offer of a guilty plea in January, when the DPP:

> offered a plea to the boys of aggravated indecent assault, whereas in December, back-up charges (made on the advice of the DPP) included aggravated sexual intercourse and sexual intercourse without consent. (If defendants admit to a form of penetration they are allowed to plea to a lesser charge.) One said yes, the others no (Lawson 2001).

Nevertheless, the story told by the agreed statement of facts was horrific. A children's court magistrate was reported as saying that there was an ongoing culture of bullying and abuse, in which victims were tied to beds and sexually assaulted in front of their peers (Connolly 2001). In passing sentence, the magistrate 'said the offences were committed in company, were ongoing, and involved the use of implements "in a most degrading way for the victim" ' (AAP/*Weekend Australian* 2001:11).

As the victims did not give evidence at the hearings, when they became disappointed at and hurt by the lenient sentences, and felt betrayed by information management and denial, they told their story instead to the press. It involved racism and bullying (Walker 11/2/01).

Two 16-year-old offenders were given twelve-month good behaviour bonds and had no conviction recorded (*Sydney Morning Herald* 2001a40; ABC News Online 24/3/01). The one youth who admitted using his school tie to bind one of two victims who had been sexually assaulted more than 75 times over four months, was found guilty of intimidation and released on a good behaviour bond of six months without a conviction recorded. A fourth boy was allowed to plead guilty to intimidation in return for the withdrawal of two charges of aggravated indecent assault, and was placed on a good behaviour bond of six months, with no conviction recorded (AAP 2001).

Each young man had his own team of lawyers. These were ruling-class boys. They and their victims had been boarders at the exclusive, Anglican, all-boys Trinity Grammar School, in whose boarding house the sexual assaults routinely occurred.

There was no moral outrage expressed in the media about the charge bargaining process. There was no shock or disgust voiced by press or politicians at the leniency of the sentences. No change was proposed to the law. The same tabloids which, in the 'ethnic gang rape' case, campaigned stridently to have the offenders publicly named (e.g. *Daily Telegraph* 2001:20), even though they were minors, seemed to accept as appropriate that the offenders not be named in this instance, in the interests of rehabilitation – certainly, there was no campaign for them to be identified. Nor were their families identified. In this instance, the media did not make an issue of the common religion of the offenders. The contrast with the media, political and juridical treatment of working-class, poorly educated Muslim boys speaks volumes.

Blind spot allows barbarism to flourish

In July 2002, as the young men convicted of the south-west Sydney rapes were awaiting their sentences in prison, the conservative *Australian* columnist, Janet Albrechtsen (2002) wrote a provocative and misleading opinion piece entitled 'Blind Spot Allows Barbarism to Flourish'. The 'blind spot' was multiculturalism and the barbarism was 'racially motivated gang-rape' practised by 'Muslim pack-rapists' from 'a culture that can treat women as second-class citizens', 'a culture which places so little value on gender equality'. The article not only took racial vilification to new depths among Australian broadsheet newspaper journalists, it regurgitated borrowed and unacknowledged material, misrepresenting the original stories and 'verballing' sources (Australian Muslim Public Affairs Committee 2001). The piece is of particular interest, because of the extent to which exactly the same ideological elements, phrases, stories, comparisons, distorted logic and common-sense cultural-political conclusions were picked up and circulated widely on talkback radio and in everyday conversations; one can find some of the very same formulations in rabid, racist letters to the editor of tabloids. The fact that the article appeared in a 'quality' broadsheet, the Murdoch 'flagship' in Australia, gave authority and apparent credibility to the ideas. The same ideas, expressions and arguments did not have either this circulation in Australia, nor this cachet, when they appeared on a US neo-Nazi website a year earlier, below the swastika and the heading 'New multiracial sport: GANG RAPE!' (Francis 2001). Both the author of this article, Sam Francis, and Janet Albrechtsen had picked up on a media story from France, about an allegedly cultural or racial practice there dubbed *tournante* (Francis) or *tournantes* (Albrechtsen), translated (by both) as 'take your turn'. Francis (2001) wrote, on the white supremacist American web page, 'It consists in the ritual gang rape of white women by non-white immigrants', and further (referring to the *Sun-Herald*'s fallacious front-page story of 31 July 2001), 'France isn't the only nation to experience the pleasures of diversity. Reports from Australia reveal that racially motivated rapes are catching on there as well'. Albrechtsen described *tournante* as 'the French term for the pack-rape of white girls by young Muslim men'. Like Francis, she took a swipe at multiculturalism: 'For 20 years the French ignored the ethnic causes of these barbaric crimes for fear of offending multicultural man. Along the way, more innocent young girls were pack-raped'. She continued:

> Now it's in Australia. Last week two Muslim brothers were found guilty of the gang-rape of a young Australian girl . . . She was invited for a drive but taken to a secluded park and gangraped while 14 Muslim boys watched (Albrechtsen 2002).

The main difference in the two accounts seems to be that Francis is more interested in race (white/non-white) whereas Albrechtsen focuses more on culture ('white' girls but 'Muslim' men) in the mode of what has been called the New Racism (Barker 1981), which in Australia is basically the form of racism of One Nation, as outlined in Chapter Five. Both refer to the press statement of French magistrate Sylvie Lotteau, undated but (northern) spring 2001, according to Francis. The latter refers to 'black male' rapists,

Albrechtsen to the religion of the young men, both attributing this meaning to Lotteau. Francis describes the typical victim as 'a white female'; Albrechtsen (purporting to quote Lotteau directly) as 'a white girl'. The French *tournante* story and its comparison to the 'ethnic gang rape' crisis in Australia had already appeared a year before Albrechtsen's effort, in the column of fellow critic of multiculturalism, Paul Sheehan (2001:20), three days after the Francis piece, and also in Jackman (2001:31).

Albrechtsen reproduces a version of the 'caught between cultures' myth, [. . .], and presents it as a cultural cause of endemic gang rape: 'French and Danish experts say perpetrators of gang rape flounder between their parents' Islamic values and society's more liberal democratic values, falling back on the most basic pack mentality of violence and self-gratification' (Albrechtsen 2002). *Media Watch* (2002) argues convincingly that she lifted this story without citation from an article by Adam Sage in the *Times*, some 16 months earlier: 'Caught between their parents' Islamic values and societies [sic] Christian and social democratic values, some youths appear to have fallen back on the most basic instincts of violence and pleasure' (Sage 2001, cited in *Media Watch* 2002). Albrechtsen falsely ascribes to the 'French and Danish experts' the identification of the rapists as Muslim and the victims as 'white'. Sage's original article had quoted French Psychotherapist Jean-Jacques Rassial as saying that, 'gang rape had become an initiation rite for male adolescents in city suburbs'. In Albrechtsen's rather more creative version, 'male adolescents' becomes 'a small section of young male Muslim youths', and 'gang rape' of unspecified victims becomes 'pack rape of white girls' (*Media Watch* 2002; Australian Muslim Public Affairs Committee 2001). The Danish expert, criminologist Flemming Balvig, receives similar treatment, with Albrechtsen, still referring to the 'young male Muslim youths', claiming that he corroborated 'the French experience of this barbaric rite of passage into manhood for some of these young men' (*Media Watch* 2002). When Balvig was presented by *Media Watch* with Albrechtsen's misuse of his work, he rejected this interpretation indignantly: 'The citation is completely wrong. What I have said is, that the main explanation of gang rape probably is social, and not cultural or religious' (*Media Watch* 2002).

Not only did Albrechtsen add to the European academics' accounts her own supposition that the rapists were Muslim, she also omitted that some of the victims whom she (but not the academics) described as 'white' were themselves Muslim. Scott Johnson's *Newsweek* report of August 20, 2001 is quoted on this by Australian Muslim Public Affairs Committee (2001):

There are increasing reports of gang rapes called tournantes by bands of adolescent boys, some no older than 14. The victims are often young Muslim girls, doubly victimized by depressed socioeconomic circumstance and the fury of the boys who haunt the abandoned buildings where the rapes take place.

We have seen some stark examples in this chapter of how racial or ethnic profiling of a particular type of crime, and the dominance of racist mindsets in the social context in which it takes place, can 'bleach' victims to 'white' and 'blacken' offenders to 'non-white'. As magistrate and Aboriginal woman Pat O'Shane wrote in her letter to the *Australian* (19/7/02), this way of looking flies in the face of history:

> Janet Albrechtsen does not let Australian history stand in the way of a few prejudices. Her comments about racially motivated gang-rapes, and that this first hit in the last 12 months, ignore 200 years of such events. Indigenous Australian women have been subject to such criminal behaviour by Anglo-Australian men, many of them in positions of control over the women and their communities, without a single bleat from the likes of Albrechtsen.

We wish to make a methodological point about appearances and ways of looking, empiricism and causality, and a political point about 'correctness', before concluding this chapter with a cautionary tale about how the assumed 'non-whiteness' of a crime can produce false conclusions about suspects.

'Open eyes to ethnic crime'

Albrechtsen's, Sheehan's, Devine's and Duffy's (2002:16) tirades about the supposed ethnic causes of gang rapes were each interwoven with an attack on 'political correctness' in relation to multiculturalism. Both the July-August 2001 and July-August 2002 rounds of this story coincided with a media campaign to have 'ethnic crime' named and dealt with as such, in the face of the suppression of this 'truth' by misguided liberals and academics and the stubborn refusal to recognise it on the part of purblind 'ethnic leaders'. An aspect of this campaign was the push to have 'ethnicity data' recorded in crime statistics in NSW.

In 2000, the present authors agreed – with reservations – with the suggestion then being floated that ethnicity data be gathered and recorded in the criminal justice system of NSW. The reservations had to do with the practical difficulties of obtaining accurate data (what would count as ethnicity and who would count 'it'?), as well as its possible ideological misuses (Collins et al. 2000). In the end, we were convinced by the arguments being put forward by Don Weatherburn of the Bureau of Crime Statistics and Research, and others, that such data would be useful in determining whether there was over-policing of certain ethnic groups, or overrepresentation in arrests, convictions, incarceration, and so on, as indeed analogous statistics had demonstrated with Aboriginal people, especially young men (Cunneen 2001). If the data were objective and 'true', why, indeed, should social scientists or the people in general fear their being known? In retrospect, perhaps we should have had more reservations about *why* the data and why these particular data were being demanded. What ethnicities and what crimes were focused upon in the popular label 'ethnic crime' or in the practical labour of data collection to which it gave rise? Imagine if, because of a few high profile cases and longstanding cultural stereotypes, the demand were raised to keep statistics on, say, Jewish businessmen in white collar crime? The proposal would rightly be rejected, with contempt and outrage, as racist. Why then, *Lebanese car theft, Muslim rapists, Middle-Eastern appearances?*

Even the ABC's *7:30 Report* became caught up in the ethnic labelling and attacks on 'political correctness'. Journalist Maxine McKew, leading into the piece with comments about 'squeamishness' over 'crime and ethnicity' and 'political correctness', put to NSW Director of Public Prosecutions, Nicholas Cowdery, that 'what makes this [the "brutal gang rapes"] case unique was a particular ethnic group targeting another exclusively' (*7:30 Report* 15/7/02). Apart from the 'particular ethnic group' coming into focus in a certain way of looking, we have also seen that the exclusive targeting of 'another' ethnic group was more folklore than reality – just as it was in the French cases. McKew made clear who that other targeted group is: '. . . there were seven women and all Anglo-Celtic'. Wrong. Cowdery assents both times. The first time, he replies:

> That was certainly the case in the recent series of matters that have been dealt with. And that of course makes it doubly relevant. How can you say it is not relevant when it seems to be a factor in the motivation of the actions of the perpetrators of offences' (*7:30 Report* 15/7/02).

Seems. Appearance is everything. What causal mechanisms have been proposed and tested? We have seen no explanations beyond the sorts of folk prejudices rightly dismissed by Pat O'Shane. What tests, beyond the market research of the successful manufacturing of 'public opinion'? Beyond social-scientific knowledge, was the purported motivation ever proven at law?

In the same interview, Keysar Trad, Vice President of the Lebanese Muslim Association, makes a telling argument, going directly to the question of causation and refuting its (ideological) link with ethnicity. McKew Asks him, '. . . what about this crime? This was a particular group targeting western women, non-Muslim women'. Trad replies:

> This is the issue that I'm getting at. That I've received reports from Muslim women who feel that they were also targeted by rape, sexual harassment, so forth. Now, the issue in this case is that the lady who came forward and reported the complaint happened to be an Anglo-Celtic woman. I believe that if we follow the case further, you will find that the motivation itself of these people, even though they are making

derogatory, racist slurs, that their motivation was the object of their gratification rather than the race of the object of their gratification.

Cowdery then concurs:

> I think that's right. I think the criminality of the crime of rape, as we used to call it, was the primary motivating factor and I think the rest was just regarded as an embellishment by the people who were involved. I have difficulty accepting that this was some sort of ethnic offence by one ethnic group against another ethnic group. I think it was delinquent male behaviour (*7:30 Report* 15/7/02).

How did the papers report this? The *Herald* headlined, 'Open eyes to ethnic crime: DPP' (Stevenson 13–14/7/02:7); the *Telegraph*, 'Racism a factor in gang rapes: Cowdery' (Hilderbrande & Morris 16/7/0:4). Racism was indeed a factor, but not the way the *Telegraph* meant.

'Gang wrongly jailed for rape'

Empiricism – the leap from the observable conjunction (say, statistical regularities) of particular ethnicities and given crimes to the assumption that the ethnicity is a causal factor in the crime – is not the only difficulty, but it is a besetting one. We also need to be especially alert to the ideological ladenness of the observations, and we need to take into account the impact of the social relations of racism pervading the State which is doing the policing, charging, trying, sentencing, incarceration, along with the intimidation, harassment, humiliation and sanctioned violence, as well as doing the statistics, objectivity, recording, reporting. We need theories which can grasp this.

The authors were impressed by the analysis of James Messerschmidt (1993), who attempts – as is in our view greatly needed – to grasp theoretically the complex interplay of class and gender (masculinity) relations in crime. In fact, we are still impressed, though chastened with a salutary lesson. In his groundbreaking study of masculinity and crime, Messerschmidt postulates that racial subordination can be ideologically inverted in acts of sexual violence, in a process by which the less powerful (racialised minority) men are made to feel more powerful in a collective practice of violence expressing momentary but significant power over women victims who come from a more powerful position in the prevailing class and ethnic relations. He may be right. It is an open question, to be tested, like all theory of any use, empirically.

The embarrassment of those of us impressed by this analysis – and doubtless now also of Messerschmidt – is that he used the 1989 New York Central Park 'wilding' case to instantiate his theory. Five black and Latino youths were jailed for up to 13 years for the rape, brutal bashing and leaving for dead of a middle-class white woman jogger in Central Park. The vicious-ness of the violence was a factor to be explained. The 'gang' of young men had been identified 'wilding' in the park, that is, carrying on in a wild manner, skylarking and scaring people. The five matched the ethnic or racial profile fitted by the police to the crime. They were interrogated and they confessed, and their confessions were recorded. Their conviction was a matter of course. The American media called them 'animals', and the rapes were invariably reported in terms of race. They fitted the profile. They were, however, inno-cent of the crime. Recently, another man has confessed to the rape and near-fatal beating, and DNA evidence has shown him to be the offender and the five who were convicted to be innocent (Gordon 2002:28; *Weekend Australian* 2002:15; Sauiny 2002:13). So, in addition to the questions about the inexplicable violence of the assault, we now need to explain why and under what circumstances the five convicted but innocent men confessed. We have no answers, but the question takes us back to the point about racism within the State. We also need to ask why Messerschmidt – and, reading him, why we – did not raise these questions then.

The point of this example is not to suggest that those convicted of the gang rapes in Sydney in 2000 are innocent. It is to say that, until proven otherwise, it is scientifically prudent and socially responsible – not merely 'politically correct' – *not to assume* that their culture is an accomplice, that their ethnicity is a causal factor in the crime. It remains an open question, and one to be investigated empirically, what interrelations were at work between the masculinities of the perpetrators and the class relations and social rela-tions of racism in which they were constructed and in which the young men lived.

[. . .]

5.4

Genocide and the social production of immorality

by Ruth Jamieson

This article is offered as a contribution to the growing literature of social enquiry into the catastrophic wars taking place in middle Europe and Africa at the end of the 20th century (Walzer, 1993; Ignatieff, 1994). More specifically, it also offers a criminological exploration of some defining aspects of those wars.

The work of Stanley Cohen in these areas draws our attention to the continuities between peace and war in respect of certain key themes in 'human rights'. My particular concern in this article, however, is to highlight two other connected issues – the idea of genocide as *social exclusion* and the problem of *victimization* in contemporary genocide.

Genocide

The UN *Convention on the Prevention and Punishment of Genocide* of 1948 defines genocide as a specific form of crime under international law which applies in both war and peace. The UN convention contains two key elements – the definitions of *protected groups* and *prohibited acts*. It stipulates that genocide means:

> any of the following acts committed with intent to destroy, in whole or in part, a *national, ethnical, racial* or *religious group*, as such:
>
> (a) Killing members of the group;
> (b) Causing serious bodily or mental harm to members of the group;
> (c) Deliberately inflicting on the group conditions of life calculated to bring about its physical destruction in whole or in part;
> (d) Imposing measures intended to prevent births within the group;
> (e) Forcibly transferring children of the group to another group.

Some of these prohibited acts (for example killing or causing serious bodily harm) involve extreme physical violence. Others (for example the forced transfer of children) do not. What distinguishes genocide from other forms of group violence is not so much the degree of violence involved, but the fact that genocide is a crime which is concerned with the 'taking out' ('the intent to destroy in whole or in part') of a targeted 'Other' group.

Genocide as a form of social exclusion

An extensive literature on the social and cultural context of genocide and the Holocaust exists, but with a few important exceptions (Milgram, 1974; Bauman, 1989; Kelman and Hamilton, 1989), this has not had a major impact on the individuating tendencies of criminological thought. In the discussion which follows I want to look at the work of Zygmunt Bauman (1995) and Heinz Steinert (1997) who are among a very small number of social theorists who have addressed contemporary (and other) instances of genocide as social exclusion.

Bauman

In the context of an essay on 'Tribal Moralities', Bauman revisits Levi-Strauss's discussion in *Tristes Tropiques* (1955), of the ways in which primitive societies deal with 'danger-carrying strangers' (Bauman, 1995: 179–92). He notes that the general tendency in such societies is to adopt strategies which we may consider 'different . . . from the one that we practise and consider normal and civilized' (p. 179). That is:

> Theirs is the *anthropophagic* strategy; they eat up, devour and digest (*biologically* incorporate and assimilate) the strangers who carry powerful, mysterious forces – perhaps hoping to avail themselves in this way of those forces, absorb them, make them their own.
>
> (p. 179)

Levi-Strauss then argued that the strategic practices of 'civilized' or modern societies, by contrast, were *anthropoemic* (i.e. that we should think of them, after the Greek, as a form of 'vomiting'). That is:

> We throw the carriers of dangers up – and away from where the orderly life is conducted; we keep them out of society's bounds – either in exile or in guarded enclaves where they can be safely incarcerated without hope of escaping.
>
> (p. 180)

For Levi-Strauss, the application of -phagic or -emic strategies was a measure of social evolution. Bauman argues instead that both these 'strategic alternatives' are 'endemic to every society', and, indeed, that they can only ever be effective as a co-present, 'either – or' pair. That is:

> To the strangers whose life conditions and choices they define, they posit a genuine 'either – or' – conform or be damned, be like us or do not overstay your visit, play the game by our rules or be prepared to be kicked out from the game altogether.
>
> (p. 180)

Bauman extends the argument further – in ways which would also be familiar to students of Gramsci – in observing that the 'rules of [social] admission' which underpin the inclusivist mode of social organization 'are effective only as far as they are complemented by the sanctions of expulsion [social exclusion] . . . but the latter may inspire conformity only as long as the hope of admission is kept alive' (p. 181). So the inclusivist mode of domination is necessarily supplemented by corrective institutions for 'the failures' and 'the recalcitrant' (p. 205) which serve to mark the possibility of their readmission under certain (often highly improbable) circumstances. In principle, then, this discussion of double-headed strategies of social domination (inclusion/exclusion) could make sense in general terms of the ways in which modern (capitalist) societies in the 20th century have responded to crises of boom and slump and mass unemployment, that is, it can make sense of the mobilization of a broad range of moral and other justificatory discourses vis-a-vis the feckless or criminal underclass (the reserve army of labour) in order to justify its exemplary imprisonment. Jock Young (forthcoming) develops Bauman's use of such terms in arguing that late modern society neither swallows nor vomits up its marginal groups, but engages in a 'bulimic' process of inclusion and exclusion, engulfing them culturally while simultaneously excluding them socially. So, for example, he suggests African-American men are absolutely 'engulfed' in American culture, especially in its consumer culture – suffering from a 'surfeit' of American values – while also being systematically excluded from the chance of full inclusion in consumer citizenship.

Beyond exclusion: elimination

For the crime of being a Tutsi, I had to beg pardon.
Diane Murebwayire (African Rights, 1995a: 314)

In what sense, however, does this conceptualization of the two different modes of the administration of strangers (and the third offered by Jock Young) help the understanding of genocide? It is obvious that the kinds of 'ethnic cleansing' recently witnessed in Bosnia and Rwanda cannot be understood merely as an extreme formulation of the 'either – or'/'conform or be damned' mode of 'inclusivist' domination described by Bauman. These *eliminationist* social or military strategies involve the complete abandonment or rescinding of the (performance-based) 'rules of [social] admission' in pursuit of a zero sum, 'them-or-us', total solution. That is to say that in this eliminationist mode the rules of admission and their 'either – or' dynamic are suspended:

> In every genocide, the victims are killed not for what they have *done*, but for what they *are*; more precisely still, for what they, being what they are, may yet become; or for what they, they being what they are, may not become. Nothing the appointed victims may or may not do would affect the sentence of death – and that includes their choice between submissiveness or militancy, surrender or resistance.
>
> (Bauman, 1995: 203, emphasis added)

What is at issue in genocide goes beyond the temporary, cyclical and reversible marginalization of the reserve army of labour described by Rusche and Kirchheimer (1939). Genocide constitutes a 'social exclusion' of a final and irrevocable kind. The conditions of existence of the move to such a solution for Bauman are those outlined in his classic enquiry *Modernity and the Holocaust* (Bauman, 1989). The twin conditions of existence of the Holocaust were, first, the existence of a racist ideological project which focused on the extermination of the Jews as a necessary element in the creation of an Aryan territory or *Lebensraum*, and, second, according to Bauman, the construction of a highly rational bureaucracy which made possible, both logistically and ideologically, this project of mass exterminism. The Holocaust, according to Bauman, has to be understood in part in terms of its apparently rational, planned, bureaucratic and hence impersonal character. This, he argues, was a creature of modernity.

Whether one accepts this particular account of the Holocaust or not, it is an account which rejects the interpretation of genocide simply as a 'spontaneous eruption of ethnic hatred' (Cigar, 1995: 6) or a 'descent into barbarism' (Hobsbawm, 1994). It is, instead, a project of elimination which involved extensive planning, co-ordination (and allocation of resources) by a few (for example Adolf Eichmann) and implementation by many. The publicly articulated and legitimizing arguments for such a process of elimination normally identifies the annihilation of a particular targeted outsider group as a rational process that will contribute to the 'public good', that is of the insider population. In addition, he argues, genocide also demands the continuous incitement of perpetrators to reach the 'end point'.

Steinert

Bauman's exposition of the genocidal process is compelling, though questions can still be posed as to whether his general theory on modernity and the Holocaust helps elucidate the specific conditions that give rise to genocidal campaigns and movements.

In a recent essay Heinz Steinert (1997: 112) argues that the basic form of social solidarity which has operated in European society during most of the 19th and 20th centuries is 'market capitalism' (the pre-conditions of which he enumerates as wage labour, private ownership of the means of production (and of labour-power) and private households). The specific forms of exclusion produced by 'market solidarity', therefore, are identified as unemployment, poverty, patriarchy (defined as capitalist domination over women and young men), colonialism and institutionalized social exclusion (in the form of military and bureaucratic discipline, including state punishment). But while market solidarity has been the historically dominant form of social solidarity in this 'troubled and bloody century of counter-enlightenment', it has also been displaced from time to time by other more malignant (or more benign, universalistic) forms of social solidarity. Thus the 'us' against 'them' *(Volks-) Gemeinschaft* solidarity of Nazism had organized fanaticism as its precondition and entailed racism, zenophobia (and ultimately genocide) as its modes of exclusion.

It is beyond the scope of this article to enter into a full account of these different relationships of correspondence (and indeed Steinert does not offer a detailed account of his own). What matters, however, is Steinert's attempt to identify different kinds of political and social movements as attempts to realize or create particular variants of inclusionary or exclusionary forms of social solidarity, set alongside his brief summary of the demonstrable correlates of these specific instances of social and political struggle. We have here the formal theoretical taxonomy of different forms of social exclusion, which could in principle provide a social account of the conditions of existence of genocide in particular types of socially constituted community, to which can be added the vital additional insight of Bauman's as to how this particular form of exclusion can be presented, in modern and rational conditions, as an impersonal bureaucratic process.

Adopting a framework of analysis deriving from Bauman, Steinert allows us to understand that it is not the *degree* of physical violence (which, after all, is also sometimes present in incidents of spree-killing) which is the defining feature of genocide per se, but the unfolding of a 'them' or 'us', zero-sum imperative. The degree of violence involved and the cruelty to individuals is not strictly relevant. As Bauman himself has remarked, the 20th century's impersonal deployment of destructive technology (for example at Hiroshima) has had the effect of 'making [personal] cruelty redundant' (1995: 183). This is not, of course, to suggest that there can be a 'humane' form of genocide.

Focusing of these forms of extreme cruelty and brutality may blind us to the aspects of these crimes (specifically the moral and subject relations to social 'Others' which are entailed in different modes of social domination) which as Nils Christie (1993) points out are also integral features of the more routine forms of social exclusion like imprisonment.

'Social exclusion', broadly defined, and genocide are both only achievable through the concerted action (and self-serving omissions) of those who *will* them and those who actually implement that will. Steinert comments on how 'the individualizing juridical mode' of dealing with 'inhuman' political events and deeds (such as the Holocaust) routinely yields up some 'culprits', in both categories (initiators and implementors), but also produces many 'false innocents' – quite often the broader institutions or the broader society. This individualizing juridical approach to war criminals obscures the fact that exclusionary projects like ethnic cleansing in Bosnia-Herzegovina are not achievable without the complicity and, indeed, the support of the whole community. Thus, although genocide and social exclusion differ in terms of the extremity and reversibility of their practices and effects, they have in common the abdication of responsibility for those defined as 'Other' (Bauman, 1989: 183). At the very least, they both represent an attempt to *reduce* the ambit of moral and social responsibility for said 'Others' (Fein, 1993). Following Steinert's approach, we could call this a form of 'zero-sum solidarity' – pitting the survival of the in group against the out. That said, it is also important to note that the exclusion of the victim from the universe of obligation is a necessary, but not sufficient condition of genocide (Fein, 1993: 36). Genocide also involves a process of essentializing, devaluing and humanizing of the excluded 'Other'.

The capacity to violence

I now want to turn to a consideration of two contemporary instances of genocide in order to consider how the forms of social solidarity which produce genocide may or may not be articulated around other categories of social domination and difference such as gender. The evidence from the two genocidal conflicts in Bosnia-Herzegovina and Rwanda, currently being placed before the tribunals investigating these two contemporary tragedies, suggests that the capacity to forsake or violate the 'Other' was universal (in terms of age and gender) within those societies – especially, that is, if one includes the full range of what Steinert and Bauman would call subject positions (from active perpetrators to passive condoners) within the frame of analysis. This same evidence also directs attention to the limitations of conducting an analysis of such events through the prism of orthodox victimological or feminist theory, particularly the limits of a diadic, 'victim-perpetrator' conception of such forms of eliminationist violence. Finally, the evidence provides further support for Stan Cohen's continuing attempts to question conventional approaches to the idea of the 'bystander' (Cohen, 1995). Not least of the concerns here must be the need to distinguish between 'bystanders' who have no stake in the outcome of conflict, and those who do. The stakes in question may be ideological, material (gain of the victim's property or job), the vicarious settling of old scores or simple self-preservation. There are pitifully few different circumstances, especially in wars where victims can be said to be authentically neutral in their 'subject positions'.

Euphemisms such as 'ethnic cleansing' notwithstanding, events in Bosnia and Rwanda meet the UN's definition of genocide ('intent to destroy [a group] in whole or in part'). Despite the fact that these conflicts have very different specific origins, closer examination reveals significant similarities in respect of the move to exclusion and the embrace of genocidal policies. Not least, there are common patterns of 'agency' and 'responsibility'. These common logics are also evident in what have been described as 'collateral' or incidental crimes such as sexual abuse, extortion, the looting of the dead and dying and the destruction and seizure of property. Let us examine the Bosnian and Rwandan implementation of genocidal projects for what they reveal about the issue of agency and responsibility.

In addition to the enormous importance which was given to the killing of all 'out group' men of military age (a feature it shared with Rwanda), the Bosnian genocide also involved the widespread and systematic use of mass rape as a weapon of war (Commission of Experts on the Former Yugoslavia, 1994: IV F. 1). It is estimated that from 1991 to the cease-fire four years later between 20,000 (EC) and 50,000 (Bosnian Ministry of the Interior) women and girls were raped in towns, police stations and other places of detention in Bosnia-Herzegovina. (See the Report of the Commission of Experts on the Former Yugoslavia, 1994 and Stiglmayer, 1994.) There is evidence of equally extreme and widespread sexual abuse (rape and sexual slavery) associated with the genocide of the Tutsi in Rwanda (African Rights, 1995a: 748–97).

But the case of Rwanda discloses another equally significant dimension of the relationship between social identity and the human capacity to violence. It is the fact that the genocide of the Tutsi involved the mobilization of virtually all of the Hutu population (women and children as well as men). This direct involvement of women and children in the genocidal violence – whether their involvement was willed or induced by greed, terror or intimidation – has been largely ignored by feminist theorists and commentators. The fact of women's (and children's) participation in the Rwandan genocide, should make us pause and reflect on the question of the 'auxiliariness' of women in operationalizing, willing and tolerating eliminationist projects (and, perhaps, in other projects of social exclusion). It is important that we try to see the role of women as members of particular social groups in *sustaining* (as well as healing) social division and conflict and also their potential for inflicting extreme cruelty on others in the contexts of armed conflict, genocide, social exclusion (African Rights, 1995c: 1). I make this point not in order to demonize 'the violent feminine' through an inversion of gender essentialism, but to open out consideration of the broader relationship between violence and social identities which happens to include gender.

Implementing the genocidal logic

There is ample and persuasive evidence that the Bosnian and Rwandan genocides followed similar logics. They were planned at the highest level, organized and co-ordinated by members of the state apparatus (the military, paramilitary groups, the police) and were implemented locally by an array of militarized groups (Commission of Experts on the Former Yugoslavia, 1994; African Rights, 1995b: 59–61; Cigar, 1995: 47–61). Both entailed the manipulation and reanimation of old ethnic or tribal hatreds and fears (Meštrović, 1996) to promote an acceptance by perpetrators and the community of the 'necessity' of eliminating the targeted 'Other'. The pattern of implementation of these projects of elimination is consistent with a progression through the three stages outlined by Hilberg (1985) in respect of the Holocaust. The first stage was the *definition* and classification of the 'out group' as 'Other' (cockroaches ['Inyenzi'] or snakes in the case of the Tutsi or 'Ustashi' in the case of the Croats in Bosnia). The second stage – the activation of the policy – involved co-ordinated action to round up and detain members of the target group – the stage of *concentration*. The last stage was that of expulsion or *annihilation*.

In both Bosnia and Rwanda, the division of labour and chain of responsibility approximated a broadly similar pyramid structure with the planners at the top overseeing the 'middle men of genocide' – the co-ordinators and tacticians who, in turn, directed those who implemented the policy on the ground (African Rights, 1995a; Cigar, 1995; Vulliamy, 1996, 1997).

The pattern of 'ethnic cleansing' in Bosnia

Cigar (1995) describes the pattern of genocide in Bosnia-Herzegovina as follows. The first step was to establish control over the cities and then extend this control into the countryside. Areas where there were large concentrations of Muslim population had to be taken by force from the outside. In localities where there were sufficient numbers of Serbs, control could be seized from within. Once an area was secured, it could be 'cleansed', often by roving paramilitary forces like those of Arkan (Željko Ražnjatović) known as 'The Tigers', or 'The White Eagles' (the Chetnik (Serb nationalist) militia loyal to Dragoslav Bokan). In some cases – for example in the Prijedor area in northern Bosnia – Muslims were taken to detention centres (concentration camps) like Omarska and Keraterm (for men) and Trnopolje (for both men and women) where many were tortured and killed. In other instances, the

(Muslim) men were subject to mass killings – for example in Srebrenica in April 1993 where 5000 men were killed in this way.

Thus far, the logic of exclusion/elimination in Bosnia and Rwanda was very similar. However, a feature of the Bosnian genocide which marked it out as 'unique' was the strategic use of mass rape – sometimes involving spectacles of mutilation and death – of Muslim and Croat women in towns, detention camps and brothels (for example in the Drina Valley at Vgosca, Foca and Brcko Luca) as part of the ethnic cleansing policy. The first cases of mass rape were perpetrated by Serbs against Muslim women in the spring of 1992 (see Mazowiecki, 1992). The following year a second wave of retaliation rapes was committed by Bosnian Croats against Serb women. The mass rapes and forced impregnation of Bosnian women were so systematic and committed on such a scale that it is difficult to see how they could be construed as anything other than an instrument of ethnic cleansing (Mazowiecki, 1992: 73), or a 'weapon of war' (Helsinki Watch, 1993: 21). Tutsi women and girls in Rwanda also were the targets of a catalogue of abuses including widespread rape, torture and mutilation and forced 'marriage' amounting to sexual slavery. But it is not clear that these crimes were perpetrated under orders or as part of a mandated and systematic policy (African Rights, 1995a: 748).

There can be little doubt that the actual implementation of genocidal policies on the ground provides a dizzying degree of licence for 'sadistic innovation' on the part of the foot-soldiers involved in such genocide and that sexual abuses are part of the not very deeply buried repertoire of many participants in these events. Catharine MacKinnon (1994: 194) suggests that, in the end, what it comes down to is that 'men do in war what they do in peace, only more so'.

A common feature of the attempts to make sense of the mass rapes in Bosnia by scholars and journalists alike is that little or no attempt is made to explain how or why 'men doing their thing' expands to include the sexual abuse and torture of 'Other' *men* (for example of the sort for which Dusko Tadic was tried at the Hague Tribunal), or why some of the most sadistic acts of cruelty were not sexual, but involved forcing both women and men to witness (or indeed be the authors of) the victimization of their own children. Nor do these commentators address the issue of whether and to what extent the mass rapes committed by members of the various warring factions may have been either approved or tolerated by the women of their respective communities. Perhaps most dramatically of all, however, the fact of the *active* participation of women in the Rwandan genocide (including episodes involving extreme brutality and sexual abuse) renders the restricted frame of analysis of these attempts at defining the meaning and dynamic of the mass rapes all too apparent.

The irony is that, despite mainstream criminology's having largely succeeded in marginalizing feminist perspectives in much the same way as it has 'human rights' work, feminist criminologists may have been so successful in colonizing the sub-discipline of 'victimology' to the extent that the refrains that it is 'men' who victimize (women) and *women who are victimized* have become paradigmatic. In this sense – so far from transforming mainstream criminology – it is arguable that feminist criminologists have succeeded only in (a) hegemonizing women as victims (and thereby silencing men as victims) and (b) blunting the analysis of the *shared human capacity* to violence by 'splitting off' violence from women and endowing it in the 'masculine' (Connell, 1985: 4). This has had the effect of stunting the conceptualization of violence and (im)morality in criminology. It is for this reason that the role of women (and children) as both targets and participants in the Rwandan genocide warrants our close attention. Therefore, I turn to a consideration of the specific division of labour in that genocidal project.

The Rwandan genocide as a gendered division of labour

The genocide of the Tutsi by the Hutu extremists in Rwanda took place over 100 days between 7 April to 4 July 1994 and followed a similar logic to that of the ethnic cleansing in Bosnia though the scale of the genocide in Rwanda (estimated to have resulted in the deaths of a million people) was greater – due, precisely, to the practice adopted of involving as much of the community as possible in the killings (African Rights, 1995c: 1). The genocide was carried out primarily by the Rwandese Armed Forces, the Presidential guard, the gendarmes and the Interahamwe militia. The first phase involved the targeting of political and intellectual leaders, opinion makers and human rights activists in the capital, Kigali, for immediate elimination and the simultaneous setting up of roadblocks to screen (according to ethnic identity) the people attempting to flee the city. These roadblocks then became centres of execution, extortion and rape (African Rights, 1995a: 770). The second phase involved local sweeps aimed at the rounding up, concentration (in schools, churches or other public buildings) and execution of local Tutsis, 'Ibyitso' (Rwandan Patriotic Front (RPF) accomplices) and 'unreliable' Hutus in the regions. This was done according to previously compiled lists of Tutsis and Hutu moderates as well as by the ad hoc denunciation of others.

The third phase of the genocide involved the exhortation of perpetrators to continue the genocidal slaughter until all of the defined out group had been identified and eliminated. Fein (1993: 37) points out that the historical evidence suggests that, by contrast with 'pogroms, lynchings and massacres' where 'victimizers have stopped when they were sated, drunk or eager to enjoy their booty; genocides on state order press perpetrators to continue'. This third, exhortatory phase of the Rwandan genocide also involved a simultaneous expansion of the definition of the 'out group' to include categories of persons who had not previously been targeted, for example children of mixed parentage. Thus Hutu women married to Tutsis were urged to kill or surrender their own children. Hutu husbands were urged to kill their Tutsi wives (African Rights, 1995c: 53–4).

It is also arguable that there was a fourth post-genocide phase, in which the project of elimination was continued, and still continues, in refugee camps in Eastern Zaire (now Congo) and Burundi. Killings of returning refugees continue in Rwanda as a means of eliminating witnesses who are likely to provide testimony at the Arusha Tribunal, or as a means of avoiding restitution of property seized from Tutsis during the conflict (see African Rights, 1996; Omaar, 1996).

The above description provides only the barest of outlines of the way in which the genocide was implemented. But the issue of *who* played what part in carrying out the Rwandan genocide is important for what it reveals about the human capacity to violence. Although most of the genocidal violence in Rwanda was perpetrated by men who were members of the army, the Intera-hamwe militia or the local gendarmerie, it is also the case that women – from school girls to old women – participated in the project of 'elimination' of the Tutsis – as did some children. Not all did so willingly, but many did. This was a result of the Hutu extremists' demand that all Hutus should participate in the killing (African Rights, 1995c: 41). Typically, the following division of labour obtained:

- Anyone could identify and denounce a neighbour as a member of the Tutsi 'out group'. For example, school girls provided lists of their Tutsi fellow pupils (African Rights, 1995c: 68–9).

- Any opinion leader/member of the central or local government could exhort others to redouble their genocidal efforts, for example Agnès Ntamabyariro, Minister of Justice admonished Hutus for their lack of zeal:

  When you begin extermination, no one, nothing must be forgiven. But here [Kibuye], you have contented yourselves with killing a few old women (African Rights, 1995c: 6).

- Some Women in crowds acted as cheerleaders to the rounding up and killing of Tutsis, ululating [vocalizing] the perpetrators into action. Some encouraged men to rape. (African Rights, 1995a: 748–97, 1995c: 72).

- Women also acted as enablers and participants in the killing (for example Sister Julienne Kizito, a nun in Sovu, Butare, has been accused of aiding in the massacre of people who had sought sanctuary in her convent, handing out cans of petrol which were used in her presence to burn people alive (African Rights, 1995c: 157).

- Women along with children acted as 'finishers off'. Their task was to locate those who were still living and kill them, using whatever – usually 'low tech' – weapons were available to them (knives, machetes, 'masus' [nail-studded clubs] or sharpened sticks).

• Women and children (typically mothers and their daughters) looted the dead and dying (African Rights, 1995c: 81).

It is absolutely and consistently the case that in war women are victims of all kinds of abuse, including sexual abuse, but the events in Rwanda suggest that this is not the whole story. What is apparent from the Rwandan example, however, is that we are unlikely to arrive at an adequate conception of the human capacity to violence if we insist on endowing it only in the masculine or the 'ethnic' rather than in the feminine, the 'human', or the 'social'. Evidence as to the role of women in the concentration camps of the Third Reich or the Vichy government in France should already have alerted us to this possibility. Moreover it is also important to problematize our taken-for-granted conception – not only of what violence is (Kappeler, 1995), but also taken-for-granted assumptions as to who has the capacity to commit or condone such violent social harm. If we admit the possibility that women and children may be induced to adhere to tribal projects with equal ferocity to men, then our analysis of the capacity to violence surely needs to be broadened.

I want to begin to explore the larger and more difficult problem of how criminology might approach the question of the social nature of harm, what Bauman (1989) calls the social production of immorality.

Conclusion

Let us now try to imagine a transcendence of positivistic criminology's commitment to the 'individuation' of criminality and a reductionist conception of the relationship between gender and violence to an understanding of the processes which 'produce' genocide and social exclusion. Bauman postulates a definition of immorality as 'behaviour which forsakes and abdicates responsibility for others' (1989: 183). Bauman develops this project at length and in detail in *Post-Modern Ethics* (1993) and *Life in Fragments* (1995), not least in respect of advancing the clear argument that any such social theory and practice (i.e. of morality) cannot hide behind the strictures of 'popular commonsense' or of what he calls 'the gardening State'.

At an historical moment like the present – in which the tribal wars of middle Europe and Africa threaten genocide for thousands – the argument is inescapable (for citizens of a 'moral world' (*sic*) as well as those who are in daily contact with such events). At an historical moment in which many 'developed societies' in the West are involved in the systematic exclusion of large numbers of people from full citizenship – for example in the escalating use of penal measures against those defined as 'criminal Others', or in the intensifying processes of exclusion directed against asylum-seekers, the issues may seem less immediate (sometimes less fatal) but they are inescapable nonetheless. In Steinert's terms, we can begin to glimpse in these shifting forms of social exclusion, the move from one form of 'social solidarity' (market solidarity) predicated upon the *exclusion* of the poor, the unemployed and the market redundant to another (zero-sum 'them or us' solidarity) which requires the *elimination* of the threatening 'Other'. The prospects may be thought to be ominous.

Conclusion: gender and crime – the legacy?

Criminology is likely to remain a challenging and exciting discipline for gender scholars to work within in the twenty-first century, not least because there is still much to achieve. On the one hand, criminology's 'gender myopia' (Stevens, 2006: 18), continues apace and is exacerbated, particularly in the USA, by what Chesney-Lind describes as the 'backlash politics of a sophisticated and energised right wing' (2006: 8). For Chesney-Lind, this backlash incorporates a 'repression of dissent', 'a grim record of racism' and 'a resistance to extending full rights to women' (2006: 8). On the other hand there are the encouraging signs of further 'awakenings', lively debates and intellectual advances which are indicative of a renewed and enduring intellectual interest with regard to gender and crime (Heidensohn and Gelsthorpe, 2007: 408). These include erudite and energetic sessions within the American and British Society of Criminology conferences and the biannual 'What Works for Women Offenders' international conference; the launch of the *Feminist Criminology* journal by the Women's Division of the American Society of Criminology and the increasingly commonplace publication of studies, chapters, articles and texts addressing gender, crime and criminology (Burgess-Procter, 2006; Heidensohn and Gelsthorpe, 2007).

Given that it is now just over 30 years since the instigation of gendered scholarship within the discipline, we would like to reflect in this concluding chapter upon a range of *achievements*, as well as *challenges*, which have accrued as a result of applying a gendered lens within criminology, and to comment on the potential futures of an engendered criminology. We conclude that gendered endeavour remains crucial within criminology as it is only through attention to individual, social and cultural differences that authentic and humane constructions of the offender and the victim are likely to emerge, and that such constructions are essential to the promotion of individual and social justice (Gelsthorpe and McIvor, 2007: 343–4).

Developing an engendered criminology

This reader introduces a canon of work which has sought to illustrate the core challenges and contributions of applying a gendered lens within criminology (see also Carlen, 1992; Gelsthorpe, 2002; 2003; Gelsthorpe and Morris, 1988; Heidensohn, 1996; 2002; Heidensohn and Gelsthorpe, 2007; Rafter and Heidensohn, 1995; Stevens, 2006). It has demonstrated how gendered scholarship has exposed the discipline as a criminology of and by men, and it has revealed how its 'amnesia' (Gelsthorpe and Morris, 1988: 97) with regard to girls and women was challenged through a critical appraisal of the omission and misrepresentation of female offenders within extant criminological theories. This reader has addressed the ways in which the emerging gendered enterprise sought to render the female offender more visible, and has outlined how the prioritisation of women's experiences and perspectives revealed the key place which fear and victimisation play within the lives of women and the profound impact which this has on their sense of well-being. This body of work is also used to show how 'gender and race create unique pathways for girl and women offenders into criminal behavior, particularly in communities ravaged by drugs and overincarceration' (Chesney-Lind, 2006: 2). Furthermore, a gendered scrutiny of the criminal justice system has not only revealed the sexualised and demonised constructions of women apparent within crime control systems, but also has exposed the discriminatory and damaging nature of many criminal justice practices.

The chosen readings have additionally demonstrated how the behaviour of women and girls has been controlled through sexist and patriarchal ideologies which portray the female as closer to nature than to science, as emotional rather than logical and as passive rather than active. Values of diversity, risk-taking, aggression and dominance have been attributed to the male and denied to the female, lending significant advantage to the male sex at the expense of the female in a society which celebrates and encourages those attributes assigned as masculine. However, as the readings on masculinities, crime and male victimisation demonstrate, this has had repercussions for the male sex too, revealing how ideological constructions of masculinity and femininity serve as powerful social tools which encourage gender-specific forms of behaviour that individuals may struggle to conform to or, indeed, to resist.

The last part of the reader focusing on international perspectives highlights a number of themes which the study of gender within criminology has revealed as significant. First and foremost it demonstrates the results of being perceived as different and as lying outside society's hegemonic norms. It exposes the reality that women are still little valued, disproportionately victimised and are used and abused for private gain both within national borders and by transnational networks of crime. It also uncovers the paradox that since women have been revealed as calculating and self-aware offenders as well as victims, they are, as Snider puts it, no longer 'innocent' (2003: 356) and are subsequently removed from protection and placed with all the 'others' within the existing and currently severe justice codes and penal establishments. It shows, too, that women and girls are made more vulnerable by their poverty, lack of power and marginalised status, and that they share this vulnerability with similarly poor and 'othered' social groups across the globe. In revealing these continuing truths, the study of gender and its intersections with race and class discloses the terrible consequences of the process which sets social groups against each other by classifying certain people, actions and beliefs as dangerous and threatening to social order.

Potential futures for an engendered criminology: the political project

Snider reminds us criminology 'has always been, a relentlessly applied discipline' (2003: 356) and this suited feminism's contribution to the field. Feminism after all has stood as a political as well as an academic project which set out to improve conditions for women in society. Indeed, there has been a marked resistance to abandoning women, and men, to their fate within the criminal justice system and a remarkable tenacity for 'doing something' (Carlen, 2002a; Hannah Moffat, 2002) which has not only been responsible for righting some important wrongs, but also continues to inspire the pursuit of gendered scholarship, reform and activism. Accordingly, Carlen's (1992) persuasive argument that a gendered criminology should link theoretical with political struggles, has more recently been incorporated in Chesney-Lind's assertion that feminist [gender] scholars need to 'seek creative ways to blend scholarship with activism' (2006: 6).

Indeed, even a brief reflection upon the substantive themes emerging within this reader with regard to the gendered nature of victimisation and offending, and their respective treatments within the criminal justice system, reveals a range of potential priorities and challenges for future gendered criminological endeavour.

The recognition of the gendered nature of victimisation, particularly with regard to domestic violence and sexual assault, and the vulnerabilities of such victims within the criminal justice system has been of crucial importance to the development of the gender-sensitive policing, forensic examination, court proceedings and conduct, and the provision of care and support to victims (Davies et al., 2005: 74; Hoyle and Zedner, 2007: 476). However, the need for an ongoing interrogation of the gendered nature of victimisation is patently clear from studies which demonstrate its shocking reality within the lives of women. One in four women are victims of domestic violence at least once in their lifetime; two women each week are killed by their partners; at least 50,000 rapes take place each year; 7,400 women in the UK have undergone genital mutilation, London's Metropolitan Police Force gets two calls each week from women and girls reporting so called 'honour crime', such as forced marriage or threats of extreme violence from other family members; and it is estimated that 1.2 million women in England and Wales were subjected to stalking in 2003 (Katcher, 2006: 9; see also Bourne, 2007; Fawcett Society's Commission on Women and the Criminal Justice System, 2003; Walby and Allen, 2004). Furthermore, the urgent need for a gendered scrutiny of the adequacy of state responses is obvious in the recognition that victims remain reticent about reporting domestic violence and sexual assault (Nash, 2006); that only 5.6 per cent of reported rapes result in a conviction – which in some areas falls to just 3 per cent (Farry, 2007: 17), and that strategic government policies, such as the Rape Crisis Plan (Home Office, 2007) and the National Plan for Domestic Violence (Home Office, 2005) are proceeding on a piecemeal basis with limited and short-term funding (Katcher, 2006).

Likewise, the recognition of the 'profound importance of gender in both the commission and correction of crime' (Stevens, 2006: 42) has provided a rich basis upon which academics, practitioners, activists and campaigners have made significant and important inroads into defining the place and shape of gender-specific criminal justice provision and interventions, asserting that what may work for men may not work very well for women, and vice versa (Batchelor and Burman, 2004; Gelsthorpe and McIvor, 2007; Hudson, 1989; Rumgay, 1996; 2000; 2004; Stevens, 2006; Worrall, 2001). The principles of 'women-centred' provision are reflected in and supported by the experiences and evidence accruing with regard to a small number of imaginative projects for female offenders, such as the Calderdale Women's Centre in Halifax (Corston, 2007: 59; Fawcett Society's Commission on Women and the Criminal Justice System, 2007: 13), Asha in Worchester (Corston, 2007: 60) and the 218 Centre in Glasgow (Corston, 2007: 60). While with regard to the issue of 'men-centred' provision, recent preoccupations with 'masculinities' and crime as a means of 'doing gender' has elicited some early development work in probation practice centred on 'relations between men and men's subjective experiences of masculinity' (Gelsthorpe and McIvor, 2007: 341). Furthermore, statutory recognition of 'gender mainstreaming' (Women's Policy Team, 2005: 5) has been forthcoming in the establishment the Women's Offending Reduction Programme (WORP) in March 2004; the dedication of £9.15 million in March 2005 to fund holistic and multi-agency initiatives for women offenders and women at risk of offending (Women's Policy Team, 2005); and the implementation of the gender equality duty in April 2007 (Corston, 2007; Fawcett Society's Commission on Women and the Criminal Justice System, 2007).

Yet there is still much to be done. A gendered scrutiny of the adequacy of the state's responses to offenders is necessitated by the fact that progress on gender-sensitive provision is characterised as 'limited and patchy' (Fawcett Society's Commission on Women and the Criminal Justice System, 2007:

13). The Fawcett Review highlights that the WORP projects are limited to only two areas – Yorkshire and Humberside, and the North West – and the '£9.15 million that has been invested is small considering that the criminal justice budget in the UK for 2007–08 totals £22.7 billion' (Fawcett Society's Commission on Women and the Criminal Justice System, 2007: 19). Furthermore, while it is as yet unclear how the newly established Ministry of Justice will respond to the gender equality duty, the efforts of its predecessor, the Home Office, to developing a criminal justice system which is responsive to gendered needs are described by the Fawcett Society's Commission on Women and the Criminal Justice System (2007: 31) as 'inadequate'. For women, in particular, their relatively low numbers and invisibility within the criminal justice system (Batchelor and Burman, 2004; McIvor, 2004; Worrall, 2000); the persistence of the idea that women, particularly girls, are difficult to work with (Alder 1998; Adler and Baines, 1996; Bachelor and Burman, 2004; Hudson, 1989; Worrall, 2001); the dearth of research into 'what works' with regard to the female offender (Rumgay, 2004); and the difficulties integral to getting accreditation for women-centred interventions (Gelsthorpe and McIvor, 2007) present daunting challenges to the development of gender-sensitive interventions.

With regard to imprisonment and its reform, recent research highlights the pressing need for continuing critical gendered interrogation of state rhetoric, policies and practices. Carlen's work has proved particularly significant in highlighting how successive governments have sought to respond to and defuse critiques of the female penal estate and the strong grounds forwarded for its reform. She argues that through a process of 'carceral clawback' (Carlen, 2002b) the state has incorporated and co-opted gendered critiques so that any reformist potential has been transformed and neutralised, and the legitimacy of imprisonment revitalised and rebranded (see also Hannah-Moffat, 2001). For example, a justifiable concern to address the complex constellation of issues and needs associated particularly with female offending has led to the development of the 'thera-punitive' prison which lays claim to added value in seeking to deliver rehabilitation, psychiatric, medical and educational services as well as secure containment (Carlen and Tombs, 2006: 342). While the idea that prisons can promote rehabilitation is intuitively disingenuous, Carlen and Tombs's (2006) work further warns that in the current climate, sentencers' acceptance of this new 'therapeutic' role for prisons is likely to increase female (and male) incarceration, not least because the push towards more vigorous and severe community disposals means that the 'thera-punitive' prison may be viewed as the easier option.

Notwithstanding the accumulated wisdom of several decades of gender-focused criminological endeavour and activism, it would seem that the potential for well-intentioned gender specific reform of the criminal justice system remains fraught with difficulties and dilemmas. Writing with particular regard to female incarceration, Carlen and Worrall (2004: 173) assert that the pursuit of gendered reform for the benefit of offenders is 'good in itself', even if this endeavour serves no other purpose than 'to keep open to the public view the working of the whole carceral machinery' in order to hold in check its 'endemic secrecy' and monitor its 'chronic tendency for periodic reversion from progressive to retrogressive practices'. Furthermore, the recognition that increasing numbers of women (and men) are being sentenced to custody has moved Gelsthorpe (2006: 424) to remind of us of the need to 'say it again, again and again' that criminal justice policy needs to be 'gender proofed' in order to ensure that the needs of women (and men) are fully recognised.

Potential futures for an engendered criminology: the theoretical project

Ultimately the scholars who contributed to the engendering of the criminological agenda have not always presented a unity in their criticism and in the solutions that they present. Furthermore, the gains that have accrued as a result of applying a gendered lens may not be as great as many commentators would wish. However, it is important to remember that progress has been achieved and that this progress carries practical and political significance. Undoubtedly gendered criminological endeavours have elicited a wealth of theoretical and empirical material and have spawned activist campaigns and reforms, however, notwithstanding the often cutting-edge nature of such criminological enquiry, for many commentators (Gelsthorpe and Morris, 1988; 1990; Heidensohn, 2002; Naffine, 1987; Smart, 1990) the discipline still holds a 'grudging tolerance of', rather than genuine engagement' with gendered perspectives (Stevens, 2006: 62).

Carol Smart, an early and important pioneer in the study of gender and crime who we have seen was convinced in 1976 of the possibility of establishing a feminist criminology, viewed this task as redundant by 1981 (Gelsthorpe and Morris, 1988: 99), and abandoned criminology in 1990 arguing that feminist incursions within the discipline had only succeeded in 'revitalising a problematic enterprise' (Smart, 1990: 70). For Smart, criminology's ongoing allegiance to positivist paradigms and a correctional imperative are indicative of its 'intellectual bankruptcy' (Smart, 1990: 76). Furthermore, she viewed the inherent conservatism of criminology, in both its traditional and more radical guises, and its ongoing commitment to 'the idea of a unified problem which requires a unified solution' (Smart, 1990: 77) as being in stark contrast to the rich variety of feminist (gendered) scholarship. Thus Smart concludes that there is no longer any need to continue 'knocking on the door of established disciplines hoping to be let in on equal terms' (Smart, 1990: 83), rather she suggests that it might be that 'criminology needs feminism more than the converse' (Smart, 1990: 84).

Yet others have argued for the opening up of the discipline to break free from its limited horizons to explore issues of control, power and conformity which are wider than the mere study of crime and the criminal justice system. For example, Cain (1990: 10–11) argues that in order for the 'criminological gaze' to truly 'see and speak gender' it must start outside the discipline of criminology, with an interrogation of the social construction of gender in order to explore the 'total lives' of its subjects. Writing specifically from a feminist perspective with a particular interest in the female experience, Cain proposes 'the transgressive alternative' which comprises a triple project of reflexivity, deconstruction and reconstruction and a clear focus on women as a means to transform the discipline of criminology (Cain, 1990: 6–8). For Cain, reflexivity involves the recognition and articulation of the dominant discourses which shape lived experiences, deconstruction involves the examination of its 'internal logic and the ways and sites in which it is deployed' and reconstruction provides a means to enable girls and women to transgress the 'binding web of co-man sense' (Cain, 1990: 8). Likewise, Heidensohn (1985b) argues that an understanding of women's offending will only be gained through the study of society as whole and, in particular, the extent and nature of controls employed to persuade all women to fit their behaviour within normative discourses of femininity.

While the concern of these scholars to promote a greater understanding of and theorisation in relation to gender, and in particular women, and crime is understandable, their proposal to pursue such aims outside the boundaries of criminology has evoked some controversy and dissent. Daly (1994: 448), for example, advocates that feminists continue to 'work within and against criminology', Naffine (1997: 153) enjoins criminology to 'bring women and other exiles in from the cold' and Stevens (2006: 62) urges criminologists to 'remain within the discipline for the sake of the women whose voices and needs would otherwise go unheard and unaddressed'. Arguably most significantly, Carlen provides a powerful riposte to what she describes the 'theoreticist, libertarian, separatist and gender-centric' tendencies of feminist writings which she argues are 'not in the interests of either the minority of women who break the law or that even smaller minority of women who are imprisoned' (1992: 61). For Carlen, such tendencies are indicative of an unwillingness to link theoretical with political struggles on the assumption that theoretical rigour and discourse will be subsumed or lost within the engagement with politics and practice (Gelsthorpe, 2003). Hence Carlen urges gender scholars to overcome their 'academic squeamishness' (1992: 63) and asserts the pressing need to engage in further theorisation and empirical studies relating to women, men and crime.

A potential future for an engendered theoretical scholarship was articulated over 20 years ago, in an article published in 1986, in which Jeanne Gregory argued for the formation of a 'non-sexist criminology'. Gregory maintains that the gender-conscious study of crime must combine the insights gained from feminist theories with those of critical criminology – the classic feminist-socialist combination of epistemology and ontology – which would allow the study of crime to forge ahead into new territories. This criminology would acknowledge distinctions of gender and place them as centrally important to the study of crime and criminality in order that the impact of gender distinctions on both male and female behaviour would be recognised and challenged. It would do so in the full knowledge that other structural elements and distinctions, most notably class and race, must also be prominently discussed at the same time. Critical criminology alone, Gregory argues, could not deliver the insights which the discipline needed. Critical thinkers within criminology, she asserts, focus on those who are unfairly targeted by the criminal justice system – most notably poor, young and minority ethnic peoples. Critical criminologists explore how the state compounds and ensures the continuing oppression of these groups by singling them out for denigration and punishment, stigmatising their behaviour, making claims as to its deviancy and attempting to 'correct' it. The critical gaze has thus remained blind to women's experiences precisely because the state does not target females – the most numerous marginalised group – through the same means, reserving a different kind of control for females. For these reasons, Gregory posits, that critical criminology misses a key dimension of oppression which it is essential to fully incorporate.

In the ensuing years, however, feminism in academia took a 'postmodern turn' and became somewhat separated from its former political project and activist base. For these reasons feminism and criminology have largely taken divergent routes, yet the insertion of gender into criminology has ensured that critical criminology is more sensitive to the requirement to acknowledge a wider diversity of experience and to fully encompass the complexities and contradictions which are a feature of the emotions, thoughts and actions of all humanity. Indeed, combining feminist insights with other critical reflections helps us to answer key criminological conundrums, for example, 'If poverty leads to crime and more women are living in poverty than men why don't women commit more crime?' Armed with more critical tools of analysis, the criminologist can consider how poverty impacts differently on men and women, how social constructions of gender place men as the breadwinners and women as the domestic care-givers, how women's sexuality is commodified and offers an alternative route to economic gain, and how the sexual division of labour has constructed criminality as men's work. Certainly clear echoes of Gregory's concern to promote a non-sexist criminology are apparent in the identification of the gender/race/crime nexus as one of the key challenges for criminological endeavour in the twenty-first century (Burgess-Procter, 2006; Chesney-Lind, 2006).

The political backdrop has changed considerably since feminists made their first forays into understanding crime and criminality from the perspective of women and girls. Engendered criminology was born out of a period of critical reflection, progressive politics and political optimism, yet it is now played out in an era of neoliberalism, a return to fundamentalist stances and an increasingly punitive stand towards those who stand outside normative moral and social values (Chesney-Lind, 2006). Indeed, the risks and challenges posed by a punitive crime-control complex and burgeoning globalisation appear to be exacerbating the concerns and inequalities experienced by both women and men in their relationships to crime, victimisation and criminal justice. As such, the continuing need to critically address gender remains a vital component of the criminological endeavour. Whether this undertaking is pursued outwith or within the discipline is not the crucial factor; rather, tenacious and innovative approaches to the study of crime are necessary in order to ensure that criminology continues to see, to speak and to hear gender and other inequalities. Indeed, it is only by exposing the abiding truths of women's and men's relationships to crime, in the fullness of their contradictions and specificities (Carlen, 1994), that any potential for securing individual and social justice for all is likely to be achieved.

Concluding comments

Overall, this reader has demonstrated that criminology was a much weaker discipline before it was shamed and coerced to pay due regard to issues of gender. While gendered scholarship has served to render 'the woman' and 'the man' question increasingly visible within the discipline of criminology, arguably gender still remains marginal to the criminological enterprise (Gelsthorpe and Morris, 1988; 1990; Heidensohn, 2002; Naffine, 1987; Smart, 1990). However, we fully agree with Stevens when she urges gender scholars to maintain their faith regarding the 'possibility of change', arguing that any gendered reform of criminology is dependent upon continued 'communicative and democratic engagement and debate' (2006: 58–9) within its, admittedly narrow, boundaries. Indeed, it is our strong belief that gendered scholarship is crucial in order to protect insights gained to date and to critically document the ongoing relationship of gender to criminology, crime, victimisation and criminal justice. Ultimately, it is only through the pursuit of reflexive, gender-sensitive and anti-discriminatory scholarship (Gelsthorpe, 2003: 9) that a more humanistic, inclusionary (Gelsthorpe, 2003: 9) and ethical (Gelsthorpe and McIvor, 2007: 342) vision of criminology and criminal justice is likely to prove forthcoming.

References

AAP/*Weekend Australian* (2001), 'Trinity culprits avoid conviction', *Weekend Australian*, 24–25 March, p. 11.

Acker, J. (1989), 'The problem with patriarchy', *Sociology*, 23(2): 235–40.

Ackland, J. (1982), *Girls in Care*. Aldershot: Gower.

Adams, P. (1996), *The Emptiness of Image: Psychoanalysis and Sexual Differences*. London: Routledge.

Adams-Tucker, C. (1982), 'Proximate effects of sexual abuse in childhood', *American Journal of Psychiatry*, 193: 1252–6.

Adkins, L. (2004) 'Gender and the post-structural social', in B.L. Marshall and A. Witz (eds), *Engendering the Social*. Maidenhead: Open University Press.

Adler, F. (1975), *Sisters in Crime: The Rise of the New Female Criminal*. New York: McGraw-Hill.

Adler, Z. (1987), *Rape on Trial*. London: Routledge and Kegan Paul.

African Rights (1995a), *Rwanda: Death, Despair and Defiance*. London: African Rights.

African Rights (1995b), *Rwanda: Who is Killing? Who is Dying? What is to be Done?* Discussion Paper No. 3. London: African Rights.

African Rights (1995c), *Rwanda: Not So Innocent*. London: African Rights.

African Rights (1996), *Rwanda: Killing the Evidence*. London: African Rights.

Albrechtsen, J. (2002), 'Blind spot allows barbarism to flourish', *The Australian*, 17 July, http://www.theaustralian.news.com.au/common/story_page/0,5744,4718201%255E7583,00.html.

Alcock, C., Payne, S. and Sullivan, M. (2000), *Introducing Social Policy*. Harlow: Pearson Education.

Alder, C. (1986), 'Unemployed women have got it heaps worse: exploring the implications of female youth unemployment", *Australian and New Zealand Society of Criminology*, 19 (December): 210–24.

Alder, C. (1998), 'Passionate and wilful girls: confronting practices', *Women and Criminal Justice*, 9(4): 81–101.

Alder, C. and Baines, M. (eds) (1996), *And When She Was Bad? Working with Young Women in Juvenile Justice and Related Areas*. Hobart: National Clearinghouse for Youth Studies.

Alder, C. and Hunter, N. (1999), 'Young Women in the Juvenile Justice System', unpublished, paper, University of Melbourne.

Allen, H. (1987), *Justice Unbalanced: Gender, Psychiatry and Judicial Decisions*. Philadelphia, PA: Open University Press.

Allen, J. (1989), 'Men, crime and criminology: recasting the questions', *International Journal of the Sociology of Law*, 17(1): 19–39.

Allen, V.L. (1974), 'The common-sense guide to industrial relations', *University of Leeds Review*, 17: 1.

American Association of University Women (1992), *How Schools Are Shortchanging Girls*. Washington, DC: American Association of University Women Educational Foundation.

American Correctional Association (ACA) (1990), *The Female Offender: What Does the Future hold?* Washington, DC: St Mary's.

Amos, V. and Parmar, P. (1984), 'Challenging imperial feminism', *Feminist Review*, 17: 3–19.

Anderson, M. (1988), *Thinking About Women*. New York: Macmillan.

Anderson, M.L. and Collins, P.H. (1995), *Race, Class and Gender*, 2nd edn. Belmont, CA: Wadsworth.

Anthias, F. and Davis-Yuval, Y. (1983), 'Contextualising feminism – gender, ethnic and class divisions', *Feminist Review*, 15: 62–77.

Archer, D. (1998), 'Riot grrrl and raisin girl: femininity within the female gang', in J. Vagg and T. Newburn (eds), *Emerging Themes in Criminology*. The British Criminology Conferences Selected Proceedings vol. 1, Loughborough.

Armstrong, L. (1994), 'Who stole incest?' *On the Issues*, 3: 30–2.

Arnold, R. (1995), 'Processes of victimisation and criminalization of black women', in B. Price and N. Sokoloff (eds), *The Criminal Justice System and Women*. New York: McGraw-Hill.

Artz, S. (1998), *Sex, Power, and the Violent School Girl*. New York: Teachers College Press.

Austin, J., Bruce, M., Carroll, L., McCall, P. and Richards, S. (2001), 'The use of incarceration in the United States', *The Criminologist*, 26(3): 14–16.

Australian Muslim Public Affairs Committee (2001), 'Exposing Janet Albrechtsen's dishonest attack', on ABC *Media Watch* website on 18 June 2002, www.abc.net.au/mediawatch/.

Bachelard, G. (1940), *The Philosophy of No: A Philosophy of the New Scientific Mind*. New York: Orion Press.

Bagley, K. and Merlo, A. (1995), 'Controlling women's bodies', in A. Merloarrd and J. Pollock (eds), *Women, Law and Social Control*. Boston, MA: Alleyn and Bacon.

Baines, M. and Alder, C. (1996), 'When she was bad she was horrid', in C. Alder and M. Baines (eds), *Working with Young Women in Juvenile Justice and Related Areas*. Hobart: National Clearinghouse for Youth Studies.

Balding, J., Regis, D., Wise, A., Bish, D. and Muirden, J. (1996), *Cash and Carry? Young People, their Friends, and Offensive Weapons*. Exeter: University of Exeter Schools Health Education Unit.

Bales, K. (2000), *Disposable People: New Slavery in the Global Economy*. California: University of California Press.

Balfour, G. (2000), 'Feminist therapy with women in prison: working under the hegemony of correctionalism', in K. Hannah-Moffat and M. Shaw (eds), *An*

Ideal Prison? Critical Essays on Women's Imprisonment in Canada. Halifax: Fernwood Press.

Balkin, S. (1979), 'Victimisation rate, safety and fear of crime', *Social Problems*, 26: 343–58.

Ballinger, A. (2000), *Dead Woman Walking: Executed Women in England and Wales 1900–1955*. Aldershot, Vermont and Sydney: Ashgate.

Barker, M. (1981), *The New Racism: Conservatives and the Ideology of the Tribe*. London: Junction Books.

Barker, M. (1993), *Community Service and Women Offenders*. London: ACOP.

Barrett, M. (1980), *Women's Oppression Today*. London: Verso.

Barrett, M. and McIntosh, M. (1982), *The Anti-Social Family*. London: Verso.

Barrett, M. and McIntosh, M. (1985), 'Ethnocentrism and socialist feminist theory', *Feminist Review*, 20: 23–47.

Barry, K. (1979), *Female Sexual Slavery*. New York and London: New York University Press.

Bart, P. and O'Brien, P. (1984), 'Stopping rape: effective avoidance strategies', *Signs*, 10(1): 82–101.

Baskin, D. and Sommers, I. (1993), 'Female's initiation into violent street crime', *Justice Quarterly*, 10: 559–81.

Batacharya, S. (2000), 'Racism, "girl violence", and the murder of Reena Virk', unpublished MA thesis, University of Toronto.

Batchelor, S. and Burman, M. (2004), 'Working with girls and young women', in G. McIvor (ed.), *Women Who Offend*, Research Highlights in Social Work 44. London: Jessica Kingsley.

Batchelor, S., Burman, M. and Brown, J. (2001), 'Discussing violence: let's hear it from the girls', *Probation Journal*, 48(2): 125–34.

Bauman, Z. (1989), *Modernity and the Holocaust*. Cambridge: Polity.

Bauman, Z. (1993), *Post-Modern Ethics*. Oxford: Blackwell.

Bauman, Z. (1995), *Life in Fragments*. Oxford: Blackwell.

Bauman, Z. (1997), *Postmodernity and its Discontents*. Cambridge: Polity Press.

Beck, U. (1992), *Risk Society*. London: Sage.

Beechey, V. and Whitelegg, E. (eds) (1986), *Women in Britain Today*. Milton Keynes: Open University Press.

Beikoff, L. (1996), 'Queensland's juvenile justice system: equity, access, and justice for young women?', in C. Alder and M. Baines (eds), *And When She Was Bad? Working with Young Women in Juvenile Justice and Related Areas*. Hobart: National Clearinghouse for Youth Studies.

Belknap, J. (1996), *The Invisible Woman: Gender, Crime and Justice*. Belmont, CA: Wadsworth.

Belknap, J. (2001), *The Invisible Woman: Gender, Crime and Justice*, 2nd edn. Belmont, CA: Wadsworth.

Belknap, J. and Holsinger, K. (1998), 'An overview of delinquent girls: how theory and practice have failed and the need for innovative change', in R.T. Zaplin (ed.), *Female Offenders: Critical Perspectives and Elective Interventions*. Gaithersburg, MD: Aspen Publishers.

Bell, D. and Valentine, G. (1995), 'The sexed self: Strategies of performance, sites of resistance', in S. Pile and N. Thrift (eds), *Mapping the Subject: Geographies of Cultural Transformation*. London: Routledge.

Bell, I.P. (1970), 'The double standard: age', *Transaction*, 8: 75–80.

Beneke, T. (1982), *Men on Rape*, New York: St Martin's Press.

Bennett, T. (1990), *Tackling Fear of Crime*, Home Office Research Bulletin, No. 28. London: HMSO.

Bernard, J. (1982), *The Future of Marriage*. New Haven, CT: Yale University Press.

Bertrand, M.A. (1967), 'The myth of sexual equality before the law', *Proceedings of the Fifth Research Conference on Delinquency and Criminality*. Montreal: Quebec Society of Criminology.

Bertrand, M.A. (1969), 'Self image and delinquency: a contribution to the study of female criminality and women's image', *Acta Criminologica*, 2: 71–144.

Bertrand, M.A. (1973), 'The insignificance of female criminality', First Conference of the European Group for the Study of Deviance and Social Control, Florence.

Bertrand, M.A (1999), 'Incarceration as a gendering strategy', *Canadian Journal of Law and Society*, 14(1): 45–60.

Bhavani, K. and Coulson, M. (1986), 'Transforming socialist feminism: the challenge of racism', *Feminist Review*, 23: 81–91.

Black Women in Prison (1985), *Black Female Prisoners and Political Awareness*. London: Black Women in Prison.

Bland, L. (1983), 'Purity, motherhood, pleasure or threat', in S. Cartledge and J. Ryan (eds), *Sex and Love*. London: Women's Press.

Block, J. (1984), *Sex Role Identity and Ego Development*. San Francisco, CA: Jossey-Bass.

Bloom, B. (2000), 'Successful gender-responsive programming must reflect women's lives and needs', *Women, Girls and Criminal Justice*, 1(1): 1–3.

Bloom, B. and Steinhart, D. (1993), *Why Punish the Children? A Reappraisal of the Children of Incarcerated Mothers in America*. Washington, DC: National Council on Crime and Delinquency.

Boritch, H. (1997), *Fallen Women: Female Crime and Criminal Justice in Canada*. Toronto: ITP Nelson.

Bosworth, M. (1999), 'Agency and choice in women's prisons: towards a constitutive penality', in S. Henry and D. Milovanovic (eds), *Constitutive Criminology at Work: Applications to Crime and Justice*. Albany, NY: State University of New York Press.

Bottoms, A.E. (1987), 'Limiting prison use in England and Wales', *The Howard Journal of Criminal Justice*, 26(3): 177–202.

Bourne, J. (1984), *Towards an Anti-Racist Feminism*. London: Institute of Race Relations.

Bourne, J. (2007), *Rape: A History from 1860 to Present*. London: Virago.

Bowker, L. (1981), 'Women as victims: an examination of the results of L.E.A.A.'s National Crime Survey program', in L. Bowker (ed.), *Women and Crime in America*. New York: Macmillan.

Bowling, B. and Phillips, C. (2002), *Racism, Crime and Justice*. London: Longman.

Box, S. (1983), *Power, Crime and Mystification*. London: Tavistock.

Box, S. (1987), *Recession, Crime and Punishment*. Basingstoke: Macmillan Education.

Box, S. and Hale, C. (1983), 'Liberation and female criminality in England and Wales', *British Journal of Criminology*, 23(1): 35–49.

Brennan, T. and Austin, R. (1997), *Women in Jail: Classification Issues*. Washington, DC: National Institute of Corrections.

Brienen, M. and Hoegen, E. (2000), 'Victims of crime in twenty-two European jurisdictions', PhD thesis, KathoHeke Universiteit Brabant, Nijmegen, The Netherlands: Wolf Legal Productions.

Brinkworth, L. (1994), 'Sugar and spice but not at all nice', *The Sunday Times*, 27 November.

Brinkworth, L. (1996), 'Angry young women', *Cosmopolitan*, February.

British Home Office (1999), *Aim 4: The Government's Strategy for Women Offenders*, pp. 189–90, www.hmprisonerservice.gov.uk/filstore/.

Brittan, A. and Maynard, M. (1984), *Sexism, Racism and Oppression*. Oxford: Basil Blackwell.

Brooks Gardner, C. (1990), 'Safe conduct: women, crime, and self in public places', *Social Problems*, 37(3): 311–28.

Brown, H.C. and Pearce, J. (1992), 'Good practice in the face of anxiety: social work with girls and young women', *Journal of Social Work Practice*, 6(2): 159–65.

Brown, L. (2000), *Sex Slaves: The Trafficking of Women in Asia*. London: Virago.

Browne, A. and Finkelhor, D. (1986), 'Impact of child sexual abuse: a review of research', *Psychological Bulletin*, 99: 66–77.

Brownmiller, S. (1975), *Against Our Will: Men, Women and Rape*. London: Secker and Warburg.

Bryan, B., Dadzie, S. and Scafe, S. (1985), *The Heart of Race*. London: Virago.

Bryson, V. (1992), *Feminist Political Theory: An Introduction*. London: Macmillan.

Bull, D. and Wilding, P. (eds) (1983), *Thatcherism and the Poor*. London: Child Poverty Action Group.

Bulman-Janoff, R. and Frieze, I. (1983), 'A theoretical perspective for understanding reactions to victimization', *Journal of Social Issues*, 39(2): 1–17.

Bureau of Justice Statistics (1983), *Report to the Nation on Crime and Justice*. Washington, DC: US Government Printing Office.

Bureau of Justice Statistics (1999), *Women Offenders*. Washington, DC: U.S. Department of Justice.

Burgess, A. and Holmstrom, L. (1974), 'Rape trauma syndrome', *American Journal of Psychiatry*, 31: 981–5.

Burgess-Procter, A. (2006), 'Intersections of race, class, gender, and crime: future direction for feminist criminology', *Feminist Criminology*, 1(1): 27–47.

Burman, M. (2004), 'Breaking the mould: patterns in female offending', in G. McIvor (ed.), *Women Who Offend*, Research Highlights in Social Work 44. London: Jessica Kingsley.

Burman, M., Brown, J., Tisdall, K. and Batchelor, S. (2000), 'A view from the girls: exploring violence and violent behaviour, unpublished final report for ESRC.

Burstyn, V. (1983), 'Masculine dominance and the state', in R. Miliband and J. Saville (eds), *The Socialist Review*. London: Merlin Press.

Burt, M. and Estep, R. (1981), 'Apprehension and fear: learning a sense of sexual vulnerability', *Sex Roles*, lib: 511–22

Butler, J. (1990), *Gender Trouble: Subversion and Identity*. London and New York: Routledge.

Butler, J. (1993), *Bodies that Matter: On the Discursive Limits of Sex*. New York: Routledge.

Byers, B. (1999), 'Hate crimes in the workplace: worker-to-worker victimisation and policy responses', *Security Journal*, 12(4): 47–58.

Cabinet Office (2002), *FY 2001 Annual Report on the State Formation of a Gender Equal Society*. Tokyo: Cabinet Office.

Cain, M. (ed.) (1986), 'Realism, feminism, methodology and law', *International Journal of the Sociology of the Law*, 18: 1–18.

Cain, M. (ed.) (1989), *Growing Up Good: Policing The Behaviour of Girls in Europe*. London: Sage Publications.

Cain, M. (1990), 'Towards transgression: new directions in feminist criminology', *International Journal of the Sociology of Law*, 18: 1–18.

Cameron, M. (2001), 'Women prisoners and correctional programmes', *Australian Institute of Criminology Trends and Issues in Crime and Criminal Justice*, no. 194, Canberra.

Campagna, D.S. and Poffenberger, D.L. (1988), *The Sexual Trafficking in Children*. Dover, MA: Auburn House.

Campbell, A. (1981), *Delinquent Girls*. Oxford: Basil Blackwell.

Campbell, A. (1984), *The Girls in the Gang*. Oxford: Basil Blackwell.

Campbell, A. (2005), 'Keeping the "lady" safe: the regulation of femininity through crime prevention literature', *Critical Criminology*, 13: 119–40.

Campbell, B. (1988), *Unofficial Secrets: Child Sexual Abuse – The Cleveland Case*. London: Virago.

Campbell, B. (1993), *Goliath: Britain's Dangerous Places*. London: Virago,

Campbell, J.C. (1999), 'Forced sex and intimate partner violence', *Violence Against Women*, 5: 1017–35.

Carby, H. (1982), 'White women listen! Black feminism and the boundaries of sisterhood', in Birmingham University, Centre for Contemporary Cultural Studies, *The Empire Strikes Back*. London: Hutchinson.

Carcach, C. and Grant, A. (1999), *Imprisonment in Australia: Trends in Prison Populations and Imprisonment Rates*. Canberra: Australian Institute of Criminology, No. 130, October: 1–6.

Carlen, P. (1983), *Women's Imprisonment: A Study in Social Control*. London: Routledge and Kegan Paul.

Carlen, P. (ed.) (1985), *Criminal Women: Autobiographical Accounts, Diana Christina, Jenny Hicks, Josie O'Dwyer, Chris Tchiakovsky and Pat Carlen*. Cambridge: Polity Press.

Carlen, P. (1987), 'Out of care, into custody', in P. Carlen and A. Worrall (eds), *Gender, Crime and Justice*, Philadelphia, PA: Open University.

Carlen, P. (1988), *Women, Crime and Poverty*. Milton Keynes: Open University Press.

Carlen, P. (1990a), 'Women, crime, feminism and realism', *Social Justice*, 17(4): 106–23.

Carlen, P. (1990b), *Alternatives to Women's Imprisonment*. Milton Keynes: Open University Press.

Carlen, P. (1992), 'Criminal women and criminal justice: the limits to, and potential of, feminist and left realist perspectives', in R. Matthews and J. Young (eds), *Issues in Realist Criminology*. London:Sage.

Carlen, P. (1994), 'Gender, class, racism, and criminal justice: against global and gender-centric theories, for poststructuralist perspectives', in G.S. Bridges and M.A. Myers (eds), *Inequality, Crime and Social Control*. Boulder, CO, San Francisco, CA, and Oxford: Westview Press.

Carlen, P. (1998), *Sledgehammer. Women's Imprisonment at the Millennium*. Basingstoke: Macmillan Press.

Carlen, P. (ed.) (2002a), *Women and Punishment: The Struggle for Justice*. Cullompton: Willan.

Carlen, P. (2002b), 'Carceral clawback: the case of women's imprisonment in Canada', *Punishment and Society*, 4(1): 115–21.

Carlen, P. and Jefferson, J. (1996), *British Journal of Criminology: Special Issue – Masculinities and Crime*, 33(6).

Carlen, P. and Tchaikovsky, C. (1996), 'Women's imprisonment at the end of the twentieth century', in P. Francis and R. Matthews (eds), *Prisons 2000*. Basingstoke: Macmillan.

Carlen, P. and Tombs, J. (2006), 'Reconfigurations of penality: the ongoing case of the women's imprisonment and reintegration industries', *Theoretical Criminology*, 10(3): 337–60.

Carlen, P. and Worrall, A. (eds) (1987), *Gender, Crime and Justice*. Milton Keynes: Open University Press.

Carlen, P. and Worrall, A. (2004), *Analysing Women's Imprisonment*. Cullompton: Willan.

Carlen, P., Hicks, J., O'Dwyer, J., Christina, D. and Tchaikovsky, C. (1985), *Criminal Women*. Oxford: Polity Press.

Carr, J. (2001), 'Theme paper on child pornography', 2nd World Congress Against the Commercial Sexual Exploitation of Children, Yokahama, Japan. Available from www.ecpat.com.

Carrigan, T., Connell, R.W. and Lee, J. (1987), 'Toward a new sociology of masculinity', *Theory and Society*, 14: 551–604.

Carrington, K. (1993), *Offending Girls: Sex, Youth and Justice*. New South Wales: Allen and Unwin.

Carrington, K. (1998), 'Postmodern and feminist criminologies: fragmenting the criminological subject', in P. Walton and J. Young (eds), *The New Criminology Revisited*. London: Macmillan; New York: St Martin Press.

Carrington, K. (2002), 'Feminism and critical criminology: confronting genealogies', in K. Carrington and R. Hogg (eds), *Critical Criminology: Issues, Debates, Challenges*. Cullompton: Willan.

Casburn, M. (1979), *Girls will be Girls: Sexism and Juvenile Justice in a London Borough*. London: Women's Research and Resources.

Cavadino, M. and Dignan, J. (2002), *The Penal System. An Introduction*, 3rd edn. London: Sage.

Cavadino, P., Crow, I. and Dignan, J. (1999), *Criminal Justice 2000: Strategies for a New Century*. Winchester: Waterside Press.

Cayley, D. (1998), *The Expanding Prison: The Crisis in Crime and the Search for Alternatives*. Toronto: Anansi Press.

Central Statistical Office (1987), *Key Data*. London: HMSO.

Central Statistical Office (CSO) (1988), *Social Trends*, 18. London: HMSO.

Chambers, G. and Tombs, J. (1984), *The British Crime Survey, Scotland*. Edinburgh: HMSO.

Channel Four Television (1996), *Dispatches: Class Wars: Schoolchildren, Violence, and Weapons*. London: Channel Four Television.

Chaudhuri, A. (2000), 'Twisted sisters', *Guardian*, 15 August.

Chesler, P. (1972), *Women and Madness*, Garden City, NY: Doubleday.

Chesney-Lind, M. (1971), 'Female juvenile delinquency in Hawaii', unpublished Master's thesis, University of Hawaii Manoa.

Chesney-Lind, M. (1973), 'Judicial enforcement of the female sex role: the family court and the female delinquent', *Issues in Criminology*, 8(2).

Chesney-Lind, M. (1981), 'Juvenile delinquency: the sexualization of female crime', *Psychology Today*, 43 (July): 6.

Chesney-Lind, M. (1987), 'Girls and violence: an exploration of the gender gap in serious delinquent behavior', in D. Corwell, L. Evans and C. O'Donnell (eds), *Childhood Aggression and Violence*, New York: Plenum.

Chesney-Lind, M. (1988), 'Girls and status offenses: is juvenile justice still sexist?', *Criminal Justice Abstracts*, 20: 145–65.

Chesney-Lind, M. (ed.) (1997), *The Female Offender: Girls, Women and Crime*. Thousand Oaks, CA: Sage.

Chesney-Lind, M. (2006), 'Patriarchy, crime and justice: feminist criminology in an era of backlash', *Feminist Criminology*, 1(1): 6–26.

Chesney-Lind, M. and Faith, K. (2000), 'What about feminism? Engendering theory-making in criminology', in R. Paternoster (ed.), *Criminological Theories*. Los Angeles, CA: Roxbury Press.

Chesney-Lind, M. and Okamoto, S.K. (2000), 'Gender matters: patterns in girls' delinquency and gender responsivity programming', unpublished.

Chesney-Lind, M. and Pasko, L. (2004a), 'Girls' troubles and "female delinquency" ', in M. Chesney-Lind and L. Pasko, *The Female Offender: Girls, Women and Crime*, 2nd edn. Thousand Oaks, CA, London and New Delhi: Sage Publications.

Chesney-Lind, M. and Pasko, L. (2004b), *The Female Offender: Girls, Women and Crime*, 2nd edn, Thousand Oaks, CA, London and New Dehli: Sage Publications.

Chesney-Lind, M. and Shelden, R.G. (1998), *Girls, Delinquency, and the Juvenile Justice System*. Pacific Grove, CA: Brooks/Cole.

Chigwada, R. (1986), 'Policing of black women', in E. Cashmore and E. McLaughlin (eds), *Policing of Black People*. London: Routledge and Kegan-Paul.

Chigwada, R. (1991), 'Policing of black women', in E. McLaughlin and P. Cashmore (eds), *Policing of Black People: Out of Order?* London: Routledge.

Chigwada-Bailey, R. (1989), 'Criminalisation and imprisonment of black women', *Probation Journal*, 36(3): 100–5.

Chigwada-Bailey, R. (1997), *Black Women's Experiences of Criminal Justice: Discourse on Disadvantage*. Winchester: Waterside Press.

Chigwada-Bailey, R. (2004), 'Black women and the criminal justice system', in G. McIvor (ed.), *Women who Offend*. London and New York: Jessica Kingsley.

Children Act Sub-Committee (1999), *Report to the Lord Chancellor on the Question of Parental Contact in Cases Where There Is Domestic Violence*. London: Lord Chancellor's Department.

Chodorow, N. (1994), *Femininities. Masculinities. Sexualities*. Lexington, KY: University Press of Kentucky.

Christie, N. (1993), *Crime Control as Industry: Towards Gulags Western Style?* London: Routledge.

Cigar, N. (1995), *Genocide in Bosnia: The Policy of Ethnic Cleansing*. College Station, TX: Texas A&M University Press.

Clark, L. and Lewis, D. (1977), *Rape: The Price of Coercive Sexuality*. Toronto: The Women's Press.

Clark, P. (2001), radio program, Radio 2GB, 30 July, 7.09 a.m.

Clarkson, C., Cretney, A., Davis, G., Jones, S. and Shepherd, J. (1991), 'The background, reporting, and criminal prosecution of assaults', paper delivered to the 1991 British Criminology Meeting, York.

Clemente, F. and Kleiman, M. (1977), 'Fear of crime in the United States: a multivariate analysis', *Social Forces*, 56: 519–31.

Cloward, R.A. and Ohlin, L.B. (1960), *Delinquency and Opportunity: A Theory of Delinquent Gangs*. New York: Free Press.

Cohen, A. (1955), *Delinquent Boys: The Culture of the Gang*. Chicago, IL: Chicago Free Press.

Cohen, S. (1995), *Denial and Acknowledgement: The Impact of Information about Human Rights Violations*. Jerusalem: Centre for Human Rights, The Hebrew University.

Coleman, W. (1990), 'Doing masculinity theory', in J. Hearn and D.H.J. Morgan (eds), *Men, Masculinities and Social Theory*. Cambridge, MA: Unwin Hyman.

Collier, R. (1995), *Masculinity, Law and the Family*. London: Routledge.

Collier, R. (1998), *Masculinities, Crime and Criminology: Men, Heterosexuality and the Criminal(ised) Other*. London: Sage.

Collier, R. (2004), 'Masculinities and crime: rethinmking the "man question" ', in C. Sumner (ed.), *The Blackwell Companion to Criminology*. Oxford: Blackwell.

Collins, J., Noble, F., Poynting, S. and Tabar, P. (2000), *Kebabs, Kids, Cops and Crime: Youth Ethnicity and Crime*. Sydney: Pluto Press.

Comack, E. (1996), *Women in Trouble*. Halifax: Fernwood Press.

Comack, E., Chopyk, K. and Wood, L. (2000), *Mean Streets? The Social Locations, Gender Dynamics, and Patterns of Violent Crime in Winnipeg*. Ottawa: Canadian Centre for Policy Alternatives.

Commission of Experts on the Former Yugoslavia (1994), *Final Report of the Commission of Experts on the Former Yugoslavia*. New York: United Nations Security Council 511994/674–27 May 1994.

Connell, R.W. (1985), 'Masculinity, violence and war', in P. Patton and R. Poole (eds), *War/Masculinity*. Sydney: Intervention Publications.

Connell, R.W. (1987), *Gender and Power: Society, the Person and Sexual Politics*. Cambridge: Polity Press.

Connell, R.W. (1990), 'The state, gender, and sexual politics: theory and appraisal', *Theory and Society*, 19(4): 507–44.

Connell, R.W. (1992), 'Drumming up the Wrong Tree', *Tikkun* 7(1): 31–36.

Connell, R.W. (1993), 'Foreword', in J.W. Messerschmidt, *Masculinities and Crime: Critique and Reconceptualisation of Theory*. Lanham, MD: Rowman and Littlefield.

Connell, R.W. (1995), *Masculinities*. Cambridge: Polity Press.

Connell, R.W. (2002), 'On hegemonic masculinity and violence: a response to Jefferson and Hall', *Theoretical Criminology*, 6(1): 89–99.

Connolly, E. (2000), 'Trinity boys tied up and raped, court told', *Sydney Morning Herald*, 21 December.

Connolly, E. (2001), 'Culture of rumbling, bullying', *Sydney Morning Herald*, 6 February.

Cook, D. (1997), *Poverty, Crime and Punishment*. London: Child Poverty Action Group.

Cook, S. and Davies, S. (1999), 'Will anyone ever listen? An introductory note', in S. Cook and S. Davies (eds), *Harsh Punishment: International Experiences of Women's Imprisonment*. Boston, MA: Northeastern University Press.

Cook, S. and Davies, S. (eds), (2000), *Harsh Punishment: International Experiences of Women's Imprisonment*. Boston, MA: Northeastern University Press.

Cornell, D. (1995), *The Imaginary Domain*. London: Routledge.

Corston, J. (2007), *The Corston Report*. London: Home Office, www.home-office.gov.uk/documents/corston-report/.

Corrigan, P. (1979), *Schooling the Smash Street Kids*. London: Macmillan.

Cossman, B. and Fudge, J. (2001), 'Introduction: privatization, law and the challenge to feminism', paper presented at the Feminist Political Economy and Law Conference, Toronto, 24 March.

Cousins, M. (1978), 'Material arguments and feminism', *M/F*, 2: 63–70.

Cousins, M. (1980), 'Mens rea: a note on sexual difference, criminology and the law', in P. Carlen and M. Collinson (eds), *Radical Issues in Criminology*. Oxford: Martin Robertson.

Cowie, J., Cowie, V. and Slater, E. (1968), *Delinquency in Girls*. London: Heinemann.

Crawford, A., Jones, T., Woodhouse, T. and Young, J. (1990), *Second Islington Crime Survey*. London: Middlesex Polytechnic.

Cunneen, C. (2001), *Conflict, Politics and Crime: Aboriginal Communities and the Police*. Allen and Unwin, Sydney.

Dahl, T.S. (1987), *Women's Law: An Introduction to Feminist Jurisprudence*. Oslo: Norwegian University Press.

Daily Telegraph (2001), 'All rapists' names must be released', editorial, 13 July.

Daly, K. (1987), 'Discrimination in the criminal courts: family, gender and the problem of equal treatment', *Social Forces*, 66(1): 152–75.

Daly, K. (1989), 'Gender and varieties of white-collar crime', *Criminology*, 27: 769–94.

Daly, K. (1994), *Gender, Crime and Punishment*. New Haven, CT: Yale University Press.

Daly, K. (1997), 'Different ways of conceptualising sex/gender in feminist theory and their implications for criminology', *Theoretical Criminology*, 1(1): 25–53.

Daly, K. and Chesney-Lind, M. (1988), 'Feminism and criminology', *Justice Quarterly*, 5(4): 101–43.

Davies, A. (1999), ' "These viragoes are no less cruel than the lads": young women, gangs and violence in Victorian Manchester and Salford', *British Journal of Criminology*, 39(1): 72–89.

Davies, M., Croall, H. and Tyrer, J. (2005), *Criminal Justice: an introduction to the criminal justice system in England and Wales*, 3rd edn. Harlow: Longman.

Davis, A. (1971), *If they come in the morning . . .* London: Orbach and Chambers.

Davis, A. (1981), *Women, Race and Class*. London: Women's Press.

Davis, K. (1966), 'Prostitution', in R.K. Merton and R. Nisbet (eds), *Contemporary Social Problems*. New York: Harcourt Brace and World.

Deakin, J. and Spencer, J. (2003), 'Women behind bars: explanations and implications', *Howard Journal*, 42: 123–52.

DeJong, A.R., Hevada, A.R. and Emmett, G.A. (1983), 'Epidemiologic variations in childhood sexual abuse', *Child Abuse and Neglect*, 7: 155–62.

Dembo, J.S., Sue, C.C., Borden, P. and Manning, D. (1995), 'Gender differences in service needs among youths entering a juvenile assessment center: a replication study,' paper presented at the annual meeting of the Society of Social Problems, Washington, DC.

Dembo, R., Williams, L. and Schmeidler, J. (1993), 'Gender differences in mental health service needs among youths entering a juvenile detention center', *Journal of Prison and Jail Health*, 12: 73–101.

Department of Health and Social Security (DHSS) (1986), *Personal Social Services: Local Authority Statistics*. London: Department of Health and Social Security.

Derrida, J. (1976), *Of Grammatology*, Baltimore, MD: Johns Hopkins University Press.

Devine, M. (2001), 'Rape, hatred and racism', *Sun-Herald*, 12 August.

Ditton, J. and Duffy, J. (1982), 'Bias in the newspaper reporting of crime news', *British Journal of Criminology*, 23(2): 159–65.

Dobash, R.E. (2003), 'Domestic violence: arrest, prosecution and reducing violence', *Crime and Public Policy*, 2(2): 313–18.

Dobash, R.E. and Dobash, R.P. (1979), *Violence against Wives*. New York: Free Press.

Dobash, R.E. and Dobash, R.P. (1992), *Women, Violence and Social Change*. London and New York: Routledge.

Dobash, R.P. and Dobash, R.E. (2004), 'Women's violence to men in intimate relationships: working on the puzzle', *British Journal of Criminology*, 44: 324–49.

Dobash, R.P., Dobash, R.E., Cavanagh, K. and Lewis, R. (2000), *Changing Violent Men*. Thousand Oaks, CA: Sage.

Dominy, N. and Radford, L. (1996), *Domestic Violence in Surrey*. London: Surrey County Council/Roehampton Institute.

Donzelot, J. (1979), *The Policing of Families*. London: Hutchinson.

Draper, P. (1975), '!Kung women: contrasts in sexual egalitarianism in foraging and sedentary contexts', in R.R. Reiter (ed.), *Toward an Anthropology of Women*. New York: Monthly Review Press.

Dubow, F. (1979), *Reactions to Crime: A Critical Review of the Literature*. Washington, D.C.: US Government Printing Office.

Duffy, M. (2002), 'When the racial reality hits home', *Daily Telegraph*, 17 August.

Dunbar, I. and Langdon, A. (1998), *Tough Justice. Sentencing and Penal Policies in the 1990s*. London: Blackstone Press.

Dunn, J. and Fahy, T.A. (1990), 'Police admissions to psychiatric hospital: demographic and clinical differences between ethnic groups', *British Journal of Psychiatry*, 156: 373–8.

Eaton, M. (1986), *Justice for Women? Family, Court and Social Control*. Milton Keynes: Open University Press.

ECPAT (2001), 'Briefing notes on child pornography: record of a crime', 2nd World Congress on Commercial Sexual Exploitation of Children, Yokohama, Japan, 17–20 December. Available on www.ecpat.com.

ECPAT (2003). Information from ECPAT website www.ecpat.com.

Edley, N. and Wetherall, M. (1997), 'Jockeying for position: the construction of masculine identities', *Discourse and Society*, 8(2): 203–17.

Edwards, S.S.M. (1984), *Women on Trial: A Study of the Female Suspect, Defendant and Offender in Criminal Law and the Criminal Justice System*. Manchester: Manchester University Press.

Efran, M.G. (1974), 'The effect of physical appearance on the judgement of guilt, interpersonal attraction and seventy of recommended punishment in a simulated jury task', *Journal of Research in Personality*, 8: 45–54.

Ehrenreich, B. (1989), *Fear of Falling*. New York: Pantheon.

Ehrenreich, B. (2001), *Nickel and Dimed: On (Not), Getting By in America*. New York: Metropolitan Books.

Ehrenreich, B. and English, D. (1978) *For Her Own Good*. Garden City, NY: Anchor.

Eichenbaum, L. and Orbach, S. (1984), *What Do Women Want?* London: Fontana/ Collins.

Elliot, A. (1994), *Psychoanalytic Theory: An Introduction*. Oxford: Blackwell.

Elliot, A. (1996), *Subject to Ourselves*. Cambridge: Polity.

Elliott, D. (1988), *Gender, Delinquency, and Society*. Aldershot: Avebury.

Erez, E. and Hassin, Y. (1997), 'Women in crime and justice: the case of Israel', *Women and Criminal Justice*, 9(2): 61–85.

Evans, J. (2003), 'Vigilance and vigilantes: thinking psychoanalytically about anti-paedophile action', *Theoretical Criminology*, 7: 163–89.

Faith, K. (1993), *Unruly Women: The Politics and Confinement of Resistance*. Vancouver: Press Gang Publishers.

Faith, K. (1999), 'Transformative justice versus re-entrenched correctionalism: the Canadian experience', in S. Cook and S. Davies (eds), *Harsh Punishment: International Experiences of Women – Imprisonment*. Boston, MA: Northeastern University Press.

Faludi, S. (1991), *Backlash: The Undeclared War against American Women*. New York: Anchor Doubleday.

Farley, L. (1978), *Sexual Shakedown*. New York: McGraw Hill.

Farrall. S., Bannister, J., Ditton, J. and Gilchrist, E. (1997), 'Questioning the measurement of the "fear of crime": findings from a major methodological study', *British Journal of Criminology*, 37(4): 657–78.

Farrington, D. and Morris, A. (1983), 'Sex, sentencing and reconviction', *British Journal of Criminology*, 23: 229–48.

Farry, E. (2007), 'Why aren't we more outraged?', *Guardian*, 5 October, www.guardian.co.uk/g2/story/0,,2184048,00.html.

Faulkner, D.E.R. (1971), 'The redevelopment of Holloway Prison', *The Howard Journal of Penology and Crime Prevention*, 12(2).

Fausto-Sterling, A. (2000), *Sexing the Body: Gender Politics and the Construction of Sexuality*. New York: Basic Books.

Fawcett Society's Commission on Women and the Criminal Justice System (2003), *Interim Report on Victims and Witnesses*. London: Fawcett Society

Fawcett Society's Commission on Women and the Criminal Justice System (2007), *Women and Justice: Third Annual Review of Commission on Women and the Criminal Justice System*. London: Fawcett Society.

Federal Bureau of Investigation (2002), *Crime in the United States – 2001*. Washington, DC: U.S. Department of Justice.

Feeley, M. and Simon, J (1992), 'The new penology: notes on the emerging strategy of corrections and its implications', *Criminology*, 30(4): 452–74.

Feeley, M. and Simon, J. (1994), 'Actuarial justice: the emerging new criminal law', in D. Nelken (ed.), *The Futures of Criminology*. London: Sage.

Fein, H. (1993), *Genocide: A Sociological Perspective*. London: Sage.

Fenstermaker, S., West, C. and Zimmerman, D.Z. (1991), 'Gender inequality: new conceptual terrain', in R.L. Blumberg (ed.), *Gender, Family and Economy*. Newbury Park, CA: Sage.

Ferguson, A. (1991), *Sexual Democracy: Women, Oppression and Revolution*. Boulder, Co: Westview Press.

Fickling, D. (2002), 'Racially motivated crime and punishment', *Guardian Unlimited*, 23 September, www.guardian.co.uk/australia/story/0,12070,797464,00.html.

Fineman, M.A. and Thomadsen, N.S. (eds) (1991), *At the Boundaries of Law: Feminism and Legal Theory*. New York: Routledge, Chapman and Hall.

Finkelhor, D. (1982), 'Sexual abuse: a sociological perspective', *Child Abuse and Neglect*, 6: 95–102.

Finkelhor, D. and Baron, L. (1986), 'Risk factors for child sexual abuse', *Journal of Interpersonal Violence*, 1: 43–71.

Finn, A., Trevethan, S., Carriere, G. and Kowalski, M. (1999), 'Female inmates, aboriginal inmates, and inmates serving life sentences: a one day snapshot', *Juristat*, 19(5): 1–14.

Firestone, S. (1981), *The Dialectic of Sex*. London: Jonathan Cape.

Flowers, R.B. (1987), *Women and Criminality*. Westport, CT: Greenwood.

Flowers, R.B. (2001), *Runaway Kids and Teenage Prostitution*. London: Greenwood.

Folbre, N. (1982), 'Exploitation comes home: a critique of the Marxian theory of family labour', *Cambridge Journal of Economics*, 6(4): 317–29.

Foucault, M. (1978), *The History of Sexuality*. New York: Pantheon.

Foucault, M. (1991), 'Governmentality', in G. Burchell, C. Gordon and P. Miller (eds), *The Foucault Effect*. Hemel Hampstead: Harvester.

Fowler, R. (1999), 'When girl power packs a punch', *Guardian*, 12 July.

Francis, S. (2001), 'Racial gang rape: another diversity disaster', 26 August, www.theneworder.org/news/rape.26.08.01.htm.

Frank, B. (1987), 'Hegemonic heterosexual masculinity', *Studies in Political Economy*, 24 (Autumn): 159–70.

Freud, S. (1933), *New Introductory Lectures on Psychoanalysis*. New York: W.W. Norton.

Frigon, S. (1996), 'A gallery of portraits: women and the embodiment of difference and deviance', in T. Fleming (ed.), *Post-Critical Criminology*. Scarborough: Prentice-Hall.

Frigon, S. (2000), 'Corps, femininites et dangerosite: de la production de "corps dociles" en criminologie', in S. Frigon and M. Khisit (eds), *Du corps des femmes: controles, surveillances et resistances*. Ottawa: Les Presses de l'Universite d'Ottawa.

Frosh, S. (1994), *Sexual Difference: Masculinity and Psychoanalysis*. London: Routledge.

Frosh, S. (1997), *For and Against Psychoanalysis*. London: Routledge.

Funabashi, H. (1992), Environmental problems in post-war Japanese society, *International Journal of Japanese Sociology*, 1: 3–18.

Fuss, D. (1989), *Essentially Speaking: Feminism, Nature, Difference*. London: Routledge and Kegan Paul.

Gadd, D. (2000), 'Masculinities, violence and defended psycho-social subjects', *Theoretical Criminology*, 4(4): 429–49.

Gadd, D. (2002), Masculinities and violence against female partners, *Social and Legal Studies*, 11(1): 61–81.

Gadd, D., Farrall, S., Dallimore, D. and Lombard, N. (2002), *Domestic Abuse against Men in Scotland*. Edinburgh: Scottish Executive.

Garland, D. (2002), *The Culture of Control: Crime and Social Order in Contemporary Society*. Oxford: Oxford University Press.

Gatens, M. (1996), *Imaginary Bodies: Ethics, Power and Corporeality*. London: Routledge.

Gelles, R. J. (1997), *Intimate Violence in Families*, 3rd edn. Thousand Oaks, CA: Sage.

Gelsthorpe, L. (1981), 'Girls in the juvenile court: defining the terrain of penal policy', *Justice For Children*, no. 23.

Gelsthorpe, L. (1989), *Sexism and the Female Offender*. Cambridge: Gower.

Gelsthorpe, L. (2001), 'Critical decisions and processes in the criminal courts', in E. McLaughlin and J. Muncie (eds), *Controlling Crime*. London: Sage/Open University.

Gelsthorpe, L. (2002), 'Feminism and criminology', in M. Maguire, R. Morgan and R. Reiner (eds), *The Oxford Handbook of Criminology*, 3rd edn. Oxford: Oxford University Press.

Gelsthorpe, L. (2003), 'Feminist perspectives on gender and crime: making women work', *Criminal Justice Matters*, 53: 8–9.

Gelsthorpe, L. (2006), 'COUNTERBLAST: women and criminal justice: saying it again, again and again', *The Howard Journal of Criminal Justice*, 45(4): 421–4.

Gelsthorpe, L. (2007), Memorandum submitted by Dr Loraine Gelsthorpe to the House of Commons Select Committee on Home Affairs, March, www.publications.parliament.uk/pa/cm200607/cmselect/cmconst/467/467we13.htm.

Gelsthorpe, L. and Loucks, N. (1997), 'Justice in the making, key influences on decision-making', in C. Hedderman and L. Gelsthorpe (eds), *Understanding the Sentencing of Woman*. London: Home Office Research Study 170.

Gelsthorpe, L. and McIvor, G. (2007), 'Difference and diversity in probation', in L. Gelsthorpe and R. Morgan (eds), *Handbook of Probation*. Cullompton: Willan.

Gelsthorpe, L. and Morris, A. (1988), 'Feminism and criminology in Britain', *British Journal of Criminology*, 28(2): 93–110.

Gelsthorpe, L. and Morris, A. (eds) (1990), *Feminist Perspectives in Criminology*. Milton Keynes: Open University Press.

Gelsthorpe, L. and Morris, A. (2002), 'Women's imprisonment in England and Wales: a penal paradox', *Criminal Justice*, 2(3): 277–301.

Genders, E. and Player, E. (1989), *Race Relations in Prison*. Oxford: Clarendon Press.

George, A. (1999), 'The new prison culture: making millions from misery', in S. Cook and S. Davies (eds), *Harsh Punishment: International Experiences of Women's Imprisonment*. Boston, MA: Northeastern University Press.

Gerard, I. (2002), 'Gang rapist handed 18-year jail sentence', *Weekend Australian*, 10–11 August.

Giddens, A. (1976), *New Rules of Sociological Method*. London: Hutchinson.

Giddens, A. (1981), 'Agency, institution and time-space analysis' in K. Knorr-Cetina and A.V. Cicourel (eds), *Advances in Social Theory and Methodology: Toward an Integration of Micro- and Macro- Sociologies*. Boston, MA: Routledge and Kegan Paul.

Giddens, A. (1989), 'A reply to my critics', in D. Held and J.B. Thompson (eds),

Social Theory of Modern Societies: Anthony Giddens and His Critics. New York: Cambridge University Press.

Giddens, A. (1994), *Beyond Left and Right.* Oxford: Polity.

Gilchrist, E., Bannister, J., Ditton, J. and Farrall, S. (1998), 'Women and the "fear of crime" challenging the accepted stereotype', *British Journal of Criminology,* 38(2): 283–98.

Gilmour, D. (1993), *Manhood in the Making: Cultural Concepts of Masculinity.* New Haven, CT: Yale University Press.

Gilroy, P. (1987), *There Ain't No Black in the Union Jack.* London: Hutchinson.

Glendinning, C. and J. Millar (eds) (1992), *Women and Poverty in Britain: The 1990s.* London: Harvester Wheatsheaf.

Glenn, E.N. (1992), 'From servitude to service work: historical continuities in the racial division of paid reproductive labor', *Signs,* 18(1): 1–43.

Goldstein, P. (1984), 'Drugs and violence among women', paper presented to the American Society of Criminology Annual Meeting.

Goode, W. (1982), 'Why men resist', in B. Thorne with M. Yalom (eds), *Rethinking the Family: Some Feminist Questions.* New York: Longman.

Goodey, J. (1997), 'Boys don't cry: masculinities, fear of crime and fearlessness', *British Journal of Criminology,* 37(3): 401–18.

Goodey, J. (2000), 'Biographical lessons for criminology', *Theoretical Criminology,* 4(4): 473–98.

Goodey, J. (2004), 'Sex trafficking in women from Central and East European Countries. Promoting a victim-centred and woman-centred approach to criminal justice intervention', *Feminist Review,* 76: 26–45.

Goodman, R. (2002), *Family and Social Policy in Japan.* Cambridge: Cambridge University Press.

Gordon, G. (2002), 'Gang wrongly jailed for rape', *Daily Telegraph,* 7 December.

Gordon, M. (2000), 'Definitional issues in violence against women: surveillance and research from a violence research perspective', *Violence Against Women,* 6(7): 747–83.

Gordon, M., Riger, S., LeBailly, R. and Health, L. (1980), 'Crime, women and the quality of urban life', *Signs,* 5: 140–60.

Gordon, P. (1985), *Policing Immigration: Britain's Internal Controls.* London: Pluto Press.

Gottfredson, M. (1984), *Victims of Crime: Dimensions of Risk.* London: HMSO.

Gottfredson, M. and Hirschi, T. (1990), *General Theory of Crime.* Stanford, CA: Stanford University Press.

Graef, R. (1992), *Living Dangerously: Young Offenders in Their Own Words.* London: HarperCollins.

Grbich, J.E. (1991), 'The body in legal theory', in M.A. Fineman and N.S. Thomadsen (eds), *At the Boundaries of Law: Feminism and Legal Theory.* New York: Routledge and Kegan Paul.

Greater London Council (GLC) (1985), *Women's Imprisonment: Breaking the Silence.* London: Women's Equality Unit and Strategic Policy Unit.

Green, P. (ed.) (1991), *Drug Couriers.* London: The Howard Journal for Penal Reform.

Gregory, J. (1986), 'Sex, class and crime: towards a non-sexist criminology', in R. Matthews and J. Young (eds), *Confronting Crime.* London: Sage.

Griffin, C. (1985), *Typical Girls?* London: Routledge and Kegan-Paul.

Griffin, S. (1971), 'Rape: the all-American crime', *Ramparts*, September.

Groombridge, N. (1999), 'Perverse criminologies: the closet of Doctor Lombroso', *Social and Legal Studies*, 8(4): 529–48.

Grosz, E. (1987), 'Feminist theory and the challenge of knowledge', *Women's Studies International Forum*, 10(5): 208–17.

Grosz, E. (1990), 'A note on essentialism and difference', in S. Unew (ed.), *Feminist Knowledge. Critique and Construct*. London: Routledge

Grosz, E. (1994), *Volatile Bodies: Towards a Corporeal Feminism*. Bloomington, IN: Indiana University Press.

Grosz, E. and Probyn, E. (eds) (1995), *Sexy Bodies: Strange Carnalities of Feminism*. London: Routledge.

Groves, W.B. and Frank, N. (1993), 'The sociology of structured choice', in G. Newman, M.J. Lynch and D. Galaty (eds), *Discovering Criminology*. New York: Harrow and Heston.

Hagan, J. (1991), 'A power-control theory of gender and delinquency', in R. Silvennan, J. Teevan and V. Sacco (eds), *Crime in Canadian Society*, 4th Edn. Toronto: Butterworths.

Hagell, A. and Newburn, T. (1994), *Persistent Young Offenders*. London: Policy Studies Institute.

Hale, C. (1993), 'Fear of crime: a review of the literature', *Report to the Metropolitan Police Service Working Party on the Fear of Crime*. Canterbury: Canterbury Business School, University of Kent.

Hall, R. (1985), *Ask Any Woman: A London Enquiry into Rape and Sexual Assault: Report of the Woman's Safety Survey Conducted by Women Against Rape*. Bristol: Falling Wall Press.

Hall, S. (1978), *Policing the Crisis: Mugging, the State and Law and Order*, Basingstoke: Macmillan.

Hall, S. (2002), 'Daubing the drudges of fury: men, violence and the piety of the "hegemonic masculinity" thesis', *Theoretical Criminology*, 6(1): 35–61.

Hall S. and Jefferson T. (1976), *Resistance through Rituals: Youth Subcultures in Post-war Britain*. London: Hutchinson.

Hamberger, L.K. and Potente. (1994), 'Counseling heterosexual women arrested for domestic violence: Implication for theory and practice', *Violence and Victims*, 9: 125–37.

Hanmer, J. and Itzin, C. (eds), (2000), *Home Truths about Domestic Violence: Feminist Influences on Policy and Practice*. London: Routledge

Hanmer, J. and Saunders, S. (1984), *Well-Founded Fear*. London: Hutchinson.

Hanmer, J. and Saunders, S. (eds) (1987), *Women. Violence and Social Control*. Basingstoke: Macmillan.

Hanmer, J. and Stanko, E. (1985), 'Stripping away the rhetoric of protection: violence to women, law and the state', *The International Journal of the Sociology of Law*, 13: 357–74.

Hannah-Moffat, K. (1999), 'Moral agent or actuarial subject: risk and Canadian women's imprisonment', *Theoretical Criminology*, 31(7): 1–94.

Hannah-Moffat, K. (2001), *Punishment in Disguise: Penal Governance and Federal Imprisonment of Women in Canada*. Toronto: University of Toronto Press.

Hannah-Moffat, K. (2002), 'Creating choices: reflecting on choices' in P. Carlen, (ed.), *Women and Punishment: The Struggle for Justice*. Cullompton: Willan.

Harding S. (1987), *Feminism and Methodology*. Milton Keynes: Open University Press.

Hartmann, H. (1979), 'Capitalism, patriarchy and job segregation by sex', in Z. Eisenstein (ed.), *Capitalist Patriarchy and the Case for Socialist Feminism*. New York: Monthly Review Press.

Hartmann, H. (1981), 'The unhappy marriage of Marxism and feminism: toward a more progressive union', in L. Sargent (ed.), *Women and Revolution: A Discussion of the Unhappy Marriage of Marxism and Feminism*. Boston, MA: South End Press.

Harwin, N. (2000), 'Families without fear: women's aid agenda for action on domestic violence', in J. Hanmer and C. Itzin, with S. Quaid and D. Wigglesworth, (eds), *Home Truths about Domestic Violence*. London: Routledge.

Hayman, S. (2000), 'Prison reform and incorporation: lessons from Britain and Canada', in K. Hannah-Moffat and M. Shaw (eds), *An Ideal Prison? Critical Essays on Women's Imprisonment in Canada*. Halifax: Fernwood Press.

Hearn, J. (1987), *The Gender of Oppression: Men, Masculinity and the Critique of Marxism*. Brighton: Harvester Wheatsheaf.

Hearn, J. (1996), 'Is masculinity dead? A critique of the concept of masculinity', in M. Mac an Ghaill (ed.), *Understanding Masculinities*. Buckingham: Open University Press.

Heath, L. (1984), 'Impact of newspaper crime reports on fear of crime: multimethodological investigation', *Journal of Personality and Social Psychology*, 47(2): 263–76.

Hedderman, C. (1990), *The Effect of Defendants' Demeanour on Sentencing on Magistrates' Courts*. Home Office Research Bulletin, No. 29.

Hedderman, C. (2004), 'The "criminogenic" needs of women offenders', in G. McIvor (ed.), *Women Who Offend*. London: Jessica Kingsley.

Hedderman, C. and Gelsthorpe, L. (eds) (1997), *Understanding the sentencing of Women*. London: Home Office Research Study 170.

Hedderman, C. and Hough, M. (1994), *'Does the Criminal Justice System Treat Men and Women Differently?'*, Research Findings 10. London: Home Office, Research and Statistics Department.

Heidensohn, F. (1968), 'The deviance of women: a critique and an enquiry', *British Journal of Sociology*, 19(2): 160–75.

Heidensohn, F. (1985a), *Women and Crime*. London: Macmillan.

Heidensohn, F. (1985b), *Women and Crime: The Life of the Female Offender*. New York: New York University Press.

Heidensohn, F. (1994), 'From being to knowing: some issues in the study of gender in contemporary society', *Women and Criminal Justice*, 6(1): 13–36.

Heidensohn, F. (1995), 'Feminist perspectives and their impact on criminology and criminal justice in Britain', in N. Rafter and F. Heidensohn (eds), *International Feminist Perspectives in Criminology: Engendering a Discipline*. Buckingham: Open University Press.

Heidensohn, F. (1996), *Women and Crime*, 2nd edn. Basingstoke: Macmillan.

Heidensohn, F. (2001), 'Women and violence: myths and reality in the 21st century', *Criminal Justice Matters*, 42: 20.

Heidensohn, F. (2002), 'Gender and crime', in M. Maguire, R. Morgan and R. Reiner (eds), *The Oxford Handbook of Criminology*, 3rd edn. Oxford: Oxford University Press.

Heidensohn, F. (ed.) (2006), *Gender and Justice: New Concepts and Approaches*. Cullompton: Willan.

Heidensohn, F. and Gelsthorpe, L. (2007), 'Gender and crime', in M. Maguire, R. Morgan and R. Reiner (eds), *The Oxford Handbook of Criminology*, 4th edn. Oxford: Oxford University Press.

Heise, L.L., with Pitanguy, J. and Germain, A. (1994), *Violence against Women: The Hidden Health Burden*, World Bank Discussion Papers. Washington, DC: World Bank.

Helsinki Watch (1993), *War Crimes in Bosnia-Herzegovina*, Vol 2. New York: Helsinki Watch.

Her Majesty's Inspectorate of Prisons for England and Wales (1997), *Women in Prison A Thematic Review by HM Chief Inspector of Prisons*. London: Home Office.

Herman, J.L. (1981), *Father–Daughter Incest*. Cambridge, MA: Harvard University Press.

Hester, M., Pearson, C. and Radford, L. (1997), *Domestic Violence: A National Survey of Court Welfare and Family Mediation practice*. Bristol: Policy Press.

Hilberg, R. (1985), *The Destruction of the European Jews*. New York: Holmes & Meier.

Hilberman, E. and Munson, K. (1978), 'Sixty battered women', *Victimology*, 2: 460–71.

Hindelang, M., Gottfredson, M. and Garofalo, J. (1978), *The Victims of Personal Crime*. Cambridge, MA: Ballinger.

Hindess, B. (1973), *The Use of Official Statistics in Sociology*. London: Macmillan.

Hirschi, T. (1969), *Causes of Delinquency*. Berkeley, CA: University of California Press.

Hobsbawm, E. (1994), *The Age of Extremes: The Short Twentieth Century, 1914–1989*. London: Michael Joseph

Hollway, W. and Jefferson, T. (1996), 'Date rape', paper presented to the American Society of Criminology Conference, Miami, November.

Hollway, W. and Jefferson, T. (1997), 'Eliciting narrative through the in-depth interview', *Qualitative Inquiry*, 3(1): 53–70.

Hollway, W. and Jefferson, T. (1998), ' "A kiss is just a kiss": date rape, gender and subjectivity', *Sexualities*, 1(4): 405–23.

Hollway, W. and Jefferson, T. (2000), *Doing Qualitative Research Differently: Free Association, Narrative and the Interview Method*. London: Sage.

Holsinger, K. (2000), 'Feminist perspectives on female offending: examining real girls' lives', *Women and Criminal Justice*, 12: 23–51.

Home Office (1970), *Treatment of Women and Girls in Custody*. London: HMSO.

Home Office (1985), *Prison Statistics England and Wales 1984*, Cmnd.9622. London: HMSO.

Home Office (1999), *The Government's Crime Reduction Strategy*. London: Home Office.

Home Office (2000a), *Criminal Statistics for England and Wales 1999*, Cm 50. London: The Stationery Office.

Home Office (2000b), *Prison Statistics for England and Wales 1999*. London: Home Office.

Home Office (2001a), *Prison Statistics: England and Wales 2000*. London: HMSO.

Home Office (2001b), *Making Punishments Work. Report of a Review of the Sentencing Framework for England and Wales*. London: Home Office.

Home Office (2005), *Domestic Violence: A National Report*. London: Home Office, www.crimereduction.homeoffice.gov.uk/domesticviolence/domestic violence51.pdf

Home Office (2006), *Statistics on Race and the Criminal Justice System – 2005*. London: Home Office.

Home Office (2007), *Her Majesty's Government's Cross Government Action Plan on Sexual Violence and Abuse*. London: Home Office, www.homeoffice.gov.uk/documents/Sexual-violence-action plan?view=Binary

Hood, R. (1992), *Race and Sentencing: A Study in the Crown Court*. Oxford: Oxford University Press.

Hood-Williams, J. (1997), 'Stories for sexual difference', *British Journal of Sociology of Education*, 18(1): 81–99.

Hood-Williams, J. (2001), 'Gender, masculinities and crime: from structures to psyches', *Theoretical Criminology*, 5(1): 37–60.

Hood-Williams, J. and Cealey Harrison, W. (1998), 'Trouble with gender', *Sociological Review*, 46(1): 73–94.

hooks, b. (1981), *'Ain't I a Woman?': Black Women and Feminism*. Boston, MA: South End Press.

hooks, b. (1982), *Ain't I a Woman: Black Women and Feminism*. London: The Women's Press.

hooks, b. (1984), *Feminist Theory: From Margin to Centre*. Boston, MA: South End Press.

hooks, b. (1989), *Talking Black: Thinking Feminist, Thinking Black*. London: Sheba Feminist Publications.

Hough, M. and Mayhew, P. (1983), *The British Crime Survey*. London: HMSO.

Hough, M. and Mayhew, P. (1985), *Taking Account of Crime: Key Findings from the 1984 British Crime Survey*. London: HMSO.

Howard League (1997), *Lost Inside: The Imprisonment of Teenage Girls*. London: The Howard League for Penal Reform.

Howden-Windell, J. and Clark, D. (1999), 'The criminogenic needs of women: a literature review', unpublished paper London: BM Prison Service.

Howe, A. (1994), *Punish and Critique: Towards a Feminist Analysis of Penality*. London: Routledge,

Hoyle, C. and Zedner, L. (2007), 'Victims, victimisation, and criminal', in M. Maguire, R. Morgan and R. Reiner (eds), *The Oxford Handbook of Criminology*, 4th edn. Oxford: Oxford University Press.

Hudson, A. (1983), 'The welfare state and adolescent femininity', *Youth and Policy*, 2(1): 5–13.

Hudson, A. (1985), 'Feminism and social work: resistance or dialogue?', *British Journal of Social Work*, 15: 635–55.

Hudson, A. (1989), 'Troublesome girls: towards alternative definitions and policies', in M. Cain (ed.), *Growing up good: policing the behaviour of girls in Europe*. Sage, London.

Hudson, B. (1984), 'Femininity and adolescence', in A. McRobbie and M. Nava, (eds), *Gender and Generation*. London: Macmillan.

Hudson, B. (1988), 'Content analysis of social enquiry reports written in the borough of Haringey', unpublished report Middlesex Area Probation Service.

Hudson, B. (1998), 'Doing justice to difference', in A. Ashworth and M. Wasik (eds), *Fundamentals of Sentencing Theory*. Oxford: Clarendon Press.

Hudson, B. (2002), 'Gender issues in penal policy and penal theory', in P. Carlen (ed.), *Women and Punishment: The Struggle for Justice*. Cullompton: Willan.

Hull, G., Scott, P. and Smith, B. (1982), *All the Women are White, All the Blacks are Men: But Some of Us Are Brave*. New York: Feminist Press.

Hutter, B. and Williams, G. (eds) (1981), *Controlling Women: The Normal and the Deviant*. Bromley: Croom Helm.

Ianni, F.A.J. (1989), *The Search for Structure: A Report on American Youth Today*. New York: Free Press.

Ignatieff, M. (1994), *Blood and Belonging: Journeys into the New Nationalism*. London: Vintage Books

Immarigeon, M. and Chesney-Lind, M. (1992), *Women's Prisons: Overcrowded and Overused*. San Francisco, CA: National Council on Crime and Delinquency.

Irigaray, L. (1994), *Thinking the Difference*. London: Athlone.

Jackman, C. (2001), 'Turning light on the dark side of life', *Daily Telegraph*, 29 August.

Jackson, D. (1990), *Unmasking Masculinity: A Critical Autobiography*. London: Routledge.

Jackson, M. (1999), 'Canadian aboriginal women and their "criminality": the cycle of violence in the context of difference', *The Australian and New Zealand Journal of Criminology*, 32(2): 197–208.

Jagger, A. (1983), *Feminist Politics and Human Nature*. Totowa, NJ: Rowman and Allanfield.

Jamieson, R. (1999), 'Genocide and the social production of immorality', *Theoretical Criminology*, 3(2): 131–46.

Janoff-Bulman, R. (1979), 'Characterological versus behavioural self-blame: inquiries into depression and rape', *Journal of Personality and Social Psychology*, 37(10): 1798–809.

Jefferson, T. (1992), 'Wheelin and stealin', *Achilles Heel*, Summer: 10–12.

Jefferson, T. (1994a), 'Theorizing masculine subjectivity', in T. Newburn and E.A. Stanko (eds), *Just Boys Doing Business? Men Masculinities and Crime*. London: Routledge.

Jefferson. T. (1994b), 'Theorising masculine subjectivity', in T. Newburn and E. Stanko (eds), *Just Boys Doing Business: Men, Masculinities and Crime*. London: Routledge.

Jefferson, T. (1996a), 'From "little fairy boy" to the "compleat destroyer": subjectivity and transformation in the biography of Mike Tyson', in M. Mac an Ghaill (ed.), *Understanding Masculinities*. Buckingham: Open University Press.

Jefferson, T. (1996b), 'Introduction', in T. Jefferson and P. Carlen (eds), *British Journal of Criminology*, 35(1): 337–47.

Jefferson, T. (1996c), ' "Tougher than the rest": Mike Tyson and the destructive desires of masculinity', *Arena Journal*, 6: 89–105.

Jefferson, T. (1997a), 'Masculinities and crime', in M. Maguire, R. Morgan and R. Reiner (eds), *The Oxford Handbook of Criminology*, 2nd edn. Oxford: Clarendon Press.

Jefferson, T. (1997b), 'The Tyson rape trail: the law, feminism and emotional truth', *Social and Legal Studies*, 6(2): 281–301.

Jefferson, T. (1998), ' "Muscle", "Hard Men" and "Iron" Mike Tyson: reflections on desire, anxiety and the embodiment of masculinity', *Body and Society*, 4(1): 103–18.

Jefferson, T. (2002), 'Subordinating hegemonic masculinity', *Theoretical Criminology*, 6(2): 63–88.

Joe, K. and Chesney-Lind, M. (1995), ' "Just every mother's angel": an analysis of gender and ethnic variations in youth gang membership', *Gender and Society*, 9: 408–30.

Joe, K. and Chesney-Lind, M. (1998), ' "Just every mother's angel": an analysis of gender and ethnic variations in youth gang membership', in K. Daly and L. Mather (eds), *Criminology at the Crossroads: Feminist Readings in Crime and Justice*. New York and Oxford: Oxford University Press.

Jones, S. (2001), *Criminology*, 2nd edn. London: Butterworths.

Jones, T., MacLean, B. and Young, J. (1986), *The Islington Crime Survey*. Aldershot: Gower.

Jones Finer, C. and M. Nellis (eds), (1998), *Crime & Social Exclusion*. Oxford: Blackwell.

Joseph, G. (1981), 'The incompatible ménage à trios: Marxism, feminism and racism', in L. Sargent (ed.), *Women and Revolution*. Boston, MA: South End Press.

Junger, M. (1987), 'Women's experiences of sexual harassment', *British Journal of Criminology*, 27(4): 358–83.

Kamler, B. (1999), *Constructing gender and difference: Critical perspectives on early childhood*. Cresskill, NJ: Hampton Press.

Kappeler, S. (1995), *The Will to Violence: The Politics of Personal Behaviour*. Cambridge: Polity.

Katcher, K. (2006) 'Making violence matter', *The Fawcett Society Magazine*, Winter: 8–9, www.fawcettsociety.org.uk/documents/StopGap_page_8_9.pdf.

Katz, P.A. (1979), 'The development of female identity', in C.B. Kopp (ed.), *Becoming Female: Perspectives on Development*. New York: Plenum.

Kelly, L. (1997), *Final Report of the Activities of the EG-S-VL Plan of Action for Combating Violence against Women*. Strasbourg: Council of Europe.

Kelly, L. and Regan, L. (2000), *Stopping Trafficking: Exploring the Extent of, and Responses to, the Trafficking in Women for Sexual Exploitation in the UK*, Police Research Series Paper, Vol. 125. London: Home Office.

Kelman, H.C. and V. Hamilton (1989), *Crimes of Obedience*. New Haven, CT: Yale University Press.

Kemshall, H. (1998), *Risk in Probation Practice*. Aldershot: Ashgate.

Kendall, K. (2000), 'Psy-ence fiction: governing female prisons through the psychological sciences', in K. Hannah-Moffat and M. Shaw (eds), *An Ideal Prison? Critical Essays on Women's Imprisonment in Canada*. Halifax: Fernwood Press.

Kennedy, H. (1992), *Eve was Framed*. London: Chatto and Windus.

Kidman, J. (2001), '70 girls attacked by rape gangs', *Sun Herald*, 29 July.

King, M.B. (1992), 'Male sexual assault in the community', in G.C. Mezey and M.B. King (eds), *Male Victims of Sexual Assault*. Oxford: Oxford University Press.

King, R. (1999), 'The rise and rise of supermax: an American solution in search of a problem?', *Punishment and Society*, 1(2): 163–86.

Klarin, M. (1997), 'Tadic sentenced to 20 years imprisonment', *Tribunal Update*, 36, 14–19 July.

Klein, D. (1973), 'The etiology of female crime: a review of the literature', in S. Datesman and F. Scarpitti (eds) (1980), *Women, Crime and Justice*. New York: Oxford University Press.

Knowsley, J. (1996), 'Girl gangs rival boys to rule the streets', *Sunday Telegraph*, 6 May.

Kokuritsu Shakai Hosho Kenkyusho [National Institute of Population and Social Security] (2003), research available on www1.ipss.go.jp/seisaku/html/112a2.htm.

Koons, R., Burrows, J., Morash, M. and Bynum, T. (1997), 'Expert and offender perceptions of program elements linked to successful outcomes for incarcerated women', *Crime and Delinquency*, 43(4): 512–25.

Kornhauser, R. (1978), *Social Sources of Delinquency: An Appraisal of Analytic Models*. Chicago, IL and London: University of Chicago Press.

Kruttschnitt, C. (1981), 'Social status and sentences of female offenders', *Law and Society Review*, 15(2): 247–65.

Kruttschnitt, C. (1984), 'Sex and criminal court dispositions', *Journal of Research in Crime and Delinquency*, 21(3): 213–32.

Laberge, D. (1991), 'Women's criminality, criminal women, criminalized women? Questions in and for a feminist perspective', *Journal of Human Justice*, 2(2): 37–56.

Lacan, J. (1977), *Ecrits: A Selection*. New York: Norton.

Laing, R.D. (1968), *The Politics of Experience*. Harmondsworth: Penguin.

Lawson, V. (2001), 'Private school, public disgrace', *Sydney Morning Herald*, 10 February.

Lea, J. and Young, J. (1984), *What is to be done about Law and Order?* Harmondsworth: Penguin Books.

Lees, S. (1986), *Losing Out: Sexuality and Adolescent Girls*. London: Hutchinson.

Lees, S. (1989), 'Blaming the victim', *New Statesman, New Society*, 1 December.

Leibrich, J. (1993), *Straight to the Point: Angles on Giving up Crime*. Dunedin: University of Otago Press.

Leonard, E. (1982), *A Critique of Criminological Theory: Women, Crime and Society*. London and New York: Longman.

Leonard, E. (1983), *Women, Crime and Society*. New York: Longman.

Levi-Strauss, C. (1955), *Tristes Tropiques*. Paris: Pion.

Lewis, D. (1977), 'Black women offenders and criminal justice: some theoretical considerations', in M. Warren (ed.), *Comparing Male and Female Offenders*. Beverly Hills, CA: Sage.

Lewis, D. and Maxfield, M. (1980), 'Fear in the neighbourhoods: an investigation into the impact of crime', *Journal of Research in Crime and Delinquency*, 17: 160–79.

Littlewood, R. and Lipsedge, M. (1979), *Transcultural Psychology*. London: Churchill Livingstone.

Lloyd, A. (1995), *Doubly Deviant, Doubly Damned: Society's Treatment of Violent women*. London: Penguin Books.

Lloyd, G. (1994), *The Man of Reason: 'Male and Female' in Western Philosophy*. London: Metheun.

Loader, I. and Sparks, R. (2007), 'Contemporary landscapes of crime, order and control: governance, risk and globalisation', in M. Maguire, R. Morgan and R. Reiner (eds), *The Oxford Handbook of Criminology*, 4th edn. Oxford: Oxford University Press.

Lombroso, C. and Ferrero, W. (1895), *The Female Offender*. Fisher Unwin.

MacInnes, J. (1998), *The End of Masculinity: The Confusion of Sexual Genesis and Sexual Difference in Modern Society*. Buckingham: Open University Press.

MacKinnon, C. (1979), *Sexual Harassment of Working Women*. New Haven, CT: Yale University Press.

MacKinnon, C. (1983), 'Feminism, Marxism, method and the state: an agenda for theory', *Signs*, 8(4): 635–58.

MacKinnon, C. (1987), *Feminism Unmodified: Discourses on Life and Law*. Cambridge: Harvard University Press.

MacKinnon, C.A. (1994), 'Rape, genocide, and women's human rights', in A. Stiglmayer (ed.), *Mass Rape: The War Against Women in Bosnia-Herzegovina*. Lincoln, NE: University of Nebraska Press.

Maguire, M., Morgan, R. and Reiner, R. (1997), *The Oxford Handbook of Criminology*, 2nd edn. Oxford: Clarendon Press.

Mair, G. and May, C. (1997), *Offenders on Probation*, Home Office Research Study 167. London: HMSO.

Malson, M. (1983), 'Black women's sex roles: the social context for a new ideology', *Journal of Social Issues*, 39(3): 101–13.

Mama, A. (1984), 'Black women, the economic crisis and the British State', *Feminist Review*, 17: 20–35.

Mandaraka-Sheppard, A. (1986), *The Dynamics of Aggression in Women's Prisons in England*. Aldershot: Gower.

Mangan, J. and Walvin, J. (eds) (1987), *Manliness and Morality: Middle-Class Masculinity in Britain and America 1800–1940*. Manchester: Manchester University Press.

Marchland, M.H. and Runyan, A.S. (2000), *Gender and Global Restructuring: Sightings, Sites and Resistances*. London: Routledge.

Margolin, G. (1987), 'The multiple forms of aggressiveness between marital partners: how do we identify them?', *Journal of Marital and Family Therapy*, 13: 77–84.

Mather, L. and Curtis, R. (1995), 'In search of the female urban "gangsta": change, culture and crack cocaine', in B. Price and N. Sokoloff (eds), *The Criminal Justice System and Women*. New York: McGraw-Hill.

Mather, L. and Daly, K. (1996), 'Women in the street-level drug economy: continuity or change?', *Criminology*, 34(4): 465–91.

Matza, D. (1964), *Delinquency and Drift*. New York: Wiley.

Maxfield, M. (1984a), *Fear of Crime in England and Wales*. London: HMSO.

Maxfield, M. (1984b), 'The limits of vulnerability in explaining fear of crime: a comparative neighbourhood analysis', *Research in Crime and Delinquency*, 21(3): 233–50.

Maxfield, M. (1987), *Explaining the Fear of Crime: Evidence from the 1984 British Crime Survey*, Home Office Research Paper No. 41. London: Home Office.

Mazowiecki, T. (1992), *Third Report of the UN Commission to Investigate the Human Rights Situation in The Former Yugoslavia*, Appx. 2. Geneva, 12 February.

McCormack, A., Janus, M. and Burgess, A.W. (1986), 'Runaway youths and sexual victimisation: Gender differences in an adolescent runaway population', *Child Abuse and Neglect*, 10: 387–95.

McGuinness, P.P. (2002), 'No one gang has monopoly on rape', *Sydney Morning Herald*, 23 July.

McGuire, J. (ed.) (1995), *What Works? Reducing Re-offending – Guidelines from Research and Practice*. Chichester: John Wiley & Sons.

McIvor, G. (ed.) (2004), *Women Who Offend*, Research Highlights in Social Work 44. London: Jessica Kingsley.

McMahon, A. (1993), 'Male readings of feminist theory: the psychologisation of sexual politics in the masculinity literature', *Theory and Society*, 22(5): 675–57.

McMahon, A. (1999), *Taking Care of Men*. Cambridge: Cambridge University Press.

McRobbie, A. (1978), 'Working class girls and the culture of femininity', in Women's Studies Group (eds), *Women Take Issue:Aspects of Women's Subordination*. London: Hutchinson.

McRobbie, A. (1982), 'The politics of feminist research: between the talk, text and action', *Feminist Review*, 12: 46–57.

McRobbie, A. and Garber, J. (1976), 'Girls and subcultures', in S. Hall and T. Jefferson (eds), *Resistance through Rituals*. London: Hutchinson.

Media Watch (2002), television programme, ABC Television, 9 July, www.abc.net.au/mediawatch/stories/default.htm.

Meiselman, K. (1978) *Incest*. San Francisco, CA: Jossey-Bass.

Merton, R.K. (1938), 'Social structure and anomie', *American Sociological Review*, 3: 672–82.

Messerschmidt, J.W. (1986), *Capitalism, Patriarchy and Crime; Towards a Socialist Feminist Criminology*. Totowa, NJ: Rowman and Littlefield.

Messerschmidt, J.W. (1993a), 'Structured action and gendered crime', in J.W. Messerschmidt, *Masculinities and Crime*, Lanham: MD: Rowman and Littlefield.

Messerschmidt, J.W. (1993b), *Masculinities and Crime: Critique and Reconceptualisation of Theory*. Lanham, MD: Rowman and Littlefield.

Messerschmidt, J.W. (1997), *Crime as Structured Action*. London: Sage Publications.

Messerschmidt, J.W. (1998), 'Men victimising men: the case of lynching, 1965–1900', in L. Bower (ed.), *Masculinities and Violence*. London: Sage Publications.

Messerschmidt, J.W. (2000), *Nine Lives:Adolescent Masculinities, the Body and Violence*. Boulder, CO: Westview.

Meštrovié, S. (ed.) (1996), *Genocide after Emotion*. London: Routledge.

Milgram, S. (1974), *Obedience to Authority: An Experimental View*. London: Tavistock.

Miller, E. (1986), *Street Woman*. Philadelphia, PA: Temple University Press.

Millett, K. (1970), *Sexual Politics*. London: Jonathan Cape.

Millett, K. (1975), *The Prostitution Papers*. Boulder, CO: Paladin.

Millett, K. (1976), *The Prostitution Papers: 'A Quartet for the Female Voice'*. New York: Ballantine Books.

Mirrlees-Black, C., Mayhew, P. and Percy, A. (1996), *The 1996 British Crime Survey: England and Wales*, Home Office Statistical Bulletin, Issue 19/96, Research and Statistics Directorate. London: Home Office.

Moffitt, T.E., Krueger, R.F., Caspi, A. and Fagan, J. (2000), 'Partner abuse and general crime: how are they the same? How are they different?', *Criminology*, 38: 199–232.

Mooney, J. (2000), *Gender and Violence*. London: Routledge.

Morash, M. (2006), *Understanding Gender, Crime and Justice*. Thousand Oaks, CA, London and New Dehli: Sage Publications.

Morgan, D.H.J. (1992), *Discovering Men*. London: Routledge.

MORI (1994), ' "Public attitudes to crime", research study conducted for *Reader's Digest* magazine', January. London: MORI.

Moriyama, Ms (2001), 'Keynote speech by the minister of Justice Ms Moriyama of Japan at the 2nd World Congress Against the Commercial Sexual Exploitation of Children', 2nd World Congress Against the Commercial Sexual Exploitation of Children, Yokahama, Japan. Available from www. ecpat.com.

Morris, A. (1987), *Women, Crime and Criminal Justice*. Oxford: Basil Blackwell.

Morris, A., Wilkinson, C., Tisi, A., Woodrow, J. and Rockley, A. (1995), *Managing the Needs of Female Prisoners*. London: Home Office.

Morris, N. (1994), *Dangerous Classes: The Underclass and Social Citizenship*. London: Routledge.

Morris, R. (2001), 'DPP to appeal on rape penalties', *Daily Telegraph*, 7 September.

Morrison, W. (1995), *Theoretical Criminology: From Modernity to Post-Modernity*. London: Cavendish.

Moulds, E.F. (1980), 'Chivalry and paternalism: disparities of treatment in the criminal justice system', in S.K. Datesman and F.R. Scarpitti (eds), *Women, Crime and Justice*. New York: Oxford University Press.

Mullender, A. (1996), *Rethinking Domestic Violence: The Social Work and Probation Response*. London: Routledge

Mullender, A., Hague, G., Imam, U., Kelly, L., Malos, E. and Regan, T. (2002), *Children's Perspectives on Domestic Violence*. London: Sage.

Muncie, J. (2000), 'Pragmatic realism? Searching for criminology in the new youth justice', in B. Goldson (ed.), *The New Youth Justice*. Lyme Regis: Russell House.

Murphy, T. (1996), 'Bursting binary bubbles: law, literature and the sexed body', in J. Morison and C. Bell (eds), *Tall Stories? Reading Law and Literature*. Aldershot: Dartmouth.

Murray, C. (1984), *Losing Ground*. New York: Basic Books.

Murray, C. (1988), *In Pursuit of Happiness and Good Government*. New York: Simon and Schuster.

Naffine, N. (1987), *Female Crime: The Construction of Women in Criminology*. London: Allen and Unwin.

Naffine, N. (1989), 'Towards justice for girls: rhetoric and practice for the treatment of status offenders', *Women and Criminal Justice*, 1: 3–20.

Naffine, N. (1990), *Law and the Sexes*. London: Allen and Unwin.

Naffine, N. (1996), *Feminism and Criminology*. Philadelphia, PA: Temple University Press.

Naffine, N. (1997), *Feminism and Criminology*. Cambridge: Polity Press.

Nagel, I. and Hagan, J. (1983), 'Gender and crime: offence patterns and criminal court sanctions', *Crime and Justice*, 4: 91–144.

Nash, M. (2006), *Public Protection and the Criminal Justice Process*. Oxford: Oxford University Press.

National Association for the Care and Resettlement of Offenders (NACRO) (1991), *A Fresh Start for Women Prisoners*. London: NACRO.

Nava, M. (1984), 'Youth service provision, social order and the question of girls', in A. McRobbie and M. Nava (eds), *Gender and Generation*. London: Macmillan.

Newburn, T. (2007), *Criminology*. Cullompton: Willan Publishing.

Newburn, T. and Stanko, E. (eds) (1994), *Just Boys Doing Business: Men, Masculinities and Crime*. London: Routledge.

O'Dwyer, J., Wilson, J. and Carlen, P. (1987), 'Women's imprisonment in England, Wales and Scotland: recurring issues', in P. Carlen and A. Worrall (eds), *Gender, Crime and Justice*. Milton Keynes: Open University Press.

O'Malley, P. (1996), 'Risk and responsibility', in T. Barry, A. Osborne and N. Rose (eds), *Foucault and Political Reason*. London: UCL Press.

O'Toole, L. and Schiffman, J. (1997), *Gender Violence: Interdisciplinary Perspectives*. New York: New York University Press.

Oakley, A. (1972), *Sex, Gender and Society*. Aldershot: Maurice Temple Smith.

Oakley, A. (1981), *Subject Women*. Oxford: Martin Robertson.

Office for National Statistics (1999), *Social Trends*, 29. London: The Stationery Office.

Omaar, R. (1996), 'Survivors of the genocide in Rwanda pay with their lives', *Guardian*, 3 April.

Orenstein, P. (1994), *School Girls*. Garden City, NY: Doubleday.

Overington, C. (2001), 'School goes on trial in unholy Trinity case: dormitory of shame', *Sunday Age*, 4 February.

Owen, B. (1999), 'Women and Imprisonment in the United States: the gendered consequences of the U.S. imprisonment binge', in S. Cook and S. Davies (eds), *Harsh Punishment: International Experiences of Women's Imprisonment*. Boston, MA: Northeastern University Press.

Pahl, J. (1985), 'Refuges for battered women: ideology and action', *Feminist Review*, 19: 25–31.

Pain, R. (1991), 'Space, sexual violence and social control: integrating geographical and feminist analyses of women's fear of crime', *Progress in Human Geography*, 15(4): 415–31.

Pain, R. (1993), 'Women's fear of sexual violence: explaining the spatial paradox', in H. Jones (ed.), *Crime and the Urban Environment*. Aldershot: Avebury.

Palmer, P. (1990), *Domesticity and Dirt: Housewives and Domestic Servants in the United States, 1920–1945*. Philadelphia, PA: Temple University Press.

Pantazis, C. (1999), 'The criminalization of female poverty', in S. Watson and L. Doyal (eds), *Engendering Social Policy*. Buckingham: Open University Press.

Pearson, G. (1983), *Hooligan: A History of Respectable Fears*. London: Macmillan.

Pease, B. (1999), *Recreating Men: Postmodern Masculinity Politics*. London: Sage.

Pease, K. (1985), 'Community service orders', in M. Tonry and N. Morris (eds), *Crime and Justice. An Annual Review of Research*, Vol. 6. Chicago, IL: University of Chicago Press.

Perloff, L. (1983), 'Perceptions of vulnerability to victimization', *Journal of Social Issues*, 39(2): 41–61.

Phelps, R.J., McIntosh, M., Jesudason, V., Warner, P. and Pohlkamp, J. (1982), *Wisconsin Female Juvenile Offender Study Project Summary Report*. Madison, WI: Wisconsin Council on Juvenile Justice, Youth Policy and Law Center.

Phillips, C. and Bowling, B. (2007), 'Ethnicities, racism, crime and criminal justice', in M. Maguire, R. Morgan and R. Reiner (eds), *The Oxford Handbook of Criminology*. Oxford: Oxford University Press.

Phoenix, J. (2001), *Making Sense of Prostitution*, 2nd edn. London: Palgrave.

Pizzey, E. (1974), *Scream Quietly or the Neighbours Will Hear*. London: IF Books.

Platek, M. (1999), 'On the margin of life: women's imprisonment in Poland', in S. Cook and S. Davies (eds), *Harsh Punishments: International Experiences of Women's Imprisonment*. Boston, MA: Northeastern University Press.

Player, E. (1989a), 'Women and crime in the city', in D. Downes (ed.), *Crime and the City*. London: Macmillan.

Player, E. (1989b), *Women and Crime in the City*. London: Macmillan.

Plummer, K. (1984), 'Sexual diversity: a sociological perspective', in K. Howells (ed.), *The Psychology of Sexual Diversity*. New York: Basil Blackwell.

Poe-Yamagata, E. and Butts, J.A. (1996), *Female Offenders in the Juvenile Justice System*. Washington, DC: US Department of Justice.

Polk, K. (1997), 'A re-examination of the concept of victim-precipitated homicide', *Homicide Studies*, 1: 141–68.

Pollak, O. (1950), *The Criminality of Women*. Philadelphia, PA: University of Pennsylvania Press, (Perpetua edition, 1961).

Pollack, S. (2000), 'Dependency discourse as social control', in K. Hannah-Moffat and M. Shaw (eds), *An Ideal Prison? Critical Essays on Women's Imprisonment in Canada*. Halifax: Fernwood Press.

Pope, C. and Feyerherm, W.H. (1982), 'Gender bias in juvenile court dispositions', *Social Service Research*, 6: 1–17.

Poynting, S., Noble, G., Tabar, P. and Collins, J. (2004), ' "You deserve it because you are Australian": the moral panic over "ethnic gang rape" ', in S. Poynting, G. Noble, P. Tabar and J. Collins, *Bin Laden in the Surburbs: Criminalising the Arab Other*. Sydney: Sydney Institute of Criminology.

Pratt, J., Brown, D., Hallsworth, S., Brown, M. and Morrison, W. (eds) (2005), *The New Punitiveness: Trends, Theories, Perspectives*. Cullompton: Willan.

Prime Minister's Office (1999), *The Present Status of Gender Equality Measures. 3rd Report on the Plan for Gender Equality 2000*. Japan: Prime Minister's Office.

Prison Reform Trust (1991), *The Identikit Prisoner*. London: Prison Reform Trust.

Prison Reform Trust (2000), *Justice for Women: The Need for Reform*, Report of the Committee on Women's Imprisonment Chaired by Professor Dorothy Wedderburn. London: Prison Reform Trust.

Puzzanchera, C., Stahl, A.L., Finnegan, T.A., Snyder, H., Poole, R.S. and Tierney, N. (2000), *Juvenile Court Statistics, 1997*. Washington, DC: National Centre for Juvenile Justice.

Quinney, R. (1980), *The Social Reality of Crime*. Boston, MA: Little Brown.

Radford, L. and Tsutsumi, K. (2004), 'Globalization and violence against women – inequalities in risks, responsibilities and blame in the UK and Japan', *Women's Studies International Forum*, 27(1): 1–12.

Radford, L., Sayer, S. and AMICA (1999), *Unreasonable Fears?* Bristol: Women's Aid Federation.

Rafter, N. and Heidensohn, F. (eds) (1995), *International Feminist Perspectives in Criminology*. Buckingham: Open University Press.

Ramazanoglu, C. (1986), 'Ethnocentrism and socialist feminist theory: a response to Barrett and McIntosh', *Feminist Review*, 22: 83–91.

Reed, B.G. (1987), 'Developing women-sensitive drug dependence treatment services: why so difficult?', *Journal of Psychoactive Drugs*, 19(2): 151–8.

Reiman, J. (1979), *The Rich get Richer and the Poor get Prison*. New York: Wiley.

Reitsma-Street, M. (1999), 'Justice for Canadian girls: a 1990s update', *Canadian Journal of Criminology*, July: 335–63.

Rex, S. (1999), 'Desistance from offending: experiences of probation', *The Howard Journal of Criminal Justice*, 38(4): 366–83.

Rice, A.F., Smith, L.L. and Janzen, F. (1999), 'Women inmates, drug abuse, and the Salt Lake County Jail', *American Jails*, 13(3): 43–55.

Rice, M. (1990), 'Challenging orthodoxies in feminist theory: a black feminist critique', in L. Gelsthorpe and A. Morris (eds) *Feminist Perspectives in Criminology*. Milton Keynes: Open University Press.

Richardson, H.J. (1969), *Adolescent Girls in Approved Schools*. London: Routledge and Kegan Paul.

Riger, S. and Gordon, M. (1981), 'The fear of rape; a study in social control', *Journal of Social Issues*, 37(4): 71–92.

Riger, S., Gordon, M. and Bailley, R. (1978), 'Women's fear of crime: from blaming to restricting the victim', *Victimology*, 3: 274–84.

Riley, K. (1981), 'Black girls speak for themselves', *Multi-racial Education*, 10(3): 3–12.

Riley, D. (1988), *Am I That Name?: Feminism and the Category of 'Women' in History*. Minneapolis, MN: University of Minnesota Press.

Robinson, R. (1990), 'Violations of girlhood: a qualitative study of female delinquents and children in need of services in Massachusetts', unpublished doctoral dissertation, Brandeis University, Waltham, MA.

Rock, P. (1988), 'The present state of criminology in Britain', *British Journal of Criminology*, 28: 188–99.

Rock, P. (1994), 'The social organisation of British Criminology', in M. Maguire, R. Morgan and R. Reiner (eds), *The Oxford Handbook of Criminology*. Oxford: Clarendon Press.

Roiphe, K. (1993), *The Morning After*. Boston, MA: Little Brown.

Rose, N. (1987), 'Transcending the public/private', *Journal of Law and Society*, 14(1): 61–75.

Rose, N. (1989), *Governing the Soul*. London: Routledge.

Rose, N. (1994), 'Expertise and the government of conduct', *Studies in Law, Politics and Society*, 14: 359–97.

Rose, N. (1999), *Powers of Freedom: Reframing Political Thought*. Cambridge: Cambridge University Press.

Rose, N. (2000), 'Government and control', *British Journal of Criminology*, 40: 321–39.

Rose, N. and Valverde, M. (1998), 'Governed by law?', *Social and Legal Studies*, 7(4): 541–53.

Rosenbaum, M. (1981), *Women on Heroin*. New Brunswick, NJ: Rutgers University Press.

Rowe, D.C., Vazsonyi, A.T. and Flannery, D.J. (1995), 'Sex differences in crime: do means and within-sex variation have similar causes?', *Journal of Research in Crime and Delinquency*, 31(1): 84–100

Rubenstein, J. (1973), *City Police*. New York: Farar, Straus and Giroux.

Rubin, G. (1984). 'Thinking sex: notes for a radical theory of the politics of sexuality', in C.S. Vance (ed.), *In Pleasure and Danger: Exploring Female Sexuality*. Boston, MA: Routledge and Kegan Paul.

Rumgay, J. (1996), 'Women Offenders: towards a needs based policy', *Vista*, September: 104–15.

Rumgay, J. (2000) 'Policies of neglect: female offenders and the probation service', in Kenshall, H. and Littlechild, R. (eds), *Improving Participation and Involvement in Social Care Delivery*. London: Jessica Kingsley

Rumgay, J. (2004) 'Living with paradox: community supervision of women offenders', in G. McIvor (ed.), *Women Who Offend*. London: Jessica Kingsley.

Rusche, G. and Kirchheimer, O. (1939), *Punishment and Social Structure*. London: Russell and Russell.

Russell, D. (1973), *The Politics of Rape*. New York: Macmillan.

Russell, D. (1982), *Rape in Marriage*. New York: Macmillan.

Russell, D. (1984), *Sexual Exploitation*. Beverley Hills, CA: Sage.

Russell, D. and Howell, N. (1983), 'The prevalence of rape in the United States revisited', *Signs*, 8(4): 688–95.

Russell, D.E. (1986), *The Secret Trauma: Incest in the Lives of Girls and Women*. New York: Basic Books.

Russell, K. (1992), 'Development of a black criminology and the role of the black criminologist', *Justice Quarterly*, 9(4): 667–83.

Rutter, M., Giller, H. and Hagell, A. (1998), *Antisocial Behaviour by Young People*. Cambridge: Cambridge University Press.

Sacco, V.F. (1990), 'Gender, fear and victimization: a preliminary application of power-control theory', *Sociological Spectrum*, 10: 485–506.

Sacco, V.F. (1995), 'Media constructions of crime', *The Annals*, 539, (May): 141–54.

Sacco V.F. (2000), 'News that counts: newspaper images of crime and victimization statistics', *Criminologie*, 33(1): 203–23.

Sauiny, S. (2002), 'After 13 years jailed five cleared of park rape', *Sydney Morning Herald*, 221–22 December.

Saunders, H. (2002), 'Making contact worse', *Safe: The Domestic Abuse Quarterly* (Spring), 14–16, Bristol: Women's Aid Federation of England.

Saunders, H. and Barron, J. (2003), *Failure to Protect? Domestic Violence and the Experience of Abused Women and Children in the Family Courts*, Bristol: Women's Aid Federation and National Society for the Prevention of Cruelty to Children.

Saunders, T. (2004) *Sex Work: A Risky Business*. Cullompton: Willan.

Saussure, F. de (1974), *Course in General Linguistics*. London: Peter Owen.

Schaffner, L. (1999), 'Violence and female delinquency: gender transgressions and gender invisibility', *Berkeley Women's Law Journal*, 14: 40–65.

Schechter, S. (1982), *Women and Male Violence: The Visions and Struggles of the Battered Women's Movement*. Boston, MA: South End Press.

Scheppele, K. and Bart, P. (1983), 'Through women's eyes: defining danger in the wake of sexual assault', *Journal of Social Issues*, 39(2): 63–81.

Schichor, D. and Sechrest, D. (1996), *Three Strikes and You're Out: Vengeance as Public Policy*. Thousand Oaks, CA: Sage.

Schrecker, T. (2001), 'From the welfare state to the no-second-chances state', in S. Boyd, D. Chunn and R. Menzies (eds), *(AB) Using Power: The Canadian Experience*. Halifax: Fernwood.

Scully, D. (1990), *Understanding Sexual Violence: A Study of Convicted Rapists*. Boston, MA: Unwin Hyman.

Seccombe, W. (1986), 'Patriarchy stabilized: the construction of the male breadwinner in nineteenth century Britain', *Social History*, 11(1): 53–75.

Segal, L. (ed.) (1983), *What Is to be Done about the Family?* Harmondsworth: Penguin.

Segal, L. (1990), *Slow Motion: Changing Masculinities, Changing Men*. New Brunswick, NJ: Rutgers University Press.

Seichi Ota (2003), reported in http://newsbbc.co.uk/go/pr/frl-/1/hi/world/asia-pacific/ 3025240.stm.

Seidler, V. (1991), *Recreating Sexual Politics*. London: Routledge.

Sharp, C. and Budd, T. (2005), *Minority Ethnic Groups and Crime: The Findings from the Offending, Crime and Justice Survey 2003*, Home Office Online Report 33/05.

Shaw, C.R. and McKay, H.D. (1942), *Juvenile Delinquency in Urban Areas*. Chicago, IL: Chicago University Press.

Shaw, M. (1993), 'Reforming federal women's imprisonment', in E. Adelberg and C. Currie (eds), *In Conflict with the Law: Women and the Canadian Justice System*. Vancouver: Press Gang.

Sheehan, P. (2001), 'Tolerant, multicultural Sydney can face this difficult truth', *Sydney Morning Herald*, 29 August.

Shiokawa, K. (1999), 'Cute but deadly: women and violence in Japanese comics', in J.A. Lent (ed.), *Themes and Issues in Asian Cartooning*. Bowling Green, Oh. Bowling Green State University Popular Press.

Shoham, S.G. (1974), *Society and the Absurd*. Oxford: Blackwell.

Simmons, J. and Dodd, T. (eds) (2003), *Crime in England and Wales 2002–2003*, Home Office Statistical Bulletin. London: Home Office.

Simons, M. (1979), 'Racism and feminism: a schism in the sisterhood', *Feminist Studies*, 5(2): 384–401.

Simon, J. and Feeley, M. (1995), 'True crime: the new penology and public discourse on crime', in T. Blomberg and S. Cohen (eds), *Punishment and Social Control*. New York: Aldine de Gruyter.

Skogan, W. and Maxfield, M. (1981), *Coping with Crime*. Beverly Hills, CA: Sage.

Smart, C. (1977), *Women, Crime and Criminology: A Feminist Critique*. London: Routledge and Kegan Paul.

Smart, C. (1977), 'Criminological theory: its ideology and implications concerning women', *Sociology*, 28(1): 89–100.

Smart, C. (1984), *The Ties that Bind: Law, Marriage and the Reproduction of Patriarchal Relationships*. London: Routledge and Kegan Paul.

Smart, C. (1989a), *Child Custody and the Politics of Gender*. London: Routledge.

Smart, C. (1989b), *Feminism and the Power of the Law*. London: Routledge.

Smart, C. (1990), 'Feminist approaches to criminology or post-modern woman meets atavistic man', in L. Gelsthorpe and A. Morris (eds), *Feminist Perspectives in Criminology*. Milton Keynes and Philadelphia, PA: Open University Press.

Smart, C. (1995), 'Feminist approaches to criminology, or postmodern woman meets atavistic man', in C. Smart (ed.), *Law, Crime and Sexuality*. London: Sage.

Smart, C., Neale, B. and Wade, A. (2001), *The Changing Experience of Childhood, Families and Divorce*. Oxford: Polity.

Smith, A. (1974), 'The woman offender', in L. Blom-Cooper (eds), *Progress in Penal Reform*. Oxford: Clarendon Press.

Smith, A. and Stewart, A. (1983), 'Approaches to studying racism and sexism in black women's lives', *Journal of Social Issues*, 39(3): 1–15.

Smith, B. (1982), 'Racism and women's studies', in G. Hull, P. Scott and B. Smith (eds), *All the Women are White, All the Blacks are Men: But Some of Us Are Brave*. New York: Feminist Press.

Smith, C. (2005), 'Gender and crime', in C. Hale, K. Hayward, A. Wahidin and E. Wincup (eds), *Criminology*. Oxford: Oxford University Press.

Smith, D. and Paternoster, R. (1987), 'The gender gap in theories of deviance: issues and evidence', *Journal of Research in Crime and Delinquency*, 24(2): 140–72.

Smith, D. and Stewart, J. (1983), 'Probation and social exclusion', in C. Jones Finer and M. Nellis (eds), *Crime & Social Exclusion*. Oxford: Blackwell.

Smith, S.J. (1989), 'Social relations, neighbourhood structure and the fear of crime in Britain', in D. Evans and D. Herbert (eds), *The Geography of Crime*. London: Routledge.

Smykla, J. and Williams, J. (1996), 'Co-corrections in the United States of America, 1970–1990: two decades of disadvantages for women prisoners', *Women and Criminal Justice*, 8(1): 61–76.

Snell, T.L. and Morton, D.C. (1994), *Women in Prison, (Special Report)*. Washington, DC: Bureau of Justice Statistics.

Snider, L. (1994), 'Feminism, punishment and the potential of empowerment', *Canadian Journal of Law and Society*, 9(1): 75–104.

Snider, L. (1998), 'Towards safer societies: punishment, masculinities and violence against women', *British Journal of Criminology*, 38(1): 1–39.

Snider, L. (2000), 'The sociology of corporate crime: an obituary', *Theoretical Criminology*, 4(2): 169–206.

Snider, L. (2003), 'Constituting the punishable woman. atavistic man incarcerates postmodern woman', *British Journal of Criminology*, 43: 354–78.

Spohn, C., Gruhl, J. and Welch, S. (1987), 'The impact of the ethnicity and gender of defendants on the decision to reject dismiss felony charges', *Criminology*, 25: 175–91

Stanko, E. (1985), *Intimate Intrusions*. London: Routledge.

Stanko, E. (1987), 'Typical violence, normal precaution: men, women, and interpersonal violence in England, Wales, Scotland and the USA', in J. Hanmer and M. Maynard (eds), *Women, Violence and Social Control*. Basingstoke: Macmillan.

Stanko, E. (1990), *Everyday Violence. How Men and Women Experience Sexual and Physical Danger*. London: Pandora.

Stanko, E. and Hobdell, K. (1993), 'Assault on men: masculinity and male victimization', *British Journal of Criminology*, 33(3): 400–14.

Stanley, L. and Wise, S. (1983), *Breaking Out: Feminist Consciousness and Feminist Research*. London: Routledge and Kegan Paul.

Steffensmeier, D. (1978), 'Crime and the contemporary woman: an analysis of changing levels of female property crime 1960–1975', *Social Forces*, 57(2): 566–84.

Steffensmeier, D. (1980), 'Sex differences in patterns of adult crime, 1965–1977: a review and assessment', *Social Forces*, 58: 1080–108.

Steffensmeier, D. (1983), 'Organizational properties and sex-segregation in the underworld: building a sociological theory of sex', *Social Forces*, 61: 1010–32.

Steffensmeier, D. and Haynie, D.L. (2000), 'The structural sources of urban female violence in the United States', *Homicide Studies*, 4: 107–34.

Steinert, H. (1997), 'Fin de siècle criminology', *Theoretical Criminology*, 1(1): 111–29.

Stevens, A. (2006), *Confronting the 'Malestream': The Contribution of Feminist Criminologies*, Issues in Community and Criminal Justice Monograph no. 7. London: NAPO.

Stiglmayer, A. (ed.) (1994), *Mass Rape: The War Against Women in Bosnia-Herzegovina*. Lincoln, NE: University of Nebraska Press.

Straus, M.A. (1993), 'Physical assaults by wives: a major social problem', in R.J. Gelles and D.R. Loseke (eds), *Current Controversies on Family Violence*. Newbury Park, CA: Sage.

Stubbs, J. (ed.) (1994), *Women, Male Violence and the Law*. Sydney: Institute of Criminology.

Sturge, C. and Glaser, D. (2000), 'Contact and domestic violence – the experts' report', *Family Law*, 30 615–29.

Sutherland, E.H. and Cressey, D. (1978), *Criminology* 10th Edn. Philadelphia, PA: Lippincott.

Swan, S.C. and Snow, O.L. (2002), 'A typology of women's use of violence in intimate relationships', *Violence against Women*, 8(3): 286–319.

Swidler, A. (1986), 'Culture in action: symbols and Strategies', *American Sociological Review*, 51(2): 273–86.

Sydney Morning Herald (2001a), 'Bullies and cowards', editorial, 10 February.

Sydney Morning Herald (2001b), 'Trinity charge reduced', 24 February.

Taylor, I. (1971), 'Soccer consciousness and soccer holiganism', in S. Cohen (ed.), *Images of Deviance*. Harmondsworth: Penguin.

Taylor, I., Walton, P. and J. Young (1973), *The New Criminology: For a Social Theory of Deviance*. London: Routledge and Kegan Paul.

Temple, W. (2001), 'Gang admits to sex attack at knifepoint', *Daily Telegraph*, 11 August.

Teplin, L., Abram, K. and McClelland, G. (1996), 'Prevalence of psychiatric disorders among incarcerated women', *Archives of General Psychiatry*, 53: 505–21.

Terry, R.M. (1970), 'Discrimination in the handling of juvenile offenders by social control agencies', in P.G. Garabedian (ed.), *Becoming Delinquent*. Chicago, IL: Aldine Press.

Thomas, W. (1907), *Sex and Society*. Boston, MA: Little Brown.

Thorne, B. (1993), *Gender Play: Girls and Boys in School*. New Brunswick, NJ: Rutgers University Press.

Thrasher, F.M. (1927), *The Gang*. Chicago, IL: Chicago University Press.

Thurston, R. (1996), 'Are you sitting comfortably? Men's storytellings, masculinities, prison culture and violence', in M. Mac an Ghaill (ed.), *Understanding Masculinities*. Buckingham: Open University Press.

Tong, R. (1996), 'Maternal-fetal conflict: the misguided case for punishing cocaine-using pregnant and/or postpartum women', in C. Sistare, (ed.), *Punishment: Social Control and Coercion*. New York: Peter Lang.

Townsend, P., Davidson, N. and Whitehead, M. (1992), *Inequalities in Health: The Black Report and the Health Divide*. London: Penguin.

Tyler, T. (1980), 'Impact of directly and indirectly experienced events: the origin of crime-related judgements and behaviors', *Journal of Personality and Social Psychology*, 39(1): 3–28.

Ulmer, G.L. (1985), 'The object of post-criticism', in H. Foster (ed.), *Postmodern Culture*. London: Pluto.

United Nations (1995), *Platform for Action*, Report of the Fourth World Conference on Women, Beijing, September (UN Publication, E96.IV.13). New York: United Nations.

US Attorney General's Task Force on Family Violence (1984), *Final Report*. Washington, DC: United States Government Printing Office.

Vulliamy, E. (1996), 'Bloodlust of Bosnia faces the reckoning', *Observer*, 12 May.

Vulliamy, E. (1997), 'Face to face with Bosnia's Doctor Death', *Observer*, 13 July.

Walby, S. and Allen, J. (2004), *Domestic Violence, Sexual Assault and Stalking: Findings from the British Crime Survey*, Home Office Research Study 276. London: Home Office.

Walker, A. and Walker, C. (eds) (1987), *A Growing Divide: A Social Audit, 1979–87*. London: Child Poverty Action Group.

Walker, A. and Walker, C. (eds) (1997), *Britain Divided. The Growth of Social Exclusion in the 1980s and 1990s*. London: Child Poverty Action Group.

Walker, D. (2000), 'Poverty traps', *Criminal Justice Matters, Millennium Justice* 38: 10–11.

Walker, F. (2001), 'Trinity victim: "We were all bullied" ', *Sun Herald*, 11 February.

Walker, L. (1978), 'Battered women and learned helplessness', *Victimology*, 2: 525–34.

Walker, N. (1973), *Crime and Punishment in Britain*. Edinburgh: University of Edinburgh Press.

Walkerdine, V. (1995), 'Subject to change without notice: psychology, postmodernity and the popular', in S. Pile and N. Thrift (eds), *Mapping the Subject: Geographies of Cultural Transformation*. London: Routledge.

Walklate, S. (1995), *Gender and Crime: An Introduction*. Hemel Hempstead: Prentice Hall.

Walklate, S. (2001), *Gender, Crime and Criminal Justice*. Cullompton and Portland, OR: Willan.

Walklate, S. (2004), *Gender, Crime and Criminal Justice*, 2nd edn. Cullompton and Portland, OR: Willan.

Walmsley, R., Howard, L. and White, S. (1992), *The National Prison Survey 1990*, Home Office Research Study 128. London: HMSO.

Walzer, M. (1993), 'Exclusion, inclusion and the democratic state', *Dissent*, 40: 55–6.

Ward, D. (1968), *'Crimes of Violence by Women': A Report to the National U.S. Commission on Crimes of Violence*. Washington, DC: US Government Printing Office,

Ward, E. (1984) *Father–Daughter Rape*. London: Women's Press.

Warr, M. (1984), 'Fear of victimization: why are women and the elderly more afraid?', *Social Science Quarterly*, 65: 681–702.

Weedon, C. (1987), *Feminist Practice and Poststructuralist Theory*. New York: Basil Blackwell.

Weeks, J. (1981), *Sex, Politics and Society: The Regulation of Sexuality Since 1800*. Harlow: Longman.

Weeks, J. (1986), *Sexuality*. New York: Tavistock.
Weekend Australian (2002), 'DNA test may set park rape gang free', 7–8 December.
Weis, K. and Borges, S. (1973), 'Victimology and rape', *Issues in Criminology*, 8(2): 71–115.
West, A. (2001), 'Meet Mr Westie, the man who put Howard in poor', *Sun Herald*, 18 November.
West, C. and Fenstermaker, S. (1993), 'Power, inequality and the accomplishment of gender: an ethnomethodological view', in P. England (ed.), *Theory on Gender/ Feminism on Theory*. New York: Aldine.
West, C. and Zimmerman, D.J. (1987), 'Doing gender', *Gender and Society*, 1(2): 125–51.
Wetherell, M. and Edley, N. (1999), 'Negotiating hegemonic masculinity: imaginary positions and psycho-discursive practices', *Feminism & Psychology*, 9(3): 335–56.
White, P. (1999), *The Prison Population in 1998; A Statistical Review*, Research Findings, No. 94. London: Home Office, Research, Development and Statistics Directorate.
White, R. and Perrone, S. (2002), 'Racism, ethnicity and hate crime', *Communal/ Plural*, 9(2): 161–81.
Widom, C. and Maxfield, M. (1984), 'Sex roles and the victimization of women: evidence from the British Crime Survey', paper presented at the annual meeting of the American Society of Criminology.
Widom, C.S. (1988), 'Child abuse, neglect and violent criminal behaviour', unpublished manuscript.
Widom, C.S. and Kuhns, J.B. (1996), 'Childhood victimisation and subsequent risk of promiscuity, prostitution and teenage pregnancy: a prospective study', *American Journal of Public Health*, 86: 1607–10.
Wiles, P.N.P. (1970), 'Criminal statistics and sociological explanations of crime', in P. Wiles and W.G. Carson (eds), *Crime and Delinquency*. London: Martin Robertson.
Wilkinson, C. (1988), 'The post-release experience of female prisoners', in A. Morris and C. Wilkinson (eds), *Women and the Penal System*. Cambridge: Institute of Criminology, Cropwood Series No 19.
Wilson, J. (1975), *Thinking About Crime*. New York: Basic Books.
Wilson, J. and Herrnstein, R. (1985), *Crime and Human Nature*. New York: Simon and Schuster.
Winkel, F.W. and Vrij, A. (1990), 'Fear of crime and mass media crime reports testing similarity hypotheses', *International Review of Victimology*, 1: 251–65.
Wockner, C. (2002), 'Gang rapes a form of torture: judge', *Daily Telegraph*, 9 August.
Wolf, N. (1993), *Fire with Fire*. New York: Random House.
Women's Policy Team (2005), *Women's Offending Reduction Programme: Annual Review 2004–2005*. London: NOMS.
Worrall, A. (1989), 'Working with female offenders: beyond alternatives to custody', *British Journal of Social Work*, 19(1): 77–93.
Worrall, A. (1990), *Offending Women: Female Lawbreakers and the Criminal Justice System*. London: Routledge and Kegan Paul.
Worrall, A. (1997), *Punishment in the Community: The Future of Criminal Justice*. Harlow:, Longman.

Worrall, A. (2000), 'Governing bad girls: changing constructions of adolescent female delinquency', in J. Bridgeman and D. Monk (eds), *Feminist Perspectives on Child Law*. London: Cavendish.

Worrall, A. (2001), 'Girls at risk? Reflections on changing attitudes to young women's offending', *Probation Journal*, 48(2): 86–92.

Worrall, A. (2004), 'Twisted sisters, ladettes, and the new penology: the social construction of "violent girls" ', in C. Alder and A. Worrall (eds), *Girls' Violence Myths and Realities*. New York: SUNY Press.

Young, I. (1981), 'Beyond the unhappy marriage: a critique of dual systems theory', in L. Sargent (ed.), *Women and Revolution*. Boston, MA: South End Press.

Young, J. (1971), *The Drugtakers*. London: Paladin.

Young, J. (1988), 'Radical criminology in Britain', *British Journal of Criminology*, 28: 159–313.

Young, J. (1996), *Imagining Crime*. London: Sage.

Young, J. (2002), 'Crime and social exclusion', in M. Maguire, R. Morgan and R. Reiner (eds), *The Oxford Handbook of Criminology*, 3rd edn. Oxford: Oxford University Press.

Zedner, L. (2002), 'Victims', in M. Maguire, R. Morgan and R. Reiner (eds), *The Oxford Handbook of Criminology*, 3rd edn. Oxford: Oxford University Press.

Zhana (ed.) (1989), *Sojourn*. London: Methuen.

Author Index

Subject Index

Related books from Open University Press

ETHNICITY AND CRIME
A READER

Basia Spalek

Basia Spalek has compiled an excellent reader about a much researched and highly sensitive subject. Crucially, she contextualises ethnicity and crime within broadly defined social and intellectual contexts, avoiding the limitation of all too frequently repeated research based solely on statistical measures and policy evaluations.

> Simon Holdaway, Professor of Criminology and Sociology, Sheffield University

Issues in relation to race and ethnicity have generated substantial and ever-growing interest from, and within, a multitude of academic, research and policy contexts. This book brings together important material in race and ethnic studies and provides different ways of thinking about race and ethnicity in relation to crime and the criminal justice system.

Ethnicity and Crime: A Reader consists of a collection of works that capture the main themes that arise from within this vast area of work. It is divided into five sections:

- 'Race and crime', racial discrimination and criminal justice
- The racialisation of crime: Social, political and cultural contexts
- Race, ethnicity and victimisation
- Self and discipline reflexivity: Ethnic identities and crime
- Ethnic identities, institutional reflexivity and crime

Each section contains recurring and overlapping themes and includes many different ways of thinking about race and ethnicity in relation to crime. It spans theoretical approaches that might be labelled as positivist, critical race analyses, left realist approaches, feminist, as well as post-modern perspectives.

This is the first title in the new series *Readings in Criminology and Criminal Justice* and follows the series format of thematic sections, together with an editor's introduction to the complete volume and an introduction to each section.

Contents

Part One: 'Race and crime', racial discrimination and criminal justice – Part Two: The racialisation of crime: Social, political and cultural contexts – Part Three: Race, ethnicity and victimisation – Part Four: Self and discipline reflexivity: Ethnic identities and crime – Part Five: Ethnic identities, institutional reflexivity and crime.

2008   352pp
978–0–335–22379–4 (Paperback)   978–0–335–22378–7 (Hardback)

THE END OF MULTICULTURALISM?
TERRORISM, INTEGRATION AND HUMAN RIGHTS

Derek McGhee

. . . the book is a brave and authoritative analysis of multiculturalism . . . McGhee successfully locates his subject in the context of recent developments in both community cohesion and human rights and shows with great skill how differing impulses within government and the wider community pull multiculturalism in various different directions . . . With this book, McGhee manages to be both topical and well-informed: it deserves a wide readership.

Professor Conor Gearty, LSE

This topical book provides a thorough examination of debates on multiculturalism, in the context of current discussions on security, integration and human rights.

Recent debates on national identity and the alleged failure of multiculturalism have focused on the social disorder in Oldham, Burnley and Bradford in the summer of 2001 and the bombings and attempted bombings in London in July 2005. Derek McGhee assesses how these events and the events that have occurred outside Britain, especially the attacks on the USA on 11th September 2001, have resulted in the introduction of a number of high profile debates in Britain with regards to immigration, integration, citizenship, 'race' inequality and human rights.

McGhee examines these debates on multiculturalism and terrorism in light of enduring questions regarding 'Muslim integration' and 'Muslim loyalty' in contemporary Britain. He also explores the nature of a diverse range of inter-related areas of public policy, including anti-terrorism, immigration, integration, community cohesion, equality and human rights, critically examining many of the Government's key strategies in recent years.

The End of Multiculturalism? will appeal to a wide readership of students and academics in sociology, politics, international relations and law.

Contents
Deportation, detention and torture by proxy: Foreign national terror suspects in the UK – In between allegiance and evilization: The Muslim question post 7/7 – Counter terrorism, community relations, radicalisation and 'Muslim grievances' – Cohesion, citizenship and integration (beyond Multiculturalism?) – Culture change: the Commission for Equality and Human Rights – future proofing the nation – Shared values, Britishness and human rights.

May 2008   208pp
978–0–335–22392–3 (Paperback)   978–0–335–22391–6 (Hardback)

IMAGINING THE VICTIM OF CRIME

Sandra Walklate

> . . . the clarity in which the wide range of relevant issues are presented throughout the book makes this must-reading for new entrants to this field and for students.
> International Review of Victimology

Concern for the victims of crime first emerged with the formation of the Criminal Injuries Compensation Board in 1964 and this has continued with the increase in crime rates since the 1970s and 1980s and in the aftermath of a number of high profile trials. In this book Sandra Walklate offers an introduction to the key theoretical, methodological and substantive issues in victimology and criminal victimisation. She situates the contemporary preoccupation with criminal victimisation within the broader social and cultural changes of the last twenty-five years.

Written in the context of post-September 11, and alongside the events in Madrid of 2004 and London in July 2005, it questions who can be considered a victim of crime and what the response to such victimisation might look like.

Topics include:

- Theoretical perspectives - positivist, radical and critical victimology
- Victimisation, risk and fear
- The re-politicisation of the crime victim
- The impact of global processes and global change on both the politics and the policy process

The book concludes with an examination of future possibilities for both victimology and victims' policies in the light of contemporary political preoccupations.

Imagining the Victim of Crime is key reading for students of criminal justice and victimology.

Contents

Why are we all victims now? - Theory and victimology - Structuring criminal victimisation - Victimisation, risk and fear - Victimisation, politics and policy - Local victim; global context - The rhetoric of victimhood and the role of the state.

2006   224pp
978-0-335-21727-4 (Paperback)   978-0-335-217281 (Hardback)